Since 1969, Antonia Fraser has written many acclaimed historical works which have been international bestsellers. These include the biographies *Mary Queen of Scots* (James Tait Black Memorial Prize), *Cromwell: Our Chief of Men* and *King Charles II*, and *The Gunpowder Plot: Terror and Faith in 1605* (St Louis Literary Award; CWA Non-Fiction Gold Dagger). Four highly praised books focus on women in history: *The Weaker Vessel: Woman's Lot in Seventeenth-Century England* (Wolfson Award for History, 1984), *The Warrior Queens: Boadicea's Chariot* (1988), *The Six Wives of Henry VIII* (1992) and *Marie Antoinette: The Journey* (Enid McLeod Literary Prize, Franco-British Society, 2001). Antonia Fraser is the editor of the series *Kings and Queens of England* (Weidenfeld & Nicolson), and wrote the volume *King James VI of Scotland, I of England*. She is married to Harold Pinter and lives in London. Antonia Fraser was made CBE in 1999, and awarded the Norton Medlicott Medal by the Historical Association in 2000. Her latest book, *Love and Louis XIV: the Women in the Life of the Sun King*, is published by Phoenix.

D0543050

'A King is history's slave.
History, that is the unconscious general swarm-life
of mankind, uses every moment of the life of kings,
as a tool for its own purposes.'

Tolstoy

Contents

Author's Note

I had two principal aims when I began to write this biography. First, being possessed since childhood by a passion for the subject of Mary Queen of Scots, I wished to test for myself the truth or falsehood of the many legends which surround her name. In order to tear away these cobwebs – or in certain cases reverently replace them – I delved into as many published and unpublished sources as I could discover, taking as my starting-point Mary's own letters and the calendars of state papers (although of course there may well be some sources of which I was unhappily ignorant). Secondly, for the sake of the general reader, I hoped to set Mary anew in the context of the age in which she lived. In the course of my own inquiries I was surprised to discover that despite the enormous quantity of research on the sixteenth century published during the last fifty years, radically changing our attitudes to certain of its aspects, no general life of Mary has yet appeared, taking it all into account. There have been detailed treatments of certain episodes in her life – notably that of the Kirk o'Field murder and the Casket Letters, and later the Babington Plot – and Stefan Zweig's fascinating psychological interpretation, written in the thirties. But the last full-length biography, giving documentation, was that of T. F. Henderson in 1905. So in the end my two aims converged, and I found myself with the single objective of showing, with as much accuracy as is possible in the light of modern research, what Mary Queen of Scots must have been like as a person.

In the interests of clarity, I have not entered into the various complications of dating in the sixteenth century, i.e. I have ignored the fact that the calendar year was held to start on 25 March during this period, and have used the modern style of dates starting on 1 January throughout. I have also ignored the ten days' difference between English and European dates in the period of the Babington Plot, due to the fact that the adjustment to the Gregorian calendar was not made in England until the eighteenth century; and, in order to avoid confusion, have given the dates of letters coming from abroad as if they originated in England.

With regard to Scots words and spelling, the documents both in Scots and French – notably Queen Mary's own letters, which were nearly always written in French – I have translated, adapted to modern spelling, and in certain cases, paraphrased the text, as it seemed to me necessary to make the meaning clear to the general reader today.

It will be found that sums of money relevant to Scotland are given in pounds Scots and those concerning England in pounds sterling – the pound Scots being worth roughly one-quarter of the pound sterling in this period.

The task of writing such a book – covering ground well-trodden by scholars of the present, as of previous generations – would not have been possible without the benefit of their works, which are listed in the bibliography, and whose assistance I gratefully acknowledge. I was also fortunate enough to be able to draw upon the advice of a number of people, whose suggestions concerning the lines of research to pursue were a major contribution to my book (although the conclusions drawn are of course all my own). In the first place I should like to thank Sir James Fergusson of Kilkerran, Keeper of the Register House, Edinburgh, for valuable advice over reading-matter as well as guidance in researches within the Register House itself; Sir Iain Moncrieffe of that Ilk on whose encyclopaedic knowledge of Scottish history I frequently drew; Archbishop David Mathew for advice and encouragement at an early stage; and Father Francis Edwards SJ, Archivist of the English Society of Jesus, for advice and help in researches within the Farm Street Library, including the opportunity to use the notes of the late Fr J. H. Pollen.

I would also like to acknowledge most gratefully the help of the following: Mr Andrews, Clerk of the Works, Westminster Abbey; the Duke of Argyll; Sir Charles Barratt, Town Clerk of Coventry; Mr and Mrs Godfrey Bostock of Tixall, Stafford; Dr C. Burns of the Vatican Archives, Rome; Fr Philip Caraman SJ; Miss Margaret Crum, Deputy Keeper of Western MSS, Bodleian Library, Oxford; Mr Stanley Cursiter; Fr Martin D'Arcy SJ; Dr Chalmers Davidson; Professor A. A. M. Duncan of Glasgow University; the Duke and Duchess of Hamilton and Brandon; Mr R. E. Hutcheson, Keeper of the Scottish National Portrait Gallery, for advice on the authenticity of Scottish portraits of the period; Mr and Mrs W. J. Keswick of Glenkiln, Dumfriesshire; Mr A. H. King of the Music Room, British Museum and Miss Marion Linton of the Music Room, National Library of Scotland for help over Riccio's music; Mr King, Northamptonshire County Archivist; Mr Eric Linklater; Dr Ida Macalpine and Dr Richard Hunter for additional help on the subject of porphyria, beyond their BMA publication; Mr John MacQueen of the University of Edinburgh, for advice on the literature of the period, and for showing me his paper on Alexander Scott in advance of publication; Dr William Marshall of Peterborough; the Earl of Mar and Kellie; Mr James Michie for his translation of George Buchanan's poem on page 223; Miss Elizabeth Millar of Jedburgh; Mr J. W. Moore, of Stone; the Duke of Norfolk and his archivist Mr Francis Steer; the Earl of Oxford and Asquith; Mr Peter Quennell; Sir Patrick Reilly, then British Ambassador in Paris, and Mr C. S. de Winton, British Council representative in France, for assistance in the course of French researches; Mr Jasper Ridley (whose own life of Knox was unfortunately published after this book went to press), for suggestions and criticism at the manuscript stage; the Marquess of Salisbury for permission to research at Hatfield House and reproduce certain documents in the illustrations, and also his librarian, Miss Clare Talbot, for special assistance over the Casket Letters; Mr F. B. Stitt, Staffordshire County Archivist;

Dr Roy Strong, Director of the National Portrait Gallery, for generous help over the complicated subject of the iconography of Mary Queen of Scots; M. Marcel Thomas, Conservateur en Chef of the Cabinet des Manuscrits, Bibliothèque Nationale, Paris; Mr Hugh Tait of the Department of British and Mediaeval Antiquities, British Museum; Mr F. A. Warner of the British Embassy, Brussels; Mr Neville Williams, Assistant Keeper at the Public Record Office; the late Mr F. Wismark of Madame Tussaud's; Mr T. S. Wragg, librarian to the Duke of Devonshire at Chatsworth; Canon A. de Zulueta.

I am grateful to G. Bell & Sons Ltd for permission to quote passages from *Queen Mary's Book* edited by Mrs P. Stewart-Mackenzie Arbuthnot.

Lastly I should like to thank the Librarian and staff of the London Library; the staff of the Reading Room of the British Museum; my aunt Lady Pansy Lamb who kindly read the proofs; and my mother Elizabeth Longford, who made vital critical suggestions at the manuscript stage, and without whose admirable example I should never have attempted to write the book at all.

ANTONIA FRASER

September 1968
52 Campden Hill Square, London W8
Eilean Aigas, Beauly, Inverness-shire

The English

showing the position of Mary Queen of Scots and

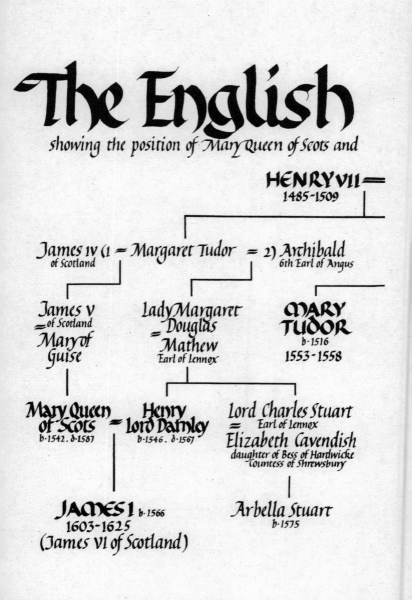

HENRY VII
1485-1509

James IV (1 = Margaret Tudor = 2) Archibald
of Scotland   6th Earl of Angus

James V
= of Scotland
Mary of
Guise

Lady Margaret
= Douglas
Mathew
Earl of Lennox

**MARY
TUDOR**
b·1516
1553-1558

**Mary Queen
of Scots**
b·1542. d·1587

Henry
lord Darnley
b·1546. d·1567

Lord Charles Stuart
= Earl of Lennox
Elizabeth Cavendish
daughter of Bess of Hardwicke
Countess of Shrewsbury

JAMES I b·1566
1603-1625
(James VI of Scotland)

Arbella Stuart
b·1575

succession

Lord Darnley, in relation to the English throne

= Elizabeth of York

HENRY VIII 1509-1547	Louis XII (1 = Mary of France	= 2) Charles Brandon Duke of Suffolk
ELIZABETH 1 b·1533 1558-1603	**EDWARD VI** b·1537 1547-1553	Lady Frances Brandon d·1559 = Henry Grey Duke of Suffolk
Lady Jane Grey Executed 1554	Lady Catherine Grey d·1568 = Edward Seymour Earl of Hertford	Lady Mary Grey d·1578 = Thomas Keys
	Edward Seymour b·1561	Thomas Seymour b·1563

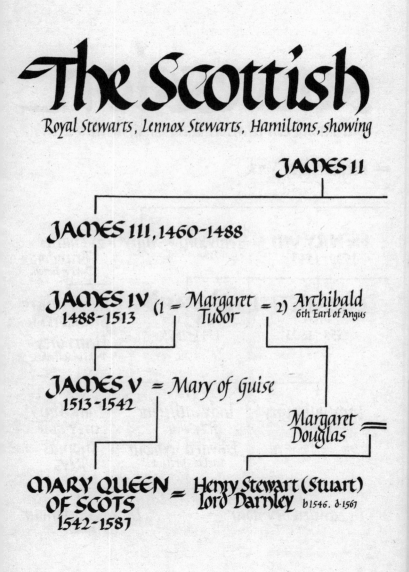

The Scottish

Royal Stewarts, Lennox Stewarts, Hamiltons, showing

JAMES II

JAMES III, 1460-1488

JAMES IV (1 = Margaret = 2) Arthibald
1488-1513   Tudor   6th Earl of Angus

JAMES V = Mary of Guise
1513-1542

Margaret =
Douglas

MARY QUEEN = Henry Stewart (Stuart)
OF SCOTS   Lord Darnley b 1546. d 1567
1542-1587

succession

their relation to the throne in the sixteenth Century

1437 – 1460

MARY = James
lord Hamilton
d·1479

Mathew Stewart = Elizabeth Hamilton
2nd Earl of Lennox
d·1513

James Hamilton
1st Earl of Arran, d·1529
= 3) Janet Beaton

John Stewart
3rd Earl of Lennox
d·1526

= Mathew Stewart
4th Earl of Lennox
d·1571

James Hamilton
2nd Earl of Arran
1st Duke of Châtelherault (the governor)
d·1575

James Hamilton
3rd Earl of Arran
d·1609

3 other sons
4 daughters

PART ONE

The Young Queen

CHAPTER ONE
All Men Lamented

'All men lamented that the realm was left without a
male to succeed.'

John Knox

The winter of 1542 was marked by tempestuous weather
throughout the British Isles: in the north, on the borders
of Scotland and England, there were heavy snow-falls in
December and frost so savage that by January the ships were
frozen into the harbour at Newcastle. These stark conditions
found a bleak parallel in the political climate which then prevailed
between the two countries. Scotland as a nation groaned under
the humiliation of a recent defeat at English hands at the battle
of Solway Moss. As a result of the battle, the Scottish nobility
which had barely recovered from the defeat of Flodden a
generation before, were stricken yet again by the deaths of their
leaders in their prime; of those who survived, many prominent
members were prisoners in English hands, while the rest met
the experience of defeat by quarrelling among themselves,
showing their strongest loyalty to the principle of self-
aggrandizement, rather than to the troubled monarchy. The
Scottish national Church, although still officially Catholic for the
next seventeen years, was already torn between those who
wished to reform its manifold abuses from within, and those
who wished to follow England's example, by breaking away root
and branch from the tree of Rome. The king of this divided

3

country, James v, having led his people to defeat, lay dying with his face to the wall, the victim in this as much of his own passionate nature, as of the circumstances which had conspired against him. When James died on 14th December, 1542, the most stalwart prince might have shrunk from the Herculean task of succeeding him. But his actual successor was a weakly female child born only six days before, his daughter Mary, the new queen of Scotland.

James v, the last adult male king of Scotland for nearly fifty years, has been treated kindly by contemporary historians, who look back to his reign with nostalgia across the turbulence of that of his daughter. He has been credited with the qualities of King Arthur, whereas on balance his character seems to have been more like that of Sir Lancelot. Since his physical description, 'of midway stature',[1] bluish grey eyes, sandy hair, weak mouth and chin, does not justify the general reputation he enjoyed among his contemporaries for good looks, he clearly possessed an animal magnetism, impossible for another century to understand through pictures. This, and his health, seems to have been his chief physical legacy to his daughter, since in all other respects, starting with her height and athletic carriage, the features and build of Mary Queen of Scots are far easier to trace among her physically magnificent Guise uncles, than in her Stewart forbears. Ronsard described him as having '*le regard vigoureux*'; James certainly possessed the cyclical high spirits and gaiety of the Stewarts – another quality which he handed on to his daughter – and the ability to fire the imagination of his subjects, an attribute generally described in monarchs as possessing the common touch. Unfortunately there is no doubt as to the reverse side of this golden coin: the evidence of the debauchery of James v is unanimous. 'Most vicious we shall call him,' wrote Knox with relish,[2] relating how he spared neither man's wife nor maiden, no more after his marriage than he did before.

James inherited a kingdom bankrupted by his mother Margaret Tudor and her second husband, the earl of Angus; unfortunately his various efforts to search about him for new sources of income brought further troubles in their train. Even his prolonged search

4

for a wealthy foreign bride set his feet firmly on the path of a foreign policy which proved in the final analysis to be disastrous. In view of the predatory attitude of his uncle, Henry VIII, towards Scotland, James determined upon the traditional Scottish alliance with the French king, in order to bolster himself with French aid against any possible English claims of suzerainty. Rightly or wrongly, James viewed Henry's offer to his daughter Mary Tudor as a bride as a further effort on the part of his uncle to envelop Scotland in his bear's hug. At one point James even dangled after the young Catherine de Médicis, niece of the Pope, lured by the thought of her magnificent inheritance.[3] The results of such a union, between Mary Stuart's father and the woman who was later to be her mother-in-law, provide an interesting avenue of historical speculation; in fact the match was doubly vetoed, by the Pope's reluctance to see his niece set off for the far land of Scotland, and by Henry VIII's anger at the idea of such a powerful match for his nephew. James's mother had been the elder of the two daughters of Henry VII; later this share of Tudor blood was to play a vital part in shaping the life story of James's daughter Mary; the deaths of two out of the three surviving children of Henry VIII meant that by the time Mary was sixteen she was next in line to the English throne after her cousin Queen Elizabeth. But in the 1530s, at the time of James V's marriage projects, these coming events had not yet cast their shadow. It was Henry VIII, in the fullness of his manhood, and with two children to his credit already branching out of the Tudor family tree, who seemed blessed with heirs. His nephew James on the other hand singularly lacked them.

The position of the Stewart monarchs in the fifteenth and sixteenth centuries was peculiarly perilous in dynastic terms, for a number of reasons. In the first place chance had resulted in a total of seven royal minorities – there had been no adult succession since the fourteenth century – which had an inevitable effect of weakening the power of the crown and increasing that of the nobility. Secondly, the Stewarts had a special reason for needing to separate themselves from the nobility, and raise themselves above it into a cohesive royal family, by the nature of their origins. These were neither obscure nor royal. On the contrary the Stewarts were no more than *primus inter pares* among the body of the Scottish nobles. They had formerly been stewards, as their name denotes, first of all to the ruling family of Brittany, and later more splendidly, great stewards to the kings of Scotland. It was Walter, sixth great steward, who by marrying Marjorie Bruce, daughter of Robert I, fathered Robert II, king of the Scots, and thus founded the Stewart royal line.

The ramifications and interconnections of the Stewart family were henceforward focused on the throne. The many inter-marriages, common to all Scottish noble families of this period, meant that by the 1540s there were descended from younger sons or daughters of the kings a number of rival Stewart families[4] – the Lennox Stewarts, who later came to use the French spelling of Stuart and thus handed it officially on to the royal line through the marriage of Mary to Henry Stuart, Lord Darnley;* the Atholl Stewarts, the Stewarts of Traquair, the Stewarts of Blantyre, and the Stewarts of Ochiltree. Even those dignitaries whose name was not actually Stewart often stood in close relationship to the crown through marriage or descent; throughout her reign Mary correctly addressed as 'cousin' the earls of Arran, Huntly and Argyll, heads respectively of the families of Hamilton, Gordon and Campbell. Kinship as a concept was all-important in Scotland of the period: unfor-tunately kinship to the monarchy was universally held to strengthen the position of the family concerned, rather than add to the resources of the monarchy. Compared to the Stewarts, how fortunate then – or how prudent – were their Tudor

* According to modern practice, Mary Queen of Scots was born a Stewart (as her father had been) and became a Stuart only through her marriage to her cousin Lord Darnley. But as the Anglo-French spelling of her name – Stuart – was adopted on her behalf during her upbringing in France, and always employed by her in the many devices and anagrams of her own name, it has been used to indicate her throughout this book. James VI and I was quite properly Stuart, rather than Stewart, taking the surname of his father Darnley. But of course too much importance should not be attached to the spelling of names in an age when many people spelt their own names in a variety of different ways on different occasions.

cousins in England. By the reign of Queen Elizabeth, her Tudor forebears had seen to it long ago that the crown was not surrounded by a host of ambitious relatives, by a policy of steady elimination directed towards possible rivals. The many Scottish minorities meant that the Stewart kings had never ruled for long enough to follow this same course.

Determined to cut his way free from this prickly dynastic hedge, on 1st January, 1537 James finally brought about his marriage to Madeleine, daughter of the French King Francis 1. Her dowry – 100,000 *livres* on the marriage day, and annual rents on a sum of 125,000 *livres* – was obviously desirable, and so was the support of her father; but the Maytime beauty and fragility of this *princesse lointaine* seems to have played on a genuine chord of romance in the nature of the Scottish king. Her hand had already been refused him by her father on the grounds of her physical delicacy, and James had actually set out for France to marry Marie, daughter of the duke of Vendôme. The sight of Madeleine prompted him to pursue his original aim with pertinacity, and at length success. Alas! her father's premonitions concerning the effect of the Scottish climate on a girl brought up in the soft air of the Loire valley proved all too correct. The sixteen-year-old queen, who arrived in Scotland in May, was dead by July; the mourning veils which were thus for the first time introduced into Scotland, remained the only permanent memorials of a summer's marriage.[5]

The woman on whom King James's matrimonial negotiations were now focused, through his envoy Cardinal Beaton, was like himself recently widowed. Mary of Guise was the eldest daughter of the large and flourishing family of Claude, duke of Guise, and his wife Antoinette of Bourbon. She had been married at the age of nineteen to Francis of Orleans, duke of Longueville, and was left a widow at the age of twenty-two by his premature death in June 1537, a month before James himself was left a widower. Unlike James, she had one small son, Francis, the new duke of Longueville, and gave birth to another son shortly after her husband's death, who died. In appearance, she was a tall well-built girl, not exactly beautiful, but of the healthy type calculated to appeal to sixteenth-century monarchs in search of heirs. Mary of Guise also possessed remarkable inner qualities of prudence and tolerance, as well as the courage and intelligence which might fairly have been expected of a Guise. However, none of these characteristics was greatly tested by her staid and happy married life with her first husband, spent placidly at his various castles at Châteaudun on the Loire, and at Amiens and Rouen. According to Brantôme, she also had her ration of Gallic gaiety, and loved to gamble and play cards. At all events she was quite happy at this stage in her life to form part of the great Guise family network, a domestic triangle at the apex of which stood the formidable Duchess Antoinette.

James had possibly met Mary of Guise in France at the time of his first marriage, which she attended, but he tendered for her hand for strictly conventional reasons: she would be provided with a dowry by Francis I, was clearly capable of child-bearing, and strengthened once again the important French alliance. So matrimonially suitable did she seem indeed in the terms of the time that in the autumn of the same year Henry VIII also offered for her hand, after the death of Jane Seymour. He referred approvingly to her fine stature, at which Mary of Guise is said to have wittily replied that although her figure was big, her neck was small. Certainly Francis had no particular wish to increase the pretensions of the Guises still further by placing one of them on the English throne. The marriage contract with James was thus prepared in January 1538, and the marriage performed by proxy, with Lord Maxwell acting the part of the bridegroom, on 18th May in the cathedral of Notre Dame in Paris.

Accompanied by a navy of ships under Lord Maxwell, and 2000 lords and barons whom her new husband had sent from Scotland to fetch her away, Queen Mary landed at Crail in Fife on 10th June, 1538, just over a year since the landing of Queen Madeleine.[6] She was formally received by the king at St Andrews a few days later with pageants and plays performed in her honour, and a great deal of generally blithe rejoicing, before being remarried the next morning in the cathedral of St Andrews.

Immediately afterwards she was received into the king's palace with trumpets and still more pageants, in all the celebrations a prominent part being played by Sir David Lyndsay of the Mount, later to become famous for his denunciation of the state of the Scottish Church, *The Satire of the Three Estates*. The next day the royal couple were conveyed on a tour of churches, colleges and universities within the town by the provost and burgesses.

These arrangements, like the steps of a formal dance, convey little of the feelings of the people concerned: but clearly Queen Mary, a woman of innate tact, was at pains to please her husband by praising his country. Fife, for example, she admired extravagantly, and confided to James that although she had been warned in France that she would find Scotland a barbarous country, destitute of comforts, ever since her arrival she had found the exact reverse, for she had never seen so many fair personages of men and women and also young babes and children, as she saw that day. Delighted with this graceful and diplomatic speech, King James swore to show her even better sights as she passed through Scotland. After forty days had been spent at St Andrews in merriment, games, jousting, archery, hunting, hawking, dancing and minstrel playing, the court then passed on to further celebrations in other towns, culminating in the queen's reception at Edinburgh, which she entered in triumph on St Margaret's Day.[7]

Despite this elaborate pageantry, despite the queen's gracious compliments to her adopted country, the marriage of James and Mary does not seem to have been a particularly happy one in its early stages. It was rumoured in England that James had a mistress at Tantallon and 'set not much store by the queen'.[8] The letters exchanged between Mary of Guise and her mother, Duchess Antoinette, give a picture of secret homesickness, the mother both advising her daughter on her role in Scotland, and trying to reassure her with an abundance of family news about affairs in France.[9] Nearly every letter contains some reference to the little boy Francis whom the queen had been obliged to leave behind. The melancholy of a mother who had to abandon a

three-year-old child for a state marriage in a far-off country may
be imagined; sadly, Mary of Guise, a woman of undoubtedly
maternal nature, was deprived of the upbringing of both her
surviving children, Francis and Mary Stuart, after the first
years of infancy. Francis was clearly a delicate child: Duchess
Antoinette's letters abound with details of his diseases. Later he
learns to say his Paternoster, has his hair cut like his uncles, has
supper with his grandfather the duke of Guise in the garden
and picks strawberries, and relates how his Uncle Aumale hid
in his room while his aunt put him to bed. As the little duke
grows up, far from his mother, he sends her a string to show
his height, and by 1547, after the battle of Pinkie Cleugh, writes
to her to say he is practising tilting to come to her rescue. The
next year, on the same theme, he is keeping up with the French
king out hunting to prove himself a man able to come to the
help of his mother.[10]

A mother's homesickness was not Queen Mary's only
problem. There was trouble with King Francis over the payment
of her dowry to the Scottish king, for Francis, in arranging for
her dowry, used the money already given to her on her first
marriage, to the annoyance of both Duchess Antoinette and her
daughter, who feared that the little duke's rights would be thus
prejudiced. There was a further problem ingenuously exposed
by Francis of Longueville, when he sent his love to Papa (James
v) and hoped that he would soon give a little brother to the
queen.[11] By the end of 1539 no royal heir had appeared, although
the marriage of James and Mary was eighteen months old; a
proposal of the duke of Guise to voyage to Scotland in January
1540, to see how his daughter was faring, indicated that Queen
Mary's parents were genuinely concerned as to her situation.

The birth of James, prince of Scotland, the longed-for heir,
in May 1540 put an end for the time being to this particular
problem. The news was received with ecstasy by Duchess
Antoinette, who bombarded her daughter alternately with questions and advice. By December of the same year, the queen was
again with child, the royal marriage thus considered satisfactory
in both countries. In the meantime Mary of Guise took a

number of steps to introduce the amenities of French life into Scotland. The material objects she sought from France ranged from pear trees and plums to wild boars for hunting; the personages included masons, miners from Lorraine to mine the 'golden strand' of Crawford Muir, where substantial amounts of gold were discovered in the sixteenth century, an armourer, tailors, and – typically of an expatriate – French doctors and apothecaries. From Antwerp one Eustating de Coquiel wrote to the queen that he was sending his servant with merchandise and certain luxuries ('*gentillesses*') – of which she was to have first choice.[12] Obviously *gentillesses* to the French way of thinking were not in abundance in Scotland, and Mary of Guise turned her practical mind to remedying the deficiency.

A double tragedy now struck both king and queen in the area in which they were most vulnerable. In April 1541 at Falkland the queen gave birth to a second son, Robert, duke of Albany, who died two days later, and within a few days the little prince of Scotland was himself dead at Holyrood. Thus King James was once more left without a direct heir; Queen Mary's feelings may be imagined to have been equally desperate, but according to Pitscottie she still managed to behave admirably: '... telling the king that they were young enough to expect to have many more children'.[13] Her mother did not fail to write immediately from France, devoutly hoping that the king had not taken it too badly, expressing her daughter's own opinion that they were both young and might have many more children, and finally ascribing the death of Prince James to overfeeding, or at least a change of nurses.[14] Contemporary opinion in Scotland advanced a more dramatic explanation for the tragic deaths of the two princes. Although there were the usual rumours of poison, common to all unexpected deaths of the period, the most general explanation was that the sins of King James v were being visited upon his children. It was said that Sir James Hamilton of Fynart, the king's former master of the works, whom he had had executed in dubious circumstances, appeared to him in a dream as he lay asleep, and warned him that he would shortly lose both his arms, and finally his head. According to Knox, Sir James Hamilton himself struck off both the king's arms in the vision with his sword, crying: 'Take that while thou receive a final payment for all thy impiety.'[15]

Although the precarious nature of infant life in the sixteenth century is a more probable explanation for the double tragedy than either poison or divine vengeance, at the same time the deaths of the young princes did mark the point at which the fortunes of King James seemed to take a final downward turn. There was no sign of another heir. While James's domestic policy had the natural effect of alienating those of his nobles who felt the corrective side of it, especially the powerful family of Douglas, headed by the earl of Angus, his refusal to join Henry VIII in plundering the Catholic Church did not endear him to the menacing forces on the other side of the border. When Henry demanded a conference at York in September 1541, James was not allowed to attend on the grounds that his person was too precious since the deaths of his sons. His own clergy, fearful that Henry would sway James towards his preda- tory policy with regard to the Church, offered to finance a war if this should be necessary. Incensed at the Scottish king's failure to appear, Henry angrily asserted that the Scots had thus broken their words, and 'not satisfied their former promises'.

By the summer of 1542 the English forces were being mobilized in the north, with vicious instructions from their king for bringing the Scots to heel, should King James continue to ignore his uncle's request for a meeting in England. Queen Mary was once again expecting a child, but in his general statement claiming suzerainty over Scotland, King Henry particularly spe- cified that this should not prevent her husband from coming to London by Christmas – there were to be no 'ifs and ands' from the king's wife, which King Henry thought would engender great uncertainty over the whole situation, considering 'the common error of women in reckoning their time'.[16] The check of the English forces by the earl of Home at Haddonrig in August was only temporary. In the autumn, as Queen Mary awaited the birth of another longed-for heir, and Duchess Antoinette wrote constantly from France advising her on her health (she is to eliminate her bad colds by washing her hair once a month, having previously cut it short, since greasy hair makes for colds; Duchess Antoinette herself is careful to cut her hair every six weeks)[17] the king of Scotland rallied his own army for the final crisis of his reign. His difficulties in assembling what was virtually a feudal host were in no way smoothed by the fact that command was given to Cardinal Beaton, who tried to invest the campaign with the character of a holy war, on the grounds that England lay under the papal interdict. Nor were the nobles any better pleased when another command was given to the king's favourite, Oliver Sinclair.

On 24th November, the forces under Oliver Sinclair encountered the English deputy warden of the West March near the River Esk at Solway Moss, and were driven back in a disorderly rout, as a result of which 1200 Scots were captured, among them many of the leading nobles, who were then taken to London for confrontation with King Henry. Although Knox discerned the hand of God in the discomfiture,[18] it was the great reluctance of the Scots to pursue a long campaign away from their homes, and the fact that as fighters they lacked not courage but endurance, which had once more defeated their efforts. The English increased in valiance as they fought, but the Scots declined. As the Scots cast aside their weapons and fled, many were drowned by the incoming tide, and others still fell in the Moss, losing either horse or rider or both. Some were so anxious to be saved by capture that they surrendered themselves to women. An English eye-witness wrote that night from Carlisle that anyone who wanted prisoners had only to follow the retreating Scots, for they were past making any sort of self-defence.[19]

The king of this stricken country, in a state of appalling mental anguish, exacerbated by worry over the fate of Oliver Sinclair, retired to Edinburgh, where he made an inventory of all his treasure and jewels. From there he went secretly to Hallyards, in Fife, the seat of Sir William Kirkcaldy of Grange, the treasurer. When Kirkcaldy's wife tried to cheer him and persuade him to take the 'work of God' in good part, the king replied with conviction that his portion of the world was on the contrary short, and he would be dead in fifteen days. When his servants asked him where he wanted to spend his Christmas, he replied with a contemptuous smile: 'I cannot tell: choose ye the place. But this I can tell you, on Yule day, you will be masterless and the realm without a king.'

The working out of these gloomy prophecies took only a short time. James went to Linlithgow where he spent some days with Queen Mary, now in the last stage of her pregnancy. From there he went to Falkland, the beloved palace which he had built for himself in admiration of the French Renaissance, and which like an animal he now chose as his lair in which to die. Incapable of digesting the disasters of his hopes, his personal humiliation and the humiliations of his country, the king now underwent a complete nervous collapse. He lay on his bed, sometimes railing at the cruel fate which had led to his defeat, at other times silent and melancholy, meditating on the wastes of despair. He heard of the capture of Sinclair and cried out: 'Oh fled Oliver! Is Oliver tane [taken]? Oh fled Oliver!'[20] It seems to have been his last true pang of earthly emotion.

Into this sad sick-room came a messenger from Linlithgow who brought the news that the queen had been confined, and given birth to a daughter. The onlookers hoped that the king's sorrow might be somewhat alleviated by the fact that he now had an heir once more. But the king observed cynically: 'Adieu, fare well, it came with a lass, it will pass with a lass'; thus alluding to the marriage of Marjorie Bruce and Walter Stewart, which had founded the Stuart dynasty.*[21] Six days later, on 14th December, King James was dead at the age of thirty. In a letter to the king in 1540, Cardinal Pole reminded him how his uncle, Henry VIII, had once been a man of promise and goodness, and what he was now; the cardinal told King James that he dreaded to see him follow the same route.[22] It is likely that the

---

* Although the throne did finally 'pass with a lass' as James v predicted, that lass was not his daughter. The Stewart dynasty, far from ending with Mary, went on through her son James to extend its power still further, over the throne of England and of Ireland.

cardinal was right in thus stressing King James's Tudor blood; if he had lived, his character too might have deepened in cruelty and sadism, to have eradicated totally the fair impression of his youth. He also seems to have included a mysterious, apparently hysterical, streak in his nature; there is no need to regard the contemporary suggestion of poison either by angry prelates, or seditious heretics, to explain his nervous breakdown after Solway Moss. Clearly a tendency to sudden physical collapse at moments of stress ran in the Stuart blood, a tendency which James handed on to his daughter, so that twenty-five years later, after Kirk o'Field, Scotland again witnessed the prostration of its monarch at the critical moment in her fortunes.

The daughter and only surviving (legitimate) child of James, who now succeeded to the throne of Scotland, had been born at the palace of Linlithgow, West Lothian, on the Feast of the Immaculate Conception of the Virgin Mary, 8th December. She was baptized Mary, by tradition in the Church of St Michael, at the gates of the palace, although one rumour stated that she had been named Elizabeth, which if true would have led in later years to two rival Queen Elizabeths on the thrones of England and Scotland.[23] A certain confusion surrounds the date of her birth, as indeed it surrounds the date of her father's death, due to the perilous political situation in Scotland at the time. The date of James's death was finally established in the seventeenth century by the discovery of the date engraved on his coffin. The date of Mary Stuart's birth, although given as the 8th by a concurrence of contemporary accounts, including Knox, is given as the 7th by her own partisan Leslie, who had special access to official records.[24] It has therefore been suggested that Mary was actually born on the 7th and that the date was altered to the 8th in order to coincide with the feast of the Virgin. Whatever the truth of this, which can never be proved, Mary Stuart herself always believed that she had been born on the 8th, heading a letter as late as 1584: 'December 8th the forty second anniversary of my birth.'[25] It certainly seems likely that she was born prematurely, the confinement of Queen Mary being brought on by anxiety over her husband: on 12th December Lisle and Tunstall reported to England from Alnwick that 'the said Queen was delivered before her time of a daughter, a very weak child, and not likely to live as it is thought'. In a private letter to King Henry on the same day, Lisle told him that the baby was actually dead. For the first ten days of her life, all the rumours spread about Mary Stuart were of an exceptionally frail baby, unlikely to survive, any more than her brothers. On 17th December, Sir George Douglas, writing from Berwick, still referred to 'a very weak child', and although by 19th December Lisle was able to tell Henry that 'the princess lately born is alive and good-looking', rumours of her ill-health continued long enough for Chapuys, the imperial ambassador in London, to write to the queen of Hungary on 23rd December that both mother and child were very ill and despaired of by their physicians.[26]

Perhaps with the English the wish was father to the thought, since the death of the infant queen would have increased the confusion of Scotland still further, to the point of the possible extinction of their government. The secret wishes of the Scots on the other hand are probably expressed by the rumour of the time that the child was actually a boy. The position of a country with a child heiress at its head was widely regarded as disastrous in the sixteenth century. As Knox put it, 'all men lamented that the realm was left without a male to succeed'.[27] The reason is not difficult to seek. In 1542, the successful reign of Queen Elizabeth I lay very much in the future. The birth of an heiress generally led to the swallowing up of the country concerned, as happened in the case of Burgundy, Spain, Bohemia and Hungary with Habsburgs, and with England, in the time of Mary Tudor. To the disadvantages of Mary Stuart's situation at birth, herself frail in health, the country divided and facing the prospect of a long minority, was therefore added the disadvantage of being of the weaker, and therefore the wrong sex.

The palace of Linlithgow, where Mary was born – in a room in the north-west corner, overlooking the loch* – and where she was destined to spend the first seven months of her life, was a traditional lying-in place of queens. James v himself had been born there. It was he who had enriched it by many improvements and who had developed it in a quadrangular form, from an earlier castle, in the course of his munificent Scottish rebuilding schemes, and it was certainly considered to be a splendid palace by the standards of the time: Mary of Guise compared it approvingly to the castles of the Loire on her arrival, and Sir David Lyndsay called it a 'palace of pleasance' worthy to be put beside those of Portugal and France. Leslie wrote warmly of its fine position, above the loch 'swimming full of perch and other notable fishes', and even in the next century, John Ray the naturalist called it 'a very good house, as houses go in Scotland'.[28] However, in December 1542, above this serene place, and its youthful incumbent, hovered a series of political thunder clouds of a highly ominous nature.

James v was buried with due pomp, says Leslie, with lighted torches and the sound of mourning trumpets (*buccinae querelae*); the nobles were in black, Cardinal Beaton hung his head down, while the people were loud in sorrow and lamentation. But with an outward delicacy of feeling which probably sprang in fact from shrewd political calculation, it was now thought unseemly for the English commander to pursue an attack against the kingdom of a dead man. Lisle reported as much to King Henry: 'I have thought good to stay the stroke of your sword until your majesty's pleasure be farther known to me in that behalf' and he included in his forbearance 'the young suckling', the late king's daughter.[29] Thus curiously enough, the premature death of King James, which had such dire results for Scotland in producing another long minority, had the short-term effect of staying the avenging hand of the English army after Solway

* Today the room where Mary Queen of Scots was born is roofless and the remaining structure of the palace of Linlithgow owes much of its beauty to embellishments in the next century.

Moss. As a result the first year of his daughter Mary's existence, instead of being threatened by English armies, was dominated by two questions of important bearing on her subsequent history – who was to govern the kingdom during her infancy, and whom she was destined to marry.

Of these two issues, it was the first which demanded immediate settlement, for while the bridals of the queen would only be a matter of speculation for many years to come, if Scotland was to survive as an independent nation the office of the governor had to be filled at once. Despite this urgency, a fierce controversy at once arose on the subject, to add to the country's troubles. It arose out of the clash of the hereditary claim of the earl of Arran, head of the house of Hamilton, to be sole governor, with the rival claim of Cardinal Beaton, which he based on a forged will supposed to have been made by the late king. This provided for four governors (Huntly, Moray, Argyll and Arran) with the cardinal himself to be the governor of the princess, and chief ruler of the Council. The prize was a rich one. The prestige and importance of the governor, or regent, was considered to be equivalent to that of the king himself; and the political powers were interwoven with the material rewards of office. It was tradition for the governor to take over the palaces, jewels and treasure of the late king during the minority of his successor; he was responsible for the administration of the crown revenues, for which he would be given a discharge signed at the end of his period of office.

As it happened, the man with the hereditary right to this important office at this critical juncture in Scottish history, James, 2nd earl of Arran and later 1st duke of Châtelherault, was singularly unfitted to hold it. Mary of Guise described him succinctly as the most inconstant man in the world: the most charitable verdict is that of a chaplain who called him 'a good soft God's man', presumably referring to the fact that for the past five years he had been a supporter of the reformed religion.[30] Yet this vacillating figure, by the very fact that he was the head of the house of Hamilton, was destined for the most prominent position among the Scottish nobles.

Arran's grandfather, James, 1st Lord Hamilton, had been married to Princess Mary Stewart, sister of James III.* If the child Queen Mary died, Arran could fairly claim the Scottish throne, as the next heir by blood. It was true that there was a complication: there was some doubt whether Arran's father had ever been properly divorced from his second wife and it was therefore conceivable that Arran, as the fruit of the third marriage, was illegitimate: in which case, the Lennox Stewarts who descended perfectly correctly from Princess Mary and Lord Hamilton – but from the daughter not a son – were the true heirs to the throne. This in turn meant that the earl of Lennox, not the earl of Arran, had the hereditary claim to be governor of Scotland, and second person in the realm. Despite this Lennox shadow across the Hamilton claim, a fact to be borne in mind when considering the perennially explosive relations between the two families during this period, the Hamiltons still managed to retain their position as heirs or next heirs to the Scottish throne for nearly a hundred years. Throughout much of the reign of Mary's father, her own reign, and that of James VI, until the birth of his quiverful of Stuart children in the 1590s, the Hamiltons were separated from the throne by only one life. Unfortunately the accidental importance of their position was in no way matched by the calibre of their blood. They possessed natural advantages other than their descent, in the shape of great estates, strategically placed close to the capital, and strong political connections in half a dozen counties. But at a time when most of the Scottish nobles made up in quickness and an eye to the main chance what they lacked in graces and civilization, the Hamiltons were strangely untypical of their kind: the Governor Arran was indecisive but his eldest son actually went mad and had to be confined. During the whole of this period, Hamilton blood was generally considered a convenient scapegoat on which to blame abnormalities of temper.[31]

There was nothing softened or indecisive about the character of David Beaton, cardinal-archbishop of St Andrews, the man

* See table of the Scottish royal succession.

who now opposed Arran's claim with the will of the late king, apparently made in his favour. The evidence that Beaton actually forged the will seems conclusive,[32] but in view of the weakness of Scotland at the time, it may be argued that Cardinal Beaton was at least making a bid to give his country some sort of strong government to combat England's rapacity. He was now a man of over fifty, having been made cardinal of San Stefano by Pope Paul III five years previously, and succeeded his uncle as archbishop of St Andrews in 1539; he had considerable knowledge of Europe, having studied in Paris and acted on various diplomatic missions abroad. Certainly the cardinal's pro-French, Catholic policy, which had led to disaster at Solway Moss, did represent the only alternative to subjugation under the yoke of Henry VIII. Knox has described the worldliness of the cardinal at length in his usual vivid phrases, referring to 'that kingdom of darkness, whereof within this realm he was the head' and how he was 'more careful for the world than he was to preach Christ ... as he sought the world, it fled him not'. Knox even goes so far as to hint at Cardinal Beaton's lascivious relations with Mary of Guise – an accusation of which the verdict of history has acquitted the queen, although undoubtedly the cardinal lived openly with at least one woman, in a way which made nonsense of his vows of celibacy.[33] Whatever the cardinal's moral deficiencies, he was certainly not a man of straw; as a prelate without any family that he might be bound to favour, he at least showed some signs of identifying his personal policies with those of Scotland, in contrast to the rest of the venal Scottish nobility.

Despite Cardinal Beaton's strength of purpose, the deciding factor in the contest for the governorship proved to be the return of those Scottish nobles captured at Solway Moss: after a sojourn in London, they were now dispatched north again by Henry VIII, like so many Trojan horses, as emissaries of his policy; they included Cassillis, Glencairn, Maxwell and Fleming, besides Angus and his brother George Douglas, who were already in England in exile. While in London they had been induced to sign a series of articles which pledged them to help

Henry bring about the marriage of Mary and Prince Edward, and generally advance the cause of England in Scotland in return for which they were given suitable pensions of English money. Ten of them had even gone further and promised to help Henry himself to achieve dominion and government over Scotland, should the young queen die. The signing of these articles seems to us by modern standards unpatriotic to the point of treachery; it is only fair to point out that they should be judged in the context of an age in which patriotism, as a modern concept, was only just beginning to exist. Xenophobia there was, a primordial dislike of the foreigner, at a period when bad communications made foreigners out of those who would seem close neighbours today; but although this xenophobia was starting to push out a few green shoots of patriotism from time to time, it certainly cannot yet be too closely identified with it.

In January Arran was confirmed in his office of governor, and a few days after the return of the English faction among the nobles, Cardinal Beaton was arrested: it seemed thus certain that the rulers of Scotland during Queen Mary's minority were to be a protestant pro-English faction. Equally, the matrimonial future of the young queen seemed to lie in the direction of England. Only eleven days after Mary's birth, Lisle had expressed the general English wish concerning her future: 'I would she and her nurse were in my lord prince's house.'[34] Henry's son, Prince Edward, then aged five, seemed the ideal spouse to unite Scotland and England firmly forever under English suzerainty, and Henry furthermore intended to bring up the Scottish queen actually at the English court, in order to check any possible fluttering for liberty in the Scottish dove-cots. This marriage, which if Edward VI had lived would have antedated the peaceful union of England and Scotland by half a century, would not necessarily have been such a terrible prospect for Scotland, had it not been for the savagely bullying attitude which Henry VIII persisted in adopting towards his neighbour. It must be recalled that at this date Mary's future husband the dauphin of France had not yet been born and his mother Catherine de Médicis, wife of the heir to the French throne, appeared to be barren, having been married ten years without producing any children at all. Thus there was no French prince in prospect whose merits could be weighed against those of Prince Edward.

If a match with a foreign prince was rejected altogether, then the other obvious matrimonial possibility before the Queen's guardians was to wed her to the son of one of her own nobles: Arran, for example, took the line that his own son would make her the best bridegroom, because the marriage would keep the crown of Scotland within the control of its own people. In March Sir Ralph Sadler came to Scotland as Henry's envoy, charged with negotiating the marriage of Edward and Mary with the Scottish Parliament. He reported that the queen dowager was far from unfavourable to the project. Indeed at the time, the behaviour of the Scottish nobility may easily have encouraged Mary of Guise to believe that a royal match with her daughter, even with England, was the lesser of two evils. She certainly took the opportunity to display the baby proudly to Sadler, anxious no doubt to contradict the rumours at the time of her birth that the princess was frail and unlikely to live. She had her daughter brought into the room, now aged three and a half months, and with determined thoroughness had her unwrapped by her nurse out of all her clothes, until she was totally naked; thus there could be no suspicion afterwards of some deformity concealed under the swaddling clothes. Sir Ralph Sadler was duly impressed by the sight. He wrote back to King Henry: 'I assure your Majesty, it is as goodly a child as I have seen of her age, and as like to live, with the Grace of God.'⁵⁵ In the meantime, lest Arran suffer disappointment at the thought of this rich matrimonial prize being wrested from his own son, Henry deliberately wooed the earl with the prospect of a match between his son and Henry's daughter Princess Elizabeth.

On 1st July the Treaties of Greenwich were drawn up, providing for the marriage of Edward and Mary. These treaties respected Scotland's independence as a country and provided for the return of Mary as a childless widow if Edward died; the main point on which the Scots insisted and on which Henry disagreed was that the child should not actually leave Scotland until she was ten years old. Henry remained avuncularly anxious to oversee her upbringing personally at the English court – or perhaps he did not trust the Scots to implement their promises in ten years' time. But in any case the point was never put to the test, since already by the summer of 1543 the internal situation in Scotland had changed radically. Opinion, although Henry VIII might be ignorant of the fact, was no longer predominantly favourable to the Protestant and pro-English cause. It was true the advent of Arran as governor had led to the extension of the reformed doctrines and practices – especially the reading of the Bible and preaching in the vernacular. Knox commented cynically on the number of those who now flaunted their Bibles with the boast, not always true: 'This has lain under my bed-foot these ten years.'[36] Protestant sympathies formed the most natural bond between those Scots and those English who shared that inclination. But by the summer Cardinal Beaton had somehow eluded captivity – the English suspected that no great efforts had been made to hold him – and in Pitscottie's words, he began to rage as any lion loosed of his bond; in short he was once more in a position to galvanize Catholic pro-French opinion.[37] Two new arrivals on the Scottish scene – the governor's bastard half-brother John Hamilton, abbot of Paisley, and Mathew, earl of Lennox, himself – only helped to poison Arran's mind further against the English alliance. John Hamilton pointed out that by abandoning the cause of Rome, Arran put himself in a vulnerable position in which his father's divorce might be questioned; Lennox, as head of the rival Stewarts, represented a positive alternative to Arran as governor. Under the circumstances Arran's vacillating wits were no match for the machinations of the cardinal. French subsidies began to enter Scotland, to vie with the English ones, and the very day after the Treaties of Greenwich had been signed, Sadler reported to Henry that the French ships had been seen lying off the coast of Scotland.

Henry reacted to this news predictably by demanding that the queen be moved away from Linlithgow, which he thought altogether too accessible to the French if they landed. Arran replied smoothly to Sadler that the baby was suffering from 'the breeding of teeth' and it might be dangerous to move her at this precise moment. Sadler noted that Arran was as much concerned for her well-being as if she had been his own child. In point of fact, Linlithgow did no longer seem a suitable place in which to guard their queen, although it was fear of abduction by the English, rather than by the French, which now prompted the Scots to move her. On 21st July, Cardinal Beaton assembled about 7000 followers at Stirling and marched down to Linlithgow, together with Huntly, Lennox, Argyll and Bothwell, with the avowed aim of putting the child in charge of some reliable guardians at Stirling Castle. There was as yet no conclusive evidence of a volte-face on the part of the Scottish government. The Protestant earl of Glencairn was deputed to make the new arrangements, and of the four lords thus chosen – Graham, Lindsay, Livingston and Erskine – Erskine was a natural choice, since the Erskines enjoyed a hereditary right to guard the person of the heir to the throne. (This same Lord Erskine had been one of the personal guardians of the young King James v as well as guardian to Mary's dead brother the prince of Scotland when his father visited the Isles in 1540.) Equally, since Stirling had formed part of Mary of Guise's dowry, there was no particular reason why she should not visit it at any time she wished, although additional care was taken to explain to Sadler that Linlithgow, that splendid palace, was actually too small to lodge both queens comfortably.

The new home of Mary, Stirling, had in the time of Edward i's invasion been considered the strongest castle in Scotland. Even that optimistic maker of promises, Sir George Douglas, thought it would be extraordinarily difficult to abduct Mary from Stirling in the autumn, and hand her over to King Henry, although he characteristically offered to try, if supplied with enough gold. In spite of its subsequent ornamentation, its commanding situation, surveying both plain and mountain, looking towards the Ochils on one side (where silver for the royal mint was mined) and the Grampian and Trossachs on the other, the castle was unaltered since the days of Edward i. Its attractions included the splendour of the great hall of James v, which in 1618 John Taylor compared favourably to Westminster Hall,[38] and the palace, a jewel of the Scottish Renaissance, today still showing King James's initials in the carved panels over its windows. But in 1543 it was the fortress aspect of the castle, high over the town of Stirling, higher still over the plain, and standing at the gateway of the impenetrable territory of the Highlands, which commended it to the lords who there incarcerated their queen for safety.

Henry VIII still felt secure enough in the terms of the treaty he had just signed to imagine that he could put Sadler in charge of the queen in her new abode, and he actually laid it down that Mary of Guise was not to be allowed to lodge in the castle with her baby, but should be kept elsewhere in the town and allowed to visit her from time to time, as the little queen's keepers should think fit.[39] Such might be the distant relationship which Henry in England considered suitable for a child and its mother. But the time when Henry would have any say in Scotland's affairs was rapidly passing. The king made a series of frantic efforts to maintain his ascendancy over Arran; he also tried to woo his former enemy Cardinal Beaton, and tempt him to throw in his lot with the English, after laying aside his cardinal's hat and his religion; but his arrest of some Scottish merchant ships sailing to France, and the impounding of the merchants and their goods, aroused popular indignation. Sadler warned him that the temper of the country was turning against him. After torments of indecision, Arran finally decided to throw in his lot with Beaton and the pro-French party, his mind probably made up in the end by the renewed promise of the little queen's hand for his son. On 8th September, in the church of the Franciscans at Stirling, 'the unhappy man', as Knox disgustedly termed him, did penance for his apostasy and received the Catholic sacrament while Argyll and Patrick, earl of Bothwell, held the towel over his head.[40]

The day after Arran's change of faith, on 9th September, 1543, Mary Stuart was solemnly crowned in Stirling Castle chapel at the age of nine months. It was an inauspicious date, being the thirtieth anniversary of the battle of Flodden, and the coronation scarcely seems to have been an occasion for universal rejoicing. Sir Ralph Sadler reported back that Mary had been crowned 'with such solemnitie as they do use in this country, which is not very costlie'.[41] Certainly the Tudor use of ceremonial which Queen Elizabeth 1 was to put to such good effect in subjugating the imagination of her subjects, was not understood in Scotland. Sixteen years later, Elizabeth's own coronation was a magnificent display of pageantry, with the uncrowned queen its centrepiece, sparkling with jewels, in cloth of gold, revealed to an admiring populace in an open litter. By contrast the coronation of the Stuart queen consisted of the hurried investiture of a tiny child, surrounded by feudal nobility at least as powerful as the crown they nominally served. At the ceremony, the earl of Arran bore the crown, the earl of Lennox bore the sceptre, and the earl of Argyll, also of royal descent from James 1, bore the sword. The pro-English party, including Angus, Gray, Glencairn, Cassillis and Maxwell, stayed away altogether.

CHAPTER TWO

England's Rough Wooing

'I perceive that proverb to be very true
Unhappy is the age which has o'er young a King'
Sir David Lyndsay of the Mount

The defection of Arran marked the first turning-point in the life of Mary Queen of Scots. It decided, among other things, that Henry would no longer woo the Scots with gifts, but attempt to constrain them by force. This was indeed the course which he furiously advised his pensioners among the Scottish nobles to pursue, when he heard the news of Arran's treachery. However, George Douglas managed to put forward a number of objections to immediate action, while continuing to profess loyalty to Henry and amazement at the turn events had taken in Scotland. The world was full of falsehood, he exclaimed, he knew not whom he might trust. Arran and Cardinal Beaton took no immediate steps to break with England, but the knowledge that they had cut themselves free from close entanglement with Protestant England encouraged both the papacy and the French king to renew their support to Scotland. The appearance of a papal legate, Marco Grimani, the patriarch of Aquileia, with a papal subsidy, and of French envoys at the Scottish court, presaged the final change of policy announced by the Scottish Parliament in December 1543. By the Treaty of 15th December, as Leslie put it, the 'auld bands' between the Scots and the French 'so long and religiously kept' since the days of King Robert the Bruce, were now once more confirmed.[1] A secondary effect of Arran's volte-face was the turning away of Lennox from the party of Scottish government. Lennox was unable to endure the fact that despite his changes of allegiance, his rival Arran still retained his position as governor of Scotland. The classical policy of the Lennox Stewarts was to ally themselves with the enemies of the Hamiltons. Lennox now veered his eyes towards England, and offered himself as a bridegroom to Lady Margaret Douglas, daughter of Margaret Tudor by her second marriage to the earl of Angus, and niece of Henry VIII. In time to come, this formidable lady was to show herself a worthy combination of the intriguing talents of Douglas and Tudor. She was also, as the mother of Henry Stuart, Lord Darnley, to play a significant part in the history of her daughter-in-law, the queen of Scots. But at the time of her marriage, in June 1544, her importance was mainly dynastic: she brought Lennox within the sphere of the English succession, and as Henry's nephew by marriage, Lennox contracted a marriage treaty with him, which put him henceforth firmly into the English camp. Among other provisions, Lennox promised to do all he could to hand over Mary Stuart to Henry, and Henry in return swore to make Lennox governor of Scotland once he had subjugated the country, with Lennox's help.

Thus by the time Mary Stuart was one year old, the pieces on the traditional chess board which lay between Scotland and England had been rearranged to form an altogether different pattern from that which was in evidence when she first succeeded to the throne. In this realignment, human frailty had played an important part – the pliable character of the Governor Arran, steadfast in one thing only – greed for his own family's advancement, the intemperate nature of Henry VIII's attitude towards Scotland, the mature cunning of the cardinal, able to play on Arran's weakness, and lastly the remarkable character of the Scottish nobles of the time, who saw no point in pursuing any policy out of principle, once it no longer suited their purpose, even if they were being bribed to do so. In twelve months the possibility of the peaceful annexation of Scotland by England, through the marriage of Mary and Edward, and the direction of Scottish affairs by King Henry, had receded with amazing rapidity. With the renewal of the French alliance, and the birth of a son to Catherine de Médicis and the future Henry II of France in January 1544, the prospect of a very different education and marriage unfolded before the child queen.

Four and a half years were to elapse before the young queen of Scots was finally dispatched to the safety of France. They were years in which the policy of Henry VIII towards Scotland did little to correct the impression he had already given, of a vindictive bully, once his will was gain-said. In May 1544 Henry's commander Hertford set out on the first stages of what has been aptly termed 'the Rough Wooing', in which Henry paradoxically attempted to win the loyalties of the Scots by a planned programme of devastation of Scottish territory. His instructions to Hertford strike a note of ruthlessness which chills the spirit,[2] and the English records make it clear that their armies were remarkably successful in carrying out this 'scorched earth' policy, until the point when they were checked by the fortress castle of Edinburgh, which withstood their siege. There was no pity in the English hearts: an eye-witness account of the campaign sent to the Lord Russell, the Lord Privy Seal, in London, exhibits a positively self-righteous spirit towards these fiery depredations – the English seem to have considered themselves taking part in a sort of holy war, as a result of the broken promises of the Scots. The burning of Edinburgh – which took two days – is vividly described, and in the course of it the abbey and palace of Holyrood were sacked.[3]

The English also broke up the pier at Leith Haven, captured the Scottish merchant ships and finally set off for home laden with booty, taking care on their way to devastate the castle of Lord Seton, including his gardens and orchards, said to be the fairest in Scotland, because he was held responsible for the release of the cardinal, the author of all this calamity. 'In these victories who is to be most lauded but God, by whose goodness the English hath had of a great season, notable victories,' exclaims Lord Russell's correspondent. Allowing for natural

English exaggeration of their success, even if half the destruction he reported took place, the Scots may surely have supposed that God had temporarily deserted the side of David for that of Goliath. The next rough embrace on the part of the English took place in November 1544. Coming up from the borders, the English forces laid about them as before; in the course of their campaign, they devastated the ancient tombs of the Douglases at Melrose, one of the string of rich abbeys along the fertile valley of the Tweed, hives of life and industry, which made them enticing bait for predatory English soldiers. It was, however, not so much this insult to his ancestors, as the fact that the Scottish government had learnt to counter the English bribes with gifts of their own, which persuaded the venal Angus to lead the Scots to victory at Ancrum Moor in February. But the effects on Ancrum Moor were not permanent: for in September 1545 Hertford himself led a second, equally destructive expedition to the south-east, at a time deliberately chosen in order to ravish and burn the newly cut harvest.

In this atmosphere of violence, the safety of the young queen continued to be a matter of concern – Hertford reported that at the time of his forays in May 1544 she had been removed to Dunkeld for greater security. In the same summer the statecraft of her mother Mary of Guise made its first effects felt. She had impressed the patriarch of Aquileia with her prudent and cheerful disposition, in view of her continuously desperate situation in such a divided kingdom as poor Scotland. 'I say poor kingdom,' wrote the patriarch, 'because it is so divided and disturbed that if God does not show his hand and inspire these nobles to unite together, public and private ruin is clearly to be foreseen.'[4] Hertford's spoilations of 1544 did nothing to heal such divisions. On the contrary, considerable dissatisfaction was now felt with the policy of the cardinal, which had plunged Scotland into such a state of physical misery. From the summer onwards, the weight of the queen dowager's counsels were also felt in the shifting scales of Scottish national policy. Many nobles were beginning to feel that she should share the regency with the weak Arran. From its first volume, the Register of the Acts of the Privy Council marks her presence – *Presentibus, Regina et Gubernator.* It is safe to assume that Queen Mary's secret wishes were by now steadily in favour of a French marriage – France, her own country, the country of her able family, and the country with enough resources to quell the English, on behalf of the Scots, if necessary. The climate of Scottish opinion was not yet ready for such a match: it needed further action on behalf of England, to point the lesson that a French alliance, however confining to their independence, was at least preferable to extinction at the hands of their neighbours. Mary of Guise had also two specific hazards to overcome – Arran's desire for the marriage of Mary and his own son, and the cardinal's steady opposition to the idea of a French marriage, as marked as had been his opposition to an English one, for the same nationalist reasons.

But Cardinal Beaton's days were numbered. Quite apart from its political confusion, religious life in Scotland was in a ferment. Not only had high office in the Church become a valuable part of royal patronage, but in a poor country such as Scotland, with a primitive economy, the Church still presented a picture of disproportionate wealth. In a report to Pope Paul IV in 1556 on the state of the Scottish Church, Cardinal Sermoneta wrote that 'almost one half of the revenue of the whole kingdom' was coming in to it; it has been calculated that the Church revenues on the eve of the Reformation must have been more than £300,000, whereas the royal lands only brought in £17,500.' Such riches had in all too many cases cut off the Scottish clergy totally from a sense of pastoral mission and many of them might well justify Knox's abusive term of 'a greedy pack'. It was felt that while monks and friars idled and were supported by the community, the true objects of social pity – 'the blind, crooked, bed-ridden, widows, orphans and all other poor, so visited by the hand of God as may not work' in the words of one contemporary complaint – were being neglected. The majority of the parish churches in the country had been assigned or appropriated to bishoprics or monasteries, and other churches had no priest at all. The provincial council of 1549 enacted a significant amount of statutes denouncing concubinage among the priesthood, or the promotion and endowing of illegitimate children. Repeated enactments by provincial councils urging the clergy to preach to the people showed both that the problem was pressing and that it was not being cured.[6]

Against this background, it is easy to understand the success of any anti-clerical movement: by 1543, the flames of unrest were being fed by a continuous fuel of books, pamphlets and broadsides advocating the reformed religion. Many were spiritual in content; the others were mere lampoons. The same parallel exists in those people who were drawn to the new religion. Many were men of the most ascetic nature, who felt they could no longer stretch their wings under the tutelage of the corrupt Scottish Catholic Church; others were merely animated by a strong dislike of the Catholic clergy. In time past the Scottish nobles had often endowed the Church with land, in order that they might be prayed for in perpetuity: their reactions, once it was explained to them by the reformers that these prayers were not necessarily an assured passport to heaven, were predictably angry; the nobility considered that the land could be rightfully returned to them. In March 1546 George Wishart, a leading Protestant preacher of outstanding gentle character, in an age not over-endowed with the pure in heart, was burned to death in the forecourt of the castle of St Andrews. Cardinal Beaton and his bishops watched from cushioned seats on the castle walls. Three months later, a band of Fife lairds, disguised as the masons whom the cardinal had commissioned to re-fortify the castle, broke into St Andrews and seized the cardinal as he was resting after a night spent with his concubine Marion Ogilvy. After holding him at sword point, and asking him to repent the shedding of Wishart's blood, they did him to death. After death the cardinal's savagely mutilated body was hung naked from the foretower of the castle for the edification of the people.* Later, the corpse was pickled in salt, and kept in a barrel in the famous

---

* 'Ane callit Guthrie loosit done his ballops' poynt and pischit in his mouth that all the pepill might sie' – *Pitscottie*.[7]

Bottle Dungeon of St Andrews for over a year, while his assassins kept the castle in their thrall.

Knox related the death of the cardinal with all the relish of an Old Testament prophet who knows that God is on his side. It was indeed an almost Biblical end for this great prince of the Church. But his murderers, whatever their motives, did not receive the immediate help from Henry VIII which they had anticipated, once they publicly announced their support of the English marriage. The murder of Beaton had the unexpected consequence of bringing the prospect of a French marriage for Mary closer. Henry VIII lagged in sending aid to the 'Castilians' as they were now termed. Arran dithered, unable to condone the murder of a prelate since his half-brother John Hamilton was bishop-elect of Dunkeld, but unwilling to send for French help, which might spoil the chances of his son's royal marriage – moreover as this very son was being held hostage in St Andrews, he had a special reason for not wishing to press the Castilians too hard. He compromised with a long but ineffective siege of the castle, which owing to its spectacular position on the Fife coast, with the sea washing round the very walls of the castle, was able to hold out for the unbelievable period of fourteen months, despite the most determined mining operations on the part of the attackers, from the land side. There was, however, a long period of armistice in the course of the siege and it was during this that Knox himself entered the castle, and began his career as a preacher in the pulpit of the parish of St Andrews: he confirms Pitscottie's account of the impudent behaviour of those within the castle, who, when the siege was not at its hottest would ride out and harry the countryside 'using their body in lechery with fair women'.[8] It took the arrival of a French expedition off the coast to bring the siege to an end: the castle fell on 30th July, 1547, as a result of which the principal defenders were dispatched to France as prisoners, and many others of its inhabitants, including Knox, were sent to the galleys.

The death of Francis I and the accession of his son Henry II to the throne of France in the spring of 1547 had made the

climate of opinion in France newly favourable to notions of
French aid for Scotland: Henry II was anxious to conciliate his
powerful Guise subjects, whose sister and niece were evidently
in such a dangerous situation there. The death of Henry VIII,
on the other hand, in January 1547, had no effect in reducing
the savagery of the English attitude towards Scotland. In late
August of that year, the former Hertford, now Protector Somerset, mounted an expedition towards Scotland which was to
rival in ferocity anything the late king had commissioned.
Throughout the summer, the Register of the Scottish Privy
Council is full of enactments to do with the coming war: to
impress the country with a sense of the emergency facing them,
the fiery cross was sent to every district, as a result of which
the divided Scots seem to have made some sort of genuinely
national effort: 36,000 people hastened from all over the country
towards Edinburgh. These also included members of the clergy,
who had a special reason for wishing to fight off the heretical
invader, and provision was made that if any kirkman died in
battle, his next-of-kin was to have his benefice. It was in this
do-or-die spirit that on 10th September the battle of Pinkie
Cleugh was engaged.[9]

Under the command of Arran, the Scots drew up in a strong
position on Edmonstone Edge, behind the town of Musselburgh.
Their ranks and spears were thick as the spikes of a hedgehog,
as an English observer, William Patten, put it: the clergy were
there, marked out by their shaven crowns, their black garments
contrasting with the white banner which they bore before them;
among the magnates Huntly was especially magnificent in gilt
and enamelled armour. Unfortunately there was nothing in the
situation now facing him to supply Arran with the backbone
which he had so singularly lacked throughout his career. Certain
of his leading nobles' names had been discovered on a list of
'assured Scots', the contemptuous English phrase for those on
their payroll, within St Andrew's Castle. Not only was he doubtful
of the loyalty of his lieutenants, including the flamboyant
Huntly recently ransomed from England, but he had no greater
confidence in the discipline of his troops. When the Scots hurled

themselves upon their traditional foes, needlessly abandoning their strong position, Arran displayed none of the qualities of leadership necessary to hold them back. The result of the clash between these courageous but scarcely disciplined troops, and Somerset's well-drilled army, was another horrifying rout for the Scots.[10]

William Patten described scornfully how the Governor Arran fled 'skant with honour', followed by Angus and the other chiefs, whereupon the whole army turned and cast down their weapons, preparatory to flight. Patten's details of the English pursuit are revolting if vivid: some of the Scots tried to elude capture by crouching in the river, with their noses breathing through the roots of willow trees. The dead had their wounds mainly in the head, because the horsemen could not reach lower with their swords, although arms were sometimes sliced off, and necks cut half asunder. Patten noted that the dead bodies lying about gave the impression of a thick herd of cattle, grazing in a newly replenished pasture. Patten takes the line that the English were playing the role of a schoolmaster chastising naughty children for their own good. But quite apart from the pillaging of the countryside which followed, the casualties suffered by the Scots at Pinkie Cleugh decimated their finest fighting men yet again, only five years after Solway Moss.

The unconscious cause of this holocaust, Mary Queen of Scots, now aged four years and nine months, was removed rapidly from the possible area of conflict, after the Scottish defeat. Stirling Castle was no longer considered safe enough, as Somerset raged about the lowlands of Scotland, like a beast of prey. The place of security chosen for her repose was a romantic and secluded island, Inchmahome, off the north shore of the Lake of Menteith, a few hours' ride from Stirling. Here, amid pleasant trees and luxurious vegetation, had been built in the thirteenth century an exquisite island priory for the monks of the Augustinian order. This priory was still in existence, but as it had been given *in commendam* to members of the Erskine family ever since 1528, it had become practically speaking their hereditary possession. Robert Erskine, commendator from 1529 onwards, was actually killed at the battle of Pinkie, but his family connections with the monarchy made Inchmahome a natural choice for a retreat. Lord Erskine was still numbered among the queen's guardians and in 1545, together with Lord Livingston, had been exempted from military service such as armies or raids against England, to look after the queen's person.[11]

Inchmahome, seen from the shore low-lying on the horizon of the lake, with its religious buildings, its sedge, its views of mountains and water, makes an ideal focus for romance. It is therefore not surprising that a number of charming legends have grown up around Mary Stuart's visit to it. Queen Mary's Garden, Queen Mary's Bower and Queen Mary's Tree all honour the memory of the child, not yet five, who spent at the most three weeks on the island. Although there are records of letters being brought to the island on matters of state, after she had been committed to the safe keeping of the commendator, Leslie makes it clear that she was only sent to Inchmahome during the time the English were at Leith, i.e. between 11 and 18th September, and returned to Stirling as soon as the English left Scotland – the English re-crossed the Tweed on 29th September. So much for the legends which have grown up that Mary Stuart first learnt Latin and other languages there under the tutelage of a stern prior, as well as finding the time and strength to plant a garden and a number of trees. In the middle of the last century, Sir William Fraser suggested to the duke of Montrose, the then owner of the island, that he should restore the bower with new boxwood plants to please 'tourists from America', who would want a cutting from plants supposed to have been planted by Queen Mary herself.[12] The best hope for the authenticity of such a bower, which cannot in honesty be attributed to Mary Stuart's short infant stay on the island, would seem to be the fact that Mary often stayed at Stirling in later years, and might then have paid some unrecorded visit to the island, in the course of which the planting took place. But the real romance of Inchmahome lies more in its genuine and touching association with Mary Stuart as a child refugee from English oppression, rather than in any specific historical relic.

After her return from Inchmahome Mary spent the winter once again at Stirling, before being transferred to Dumbarton Castle on the west coast of Scotland, in February 1548. The victory of the English at Pinkie Cleugh was making it increasingly clear to many of the Scots that a French alliance, at the price of a French marriage for their queen, was their best hope of extricating themselves from the morass of defeat and disunity in which they now found themselves. They could not even call all the country their own: ever since Pinkie, the English troops had occupied Haddington, uncomfortably near Edinburgh, from where they were able to exert a stranglehold on the south-east of Scotland. A council was held in November 1547 at which the queen's removal to France was discussed, as well as the necessity of placing the Scottish strongholds in the hands of the French. By the end of December, fifty French captains had arrived in Scotland, and on 27th January a contract was signed between Arran and Henry II by which Arran bound himself to assemble the Scots Parliament, in order to give its consent to the marriage of the queen with Henry's son, her deliverance to France, and the handing over of the crucial fortresses. In return Arran was to receive a French duchy.

By June 1548 the French were actually landed in Scotland, under the command of an experienced soldier, André de Montalembert, Seigneur d'Essé. D'Essé was to show admirable sangfroid as a general, the quality hitherto most lacking in the Scottish command. When messengers came to him crying: '*Monsieur, voici les ennemis qui viennent a vous*', he replied without a flicker of astonishment: '*Et nous a eux*'.[13] He also brought with him an extremely well-equipped body of 6000 men, including German and Italian mercenaries, the latter probably engineers, as well as a quantity of light horsemen under two French captains. D'Essé's friend, Jean de Beaugué, who accompanied him, and witnessed the campaign, formed the impression that the Scots' troubles as fighters sprang not from their lack of courage, nor from the fact that they were less '*belliqueux*' than the English, but simply from the '*ligues*' and '*partialités*' with which they were plagued. He concluded that they had been chastened by God deliberately during their recent misfortunes, to teach them the error of their ways, going on to observe with irritating superiority, typical of the French attitude to Scotland at this period, that luckily for them things took a better turn immediately the French came to their rescue.[14] Whether or not the Scots themselves shared this view of their predicament, their Parliament finally gave its assent to the marriage of Mary and Francis in July 1548, on condition that the king of France should defend Scotland as he did his own realm, and at the same time respect Scotland's independence. On these terms, the marriage was described as being 'very reasonable'.

In March of the same year, the cornerstone of the Scottish–French alliance nearly fell from its arch when Mary became suddenly and dangerously ill. The disease, whatever its nature, was violent enough for there to be rumours that she was actually dead. Huntly told Somerset that she had smallpox, but as Mary was to suffer a much better attested attack of smallpox later in her childhood, it seems to have been measles, the explanation given to La Chapelle in Edinburgh, which was responsible for her collapse on this occasion.[15] The whole incident illustrates the perils in the sixteenth century of founding foreign policy on the lives of children. However, by the time the informative Frenchman de Beaugué saw Mary at Dumbarton, when she was being prepared for her journey to France, he was able to wax lyrical in her praises. Even allowing for Gallic gallantry, the unanimity of all the early reports on Mary as a child, both now and on her arrival in France, concerning her physical perfection and conspicuous health, make it clear that she was an exceptionally attractive and above all energetic little girl. De Beaugué called her one of the most perfect creatures he had ever seen, and felt that with such splendid beginnings anything could be expected of her. 'It is not possible to hope for more from a Princess on this earth,' he wrote. Looking beneath the natural hyperbole of a courtier faced with a queen, it is obvious that observers confronted with the child Mary Stuart for once did not have to work out guardedly enthusiastic phrases for some delicate and sickly prince: able to be genuine in their appreciation, they were further spurred on by poignant thoughts of her destiny.

In July the French galleys arrived at Dumbarton, on the west coast of Scotland, King Henry having sent his own royal galley for Mary's use, to demonstrate the honour which he intended to pay to her in France. On 29th July Mary embarked on her ship, after a tearful farewell to her mother, and with her went the suite which was considered suitable for her new estate in France. Two of her royal half-brothers – Robert and John Stewart – went with her, demonstrating the closeness felt by the monarchy to its own kin, and it seems virtually certain that her eldest half-brother, James Stewart, later earl of Moray, went for a short visit, although he was back in Scotland by November of the next year. Also included in Mary's suite were her guardian, Lord Erskine, and her governess, Janet Stewart, Lady Fleming, an illegitimate daughter of James IV by the countess of Bothwell, and widow of the Lord Fleming who had fallen at Pinkie. Her natural royal blood once again was considered to fit her for a post in the queen's immediate entourage. In France the nubile charms of the volatile Lady Fleming – to the Venetian ambassador's admiring gaze 'a very pretty little woman' – were to be the source of controversy; she showed her mettle even at the outset of the journey, when she became thoroughly discontented with the long delay between embarkment in the Clyde at the end of July, and sailing on the desired west wind on 7th August; growing bored with life on board ship Lady Fleming demanded to be put ashore 'to repose her'. The captain of the ship answered smartly that Lady Fleming, so far from being able to go on land, could go to France and like it, or drown on the way.[16]

Mary's departure to France also marks the first appearance in her story of those romantic concomitants of her adventures, the four Maries. A train of noblemen's sons and daughters, about Mary's age, were taken with her to France, it having been long traditional for young men of good family to be sent to France for a sort of chivalrous education. The Maries, in Leslie's words, were considered 'special', not only because they all bore the queen's Christian name, but because they came from four notably honourable houses. Thus Mary Fleming, Mary Seton, Mary Beaton and Mary Livingston are introduced into Mary Stuart's history. In point of fact Maries, or maids, had been known before in the train of a Scottish queen. The word Marie has its etymological derivation in the Icelandic word *maer*, the official designation given to a virgin or maid; from there it had come to be used in Scots especially for the maids-of-honour attendant on the queen. Pitscottie describes how Queen Madeleine, the first wife of James v, was called on by her father the king of France to pass to his wardrobe and take his rolls of cloth of gold, velvet and satins as he pleased, 'to clothe her and her Maries'.[17]

All four little Maries were of noble birth, but Mary Fleming was considered chief among them by reason of the royal blood which flowed in her veins, through her mother Lady Fleming. Mary Seton came from one of the grandest Scottish families, being the daughter of George, 6th Lord Seton, by his second marriage to a French woman, Marie Pieris, who had come to Scotland as one of Mary of Guise's maids-of-honour. Mary Beaton was the daughter of Robert Beaton of Creich, and granddaughter of Sir John Beaton, the hereditary keeper of the royal palace of Falkland; the Beatons of Creich were a younger branch of that family whose senior line had given to Scotland Cardinal David Beaton, and were to provide Queen Mary with her faithful ambassador, Archbishop James Beaton; Mary Beaton's mother like that of Mary Seton had been a French lady-in-waiting. Mary Livingston was the daughter of Mary's guardian, Lord Livingston, and thus also lay within the magic inner circle of families who could expect to attend on the queen. Mary Stuart's Maries were very far from being four ciphers, who could be dismissed by one generic name; of widely different characters, they were able to enjoy widely different adventures. Although their public lives all began at the same point on a galley sailing to France in 1548, they ended at points far from each other, and in all but one case, far from the queen they were appointed to serve.

Accompanied by her train of lords, and her miniature train of children, Mary Stuart embarked for France. Her mother's sorrow was extreme, as the Englishman Henry Jones noted when he wrote to Somerset, on 9th August. 'The Old Queen do lament the young Queen's departure, and marvelleth she heareth nothing from her.'[18] Mary of Guise's feelings can be readily understood. For the second time in her life she had to endure the keen pain of being parted from her child, to be brought up in a distant land, by other hands than hers. Furthermore, her daughter's journey was believed to be hazardous, and there was no certainty that she would arrive safely in France, since it was thought that the English intended to intercept the galleys. It is true that this danger proved in the end to be illusory: the English, who must have known that the Scottish queen would shortly be dispatched to France, once Parliament had given its assent to the marriage, made no serious efforts at interception. But this was not appreciated at the time of Mary Stuart's departure, and elaborate precautions were taken to send her on the longer western route from Dumbarton, rather than the natural short route from the east coast, in order to elude the English. Mary of Guise had to suffer the natural pangs of a mother's loss coupled with fears for her daughter's safety, at the same time as the political situation in Scotland, even with French aid, was scarcely such as to promote peace of mind. The combination of anxieties called forth all the resources of this stoical lady, who returned for a short while to the pleasant palace of Falkland to ease her sorrow.

For the alleviation of her unhappiness, the French commander sent by Henry II, the Seigneur de Brezé, wrote a series of letters to Mary of Guise, for which we are indebted for an account of her daughter's behaviour on the journey.[19] On 31st July de Brezé reports that Mary is 'as cheerful as you have seen her for a long time'. Whether out of diplomacy or genuine feeling, de Brezé announced that in the ten days in which the queen and her retinue remained at sea without sailing, it was only Mary who did not fall sea-sick. On 3rd August, de Brezé reports that Mary is still in good health and has still not been sea-sick, in spite of the storms, which makes him think she will do well on the open sea. Finally, on 7th August, they departed, although the weather was still far from settled, and de Brezé wrote to the queen dowager that on two or three occasions he even thought they would have to go back to Dumbarton again. The route taken led them westwards, right round the coast to the Isle of Man, Wales, the point of Cornwall, and so to the English Channel and the coast of France. The stormy weather chased them all the way, and one night, when they were about ten leagues off the Cornish point, the sea was so remarkably wild, and the waves so high and vast, that the rudder of the ship was smashed. Dismay was universal. According to de Brezé, it was only due to divine intervention that they were able to replace the rudder almost at once, and so proceed in safety, in spite of the heavy seas which were running. In all this drama, Mary Stuart alone seems to have remained unmoved, unknowing of the dangers ahead, uncaring of the dangers around her. In high spirits, untroubled by the maladies which laid low her attendants, she was even able to poke fun at them for their sea-sickness.

The company finally landed on the coast of France on 13th August. The poet Joachim du Bellay mentions that general relief of the French at reaching dry land in his *Epithalamion* on the marriage of Mary and Francis ten years later.

> Estant au bout d'un voyage si long
> Sans craindre plus ny les vents ny l'orage
> Chacun joyeux saute au front du rivage

he wrote, with a vividness which suggests some member of the court had provided him with a personal description of the incident. On balance of probabilities it is to Roscoff, a little fishing village near Brest which sits out into the sea like a ship riding at anchor, that the honour of receiving Mary's first footsteps on French soil must be given.* But there is no contemporary evidence to support the story that this famous footstep was actually traced on the rock on her arrival, nor the tradition that the chapel of St Ninian, now standing to mark the spot, was founded by Mary later in the year. As Mary did not return to Brittany in 1548, the chapel's origins seem to lie among the many pleasant cobwebs of fantasy which surround her story.[21]

According to John Knox, Mary Stuart had thus been sold to the devil, and dispatched to France 'to the end that in her youth she should drink of that liquor, that should remain with her all her lifetime, for a plague to this realm, and for her final destruction'.[22] In the eyes of Mary of Guise, whatever her personal unhappiness, her ewe-lamb had thus been snatched from danger in ever-changing and ever-perilous Scotland, and sent on her way to the glorious future which awaited her at the French court. Of Mary herself, nothing is known of her feelings beyond her high spirits on the journey itself. As she was five years and eight months at the time of her landing in France, it may be conjectured that Scotland, Scottish life and all it stood for, for better or for worse, must quickly have faded from her mind, in favour of new and vivid French impressions. Some memories there were which must have remained, and the visit of her mother to France two years later brought them back to the surface. But in general her recollections were at the mercy of the tales told to her by her Scottish attendants in France, since stories, often repeated, soon achieve the status of memories in the minds of young children. Presumably Mary's remembrances of her native land became rapidly formalized. The next thirteen years of her life, from the age of six to nineteen, were

---

* It was Roscoff which Henry II named as the landing-place, when he reported the news in a latter written from Turin. Since de Brezé wrote to Mary of Guise from S. Pol de Leon on 15th August, the royal party may have travelled on to the port by sea; W. M. Bryce suggested that de Brezé decided to date his letter from the larger town for the better information of the dowager.[20] At Roscoff, two hundred years later, another Stuart landed, this time in flight – Prince Charles Edward, after the battle of Culloden.

to be spent in France. The development of her character is therefore predominantly a French creation. Up till now, vague events of violence, political intrigue and flight have swirled above her unconscious head. From the moment of her arrival in France, the career of Mary Stuart embarks on a more positive course.

CHAPTER THREE

The Most Perfect Child

'The little Queen of Scots is the most perfect child
that I have ever seen'

King Henry II *of France*

From the moment of her arrival in France, and indeed for
the next twelve years, Mary Stuart was the focus of
excited happy interest. The eulogistic poems and formal
epithalamia which poured forth from the pens of French poets
such as du Bellay and Saint-Gelais on the occasion of her
marriage in 1558 were not more laudatory than the enthusiastic
descriptions which were now penned by the entire French court
as well as her Guise relations. Henry II himself set the tone.
When asked what precedence Mary should be given, he ruled
that '*ma fille, la Royne d'Ecosse*' should walk before his daughters,
the princesses of France, first of all because the marriage with
the dauphin had already been decided on, and secondly because
she was herself a crowned queen of an independent country.
'And as such,' he wrote, 'I want her to be honoured and served.'¹
In marked contrast to her childhood treatment in Scotland,
where she was considered at first a sickly child, unlikely to live,
and later a pawn in a dynastic game, even at five years old Mary
was hailed as a figure of romance in France, a brave little queen
who had been forced to flee the barbaric Scots, the cruel
English, for the safe arms of all-embracing France. The stage
was already set in French minds for the appearance of a childish

heroine; to their satisfaction, Mary Stuart with her charm, her prettiness and the natural docility of youth, was ideal material to be moulded into the playing of this golden role.*

The first stage of her two-month journey towards the French court took Mary merely to Morlaix, where she was received by the lord of Rohan, accompanied by the nobility of the country, and lodged in a Dominican convent. She was then taken to the church, where a *Te Deum* was sung in honour of her safe arrival, which appears to have had but a limited effect, since on her route past the town gate, the drawbridge broke and fell into the river under the weight of horsemen. The Scottish lords in her suite, their natural suspicions of the foreigners unassuaged after a week in France, immediately started to shout 'Treachery! Treachery!', at which the lord of Rohan shouted out indignantly, 'No Breton was ever a traitor!' However, for the few days Mary remained at Morlaix, to pacify the Scots all the gates of the town were taken off their hinges and the chains of the bridges were broken.²

From Morlaix, Mary's route lay overland to the Seine, and she then proceeded up the great river by boat towards the castle of Saint-Germain-en-Laye, where the royal children were then in residence. King Henry himself was absent from his family throughout the summer and autumn campaigning. A request for M. de Brezé to join him meant that Mary's companion during her sea voyage now handed her over in turn to the care of her grandmother, Duchess Antoinette of Guise, who, it was planned, should smooth over the next period of transition before she reached Saint-Germain. Although we learn from de Brezé's report to Mary of Guise, made many months later, that the whole journey was punctuated with tragedy – both guardians,

* It is noticeable that the French love affair with Mary Stuart has been gallantly continued by many French historians; this point of view may be summed up by the words of the eminent chronicler of her childhood, Baron de Ruble, who, writing in 1891, describes: '*les belles années qu'elle passa en France, jusqu'à la date néfaste où elle fut obligée d'échanger le séjour de son pays d'adoption, un riant climat, la cour galante et polie des Valois, l'espérance d'un règne glorieux, contre l'Ecosse, un ciel brumeux et le commerce plein d'aigreur et de perfidie des lairds presbytériens*'.

Lords Erskine and Livingston, were severely ill, and one of the queen's train '*le petit Ceton*' (young Seton) died at Ancenis[3] – this decimation of Mary Stuart's suite seems to have passed comparatively unnoticed, since into her life now swept the formidable lady who was to exert one of the strongest influences on her childhood.

The kindly interference of Antoinette of Guise in her daughter Mary's Scottish affairs, at the time of her marriage to James v, has already been noticed. Alone of Mary Stuart's close relations, she was blessed with longevity, dying only in 1583, four years before her granddaughter's execution, at the age of eighty-nine, though perhaps she herself did not view her longevity as such a blessing, since in the course of her life she was fated to witness time's sickle cut such terrible swathes in her family that she in fact outlived all of her twelve children except one. The daughter of Francis, count of Vendôme and Marie of Luxembourg, she was married to Claude, duke of Guise at the age of sixteen. The birth of twelve children, between 1515 and 1536, was not a particularly remarkable feat by the standards of the time, but the vigorous strain of the Guises appears to have resisted the inroads of infant mortality with unusual vitality and of the twelve, ten survived; the mother of this remarkable brood was, in herself, a remarkable woman. She exhibited considerable administrative talent, which she handed on to her daughter Mary of Guise – not only at domestic economy, a subject at which she was considered to excel, but in the running of the vast and increasing Guise dominions, surrounding their palace of Joinville. Unlike her sons, she seems to have had a genuine streak of austerity in her disposition, and the great life of the court, the magnificent but insubstantial rewards of human glory, seem to have plucked no chord of sympathy in her nature. Her family pride, on the other hand, was enormous, and her sense of her sons' destiny on a similar scale. Much later in her history, when Charles ix offered her a choice of rank as a princess of the blood, to which in spite of the pretensions of the Guises, she was not strictly entitled, she replied loftily that no rank could be more honourable to her than that of her husband.

Traditionally, she kept her coffin in the gallery which led the way to Mass, dressed herself in black and with a proper sense of her own end, reminiscent of Philip II of Spain, surrounded herself with objects necessary to her own funeral.[4]

Antoinette of Guise also possessed a vein of wry humour which doubtless enabled her to endure the many stresses to which a matriarch is subject, and maintain her health and courage intact. At Joinville, for example, her famous charity was dispelled with a certain amount of common sense. When a convent of nuns applied to her for funds for building, she is said to have remarked dryly: '*Edifiez vos moeurs, et j'édifierai vos murs.*' Masculine frailty met with an equally practical approach: on one occasion Antoinette discovered that her husband was having a liaison with a village-girl, and that their trysting place was a certain little hut on the edge of the estate, called '*La Viergeotte*'. Without raising the subject of the girl with the duke, Antoinette merely asked him to meet her also at this particular hut; with some embarrassment, the duke agreed, only to find that the hut had been transformed into a luxurious nest of pleasure, decorated in palatial style, and now in his wife's opinion worthy of his ducal position. Subsequently Duke Claude built a little castle on the spot, with the significantly interlaced initials, A and C, and the motto: '*Toutes pour une: là, et non plus*'.

Duchess Antoinette was in ecstasies at the appearance of her granddaughter, and wrote immediately to Mary of Guise in Scotland to express the measure of her approval; she also assured her that she would see about the little girl's wardrobe, which, coming from Scotland, Mary of Guise obviously suspected might not be up to the elegant standards of the French court. The duchess was, however, a great deal less enthusiastic over Mary's Scottish train, whom she described as thoroughly ill-looking and *farouche*, and with the exception of the captivating Lady Fleming, not even, in her opinion, properly washed. The duchess clearly shared the general desire of the French, whether on the part of the Guises or the court, to have the complete education of this child, and thoroughly expunge from her all traces of her Scottish past, which it was felt would ill equip her for her glorious future role as queen of France. The possibility that she might also one day have to act as queen regnant to her native land of Scotland was felt to be definitely subordinate. No qualms were therefore felt at the prospect of cutting the little Scottish queen off immediately from her Scottish attendants. Mary of Guise, however, with superior foresight, had sent instructions that Lady Fleming was to continue as her governess, despite the claims of a French woman, Mlle Curel. The duchess wrote back to say that her daughter's wishes were being respected. Mary Stuart also retained a Scotswoman, Jehane St Clare (or Jean Sinclair), as her nurse; de la Brousse hinted to Mary of Guise that the nurse was difficult to please, for which he blamed her Scots blood ('You know that nation,' he wrote. 'I need say no more.'), but Jean Sinclair was presumably merely grumbling at novelty, in the universal tradition of her profession, when finding herself in a foreign land.[5]

Antoinette has left us a physical description of Mary as she appeared to French eyes on her first arrival, in a letter to her son written in October. She is described as 'very pretty indeed' as well as being extremely intelligent, and her grandmother hastens to prophesy that she will actually be a beauty when she grows up, especially as the little queen is also graceful and self-assured in her movements. With the help of this letter, which as it was not written to the child's mother seems candid enough, and the earliest picture of Mary Stuart, dating from July 1552, when she was nine and a half years old, it is possible to form a definite impression of her childish, preadolescent appearance. This drawing, in the Musée Condé at Chantilly, was done in response to a request from Catherine de Médicis for portraits of all her children, to include her future daughter-in-law, Mary; as the French queen was apparently weary of endless identical stylized profiles of her children, she asked that the picture should be done swiftly in crayon, to give some sort of genuinely child-like impression.[6] The charming oval of Mary's girlhood face is well captured: it is evident that her features were of the type inclined to be hawk-like in later life, which had a special attraction when still enveloped by the softness of youth. Her complexion was glowingly white, and the texture of the skin, as her grandmother noted, especially fine. The nose, which was to lengthen considerably as Mary grew older, was now still delightfully balanced in the contours of her face and Duchess Antoinette also commended her mouth and chin as being particularly well formed. The deep-set eyes of which her grandmother wrote were prettily set like two almonds beneath her high forehead; and their bright golden-brown colour contrasted with the fair, almost ash-blonde, hair which Mary enjoyed as a young girl. All in all, it was not surprising that the French court and Mary's doting relations were alike well satisfied with what they saw.

Duchess Antoinette now set in train the second part of the journey to Saint-Germain, which she reported to her son on 9th October she was making by slow stages. The care of the Guises for their nursling was more than matched by the solicitude which King Henry himself was showing, by letter, from a distance.[7] So thoroughly were the cleaning operations of the castle of Saint Germain taken in hand on his instructions, that the children of France were still at the medieval fortress of Carrières when Mary arrived there on 16th October. Two months from her arrival on the soil of France, she was now propelled into the royal nursery. It is difficult to believe that any set of young princes in the history of Europe had been so fussed over, so lavished with care and attention, as the children of Henry II and Catherine de Médicis. The letters of their mother are replete with maternal anxieties of the sort most generally associated with mothers who have no nurses, rather than with a queen, who might be supposed to have at least the duties of the court to distract her. This devotion, this concentrated attention to the minutiae of a child's existence, was fully shared during her childhood by Mary, who received in addition the extra care of her Guise relations: so concerned were they over her welfare that her uncle the cardinal, that great prince of the Church, appeared as worried over her toothache and her swollen face as about matters of national policy. Her grandmother, dedicated to the cause of her moral welfare, and her uncle, bestowing on her in youth the tenderness of a father, combined with the king of France himself, and the governors of his children, to make Mary Stuart's upbringing one of rigorous supervision.

The solicitude bestowed in such rich measure on the royal nursery of France arose to some degree from the special circumstances of the children's birth. Catherine de Médicis, a woman who has gone down to history as a mother before all else, and to whom much has been forgiven on these grounds, was for many years denied by fate the very role she most craved. Married off to a dauphin, Henry of France, with nothing to commend her but her relationship to the Pope and her dowry, lacking birth in the strict aristocratic sense, and lacking beauty in even the most prejudiced eyes of her allies, her early years at the French court were made still more unbearable by the additional torture of sterility. By 1538 there were rumours that she was to be sent back to Italy, to make room for some more nubile bride for the dauphin, one who would at least have achieved the state of puberty, unlike the wretched Catherine. What potions, what prayers, what magic arts Catherine summoned to her aid in her struggles with her cruel destiny will never be fully known. By 1540, with the help, it was said, of pills of myrrh given her by the famous Jean Fernel, she finally reached the state of puberty; by April 1543 she was at last pregnant. Finally, in 1544, Francis of Valois was born. He was sickly from birth, it was true, a weakness generally attributed to the many remedies his mother had taken both before and during her pregnancy, but for all that he represented security – he was a child, and he was an heir. The royal children of France followed in quick and satisfying succession. Elisabeth, later to be the third wife to Phillip II of Spain, in April 1545, Claude, who married the duke of Lorraine, in 1547, the future Charles IX in 1550, the future Henry III in 1551, Francis, duke of Alençon, in 1554, and Marguerite, the bride of Henry of Navarre, in 1553. Three other children died at birth. The princes and princesses thus made up in numbers what they lacked in rude health: none of them was robust and together they gave Catherine ample material for concern, from the right clothes for little

Henry in hot weather, to the correct amount of food which each child should consume to make it either thinner or fatter.

Tenderness towards the royal children was not the sole prerogative of their mother. The constable of France, Anne de Montmorency, was also deeply involved in their welfare – it was indeed to the constable that Queen Catherine broke the moving news of her first pregnancy, saying that she knew that he desired to see her with children just as much as she did.[8] Another powerful force in the royal nursery was that of Henry II's mistress, the legendary Diane de Poitiers. The enemies of Mary Stuart, in her later career, have sometimes suggested that she was debauched in early childhood by the corrupting influence of this woman, who although already aged forty-eight when Mary arrived in France, exerted and continued to exert till his death the most total fascination over her royal lover. Diane de Poitiers, as her letters show, was a woman who, quite apart from her attractive interest in the arts, took an enormous interest in every part of the kingdom's affairs. This was indeed a considerable part of her attraction for the king: she interpreted the role of mistress in the true Renaissance sense, rather than in the nineteenth-century style of a grand voluptuary. She herself had been married at the age of fifteen to a man much older than herself, Louis de Brezé, by whom she had two daughters, and with whom, as historians now agree, she led a blameless life. She has also now been acquitted of the accusation that she subsequently sacrificed her honour to Francis I, in order to save the life of her father, the Seigneur de Saint-Vallier; it was this smear which gave rise to the story that she acted as the mistress of two kings in her lifetime.[9] Diane should be judged as the mistress of Henry II only, a position which she undertook as though she felt it her duty to exploit her undoubted assets – the beauty which age could not dim, intelligence, energy, and abounding health to support it all, health over which she took great trouble.

Her flagrant adultery with the king may contrast paradoxically to our notions with the excellent upbringing which she gave to her own daughters – Françoise who married the duke of Boillon in 1547 and Louise who married Duke Francis of Guise's son in the same year – but to the age in which she lived, the paradox was not apparent. Equally, she exhibited, without any sense of impropriety, strong maternal instincts towards the king's own children, and even on occasion towards his wife – for stories were told that she actually hustled the king towards the royal marriage bed, so seriously did she take the role of mistress. Certainly, she took infinite trouble to make both the Dame and Seigneur d'Humières her allies; she recommended a nurse for the royal children, and actually trained her at Anet first, to make sure she would give satisfaction; she inquired ceaselessly over Mme Elisabeth's measles and other domestic matters; the subject of Charles d'Orléans's wet nurse, and her suitability or otherwise for her task, runs through a whole summer of letter-writing. As Mary Stuart arrives at Carrières, we find that it is Diane who passes on the king's request that Mary and Elisabeth should share a room, since it is the king's dearest wish that they should become friends; again it is Diane who expresses Henry's desire that the Scottish suite should be sent away, and the situation is accepted as perfectly natural.[10]

The first crucial encounter for Mary at the French court was with her intended husband, the Dauphin Francis. It is to be presumed that if these two children, aged nearly six and nearly five respectively, had heartily disliked each other on sight, the Scottish–French marriage alliance would still have proceeded. Nevertheless, the French courtiers hung over the meeting of the two royal children like so many sentimental cupids: whatever the contrast between the bouncing and healthy little girl, and the timid, sickly boy a year her junior, whose health had already been the matter of much concern, owing to the abnormalities of his birth, the meeting was nevertheless pronounced to be a great success. At the wedding of Francis of Guise and Anne d'Estea in December 1548, they danced happily together, as Henry II hastened to report to Mary's mother, while the English ambassador looked on sardonically. A few weeks after the first meeting, Henry was writing to the duke of Guise that Francis and Mary already got on as well as if they had known each other all their lives. By the March of the year following, Constable de Montmorency, commenting on the love that the dauphin bore for his little bride, described him as feeling as much for her as though she were both his sweetheart *and* his wife – '*sa mie et sa femme*' – a touching commentary on the contemporary conventions of feeling.[11] On the principle of the sunflower and the sun, a frail child naturally rewards a more healthy specimen of the race with its admiration; a younger child hero-worships an older one; an unattractive child responds to a beautiful one by loving it. On all these counts, it was natural for Francis to love Mary Stuart, even if he had not been heavily encouraged to do so. As it is, the constant reiteration of tales of his somewhat pathetic passion for her, from many sources, make it certain that his adoration for her was indeed genuine, and not just the projection of courtly wishful thinking.

Since we have Brantôme's word that Mary Stuart could only speak Scots when she arrived in France – barbarous and ill-sounding, he called it – she had evidently picked up enough French in the past two months, with the facility of childhood, to communicate with a fellow-child. Later, she was to be described, also by Brantôme, as speaking French with perfect grace and elegance: although she did not lose her Scots, French became the language which Mary naturally wrote and spoke for the rest of her life.[12] Possibly it was the hope of bringing this about which had influenced Henry in his decision to send away the Scottish suite; even the four Maries were sent to the convent of the Dominican nuns at Poissy, where Prior François de Vieuxpont was charged with their education, instead of being kept permanently at their mistress's side. It thus came about that the most intimate female friend of Mary Stuart's childhood and adolescence was Elisabeth of France, younger by two and a quarter years, a friendship shared, to a lesser extent, by her younger sister Claude. With these two princesses, Mary Stuart had in common the elevating but separating gift of royal blood; the fact that Elisabeth also shared the same nurtured golden childhood made her the female human being of whom Mary Stuart felt herself afterwards to be most fond, and of whom she retained the most nostalgic memories in later life.

The portrait of Elisabeth by Clouet gives an attractive impression of her lively face, full but slanting eyes, dimpled chin and large faun-like ears: she has an air not so much of beauty as of enjoyment of life, as she looks coolly across her stiffly jewelled dress. In girlhood, she was a sweet-natured child, who loved to draw with Clouet, and also, according to Brantôme, was fond of poetry and music. Claude was also reported by Brantôme to be fond of learning, as had been her Aunt Marguerite, Henry's sister, who did not marry the duke of Savoy until 1559, and was thus still part of the royal family at this date. Henry's own daughter, Marguerite, the high-spirited heroine of many later adventures in French court life, was over twelve years younger than Mary Stuart, and only came into the royal nursery when the Scottish queen had already left it for the court; her exotic character can therefore have played no part in Mary Stuart's actual childhood. The three brothers of the dauphin, whose tender health caused their mother such agonizing concern, were also sufficiently younger than Mary to play no effective part in these early nursery years, which are thus dominated by Francis and Elisabeth.

As yet, Mary had not encountered the father of the young family into which she was now adopted. This meeting finally took place in November. The confrontation from both points of view was eminently satisfactory. Mary Stuart saw a man of thirty years, swarthy and melancholy of visage, seldom smiling, obsessed either with the troubles of his government, or with the physical exercise for which he had a mania. Henry II, as one Venetian ambassador observed, found conversation with women difficult; it was part of Diane de Poitiers's prolonged and successful hold over him that he enjoyed her somewhat masculine intelligence, where other women bored him. In children, however, he took a genuine and tender delight. Mary Stuart was fortunate in that she charmed him as a child, and successfully converted later the appeal of childhood into the more alluring appeal of femininity. Of Mary, he wrote quite simply that she was the most perfect child he had ever seen. Soon the cardinal

of Lorraine was writing happily off to the child's mother that
the king had taken such a liking to her daughter that he spent
much of his time chatting to her, sometimes by the hour
together, and by the time Mary was eleven the cardinal was able
to report proudly that she knew so well how to entertain the
king with suitable subjects of conversation that she might have
been a woman of twenty-five.[13]

The next ten years in the state of France were among the most
ominous in her history – for they were the years in which the
seeds of civil war were sown. As the realm floundered in
inflation brought about by an endless series of foreign wars and
rising prices due to the influx of silver from the New World,
the lesser nobility turned away in vain from the crown, which
could no longer support them financially, to the menacing circle
of great nobles which surrounded the throne; now religious
division also reared its head, to augment the nation's woes. But
although Mary arrived in France at the very outset of this
disastrous period it would be wrong to paint these years in her
life as anything but a time of untroubled private happiness, in
which all the dramas were domestic, and the griefs and pleasures
only the inevitable ones of every childhood.

It is often said that a secure childhood makes the best
foundation for a happy life. In marked contrast to her cousin
Elizabeth Tudor, Mary Stuart enjoyed an exceptionally cosseted
youth. It is left to the judgement of history to decide whether
it did, in fact, adequately prepare her for the extreme stresses
with which the course of her later life confronted her. What is
certain is that the next six years of her life have a dream-like
quality, in which she appears to have been cut off from the
rough events of politics by a cocoon of servants and other
satellites, whose only duty was to nurture the royal nurslings in
as great a state of luxury as possible. Her life divided into two
parts – at court with the princesses and with her Guise relations.
The Guises were, however, fully aware of the value of maintaining their little half-royal cuckoo well and truly in the royal
nest, and made no difficulties at the prospect of having her

brought up so much at court – as Duchess Antoinette pointed out in January 1549, on hearing that Mary was sharing a room with Elisabeth, nothing was better for her future prospects.[14]

At this time the establishment of the royal children was by no means a fixed entity: it was essential that a household of such dimensions should be moved every few months in order that the castle which it had inhabited might be literally spring-cleaned. Mary's life consisted largely of a series of glamorous journeyings under their aegis: for example, the royal accounts for the year 1550 show that in January all the children were at Saint-Germain until April, when they went to Fontainebleau. On 1st May they were back at Saint-Germain, on 4th October they were at Mantes-sur-Seine, and on 24th November at Bury in Touraine, to avoid an epidemic, staying on the way at Diane de Poitiers's new palace at Anet. 1551 shows the same pattern of movement, with the children beginning the year at Meudon, in April at the palace of Blois, Mary herself at the court in June, then back to Blois, with the dauphin going to Chambord. In January 1552, the king took them all again to Saint-Germain.[15]

Unconsciously, Mary began to form the impression that these palaces of such splendour, such dimensions, were the natural habitat of royalty. To one who still dimly remembered the infinitely smaller castles of Scotland, the French palaces seemed like the grandiose dwellings of another planet. Fontainebleau and James v's palace of Falkland, in Fife, for example, both had their original in the traditional royal passion for the hunt, yet how different they were in scale. Although Fontainebleau was far from completed in its ultimate estate when Mary Stuart first arrived there, the magnificent structure laid down by Francis I, the two wings joined by the lofty, painted gallery of Primaticcio, cannot have failed to impress her with its sumptuous display of Italian opulence grafted on to the French imagination. The completion and decoration of the famous ballroom, under the direction of Philibert de l'Orme, continued throughout the reign of Henry II: there the interlaced Hs and Cs still commemorate to questioning modern eyes either the king and his wife or the king and his mistress, Diane the huntress, whose symbol was the crescent moon. In the same way, the palace of pleasure which Henry built over the vast fortress of Francis I at Saint-Germain, safe on its strategic escarpment, was in the course of construction during Mary's French life: but the immensity and scale of the buildings were already in existence. The *châteaux* of the Loire had in the main already been endowed with their fabled beauty and dimensions in the previous reign: to Francis I is owed the staircase at Blois and its exquisite Renaissance wing, another triumph of the Italian style in France. Chambord, with over 400 rooms, seems to foreshadow Versailles in the flourish of its enormous scale, the most spectacular of all Francis's creations, for which work went on steadily despite the growing bankruptcy of the crown. The richness of its decoration, the impressive white mass of its building, the unforgettable north-west façade across the water, cannot have failed to leave an indelible impression on the mind of a child – that this was how monarchs lived.

It would seem that the favourite *château* of the royal children, the place they regarded as the source of supreme amusement, was in fact none of the actual royal dwellings, but Anet, the home of Diane de Poitiers, which she had built for herself as a sort of monument to the spirit of the goddess Diana with Philibert de l'Orme as architect. Du Bellay called it 'Dianet', playing on the name of the house and its beautiful creator, and the dauphin wrote with boyish enthusiasm of the pleasures of Anet – what a beautiful house; beautiful gardens! beautiful galleries! so many other beauties! Indeed, he has never slept better than when at Anet, in a huge bed, in the king's own chamber.[16] The position of Anet on the river meant that some endless journeyings of the court could be made conveniently there by barge. Today, even what still exists of sixteenth-century Anet dazzles the eye with the perfection of its detail, the exquisite gateway with its balustrade, the marble dome with marble brought from Rome, the statues of Germaine Pilon, the chastely elegant memorial chapel to Diane's favourite colours of black and white. But under the sway of Diane de Poitiers, Anet was as remarkable for its reputation for *douceur de vivre*, as it was for the novelty and beauty of its buildings.

These constant journeyings meant that each month dawned with new pleasures for the children. Their daily trappings were equally exotic. They were, for example, surrounded with pets – in 1551 there were four big dogs and twenty-two little lap dogs, as well as falcons and pet birds. Horses there were in abundance, Fontaine and Enghien being the dauphin's favourites, and Bravane and Madame la Réale the favourites of Mary Stuart; horses also frequently formed the subject for presents, since the dauphin, despite his frail physique, had the typical burning passion of the Valois for the chase. At one point the royal nursery was even sent two bears by the Marshal de Saint-André, although the cost of keeping them in food proved to be prohibitive, and in addition there were tiresome reparations to be made for the damage they did, as for example at Blois, where the home of one Dame Pillonne suffered from their ferocious attentions. The children were shown wolves and boars, wild animals from Africa. There were also two-legged amusements – troops of travelling actors and Italian acrobats were stopped on their route by the royal governor to entertain his charges, by performing '*farces et buffoneries*'; a *maître de danse* was dispatched from the court by the king; there were bills also for choirs of singers, and the players of tambourins. There were bills for materials for the royal children to make the sweets of which they were particularly fond. 83 *livres*, spent on a ball for the marriage of one of the princesses' chambermaids, gives the impression that the slightest occasion for rejoicing was seized on by this pleasure-loving household.*[17]

The moves of the royal household, delightful as they may have been for the children, meant endless upheaval for their

---

* One charming tradition concerning the childhood of Mary Queen of Scots is not founded on fact: there is a story that the word 'marmalade' originated when a chef in the royal kitchen stirred and stirred his oranges muttering over and over again the words: '*Marie est malade*', until the oranges turned into a delicious golden mixture. Unfortunately, the word 'marmalade' was already in use in 1480, deriving from the Portuguese *marmelo* (a quince).[18]

servants: they frequently entailed staying at meagre villages *en route*, where villagers were apt to be angry at the loss of their food to the grand strangers. Roads were difficult and the quantity of luggage involved was a constant problem, as were the beasts to carry the luggage, whom the stable men had somehow to find or commandeer. Consequently transport, wherever possible, was made by river, as at Anet. The mountain of luggage used by the children was in part accounted for by their wardrobes. It was thought right that Mary Stuart should be more richly attired than the princesses, to mark her future position as their brother's bride. Her accounts reveal both the abundance and the formality of a royal child's wardrobe: yards of shot red and yellow taffeta for dresses, dresses of gold damask, dresses of black edged with silver, canvas and buckram to stiffen the dresses, white Florentine serge stockings, a *vasquine* or type of farthingale to hold out the dresses, shot taffeta petticoats and orange taffeta petticoats lined with red serge. Her accessories are equally elaborate: there is mention of bonnets of silver thread and black silk, orange wool to be dyed scarlet for stockings, furs to trim her clothes. Shoes are plentiful – ten pairs of ordinary shoes in the accounts of 1551, three white, three purple, two black and two red and also white, yellow, red and black velvet shoes. There are bills for exquisite embroideries on the clothes – rose leaves of gold thread for caps, and a bill for the embroidery of a device on a favour of white taffeta which Mary gave to the dauphin. There are bills for leather gloves of dog-skin and deerskin. The accessories are in keeping with the rest: a black velvet purse to keep the combs of the queen of Scots in, a crystal mirror covered with velvet and silk ribbons, gold and silver paillettes to be sewn on to her clothes, endless chains, collars and gold belts, as well as three brass chests to hold her jewels, which included a chain of pearls and green enamel, a gold ring with a ruby in it, and jewelled buttons of many different colours and shapes.[19]

The attendants who surrounded Mary Stuart and the French princesses were on the same lavish scale: indeed much of the troubles of their peregrinations arose from the enormous quantities of servants who were thought necessary to maintain their estate. The royal household had already grown to alarming proportions before Mary Stuart's arrival, so that by the end of 1547 Henry was forbidding d'Humières to engage any more servants; but it swelled again on the Scottish queen's appearance. Chamberlains rose from four in 1550 to ten in 1558, and *maîtres d'hôtel* from four to seven. The stables were burdened with attendants to cope with the royal baggage, and the baggage of the household. There were five doctors, thirty-seven pages of honour to grow up alongside the dauphin (although these at least received no wages), porters, four masters of the wardrobe, two general controllers, and twenty-eight *valets de chambre* at differing wages to carry the infant princes, feed them and serve them. In order to attend to the babies the Dame d'Humières had twenty-two ladies of various ranks under her command. The number of apothecaries rose from one to three, barbers from one to four, pantry aides from two to six – although it may be noted that in all this panoply of service, there was provision for only two laundresses and one bearer of water, leading one to suppose that the royal nurseries were more luxurious than they were hygienic. The kitchen was especially well endowed with roasters, soup-makers and the like, the numbers once again perpetually on the increase. Indeed, when one considers the vast amount of food consumed either by the children or more probably by their attendants, one can see that in the royal nursery of France, wages, attendants, children and cost chased each other upwards in a spiral reminiscent of the economy of a modern state. On one day alone, 8th June, 1553, the household consumed over 250 loaves of bread, eighteen pieces of beef, eight sheep, four calves, twenty capons, 120 chickens and pigeons, three deer, six geese and four hares.[20]

Despite all this concern for material well-being, the need for more spiritual attainments was not neglected. Education was taken seriously at this Renaissance court, and Catherine de Médicis, herself nourished in the atmosphere of Italian learning, was a considerable patron of the arts. In the past it was considered that Mary must have been a child of considerable academic brilliance, since Brantôme described her reciting a Latin speech of her own composition before the king and entire court, before she was twelve years old. Certainly she learnt Latin, but the discovery of a book of her Latin themes in the last century has corrected the impression somewhat and shows that, with respect to Latin, Mary was more of an earnest student than a prodigy.²¹ These Latin themes now exist in the shape of a bound book, with the original French themes set by M. de Saint-Estienne or some other tutor on the left-hand page, and the Latin on the right-hand page. Some are in the form of letters to Princess Elisabeth, occasionally jointly with her sister Claude. Two letters are directed to the cardinal of Lorraine, one containing the suitable, if somewhat priggish sentiment: 'Many people in these days, *mon oncle*, fall into errors in the Holy Scriptures, because they do not read them with a pure and clean heart.' Curiously enough, one of the letters is actually addressed to John Calvin: but there is no evidence that the letter with its solemn, childlike invocation, '*Christus filius Dei te avocet, Calvine*', was ever actually dispatched and it seems extremely improbable that it should have been more than a youthful exercise, the original inspiration for which remains obscure.* Many of the themes are occupied with the names of learned women and girls, as befits a princess of the Renaissance, and probably many of them were actually done in preparation for the famous Latin speech.

Mary Stuart as a child neither had nor was trained to have the brain of the calibre of, for example, an Elizabeth Tudor. She was, however, by nature bright and quick, with a pliant turn of mind which her governess praised, because it made her eager to learn. Her schoolmasters, chosen by Catherine, included Claude Millot and Antoine Fouquelin. In true Renaissance fashion, she was given all-round education; she learnt not only

---

* The editor of Mary's Latin themes, A. de Montaiglon, suggested that Mary might have heard the name of Calvin often mentioned since an edition of his Institutes was published in Paris in 1553. But there is no record of any such edition in France, either in French or Latin, before 1562. An edition of the Institutes was published in Geneva in 1554.

Latin, but Italian, Spanish and apparently some Greek;* she learnt to draw; she learnt to dance, an art at which she was universally agreed to excel both in childhood and in later life; she learnt to sing – the songs of Clément Marot were special favourites; she learnt to play the lute, for which Brantôme described her long white fingers as being ideally suited.[22] Graceful, athletic, she was above all anxious to please those around her.

Her letters to her mother, the earliest, preserved in the Register House at Edinburgh, dating from the age of seven, show her as having a clear, legible hand, remarkably like the even, rounded hand-writing which she retained for the rest of her life (although with age the writing grew considerably larger). This early, polite little note – whose neatness probably bears witness to some sort of overseer – ends with the characteristic salutation of any seven-year-old child to its mother – M. de Brezé will give her all the rest of her news, thus saving her daughter a longer letter.[23] Mary Stuart's letters to Mary of Guise bear witness to the enormous interest which the mother took in the smallest details of her daughter's upbringing, despite the distance which separates them: the sphere in which she appears to have exerted the strongest influence of all is that of her daughter's religious education. Mary of Guise laid it down that her daughter was to hear daily Mass; she was given a French chaplain of her own, Guillaume de Laon, as well as retaining her Scottish one, the prior of Inchmahome, who stayed with her in France out of devotion, and without wages. In all the travels of the court, care was taken to transport the young queen's own communion vessels, so that she could receive the sacrament from them, without any risk of infection; her accounts include payments for a coffer in which to carry these vessels around.[24] The religious education of the royal children was supervised among others by Pierre Danes, professor of Greek and later bishop of Lavane, and Jacques Amyot, abbot of Bellosaire and translator of Plutarch.

* Her Scottish library contained Greek books.

Happily, Duchess Antoinette was able to report to Mary of Guise that her daughter was extremely devout. When the duchess and the cardinal felt that it was time for the child to make her first Holy Communion, Mary wrote to her mother eagerly of her desire to do so. She was at her grandmother's at Meudon for the feast of Easter, and requested the necessary permission, not only because her grandmother and her uncle thought it right, but also because she herself fervently desired to 'receive God'. Mary signed herself: 'Your very humble and obedient daughter, Marie'.[25]

In 1550 Mary of Guise herself came to France to judge the progress of her very humble and obedient daughter. Her letters of 1549 show her to have become increasingly depressed and lonely in Scotland, for which the internal situation certainly gave her just cause; she longed to consult with her brothers on her best course of action, as well as to see her daughter and son Francis again; furthermore, there was the perennial vexed question of her French dowry, whose emoluments were more than ever necessary, as a result of her financial straits brought on by maintaining the French troops in Scotland. This visit represented the central point of Mary's childhood; overjoyed at the prospect, she wrote off ecstatically to her grandmother: 'Madame, I have been very glad to be able to send these present lines, for the purpose of telling you the joyful news I have received from the Queen my Mother, who has promised me by her letters dated April 23rd that she will be here very soon to see you and me, which is to me the greatest happiness which I could wish for in this world, and indeed I am so overjoyed about it, that all I am thinking about now is to do my whole duty in all things and to study to be very good, in order to satisfy her desire to see in me all that you and she hope for ...'[26] Evidently Mary had conceived a sort of hero-worship for her mother, a superior being, the female equivalent of her splendid uncles, an image of strength, reliability and comfort, whom she wished to do her best to impress.

Mary of Guise landed at Dieppe in September, and arrived

at the court, which was then at Rouen, on 25th September. Her household had made detailed preparations for the journey to fashionable France – although the recent death of the dowager's father, Duke Claude of Guise, meant that her own clothes were all of black, and her ladies at brightest in grey velvet and taffeta.[27] Mary Stuart had had a dangerous attack of flux in early September, but she was apparently well enough to be present at the regal reception which Henry and Catherine gave to her mother in Normandy. Throughout all the next winter, the dowager queen of Scotland enjoyed the plentiful pageantry of the court ceremonies, and enjoyed also the company of her daughter. Nothing seems to have marred the love which existed between mother and daughter, when a year later Mary of Guise sailed back to Scotland again; having had what turned out to be the last sight of her daughter in her lifetime, she left behind such strongly growing roots of love in her daughter's heart that the young Mary had a virtual nervous breakdown with grief at the news of her death in 1560, even though she had not actually seen her for nine years.

In other spheres than that of mother and daughter relations, the visit of Mary of Guise to France was considerably less successful. She herself marred it to a certain extent by her financial importunities towards the French king: anxious as she was to pave the way for her final assumption of the regency of Scotland as soon as possible, she was determined to secure as many honours and as much French money as might be available for her Scottish train, in order to bind them to her. Her personal finances were also desperately in need of succour: her servants' wages were in arrears, she was forced to borrow from her friends such as the countess of Montrose and Elizabeth, countess of Moray, who could ill afford it, and also to lean on the Scottish merchants as a possible source of aid.[28] The lawlessness of Scotland had increased mightily in the last two years, and hatred of the new foreigner – the French who were now attempting to administer this apparently barbaric country, by their own lights – was succeeding ripely to the previous hatred of the English. In May 1551 Sir John Mason reported from Tours that the dowager of Scotland was making the whole court weary of her, from the highest to the lowest, by being such an importunate beggar for herself and her chosen friends. 'The King,' said Sir John, 'would fain be rid of her, and she, as she pretendeth, would fain be gone.'[29]

Two untoward incidents also marred the atmosphere of the visit. In the first place – although no hint of it reached the young Mary's own ears – her daughter's safety did not seem to Mary of Guise to be totally secure. At the end of April 1551 a mysterious plot for poisoning the young Scottish queens was discovered;[30] it was devised by an archer of the guard named Robert Stuart, but a certain mystery hangs over the whole conspiracy, and it has never been made clear exactly why, or at whose instigation, the murder was supposed to take place. The French ambassador in London reported to the Constable de Montmorency in France that a Scot named Henderson had revealed to him Stuart's fell design. The would-be assassin had suggested to Lord Warwick and Lord Paget that by committing such a crime he might render valuable service to the English Council. Warwick, by his own account, expressed horror at the proposal, and sent Stuart to prison, but finally let him be extradited to France. Stuart was thus imprisoned in the castle of Angers, and finally hanged, drawn and quartered, without the enigma of his true inspiration or purpose ever being cleared up. It seems an unlikely moment for the English government to have sponsored any such plan: firstly, the English had not yet given up all hope of the eventual marriage of Mary Stuart and Edward vi, and when Lord Northampton came on a formal embassy to France in the summer of 1551, to convey the Garter to Henry ii, he once again applied for the Scottish queen's hand. Secondly, the English were not noticeably enraged by the refusal of the French to entertain the proposal – a refusal which they had certainly anticipated. Northampton took the denial calmly, and according to his instructions, merely applied formally for the hand of the Princess Elisabeth for the English king, in the place of that of Mary Stuart.[31]

The second untoward incident was the flagrant love affair which sprang up between Henry II and Mary's governess, Lady Fleming. The king's eye lighted on the pretty Scotswoman comparatively early in her stay at the French court, for de Brezé reported on the success she was having, and with perhaps a certain lack of taste, Henry himself took the trouble to write to Mary of Guise and tell her what an excellent job Lady Fleming was making of her task as her daughter's governess. Regarded as captivating by her admirers, Lady Fleming also appears to have had a strongly irritating streak, which involved her enjoying her success at the French court to the full, but making little effort to accommodate herself to French ways in a manner which would smooth the path of the Scottish queen's household. When the question of a doctor for Mary Stuart arose, a letter from Giovanni Ferreri to the bishop of Orkney puts forward the name of a certain Scotsman, William Bog – 'so learned he will bear comparison with any Frenchman' and also particularly adept at 'diagnosing Scottish temperaments'.[32] The understanding of Scottish temperaments was felt to be particularly essential in this case, because not only was Mary's 'temperament' held, for medical purposes, to be Scottish, but also Lady Fleming would not otherwise be able to explain what was wrong with her mistress, as she was incapable of communicating with a French doctor.

Constable de Montmorency saw in Lady Fleming's charms, and their effect on the king, an excellent opportunity of spiting his established enemy, Diane de Poitiers. The liaison did not succeed in toppling the favourite, but it did result in the incautious Lady Fleming giving birth to a son, Henry, later known as the Bastard of Angoulême, whose famous agility in later life at Scottish dances at the French court bore permanent witness to his hybrid heredity. According to Brantôme's wittily malicious report, Lady Fleming scandalized the court by exclaiming aloud in French, which she spoke with a broad Scottish accent: 'I have done all that I can, and God be thanked, I am pregnant by the King, for which I count myself both honoured and happy.'[33] Her happiness at her condition was short-lived:

her indiscretion was punished by her being sent home to
Scotland, as a result of the combined wrath of Catherine and
Diane, to whom no interloper was tolerable, and Mary was given
a new governess in the shape of Mme de Parois.

The departure of Mary of Guise first to London, where the
French fashions of her ladies impressed the English court, and
then to Scotland for a renewal of the harsh struggle for stable
government, marked the breaking of one more Scottish link in
Mary Stuart's childhood. Even Mary of Guise's last weeks in
France were marked by tragedy, for her son Francis of Longueville, who had greeted the arrival of his half-sister in France
with such generous boyish enthusiasm, and declared her to be
the most charming sister in all the world, died suddenly in
September 1551, the victim of some swift, childish disease. 'I
think, Madame, that Our Lord will that I should be one of His
own,' wrote Mary of Guise sadly to her mother on the subject,
'since he has visited me so often and so heavily.'[34]

The substitution of Mme de Parois for the errant Lady
Fleming marked a further step in the obliteration of Mary's
Scottish personality. Mary still loved to dress herself up in
Scottish national dress. She even managed to charm the French
with the spectacle, although to their critical gaze her attire
seemed dreadfully outlandish, if not downright bizarre: however,
as, according to a French print current at the time, 'Scottish
dress' for a girl consisted merely of a series of wild animals'
skins draped about the person,* perhaps the dismay of the
sophisticated French court is not too difficult to understand. At
all events it was the graceful deportment and queenly bearing
which Mary brought to her garb which was generally felt to
carry the day. But for all Mary's enthusiasm for her native
country or its customs Scottish clothes were by now for her
definitely a form of fancy dress. Patriotism, wilfulness or the
desire to please might lead her to don them: nothing could alter
the fact that with the passing of every year, the progress of

* Plaid of a sort was already known at this date, and Mary later wore it in Scotland;
but tartan, in the form we know it today, was not, and nor was the kilt.

Mary towards becoming a French woman – a child of the smooth land of France rather than of the rugged land of Scotland – became still more marked.

CHAPTER FOUR

Betrothal

'How happy oughtest thou to esteem thyself, O kingdom of Scotland, to be favoured, fed and maintained like an infant on the breast of the most magnanimous King of France...'

Estienne Perlin, 1558

By the end of 1553, when she entered her twelfth year, Mary Stuart's charmed childhood was drawing to a close, in favour of a more troubled adolescence. As the princesses of France grew older, Queen Catherine decided that they should spend more time at court in order that she should supervise their development personally. The question therefore arose whether Mary should not at this point be awarded her own household since with the departure of the princesses, her domestic arrangements seemed on occasion almost threadbare. The main drawback to the establishment of such a household was that it would entail an extra financial burden on the Estates of Scotland, who were scarcely in the mood to find still further funds for the maintenance of their young queen in France, while the budget for the French troops in Scotland remained high. The cardinal of Lorraine was obliged to write a series of letters to his sister before the final permission was granted. One of his arguments was the keen desire of Mary Stuart herself to be thus set up since at present she felt herself to be shabbily treated – the first hint of a rebellious character in this otherwise docile little paragon.' The pleadings of the cardinal prevailed. On 1st January, 1554 Mary Stuart entered into her new estate, and to celebrate the occasion she invited her uncle to supper that evening.

The choice was significant. Up till now the Guises had been content to let their nursing spend much of her time in the royal household: but from now onwards it was important that her character should be formed in accordance with their wishes, and that she should receive her early lessons in statecraft from the people who stood to gain so much from her future high position in France – the Guises. On her mother's side, Mary formed part of one of the most fascinating family nexus in French history, and it is impossible to understand the extremes of hostility and popularity which the Guises aroused during this period without considering briefly their antecedents. The family of Guise only entered France at the beginning of the sixteenth century when the widow of a younger son of the duke of Lorraine (then an independent duchy) applied to the French king to become naturalized French, along with his family of twelve children. The eldest of this family was Claude de Guise, grandfather of Mary Stuart, who was not only a highly successful general himself, but was supported on the secular flank by his ambitious brother the Cardinal Jean of Lorraine. But with success inevitably came jealousy. The Guises were accused of being foreigners by their enemies – Lorrainers rather than true Frenchmen. The Guises riposted by claiming that the royal blood of Charlemagne flowed in their veins, which, they said, entitled them to the highest place at the French court. This in turn led their detractors to accuse them of aiming at the very throne of France.[2] In truth nothing as thin as the last *fainéant* drops of Charlemagne's blood flowed in the veins of the Guises: they possessed something infinitely more potent – a furious life force and an admirable feeling of blood brotherhood. It is possible that the manner in which they upheld each other may have tempted Mary Stuart later in Scotland to suppose that all relatives supported each other as the Guises had done – a theory which the behaviour of the Stewarts sadly disproved. At all events, contemporary historians began to refer to the Guises as the Maccabees.

Mary's future was affected politically by the power of the next generation of Guises at the court of Henry II, principally the two eldest sons of Duke Claude's enormous family – Francis, second duke of Guise, and Charles who followed his uncle into the Church, and became first cardinal of Guise, later cardinal of Lorraine in his turn. During her childhood Mary also formed deep attachments to some of her Guise aunts and their children. For lack of any brothers and sisters she came to regard these young Guises as her own intimate family, especially once she was grown up, and back in Scotland, no longer in such close touch with the French royal family. Her gentle and cultivated aunt, Anne d'Esté, wife of Duke Francis, she loved with an especial warmth. The attachment was reciprocated: Duchess Anne wrote rapturously to Mary of Guise that her nine-year-old niece was 'the most beautiful and prettiest little Queen that anyone could want',[3] and she only hoped that her own daughter Catherine would be allowed to serve her when she grew up. When Mary was older, she used to dance with her aunt in front of the court, a sight which Brantôme romantically compared to the two suns of Pliny appearing together in the heavens to astonish the world – Mary being all grace and slenderness, and Anne having the statelier, fuller figure and the more apparent majesty of bearing. One effect of Mary's friendship with her aunt was to throw her together with her little Guise cousins, despite the disparity in their ages. The future Duke Henry of Guise was eight years younger than Mary, a handsome, blond, curly-haired little boy whom Marguerite de Valois, his contemporary, considered arrogant and overbearing. Mary Stuart, however, from the vantage point of superior age, described Henry and his brothers more sentimentally as the best-looking little boys in all the world.[4]

The three main centres of Guise family life were the palace of Joinville in the north-east of France whose gardens and parks were much beloved of Mary and her cousins, the palace of Meudon, close to Paris, and the Hôtel de Guise in Paris itself. Meudon was in the course of construction under the direction of Primaticcio and his pupils in the 1550s, at the cardinal's behest to include an exquisite grotto: Mary boasted of its coming marvels in a letter to her mother. The magnificent Hôtel de Guise occupied the site of four previous hotels: on the vast quadrangular space, the duke and duchess of Guise built a splendid new hotel, in which the chapel, decorated by Niccolò del Abbate from drawings by Primaticcio, showed them to be patrons of the arts, and the staircase, decorated by their emblem of the Cross of Lorraine, signified their conscious pride in their family. In each of these three magnificent homes, Mary was welcomed as the young and promising member of the Guise connection, from whom much could be expected.

The influence of the Guise family was marked at the very outset of the reign of Henry II: at his coronation, the new king received his crown from the hands of Charles of Guise, who was created cardinal five days later. At the royal tournament in celebration of the event, it was Francis of Guise who made a particularly brilliant appearance. The glamour of Duke Francis was indeed such that anti-Guisard historians like de l'Aubespine, the courtier, could not bring themselves to condemn him totally, but were inclined to ascribe his actions, of which they disapproved, to the ambitions of his brother Charles.⁵ The spell which he cast over his contemporaries was, however, due not only to his pre-eminent generalship, but also to the fact that he was fortunate enough to be able to come to his country's rescue on two dramatic occasions. The history of Europe in the early part of the 1550s was dominated by the rivalry between the house of Austria, personified by the Emperor Charles V, who included Spain in his vast dominions, and the house of Valois under Henry II. When the Emperor Charles handed over Spain and the Netherlands to his son Philip in 1556, this struggle narrowed to a rivalry between Spain and France. In this rivalry both England and Scotland were involved as pawns – England was linked to the side of Spain by the marriage of the English queen, Mary Tudor, to the Spanish King Philip; Scotland was linked to France by the planned marriage of their queen, Mary Stuart, to Henry's son Francis. But at the beginning of 1552, by making an alliance with the federation of Protestant German princes, who applied for help against the emperor, which allowed him to occupy the key border fortresses of Metz and Verdun, King Henry had brought to an end the uneasy peace which existed between France and the Empire. In reply, the emperor massed his troops with a view to regaining possession of Metz; and it was Francis of Guise who gallantly held the fortress during the prolonged siege which followed. In February the next year, the duke of Guise was solemnly thanked by the French Parliament for saving his country; he seemed indeed to justify the verdict of his brother, that he was 'the most valiant man in the whole of Christendom'.[6]

The character of the cardinal is both more complex and less outwardly attractive than that of his brother. He certainly possessed intelligence, erudition and statecraft, amply illustrated in his letters, but there was also another side to his character on which anti-Guisards loved to dwell: he was accused of avarice, probably with truth (despite the fact that he died deeply in debt and did not show much skill in managing his own financial affairs or those of Mary) since he was in perpetual need of funds to keep up his army of couriers bringing him political news from every corner of Europe. His ecclesiastical career certainly provided an example of pluralism: however, as even in youth he showed sufficient precocity to present King Francis 1 with a thesis on morals and theology, perhaps his ecclesiastical advancement was not totally unjustified. His sermons aroused the general admiration of the French court; in Holy Week 1560 the Venetian ambassador reported that no one could think of anything else except these uplifting discourses, which were attracting huge audiences – although at the same time the cardinal's enemies were busy in the streets pinning up scurrilous placards against him.[7] In his career the cardinal of Guise summed up most completely of all his brothers the dichotomy in the Guise character: on the one hand lay their superb endowment of natural gifts, to grace the public life which they craved; on the other side of the balance lay their remarkable family ambition, which was capable, under certain circumstances, of vitiating all their services. This dichotomy is seen in the two contemporary explanations of the family emblem – the two-barred Cross of Lorraine. At the funeral oration of Duke Claude of Guise, it was pronounced that the cross meant that the Guises would die twice for Christ, once in France and once in the Holy Land. But at the time of the Holy League, under Duke Henry, it was cynically suggested the double cross meant that Christ had been crucified twice, once by the Jews, and once by the Leaguers.[8]

It is difficult to estimate the true nature of the cardinal of Lorraine's religion, since by modern standards his determined persecution of the French heretics arouses abhorrence, and by the political standards of the day they led not to peace but to the disastrous civil wars of the next ten years. The word tolerance has a mellifluous ring in modern ears. To us, tolerance of another's beliefs has become a touchstone of liberalism, and intolerance is considered, by many, to be the final crime in a civilized society; but in the sixteenth century tolerance was certainly not among the public virtues expected in a ruler. As Father Pollen pointed out, what to us may seem like defence of the weak, seemed to them more like allowing vice to flourish; liberty of conscience was scarcely worthy of discussion, let alone worth fighting for. Sufferers on both sides of religious issues certainly did not expect to find that their ordeals had resulted in the spread of religious tolerance; they merely bore witness to their faith. The question of how far diversity of religion could be tolerated was indeed largely a question of public order: the Guises believed that French Catholicism was strong enough to eliminate Calvinism altogether, whereas in the next decade, Catherine de Médicis was obliged to exhibit political tolerance because she found that on the contrary neither religion was strong enough to drive out the other. In neither case can true conclusions be drawn about their private qualities of mercy. It is an interesting fact that Mary Stuart, whose religious views, as well as her views on statecraft, were formed with such care by the cardinal during her adolescence, showed throughout her career a quite remarkable clemency and lack of bigotry towards her subjects of a different religion, marking her off from almost all her contemporaries, except possibly her own mother. Every letter to her mother bears some sort of witness to the detailed supervision which her uncle was now giving to her upbringing: deeply impressionable as she was by nature, Mary Stuart's admirable innate quality of mercy could certainly have been tempered by the teachings of the cardinal, had he so wished. On the contrary, it was allowed to flourish, and guide her actions as ruler of Scotland in her later career, for better or for worse.

The cardinal's lessons in statecraft encouraged the young queen to take an interest in Scottish affairs. In her letters to her mother on the subject, she shows aptitude and application, rather than any marked independence of judgement, and at every juncture quotes, or refers back to, the opinion of one of her uncles. Scottish affairs were also the more vivid to Mary Stuart now that her mother had at last succeeded in ousting the ineffective Arran from the official role of regent, and in April 1554 her appointment was ratified by the Estates of Scotland. At the end of one letter on the subject of some presents she heard were coming from the Duke Châtelherault (Arran had been granted this French dukedom in 1549 and was now known by his new title) Mary told her mother that she had shown the missive to her uncle of Guise as she knew this was what her mother would wish her to do. On another occasion, she paid tribute to the enormous care her uncle and aunt of Guise had taken of her – and most of all her uncle the cardinal. In 1555 specifically on the advice of her uncle the cardinal she sent back blank letters to her mother signed MARIE* for administrative purposes.[9]

Despite the agreeable tutelage of the cardinal, and her modest advance into the realms of statecraft, Mary Stuart's adolescence was marred by a tiresome domestic drama, the more enervating because it occurred right in the heart of her little household. Mme de Parois, the governess who replaced Lady Fleming, proved to be admirably lacking in the human frailty of her

---

* Throughout her life, Mary used the name in its French form in her signature. A feature of this signature, seen already in her earliest letters, is the fact that all the letters, including the first M, are made to be of the same size. She may have modelled her signature on that of her mother: the two signatures are not unalike.

predecessor, but she had defects of character of her own which were considerably less beguiling. Money matters led to constant troubles. On one occasion Mme de Parois was forced to write to Mary of Guise and ask for more money to buy her mistress's clothes; Mary Stuart positively had to have a dress of cloth of gold for the approaching marriage of the Count de Vaudermont since she had been so annoyed at lacking a dress of cloth of silver for the marriage of the governor's son. On another occasion Mme de Parois bemoaned the fact that the princesses' dresses were now lined with cloth of gold, which made them so dear to copy, and she explained that the Scottish queen was very anxious to have embroidered ciphers on her dresses, also an expensive luxury. Permission was sought for two new outfits a year, for reasons of prestige, whatever the lack of finance at home.[10]

There was another side of the story: some of Mary's entourage took the line that there was quite enough money to go round if only Mme de Parois had employed it more economically. The controversy was at times bitter and at times petty. In one letter, Mary of Guise's controller inquired angrily what had happened to some money which the French king had given to Mary to spend at the fair at Saint-Germain. Mme de Parois continued to grumble over the general shortness of funds, although she pointed out primly that she took care to keep her young mistress in happy ignorance of the situation. The fact that Mary's accounts for the year 1556–7 showed outgoings of 58,607 *livres* and incomings of only 58,000 *livres* showed that wherever that fault lay, the financial situation was certainly not a satisfactory one.[11]

But now the governess fell out with her mistress. In their fractious disputes, which read like a domestic storm in a teacup, the real irritant seems to have been Mme de Parois's ill-health. When she finally surrendered the post of governess it was due to advancing dropsy; no doubt her declining health exacerbated her troubles with her charge in her own mind, and equally made her difficult to deal with. The trouble began with the distribution of the Scottish queen's outworn clothing, which Mme de Parois felt to be her own perquisite. Mary had other ideas. In a furious letter to her mother she complained that she had given some of the dresses to her Guise aunts, the abbesses of Saint Pierre and Farmoustier, to make vestments, and others to her servants, all according to her mother's instructions. In April 1556 the cardinal himself intervened and wrote to Mary of Guise that in his opinion Mme de Parois was no longer suited to be her daughter's governess. Nevertheless, in the May of the following year, Mme de Parois still had not been dislodged; and Mary wrote again to her mother complaining that Mme de Parois was now making such bad blood between Mary, Duchess Antoinette and Queen Catherine, that Mary was terrified that the malicious governess would go further and stir up trouble between mother and daughter.[12]

The dispute does reveal significantly the direction in which Mary Stuart's character was developing. There is a vein of near hysteria in some of her letters to her mother on the subject: she was passionately upset at the notion that the love of her mother might be turned away from her by the trouble-making efforts of this woman. She rebuts with anguish the notion that she who is generous should be so unfairly described as mean. The episode suggests that from adolescence onwards, Mary Stuart was peculiarly sensitive to the onslaughts of criticism which she had good reason to feel were unfair. This feminine and perfectly understandable sensitivity had dangerous possibilities for one who was, after all, destined to be a queen regnant: for there was no certainty that she would always be surrounded with the right sort of advisers to provide a balancing stability of attitude. The suggestion that the young queen had become positively ill as a result of this domestic fracas is also of interest for her future. She told her mother that Mme de Parois had almost been the cause of her death 'because I was afraid of falling under your displeasure, and because I grieved at hearing through these false reports so many disputes and so much harm said of me'.[13] This tendency of apparently nervous stress to show itself in physical symptoms almost approaching a breakdown was something she clearly inherited from her father, since the Guises were remarkably free from it: as a characteristic it was to play a marked part in her later career.

After a robust childhood, Mary Stuart's general health began to show cause for concern in adolescence. When she was thirteen, her uncle thought it necessary to write angrily to her mother in order to contradict reports that she was generally ailing; he told her that the verdict of the doctors was that she would outlive all her relations, although she sometimes got a certain heartburn or plain indigestion, due to a hearty appetite which would certainly lead to her overeating if the cardinal did not watch her carefully. 'I am astonished at what you have been told about her being sickly,' exclaimed the cardinal, in disgust at the very idea of such tale-bearing behaviour. 'It can only have been said by malicious persons out of ill nature.'[4] The truth was that, despite the cardinal's vehement protests, all her life Mary Stuart was to suffer from gastric troubles, of which these were only the first ominous symptoms, and her fierce appetite, coupled with sickness, stood for something more sinister than the mere hunger of a healthy adolescent girl. Other illnesses from which Mary suffered during adolescence included small-pox – possibly for the third time, if the two other reported attacks in Scotland are correct, but more probably for the sole occasion in her life. She told Queen Elizabeth in 1562 that she had been cured and her beauty preserved by the action of the famous physician Jean Fernel – certainly in all the tributes to the famous complexion of the queen of Scots, there is no suggestion that it was ever marred by the pox. In the summer and autumn of 1556 she fell ill with a series of fevers, possibly the precursor of the tertian fevers which haunted the rest of her life, and for all his angry denials to outsiders the cardinal's letters to Mary of Guise in Scotland show that he felt extreme concern at the time.[5]

In 1556 peace was once again temporarily established in Europe by the Truce of Vaucelles: the Emperor Charles V, anxious to retire from the world and hand over his vast dominions to his son Philip, agreed to accept the general results of the war between France and the Empire for five years. The cardinal of Lorraine was absent in Rome, and his counsels had not been felt effectively at the French court for six months; Henry II was swayed in his absence by the advice of the great rival of the Guises, the Constable Anne of Montmorency. On his return home the cardinal determined to undo the peace, which meant the virtual wrecking of his work in Rome, where he had at last persuaded the aged Pope Paul IV to enter into an alliance with France against the imperialists. As it happened, even the constable was not totally reluctant to see the great duke of Guise wasting his reputation in a series of fruitless Italian campaigns: so that once more war was resumed, and in Italy, for once, the duke was not immediately successful. The importunity of Philip of Spain to his wife, Mary Tudor, queen of England, eventually succeeded in bringing England also into the war on the side of Spain. In August 1557 the army of the constable, on its way to relieve beleaguered Saint-Quentin, was routed by King Philip's army, which included English units. Philip now captured Saint-Quentin and seemed set to march on Paris. Once more it was Duke Francis of Guise who came to the rescue of the French people. By turning the tables of the war, and finally capturing Calais itself from the English in January 1558, after 220 years, Francis of Guise not only confounded those anti-Guise critics who had rejoiced at his Italian failure, but also elevated the prestige of his family to new heights.

The victory of Francis of Guise at Calais and the reappearance of the bright star of the Guises had an important effect on the fortunes of his niece Mary. She was now, in the spring of 1558, over fifteen, and the dauphin was just fourteen. By the standards of the age, Mary was marriageable, but Francis only marginally so.* But Henry II now had two strong motives, both political,

* It has been suggested, on the evidence of a letter from Henry to Mary of Guise, that the French king had even contemplated carrying out the marriage a year earlier, when the bride and groom would have been only fourteen and thirteen respectively. This letter has now been convincingly re-dated to the next year, and thus disposes of the theory that Henry did ever in fact consider such a union of children.[16]

to persuade him towards the finalization of this marriage which had been arranged in theory nearly ten years previously. The words of the Venetian ambassador Giacomo Sorenzo, writing on 9th November, 1557, sum up the situation: 'The causes for hastening this marriage are apparently two; the first to enable them more surely to avail themselves of the forces of Scotland against the kingdom of England for next year, and the next for the gratification of the Duke and Cardinal of Guise, the said Queen's uncles, who by the hastening of this marriage, choose to secure themselves against any other matrimonial alliance which might be proposed to his most Christian majesty in some negotiation for peace, the entire establishment of their greatness having to depend on this; for which reason the Constable by all means in his power continually sought to prevent it.'[17] Henry sent to Scotland, to remind the Scottish Parliament that the time had come to implement their promises. In years gone by, there had been other matrimonial possibilities suggested for Mary Stuart, despite her theoretical betrothal to the dauphin. In July 1556, the French ambassador at Brussels threatened that if the king of Spain married the Archduke Ferdinand of Austria to Elizabeth Tudor, Henry II would give Mary Stuart to Lord Courtenay, an English aristocrat in the line of succession to the English throne.[18] The aim of this dynastic and diplomatic marriage roundabout was to prevent the house of Austria establishing itself in England, from which position it was felt it could effectively threaten France. But in the end Mary Stuart was not forced to ride on the roundabout. The death of Lord Courtenay, a few months later, put an end to this interesting possibility. Mary Stuart was given back her original position on the chess board of the French king's policy as the Scottish pawn who would help to checkmate England by marrying his son.

Commissioners were duly appointed in Scotland to come to France, in order to carry out the marriage negotiations. The nine envoys thus chosen included three supporters of the Reformation – the queen's half-brother, James Stewart, the earl of Cassillis and John Erskine of Dun; for in her anxiety to arrange the marriage contract of her daughter smoothly, Mary of Guise determined to exhibit the utmost conciliation towards the reformers, who might otherwise upset the design to which she attached such importance. The reformers took full advantage of her quiescent mood, and as the marriage negotiations proceeded, so did the reformed religion and its preaching spread in Scotland. The First Band of the Congregation which pledged the signatories to work for the cause of the reformed religion in Scotland was actually signed by Argyll, his son Lord Lorne, later the 5th earl of Argyll, Morton, Glencairn and others, in the same month in which the commissioners left for France.

Unable to leave Scotland herself, Mary of Guise appointed her mother Antoinette to act as her proxy during the arranging of the marriage contract. As a result the formal betrothal of the young pair took place on 19th April, 1558, in the great hall of the new Louvre, with the cardinal of Lorraine joining their hands together. A magnificent ball followed, at which Henry II danced with the bride-elect, Antoine of Navarre with Catherine de Médicis, the dauphin with his aunt Madame Marguerite, and the duke of Lorraine with the princess Claude whom he later married. By the terms of the betrothal contract, the dauphin declared that of 'his own free will and with the fullest consent of the King and Queen his father and mother, and being duly authorized by them to take the Queen of Scotland for his wife and consort, he promised to espouse her on the following Sunday April 24th'.[19]

Despite the formality of the language, and the political considerations which had prompted his elders to hurry forward the match, the young groom does seem to have felt genuine affection for his bride. His mother, Catherine de Médicis, and Mary Stuart seem to have been indeed the only two human beings for whom this pathetic, wizened creature felt true emotion. Sickly in childhood, he had become difficult and sullen in adolescence; his physique was scarcely developed and his height was stunted; furthermore there is considerable doubt whether he ever actually reached the age of puberty before his untimely death, when he was not quite seventeen.* The dauphin showed little enthusiasm or aptitude for learning, although his enthusiasm for the chase astonished the courtiers, considering his frail physique. All the Venetian ambassadors in turn commented on the fact that he was an invalid, from Matteo Dandolo who saw him when he was three, to Sorenzo who was at the wedding. Dandolo described him as being pale and swollen rather than fat, but rather dignified (as child invalids do often acquire a certain pathetic dignity). Obviously, for better or for worse, he soon became conscious of his high position: in 1552 he was described as having a considerable sense of his own importance, and Capello commented again on the fact when he was eleven: 'He shows that he knows he is a prince', before going on to say that he spoke little, and seemed generally '*bilieux*'.[21] This taciturn and stubborn character suffered from a chronic respiratory infection, resulting from his difficult birth, which cannot have added to his appeal, since it prompted his mother Catherine at one point to write to his governor and urge that the dauphin should blow his nose more, for the good of his health.

However, the same ambassadors who described him as a rather unattractive and self-important invalid also commented on the real signs of love which he exhibited towards his future bride. Capello wrote that he adored '*la Reginata de Scozia*' who was destined to be his wife, and whom Capello called an exceptionally pretty child. He paints a touching picture of the pair of them drawing apart into a corner of the court, in order to exchange kisses and childish secrets. When he was eleven, the cardinal referred to him jokingly as '*l'amoureux*', and when he was only six, he was hoping to joust with the duke of Guise in order to enjoy the favours of '*une dame belle et honnête*', his niece Mary Stuart.[22] They played childish games of chance

---

* He probably suffered from the condition known medically as undescended testicles. The Protestant historian Regnier de la Planche used these words to describe the formation of his body: '*Il avoit les parties génératives du tout constipées et empeschés sans faire aucune action.*' Although deeply hostile to the Guises, and thus prejudiced in many of his views of history, la Planche was likely to be well-informed on this subject through his friendship with Catherine de Médicis.[20]

together: on one occasion Mary won 74 sols, and on another lost 45. In short, she was the companion to whom he was accustomed, and she was in addition young, romantic and beautiful – increasingly so, in the eyes of the courtiers. It would have been odd indeed if the dauphin had not loved and admired this exquisite and radiant bride being presented to him, who was in addition a comforting friend from his childhood.

What were Mary's own feelings for her bridegroom? First of all it must be said that it is not difficult for the young to be fond of those who are fond of them, and openly display this fondness. Furthermore, as a character, Mary responded exceptionally easily to love all her life. She was used to being loved in the widest sense, since her childhood; she desired to continue being loved, since it was a state she enjoyed; where she saw love, or thought she saw it, she found it easy to bestow her own generous affections in return. The dauphin loved her, of that she felt certain enough in herself, but in any case the Guises and the French court combined were always assuring her that he did. Her feminine wish to charm and please those around her made her naturally want to show the conventional affection for her bridegroom which was clearly expected of her. And as she showed the affection, the imitative side of her nature made her begin to feel it. To those who have never known the transports of romantic love, companionship and the feeling of general approval are agreeable substitutes: Mary felt that she loved her bridegroom in the most worthy manner, although his infantile physique and immaturity make it unlikely that he actually aroused in her any of the feelings with which most adults would endow the word.

While the two protagonists of the match were thus perfectly content to be united, there were certain political undertones to the arrangements which were considerably more sinister than the innocent childlike emotions of Francis and Mary. Two marriage treaties were in fact signed, one open and one secret. The first official marriage treaty, whose witnesses included Diane de Poitiers, provided terms with which the Scottish delegates were adequately satisfied: the young queen bound herself to preserve the ancient freedoms, liberties and privileges of Scotland; so long as she was out of the country, it was to be governed by the regency of the queen mother, and the French king and the dauphin both bound themselves and their successors, in the case of Mary's death without children, to support the succession to the Scottish throne of the nearest heir by blood – still the head of the house of Hamilton, the duke of Châtelherault. Mary was given a satisfactory jointure. It was further agreed that the dauphin should bear the title of king of Scotland and that, on his accession to the French throne, the two kingdoms should be united under one crown, and the subjects of both countries should be thus naturalized with each other, in anticipation of the joint reign. Letters of naturalization were granted to Henry in June, and confirmed by the parliament of Paris on 8th July. In November the Scottish Estates in their turn granted letters of naturalization to all the subjects of the king of France. Up till the death of Henry, Francis and Mary were to be known as the king-dauphin and the queen-dauphiness. In the case of the death of her husband, Mary was to be allowed to choose whether she remained in France or returned to her kingdom; as a widowed queen, Mary was to receive a fortune of 600,000 *livres*; should there be male issue, the eldest surviving child should inherit both crowns, whereas if the couple bore only daughters, owing to the workings of the Salic Law in France, the eldest daughter would inherit the Scottish crown alone.

All these terms were nothing more than those the standards of the time dictated, when a female heiress married the representative of a more powerful kingdom. The only condition at which the Scottish commissioners demurred was Henry's suggestion that the crown of Scotland be sent to France, to be used for the coronation of the dauphin. As by the following November the Scottish Estates had agreed that the dauphin should be granted the crown matrimonial – which gave him equal powers as king of Scotland with his wife as queen – even this objection seems to spring from an admirably cautious attitude towards sending away a valuable object to a foreign country, rather than a disinclination towards granting the office itself. The state documents of Scotland were henceforth signed by both Francis and Mary jointly: Francis's signature, however, always appeared on the left hand and Mary's on the right – the left hand in this case, as dexter in heraldry, being the more important position, because it was read first.

At the same time, a second secret treaty was drawn up, of which the Scottish commissioners were given no official knowledge. Before the marriage contract was actually signed, Mary signed three separate deeds by which, first of all, in the event of her death without children, Scotland and Mary's rights to the throne of England were made over freely to the crown of France; secondly Scotland and all its revenues were made over to the king of France and his successors until France should be reimbursed of the money spent in Scotland's defence; and thirdly, Mary actually renounced in anticipation any agreement she might make at the Estates' behest which might interfere with these arrangements. If implemented, these secret agreements would certainly have had the effect of transforming Scotland into a mere French dominion, in the pocket of the French king. To some, the fact that Mary Stuart signed these deeds represents the first blot on her character. Yet surely Mary, aged fifteen years and four months at the time of her marriage, should not be judged too harshly on this issue, and condemnations should rather be saved for the French king and French statesmen who presented her with the deeds. She was given them to sign by an older man whom she had been trained from childhood to love and admire, and by the uncles who had been as parents to her, and had given her for the last ten years every proof of their devotion and welfare. She also had been brought up to believe that although she was virtually born reigning queen of Scotland, her actual destiny was to be queen consort of France. France was her adopted country, and half of her blood was French; as we have seen, little attempt had been made to preserve in her a sense of the true importance of Scotland. Although she had been conscientiously inculcated in statecraft by her uncle, the net result of hearing about her mother's troubles must have been to lead her to believe that Scotland was not much more than a tiresome colony or protectorate; it needed firm government, but had little right to sovereign interests, so long as the French existed to provide it with a wise administration, through the queen regent, and the French officials in power in Scotland.

All Mary's emotional inclinations led her to believe that the happiest fate of Scotland would be to be united with France – this was, after all, the union which she was about to effect by her marriage. She was far from unique in this attitude, in her age. The French panegyrics on her marriage exhibit exactly the same half-patronizing approach towards Scotland.²³ There are conventional tributes to the young queen's charms – she is Helen in beauty, Lucrece in chastity, Pallas in wisdom, Ceres in riches, Juno in power. But the panegyrists agree that while the bride is beautiful, her country is a minor one, which must consider itself fortunate to be governed for the future by France. The wedding hymn of Michel l'Hôpital puts forward the political gain to France in acquiring new territory and revenues, it is true, but also expresses the view that the Scots will be delighted to gain a new set of rulers in the French. With perhaps a certain overconfidence, he suggests that even Mary's father James v will be pleased to notice Scotland now taking second place to France, as he looks down from his eternal resting-place:

> Nor would he shrink his ancient realm to see
> Ranked second in his regal blazonry.

A work of Estienne Perlin, published in 1558, and dedicated to Henry's sister, the duchess of Berry, observes patronizingly: 'How happy oughtest thou to esteem thyself, O kingdom of Scotland, to be favoured, fed and maintained like an infant on the breast of the most magnanimous King of France, the greatest lord in the whole world, and the future monarch of that round machine, for without him thou wouldn'st have been laid in ashes, thy country wasted and ruined by the English, utterly accursed by God'.²⁴

In such a climate of opinion, it would have needed a woman of maturity, and of stubbornly independent political opinions, not a young girl who had been trained to act in feminine obedience to her powerful uncles, to hold out against the signing of the secret treaties. In April 1558, Mary Stuart can scarcely be blamed for thinking more of the gorgeous pageantry of her wedding celebrations than of the true implications of the three deeds which she had just been led to sign.

CHAPTER FIVE
Queen-Dauphiness

Just as we see, half rosy and half white
Dawn and the Morning Star dispel the night
In beauty thus beyond compare impearled
The Queen of Scotland rises on the world

Ronsard to Mary Queen of Scots,
translated by Maurice Baring

The French court, in true Renaissance fashion, desired its principals to shine out luminously against a background of endless pageantry; never were its wishes more splendidly gratified than in the marriage ceremonies of Francis, dauphin of France, and Mary Queen of Scots. The wedding itself took place on Sunday, 24th April at the cathedral of Notre Dame. The contemporary *Discours du Grand et Magnifique Triomphe faict du Mariage* gives a full description of the festivities, in which the writer himself seems to be frequently awed by the magnificence of what he is recounting.[1] Already in March, Henry had asked the French Parliament to stay at the convent of the Augustins, in order that its palace could be adequately and conveniently prepared. Notre Dame itself was embellished with a special structure outside in the antique manner, to make a kind of open-air theatre, and an arch twelve feet high inside. The royal *fleur-de-lys* was embroidered everywhere, and positively studded the canopy in front of the church.

The first sign to meet the eyes of the eagerly waiting crowds were the Swiss guards, resplendent in their liveries, who entered the theatre to the sound of tambourins and fifes. Then came Francis, duke of Guise, hero of France, uncle of the bride, and in the absence of the Constable de Montmorency, in captivity in Brussels since the defeat of Saint-Quentin, actually in charge of the proceedings. Then came Eustace du Bellay, the bishop of Paris, who considerately made sure that the view of the common people was not impeded so that they could see the show. Then came a procession, headed by a series of musicians, all dressed in yellow and red, with trumpets, sackbuts, flageolets, violins and other musical instruments. Then followed a hundred gentlemen-in-waiting of the king. Then came the princes of the blood, gorgeously apparelled, to the wonder, and presumably satisfaction, of the onlookers. Then came *abbés* and bishops bearing rich crosses and wearing jewelled mitres, and after them the princes of the Church, even more magnificently dressed, including the cardinals of Bourbon, Lorraine and Guise, and the cardinal legate of France (who had given the bride and groom the necessary papal dispensation for the marriage since they were cousins) who entered with a cross of gold borne before him.*

Now entered the King-Dauphin Francis, led by the King Antoine of Navarre and his two younger brothers Charles, duke of Orléans, and Henry, duke of Angoulême. Finally entered the centrepiece of the occasion, Mary, queen-dauphiness, led by Henry II and her cousin the duke of Lorraine. Mary Stuart, on this the first of her three wedding-days, was dressed in a robe as white as lilies, so sumptuous and rich that the pen of the contemporary observer fell from his hands at the thought of describing it. Since white was traditionally the mourning colour of the queens of France, Mary Stuart had defied tradition to wear it on her wedding-day; it certainly remained a favourite shade with her throughout her youth, and even in later years she loved to have something white about her face and neck: perhaps of all colours she felt that it set off her brilliant colouring to best advantage. On this occasion, her immensely long train was borne by two young girls; tall and elegant, she herself

---

* Mary's grandmother, Duchess Antoinette of France, and Francis's maternal grandmother were first cousins; Mary and Francis were thus third cousins.

must have glittered like the goddess of a pageant, with diamonds round her neck, and on her head a golden crown garnished with pearls, rubies, sapphires and other precious stones, as well as one huge carbuncle worth over 500,000 crowns.

The young queen was followed by Catherine de Médicis, led by the prince of Condé, Mme Marguerite, the king's sister, the duchess of Berry, and other princesses and ladies dressed with such grandeur that once again their robes could hardly be described for fear of repetition. The queen of Navarre had brought with her to Paris her six-year-old son, the future Henry IV, who at this wedding had his first sight of the capital which he was one day to make his own. At a given moment, the king drew a ring off his finger and gave it to the cardinal of Bourbon, Archbishop of Rouen, who thus espoused the pair, in the presence of the bishop of Paris; the bishop then made a wedding oration, described as being both 'scientific and elegant'.

All the while, with typical concern for the reactions of the populace, the duke of Guise was touring the whole theatre with two heralds, making sure that the nobles were not blocking the view of the people in the streets or at the windows. When he was satisfied the heralds cried out loudly: '*Largesse! Largesse!*' and threw a mass of gold and silver pieces to the crowd, at which there was an immediate tumult and clamour as the people scrambled over each other to help themselves – so much so that some fainted and others lost their cloaks in their greed. Meanwhile all the nobility entered the church itself in the same order as before, to find another resplendent royal canopy, as well as gold carpets, within. The bishop of Paris then said Mass with King Henry and Queen Catherine on one side of the altar, and King-Dauphin Francis and Queen-Dauphiness Mary on the other; during the offertory, further sums of gold and silver were distributed outside. When Mass was over, the fine display of nobility paraded all over again, with Henry taking the greatest care to show himself to his people, although in the words of the *Discours* – 'Monseigneur de Guise arranged everything'.

A long and Lucullan banquet followed in which only one

jarring note occurred to mar the general rejoicing: in the course of the meal, the gracefully leaning head of the queen, on its frail neck, started to ache under the weight of the heavy crown which adorned it. King Henry had to command a lord-in-waiting, M. de Saint-Seuer, Chevalier de Saint-Crispin, to take the crown and hold it. If this ominous incident portended the danger of placing too heavy a crown on too young a head, no one at the time commented on the symbolism. Otherwise nothing untoward marked the celebrations, except that the Sire de Saint-Jehan, favourite of the dauphin, had his eye put out during the jousting: but even this minor tragedy was not held to mar the general sense of accomplishment. At the ball, Henry danced with Mary, Francis with his mother, the king of Navarre with the Princess Elisabeth, the duke of Lorraine with the Princess Claude, and so on down the royal scale. This was only the beginning: when the ball was over at four or five in the afternoon, the entire court then processed to the palace of the parliament, the gentlemen on horseback and the ladies in litters. In order to give the maximum pleasure to the people, they travelled by a different route, and the crowds who rushed in vast numbers to watch them pass, almost blocking their progress by their density, were rewarded by a sight of the new queen-dauphiness in a golden litter with her mother-in-law Catherine, and the new king-dauphin following on horseback with his gentlemen, their horses adorned with crimson velvet trappings.

A new order of entertainment now followed, organized by the duke of Guise as grand master of the ceremonies: indeed, although the dauphin wrote sadly to the constable at Brussels, regretting that he would be absent on the wedding-day of his '*bon compère Francôis*',[2] it is doubtful whether the Duke of Guise shared his new nephew's sorrow, since the marriage celebrations thus entrusted to him gave him a renewed opportunity to shine in the popular eye. The president, counsellors and officers of the Parliament were all present at the supper which now ensued, their scarlet robes mingling with glittering robes of the court. After a supper, a second celebratory ball was held, even more splendid than the first, and punctuated by an endless series of masks and mummeries, in which the royal family themselves took part. Twelve artificial horses made of gold and silver cloth were brought into the ball-room: the dauphin's brothers, Charles and Henry, the Guise and Aumale children, and other princelings then mounted the horses, and proceeded to draw along a series of coaches with them which contained a number of bejewelled occupants singing melodiously. After this spectacle, in which the fact that the gem-studded passengers were intended to be pilgrims struck the only conceivable note of austerity, six ships were drawn into the ball-room; their silver sails were so ingeniously made that they seemed to be billowing in an imaginary wind, and the ships themselves gave the impression of truly floating on the ball-room floor. Each of these magic barques had room for two voyagers, and after touring the ball-room, the noble gentlemen at the helm selected the ladies of their choice, and helped them into their boats. Once again, however, in spite of the delicate fantasy of the scene, choice was dictated more by court ceremony than by the promptings of romance. The duke of Lorraine chose Mme Claude, the king of Navarre chose his wife, the duke of Nemours chose Mme Marguerite, King Henry chose his daughter-in-law and Francis chose his mother. The further magnificence of the occasion proved once again to beggar description – for as the author of the *Discours* observed, no one could really decide which was lighting up the ball-room more brightly – the *flambeaux*, or the flash of the royal jewels.

While distinctions of this esoteric nature occupied the contemporary observers, it is, however, possible for us, with hindsight, to see behind these elaborate ceremonies, which continued for several days, and discern the tarnish behind the tinsel. The land of France was virtually bankrupted by its prolonged struggle against the Empire, which had involved it in such time-, men- and money-consuming Italian wars. Yet Henry felt it essential to make this luxurious display, to uphold the prestige of the monarchy in the eyes of the people, and indeed the nobility. The king of Navarre whispered malevolently into the ear of the Venetian ambassador at the celebrations, 'Thou seest the conclusion of a fact which very few credited till now,' and hinted that the constable had steadily opposed this Guise marriage. The ambassador commented that the special pomp and display of the occasion was due to the fact that no dauphin of France had been married in Paris for two hundred years since they had all brought wives from abroad.[3] It is, however, likely that King Henry was less impressed by the historical nature of the occasion than by his desperate need to wipe out the defeat of Saint-Quentin in the imagination of the populace.

There is no reason to suppose that this canker at the centre of the gilded apple of fortune which now lay within her palm was apparent to Mary herself. During the wedding ceremonies, she had fulfilled the role to perfection for which she had been trained since childhood. Her new husband loved her, and was scarcely likely to treat her as Henry had treated Catherine, since the danger of a Diane de Poitiers was remote in such an immature bridegroom. Boy-husband or not, he was nevertheless the dauphin of France, and Mary thoroughly enjoyed her elevated rank as queen-dauphiness, for which she felt herself to be eminently fitted, being unable to remember a time when she was not treated with deference as a queen in her own right. When she needed advice, her uncles were to hand, anxious to supply it. She enjoyed the feminine friendship of her sister-in-law Elisabeth, or her Aunt Anne of Guise. She was young. She was beautiful. She was admired. An ecstatic letter to her mother in Scotland, written on her actual wedding-day, is almost incoherent with happiness at her new state and mentions how much honour not only Francis but her new father-in-law and mother-in-law continually do to her.[4] Scotland itself seemed far away. Although on her wedding-day, the great cannon of Edinburgh Castle, Mons Meg, was fired, the shot reaching as far as Wardie Moor, not many reverberations of either this or any other Scottish explosion were liable to be heard at the French court of which Mary was the most lucent ornament. The first few months of her new existence as queen-dauphiness were among the happiest and most carefree in a lifespan which did not turn out to include many such oases: this was indeed the time when

Mary, like Faust, might have addressed the passing moment: 'Linger awhile, you are so fair.'

The legendary beauty of Mary Stuart has been much vaunted. She was praised in her own day by her contemporaries, and in the four centuries since her death her charms have often been extolled in literature and poetry. It is interesting to consider whether she was, in fact, a beauty in the classical sense of the word, or whether her reputation was based on courtly flattery in her own day, and the romantic circumstances of her history ever since. A true estimate of her appearance is the more difficult to make because no authentic portraits of her exist, dating from the years of her personal reign in Scotland. We have no record at all of her beauty or otherwise from the age of nineteen to twenty-five, generally held to be the peak years of a woman's appearance. The authentic portraits of her as dauphiness and queen of France, all done before she was twenty years old, are also comparatively few in number; yet it is on these we must rely in order to acquire an accurate impression of her appearance when she was in her prime, since the next series of pictures were done nearly twenty years later and spring from the years of captivity. Her beauty has sometimes been judged disparagingly on the evidence of these portraits – unjustly so, since by then it had naturally been somewhat impaired by the ravages of ill-health, and imprisonment, to say nothing of middle-age itself. The beauty of Mary Stuart should be judged firstly on the evidence of the French portraits of her youth; secondly, since beauty, that insubstantial quality, exists so powerfully in the eye of the beholder, it should be judged from the verdicts of her contemporaries who, flatterers or otherwise, had at least an opportunity of estimating her quality for themselves.

Whether she was a beauty by our standards or not, Mary Stuart was certainly rated a beauty by the standards of her own time: even the venomous Knox, never inclined to pay compliments to those with whose convictions he disagreed, described her as 'pleasing', and recorded that the people of Edinburgh called out 'Heaven bless that sweet face' as she passed on her way. Sir James Melville, an experienced man of the world who prided himself on his detachment, called her appearance 'very lovesome'. Ronsard paid her superb tributes: he wrote of her hands which he particularly admired and their long, ringless fingers, which he compared in a poetic phrase to five unequal branches; he wrote of the unadorned beauty of her throat, free of any necklace, her alabaster brow, her ivory bosom. When she was a young widow, he wrote of her pacing sadly but gracefully at Fontainebleau, her garments blowing about her as she walked, like the sails of a ship ruffled in the wind.' The word goddess was the one which seemed to come most naturally to Brantôme in writing of her: she was '*une vraie Déesse*' of beauty and grace; he picked out her complexion for special praise, and described its famous pallor which rivalled and eclipsed the whiteness of her veil, when she was in mourning. Furthermore Mary had the additional charm of a peculiarly soft, sweet speaking voice: not only did Ronsard and Brantôme praise her '*voix très douce et très bonne*' in France but even the critical Knox admitted that the Scots were charmed by her pretty speech when she made her oration at the Tolbooth at the opening of Parliament, 'exclaiming *vox Dianae*! The voice of a goddess ... was there ever orator spake so properly and so sweetly!' It was also a point on which even the most hostile English observers commented on her first arrival in that country, including Knollys and Cecil's own emissary White.[6]

Her effect on the men around her was certainly that of a beautiful woman: the poet Châtelard fell violently, if slightly hysterically, in love with her; not only on the eve of his execution did he call her 'the most beautiful and the most cruel princess in the world', but on their journey back to Scotland he exclaimed that the galleys needed no lanterns to light their way 'since the eyes of this Queen suffice to light up the whole sea with their lovely fire'. The Seigneur de Damville was also said to have been so enamoured of the young queen that he followed her to Scotland, leaving his young wife at home, and if we are to believe Brantôme, Mary's little brother-in-law Charles was so much in love with her that he used to gaze at her portrait with longing and desired to marry her himself after the untimely death of Francis.[7] In Scotland Mary's beauty as well as her position was said to have captured not only the obsessional Arran, but the dashing Sir John Gordon and the youthful, handsome George Douglas. Her first English jailer, Sir Francis Knollys, although unpromising material for female wiles, was considerably seduced by the charming personality of his captive; and although the later so-called *affair* with Lord Shrewsbury was undoubtedly the creation of his wife's malicious imagination, nevertheless the fact that the accusation could be taken so seriously by the English court shows that all her life Mary was considered a beautiful and desirable woman, whose physical attractions could never be totally left out of account. At the time of her illness at Jedburgh when she was twenty-three, the Venetian ambassador wrote of her being a princess who was 'personally the most beautiful in Europe'.[8] There seems no reason to doubt that this was the general verdict of Europe during her lifetime, and that Mary Queen of Scots was a romantic figure to her own age, no less than to subsequent generations.

Despite these tributes, a consideration of her physiognomy leads one to believe that Mary Stuart was not a beauty in the classical sense – to use the language of our own day, she was an outstandingly attractive woman, rather than an outstandingly beautiful one. Her most marked physical characteristic to outside eyes must have been her height, and it is said that when she fled to England from Scotland after her defeat at Langside, strangers recognized her by it. In an age when the average height of the men was considerably shorter than it is today, Mary Stuart was probably about five feet eleven inches tall, that is to say, taller than all but the tallest women today. She grew fast in adolescence, as her grandmother indicated in her letters. At her French wedding she is said to have stood shoulder to shoulder with her Guise uncles: obviously she inherited this height from her mother, Mary of Guise, who in her day was celebrated for her upstanding stature throughout Europe. Even at the date of her execution, when Mary was humped by age and rheumatics, an English eye-witness still noted that she was 'of stature tall';[9]

and the figure on her tomb in Westminster Abbey, modelled from details taken immediately after her death, is five feet eleven inches long. Yet clearly, this stature was never considered to be a disadvantage, and her height, when described, is always commented on with admiration.* This may be in part due to the fact that although tall, Mary had extremely delicate bones, unlike her mother who had much sturdier proportions. Mary's height, and the slenderness of her youth, which lasted until ill-health and the troubles of captivity made her put on weight in middle-age, combined to give an appearance of graceful elongation: it also made her an excellent dancer, as both Conaeus and Melville bear witness, and a good athlete, who could hunt, hawk and even ride at the head of an army, in a manner calculated to dazzle the public eye at a time when the personal image of a sovereign was of marked consequence.

The portraits of Mary Stuart show that she had a small, well-turned head, and beautiful long hands; coins in particular reveal that she had a neck which was positively swan-like. One of her special charms was her colouring; the blonde hair of her childhood had darkened by the time of her marriage to a shade just lighter than auburn – a bright golden-red. The Deuil Blanc portrait† shows that her eyes were almost the same colour as her hair, a colour like amber, which today would probably be described as hazel, and this colouring was of course certainly set off to brilliant advantage by her incomparable complexion. Curiously enough Mary seems to have had rather similar colouring to her cousin Elizabeth, yet one woman was generally

---

* When Melville told Queen Elizabeth that Mary was 'higher' than her, Elizabeth remarked jealously that the rival queen must be 'over high'. But, of course, Elizabeth, despite her obsession on the subject of Mary's beauty, never actually met her: no man who saw her ever suggested that the queen of Scots was 'over high'.

† It has recently been pointed out that Mary was not wearing her white mourning in this portrait for Francis II, since the picture was painted some time prior to August 1560 when Throckmorton reported Mary's intention of sending her portrait to Elizabeth, and how she commented to him: 'I perceive you like me better when I look sadly than when I look merrily, for it is told me that you desired to have me pictured when I wore the Deuil.' Mary was therefore in mourning for her father-in-law Henry or her mother, Mary of Guise.[10]

accounted a beauty by her contemporaries, and the other was engaged in a constant, tenacious battle to extract the reassurance of compliments from her courtiers, having been so deprived of them in youth. Possibly it was the quality of the skin which distinguished the cousins as young women: Elizabeth as a young girl was described as having a good skin of somewhat sallow ('olivastra') tint by the Venetian ambassador at the English court – and this was an age when a luxurious skin was considered a prerequisite of beauty.[11]

It was Mary's heavy lowered eyelids, under their delicately arched brows, which gave a brooding almost sensual look to her face, a physical characteristic which was to increase with age. Otherwise her features were extraordinarily firm and regular. The drawing of Mary as dauphiness shows that by the time she was fifteen, the soft roundness of her childish face had formed into a perfect oval. Although her nose was long, it was not yet pronouncedly so, and the slight aquiline tendency is only just perceptible in the drawing (illustration 7). Her chin was well-modelled, her mouth, fashionably small, had a pretty curve; she had a beautiful high '*bombée*' forehead, which the caps and veils of the time set off to perfection; and her ears, although large, were elegantly made, and seemed indeed specially designed to bear the lambent ear-rings of the time.

Above all, in her length, her small neat head, her grace, we may suppose that Mary Stuart resembled the contemporary Mannerist ideal. A small bronze bust of her in the Louvre, possibly by Germain Pilon, which is regarded as an authentic if not necessarily contemporary attempt at her features when queen of France, shows the lovely leaning head, the long almond-shaped eyes, and the beautiful disposition of head, neck and shoulder. How significantly she resembled the Mannerist figures of the time, the elongated figures and angular disposition of Primaticcio's designs, the long and delicate forms, the tapering limbs, thin necks and small hands of the figures in the Galerie d'Etampes at Fontainebleau, or the sculptures of Jean Goujon. It was the same grace and elegance which her contemporaries admired in Mary Stuart, the type of beauty which they were already learning to admire in art, and could now appreciate in life, all the more satisfyingly because it was in the person of a princess. Nor must it be forgotten that to these physical attributes she added the essential human ingredient of charm, a charm so powerful that even Knox was openly afraid of its effects on her Scottish subjects – and perhaps, in his heart of hearts, also upon himself. It was the charm of Mary Stuart, that charm which is at once more dangerous and the most desirable of all human qualities, which put the finishing touches to her beauty in the eyes of her beholders.

Not only the appearance, but also the character of Mary Stuart made her admirably suited to be a princess of France in the age in which she lived. The years she spent in France represented the classical period when art and architecture flourished there; it was a time when there was a remarkable flowering in all intellectual fields as writers and artists began to free themselves from the tutelage of Italy. Nor only did Primaticcio and Serlio prosper, but individual figures appeared like Philibert de l'Orme whose art was not only classical but genuinely French. Philibert de l'Orme and Goujon, on the one hand, and Ronsard and the Pléiade on the other, created the first original and independent movements since the Renaissance first touched France. This culture was firmly centred round the court, the court at which Mary Stuart glittered, and the tributes paid to her by the poets of the time make it clear that she was the ideal star to be shining in the firmament at this particular moment. She loved their company: 'Above all,' wrote Brantôme, 'she delighted in poetry and poets, and most of all in M. de Ronsard, M. du Bellay and M. de Maisonfleur, who had made such fine poems and elegies for her, which I have often seen her read to herself in France and Scotland, with tears in her eyes and sighs in her heart.'[12] Mary was exactly the sort of beautiful woman, not precisely brilliant, but well-educated and charming, who inspired and stimulated poets by her presence to feats of homage, which were also able to take their place in the annals of literature. It was an admirable combination of artist and subject, of the sort which occurs throughout history; and Mary Stuart's own verses, although of a simple and modest nature,* do at least illustrate her love and sympathy for the art of poetry.

The odes of Maisonfleur in praise of Mary Stuart have vanished from the eye; du Bellay, however, celebrated her personal attractions in several poems, including a sonnet in 1557, and a Latin poem celebrating her forthcoming marriage, in which he described heaven as endowing her with beauty of spirit and of face, together with royal grace and honour. With Ronsard the young queen enjoyed a genuine and long-lasting friendship: the fact that Ronsard had been in Scotland at the court of James v added a special poignancy to their relationship, since Ronsard understood the very different conditions of the island from which she had sprung, and to which she might one day return. In the first verses he dedicated to her, which appeared in 1556, he certainly reminded her of the fact, and how, since her arrival in France, he had served as her tutor in poetry, hailing her in lavish terms as '*o belle et plus que belle et agréable Aurore*'. It has been suggested that it was in response to a request from Mary that Ronsard published the first collected edition of his works in 1560;[14] when she departed from France, he denounced the cruel fortune which had led Scotland to seize her. When Châtelard faced the executioner, according to Brantôme, he refused all other consolation except the hymns of Ronsard, which he had been asked by Ronsard to present to the Scottish queen. Four years after her departure, Ronsard sent Mary his newest volume by the French ambassador, and he boasted that he kept her portrait continually in front of him in his library.

It is sad to record that even Ronsard, despite these high-flown sentiments, occasionally deserted Mary's shrine. In July 1656 he published a verse collection *Elégies, Mascarades et Bergeries*; although *Bergeries* is dedicated to the queen of Scotland, the first

---

* The poem most commonly attributed to her, *Adieu, plaisant pays de France*, has been shown to be the work of an eighteenth-century French journalist. The authentic poetry of Mary Stuart can best be judged from the poignant lines she wrote on the death of Francis, the sonnet by her to Queen Elizabeth in 1568, and the poems written during her captivity, published by John Leslie.[15]

two portions are dedicated to the queen of England, and contain a quatrain suggesting that Queen Elizabeth rivalled in beauty the queen of Scotland, being two brilliant suns contained within the same island. For this outburst, he received a fine diamond from the queen of England. He may perhaps be forgiven for this temporary disloyalty for the beauty of his sonnet to Mary in captivity: he wrote that nothing now remained to him except the sorrow which unceasingly recalled to his heart the memory of his fair princess, and harangued with anger the queen who had imprisoned her – '*Royne, qui enfermez une Royne si rare*'. It was probably for this pledge of ancient loyalties, romantically renewed, that Mary's secretary sent Ronsard 2000 crowns and Mary herself responded:

> Ronsard, si ton bon cueur de gentille nature
> Tement pour le respect dun peu de nouriture
> Quen tes plus jeunes ans tu as resceu d'un Roy
> De ton Rooy alie et de sa mesme loy...*

Her friendship with Ronsard illustrates how fully Mary enjoyed the pleasures of the French court to which she was so well suited. As Castelnau de Mauvissière, an experienced diplomat and man of the world, noted in his memoirs, she turned herself so completely into a French woman that she seemed not only the most beautiful of all her sex, but also the most delightful, both in her speech and in her demeanour.

There was only one small cloud in this summer's sky – and still no bigger than a man's hand. The exquisite fifteen-year-old queen-dauphiness who danced and hawked and hunted her way through the changing routine of the court's pleasures, was able to pursue these pastimes more by the light of will-power than that of robust physical strength. The warning signs of ill-health which had existed during her adolescence had not been successfully brushed away. Her beauty was touched, and possibly

---

* Ronsard! Perchance a passing note of pain Speaks sometimes to thy heart in days gone by, When he who was thy king did not disdain To do thee honour for thy poesy..."

enhanced, by a certain fragility. In the spring of 1559, Sir John Mason wrote complacently to Cecil: 'The Queen of Scots is very sick, and men fear she will not long continue.' He added the pious hope: 'God take her to Him so soon as may please Him.' In May, the English ambassador, Throckmorton, mentioned that the queen-dauphiness had been ill again, and when on 24th May the English envoys were conducted before the queen, Throckmorton pronounced a grave opinion: 'Assuredly, Sir, the Scottish Queen in my opinion looked very ill on it, very pale and green, and withal short breathed, and it is whispered here among them that she cannot live long.'[16] In June 1559, she was twice reported as swooning: once she had to be given wine at the altar, and on the second occasion the Spanish ambassador said he had heard that she was suffering from an unspecified but incurable malady. The following autumn Mundt wrote to Elizabeth in London that Mary was 'in a consumption ...'[17] Yet whatever the young queen-dauphiness suffered from at this stage, it is clear that despite her pallor, her dizzy spells and her short breath, Mary also brought to her life an intense nervous energy which enabled her to lead an enormously active life when she was not actually suffering. A dangerous accident while out hunting in December 1559 when she was swept off her horse by a bough showed both her reckless courage and the straits to which it could lead her. This combination of a weak physique and overriding will was one which she shared, to some degree, with her husband Francis: it must have led to a bond between them.*

In September 1558 the first sour note was struck in the political existence of the dauphiness. On their way home to Scotland,

---

* For a discussion of Mary's health in later life and the subject of porphyria see Chapter 22, pp. 551–4. It has been suggested that in youth Mary suffered from chlorosis, or 'green sickness', on the basis of Throckmorton's description.[18] Chlorosis is, however, usually associated with malnutrition and general lack of exercise, fresh air and sunlight in adolescents living in slum conditions. In her upbringing at the French court Mary certainly did not lack proper exercise, fresh air or substantial meals: nor is the puffiness of the face, generally associated with chlorosis, mentioned in any of the contemporary descriptions of her appearance.

the ranks of the nine Scottish commissioners who had come to France to arrange the marriage contract were suddenly struck by illness, as a result of which four of them died in one night, and James Stewart himself fell ill, although he recovered. In a letter to her mother of 16th September, Mary spoke of this decimation as being God's will,[19] but at the time another more sinister explanation was advanced. Knox murmured of poison, either Italian or French, as did Herries and Buchanan, and even Leslie noticed 'through suspicion of venom, many wondered'.[20] It was suggested that the brothers of the queen-regent, the Guises, had determined to poison the commissioners because they had discovered something about the secret treaties which signed away the birthright of Scotland. It is true that it was vital to the Guises' plans that the secret of the treaties should be preserved; on the other hand, almost every sudden death in this century was attributed to poison, on principle, by the commentators: if there was anything to the suspicions at all, it was curious that when the remaining commissioners presented themselves to the Scottish Parliament in November, they suggested no further inquiry into the matter, and put no obstacle in the way of the crown matrimonial being granted to Francis.

Another phrase used by Mary in the same letter to her mother showed that the realities of the French international situation were beginning to come home to her: she described how the French court were all 'hoping for a peace, but this is still so uncertain, that I shall say nothing to you about it, except that they say the peace should not be arranged by prisoners like the Constable and the Marshal Saint-André'. The summer of 1558 had indeed been occupied with the general European desire for a peace settlement. Henry listened the more eagerly to the counsels of the peace party in France, not only because of the desperate state of his finances, but also because he was anxious to secure the return of his favourite, the constable, from captivity. The Guises, on the other hand, were far from anxious for a peace with England and Spain by which they feared that France would surrender many of her conquests abroad, and the rival Montmorency would triumph at home, and as Mary Stuart stressed to her mother, they felt it unworthy that a prisoner like the constable should have so much say in a peace settlement, whose main provision seemed to be to secure his return to France. Even when the negotiations for peace were begun at Cercamp, the open rivalry between Guises and Montmorencys was a feature of the French king's entourage, Diane de Poitiers having by now thrown in her lot firmly with the Montmorencys. The negotiations at Cercamp did not culminate in peace until the April of the next year, when the Treaty of Cateau-Cambrésis was finally signed.

In the interval, an event occurred of profound importance in the history of Mary Stuart. On 17th November, 1558 Mary Tudor, queen of England, died leaving no children. Her throne was inherited by her half-sister Elizabeth, an unmarried woman of twenty-five. Until such time as Elizabeth herself should marry and beget heirs, Mary was thus the next heiress to the English throne, by virtue of her descent from her great-grandfather Henry VII of England.* But the actual situation was more complicated than this simple statement reveals. Elizabeth was the daughter of Henry VIII and his second wife Anne Boleyn; as Henry's divorce from his first wife Catharine of Aragon had never been recognized by the Catholic Church, so Henry's marriage to Anne was considered void by Catholic standards, and so Elizabeth herself was held by strict Catholic standards to be illegitimate and thus incapable of inheriting the English throne. By this process of reasoning, Mary Stuart should rightly have inherited the throne of Mary Tudor. The actions of Henry VIII himself did not help to clear up the confusion: in 1536 the English Parliament itself had debarred Elizabeth from the succession as illegitimate, and the Act which restored her to the succession in 1544 did not remove the stain of bastardy. Yet by the will of Henry VIII the throne was also debarred from going to a foreigner – which by English standards also ousted Mary herself from the succession. The troubles over this will, and Mary's claim to have her place in the English succession after

* See genealogical table.

Elizabeth, lay in the future. At the moment of Mary Tudor's death, the troubles were all the other way about, and involved Elizabeth's right to be queen in the first place.

Immediately on the death of Mary Tudor, Henry II of France formally caused his daughter-in-law Mary Stuart to be proclaimed queen of England, Ireland and Scotland, and caused the king-dauphin and queen-dauphiness to assume the royal arms of England, in addition to those of France and Scotland. Up till the death of Queen Mary Tudor, England had been firmly allied to Spain, through Mary's marriage to the Spanish king; Henry now hoped to redress the balance by making a French claim to English dominion. This eminently political action on the part of the French king was to be flung in Mary's face for the rest of her life, down to the moment of her trial in England nearly thirty years later. Yet it seems certain that she had even less opportunity for judging the wisdom of her father-in-law's behaviour on this occasion than over the matter of the secret treaties. 'They have made the Queen-Dauphiness go into mourning for the late Queen of England,' commented the Venetian ambassador, who was in no doubt as to where the initiative for these moves came from.[21] At the time, the climate of French opinion was certainly such that Mary's claims were considered no more than just: the French writers eagerly commented on the dauphiness's English connection, and celebrated her accession to the triple crown in enthusiastic verse – as one of the Pléiade, Jean de Baïf, wrote, in a celebratory wedding song: 'Without murder and war, France and Scotland will be with England united.' Ronsard imagined that Jupiter had decreed that Mary should govern England for three months, Scotland for three and France for six. In another nuptial song, René Guillon described the match as the union of the white lily of France with the white rose of the York-ists – an allusion to Mary's Tudor descent.[22]

The letters of the English ambassador were full of details to illustrate the manner in which these infuriating pretensions were being upheld by the French king: at the wedding of the Princess Claude at the beginning of the next year, a feature of the proceedings was that the dauphin and dauphiness bore the arms of England quartered with those of France. The state entry to the town of Châtelherault in November 1559 was marked by a canopy of crimson damask carried over Mary's head with the arms of England, France and Scotland emblazoned on it. A canopy of purple damask with the French arms only was carried over Francis (by now the king of France) and the arms were painted on the gates of the town in the same fashion.[23] The English state papers show a definite preoccupation with the subject, understandable in view of the shaky English policy at the start of a new reign. But Melville also reported in his memoirs that the cardinal caused the arms of England to be engraved on the queen's silver plate;[24] a great seal was struck bearing the royal figures of Francis and Mary, the date 1559 and the inscription round it referring to Francis and Mary, king and queen of the French, Scottish, English and Irish. Even while the treaty of Cateau-Cambrésis was being negotiated the cardinal and others made it their business to say that they doubted whether they should treat with any of England, save the dauphin and his wife.

The matter continued to be wrangled over after the accession of Francis. In February 1560 the government in London decided to point out to the French ambassador that although the English arms had first been borne by Mary under Henry II, she had not stopped bearing them with his death. Throckmorton had a long interview with the cardinal when he argued over the matter, saying that despite Mary's admittedly English descent, she ought not to use the arms without any difference. In March the Council told Throckmorton to point out to Mary that 'her father, the King of Scots, being higher than she, never bare the same; nor by the laws of the land is she next heir'. To this the bishop of Valence, on behalf of the French king and queen, made the somewhat disingenuous counterpoint that 'the bearing of the English arms by the French Queen, was thought in France to be done for the honour of Elizabeth and to show that the French queen was her [Elizabeth's] cousin'.[25]

However, when peace was proclaimed between England, France and Scotland in 1560, Elizabeth herself consented to believe that Mary's 'injurious pretensions' to the English throne sprang from the 'ambitious desire of the principal members of the house of Guise', rather than the wishes of either Francis, 'by reason of his youth incapable of such an enterprise', or the queen of Scots 'who is likewise very young'.[26] The explanation which satisfied the English queen two years later we may also accept as being the true one. Unfortunately, once political necessity dictated another course, it no longer satisfied either Queen Elizabeth or her advisers, and the subject of Mary's pretensions to the English throne, made on her behalf by her father-in-law before she was sixteen years old, continued to haunt her for the rest of her career.

1559, which became a year of death at the French court, seemed destined at its outset to be a year of weddings. The marriage of Princess Claude to the young and handsome duke of Lorraine was celebrated with magnificence in February. The Peace of Cateau-Cambrésis, finally signed in April between England and France on one side and France and Spain on the other, provided that all the French conquests in Italy made during the last eighty years should be surrendered, and made arrangements for two further royal weddings. Mme Marguerite, the long-unmarried sister of Henry II, was to wed the duke of Savoy; Princess Elisabeth at the age of fourteen faced the prospect of marriage to Philip of Spain, freed for matrimony once more by the death of Mary Tudor. Mary Stuart's last summer as dauphiness was spent in planning for the double wedding of these two beloved companions of her childhood, to be celebrated with the full regal panoply to which the French court was so well suited. As the Venetian ambassador commented, nothing was discussed at the French court but handsome and costly apparel.[27]

Beneath these eddies of sartorial rivalry there were the undercurrents of more dangerous enmities. The constable and Diane de Poitiers were now all-powerful with Henry II, and their own alliance was symbolized by the marriage of a grand-daughter of Diane with the son of the constable. Moreover, the Montmorency faction was beginning to have Protestant affiliations, in contrast to the strong Catholicism of the Guises, since Montmorency's own nephew Admiral Coligny had become a Huguenot. These Huguenot connections were also starting to be shared by the third powerful French family, the Bourbons, through their head, King Antoine of Navarre and his wife Jeane d'Albret. As the cardinal busied himself with preparations for the double wedding, it must have seemed to him that the fortunes of the Guises had taken a definite downward trend. At this moment, the volatile wheel of fortune, which the Guises had so often observed turning to their advantage in the past, was once again to take a dynamic revolution in their favour.

On 15th June the duke of Alva arrived to claim Elisabeth by proxy for his master Philip II, and on 21st June the proxy wedding took place, although as the young bride had not yet reached the age of puberty, it was decided that she should not depart for the Spanish court until the autumn. On 27th June the marriage contract was signed between Mme Marguerite and the duke of Savoy. There were endless tournaments and festivities, and the culmination of the double event – the wedding of Marguerite – was only a few days away. On 30th June, the king, magnificent in the black and white which he wore because they were the favourite colours of Diane de Poitiers, mounted his horse Le Malheureux and entered the lists along with the duke of Guise wearing red and white, the duke of Ferrara in yellow and red, and the duke of Nemours, commonly known to be enamoured of the duchess of Guise, in yellow and black. The king's love of jousting amounted almost to a mania.* He broke three lances with the duke of Savoy, the duke of Guise, and Jacques de Lorge, count of Montgomery, a Norman with Scottish blood who was colonel of the archers of the guard and a man of renowned courage.

All went well until, on a sudden whim, the king challenged Montgomery to break a last lance with him. Apparently, with some presentiment of evil, Montgomery tried to excuse himself

---

* He seemed to be in excellent health at the time although as Throckmorton had reported to London in May that the king was ill with vertigo, it is just possible that some giddiness afflicted him to explain the events that followed.[18]

from the encounter, until Henry finally commanded him to obey as his sovereign. Now Catherine de Médicis tried to dissuade her husband, having had two visions of ill-omen about the tournament. Her daughter Marguerite tells us in her memoirs that on the previous night Catherine had actually dreamt of the death of Henry, pierced in the eye by a lance, exactly as it transpired. Henry merely replied that he would break one more lance in the queen's honour. Catherine's forebodings were justified: the shock of the meeting between the two resulted in Montgomery's lance splintering; one splinter went into the king's right eye, another into his throat. Throckmorton, the English ambassador, described the scene; Henry was borne off, 'nothing covered but his face, he moved neither hand nor foot, but lay as one amazed'.²⁹

The king was carried to the nearby Hôtel des Tournelles, and here lay in a state of virtual unconsciousness for nine days. On 8th July, in a lucid moment, he ordered Queen Catherine to proceed with the marriage of Mme Marguerite and the duke of Savoy. The ceremony was bathed in extreme gloom: the church of St Paul, close by the Hôtel des Tournelles, was hastily decorated and at midnight the young couple knelt at the altar. Catherine sat alone on the royal dais, in floods of tears, while Francis and Mary did not even attend, but remained within earshot of the king. Jérôme de la Rovère, bishop of Toulon, said a Low Mass, trembling all the while lest he should find the herald at arms announcing the death of the king at the door of the sanctuary. As Henry felt himself dying, he called for his son and began 'My son, I recommend to you the Church and my people ...' but he could not go on. He gave the dauphin his blessing and kissed him. That evening he became paralysed, his breathing was painful, and at 1 a.m. on 10th July he died with grossly swollen hands and feet, all showing signs of a virulent infection.

Queen Catherine was left to find gloomy consolation in the fact that the death of Henry II represented a signal triumph for the art of astrology to which she attached such importance. The king's death had twice been predicted accurately, although of course neither prediction had served in any way to avert the king's fate, this being a common disadvantage of this absorbing science. Catherine kept a tame astrologer, Luc Gauric, who predicted the death of the king in a duel – which was thought at the time to be extremely unlikely, as a king was seldom to be found in single combat.*

In 1555 the famous Nostradamus first published his prophecies, including the rhyme:

> The young lion shall overcome the old one
> In martial field by a single duel
> In a cage of gold he shall put out his eye
> Two wounds from one, then he shall die a cruel death.

Afterwards, it was pointed out that the tilting helm strangely resembles a cage, and that the king's visor was actually gilded; the two wounds were held to refer to the splintering of the lance, piercing the throat and the eye. There was actually one outcry demanding the burning of Nostradamus, the man who had prophesied 'so ill and so well'.†

Francis II was now king of France at the age of fifteen and a half, and Mary Stuart queen at the age of sixteen. In one blow of a lance, the fortunes of the Guises had changed. Their niece was now in the very seat of power. The stage was now set for their triumph, however short-lived. The day of Henry's death was referred to afterwards by one wit as 'the eve of the feast of the three kings', and it was commonly asserted that there were

---

* Gauric also prophesied the death of Duke Francis of Guise correctly, saying that he would be struck down from behind. This met with annoyance as well as scepticism since Francis thought that the prophecy carried with it some implication of cowardice. He forgot that although only the back of the coward is turned towards the enemy, the dagger of the assassin also strikes from behind.

† Queen Catherine was not always so fortunate, in astrological terms, in the truth of the predictions which were made to her. When the future Charles IX was born, it was prophesied that he would one day be as great a king as Charlemagne – a prediction which he did very little to fulfil during his days as king. Another son, for whom Nostradamus equally prophesied a brilliant future, died only eighteen months after his birth.

now three kings in France, Francis of Valois, Francis of Guise, and Cardinal Charles of Lorraine – 'one king in name only and two kings of Lorraine in effect'.[30] Immediately after his father's death, Francis entrusted his father's body to the constable, the Cardinal de Chastillon, Admiral Coligny and the marshal of Saint-André, and entered the coach which had come from the court on the Guises' orders. King Francis entered first, and as Queen Mary hung modestly back, Queen Catherine forced her into the place of honour. The young king was taken to the Louvre, and by the time the deputation from the Parliament arrived, the government was already in the hands of the Guises.

When the Spanish ambassadors visited Queen Catherine to pay her their condolences, they found the room draped in black, the floor as well as the walls.[31] The windows were shut, and there was no light except two candles burning on an altar draped in black. Catherine herself sat in a severe black dress with no ornament except a collar of ermine. The new queen of France on the other hand was dressed in white, the white which she had insisted on wearing for her wedding only fifteen months before, and which now she could wear in earnest as the colour of mourning. Catherine responded only faintly to the ambassador's condolences, but the new queen, prompted by her uncles, made a gracious little speech, urging them to come often to court, and asking them to give her compliments to the king of Spain. In the course of her speech she took care to sing the praises of her uncles. At the funeral of Henry II, begun at Notre Dame on 11th August, and completed at Saint-Denis on 13th August, the role of the Guises was even more significant than it had been at the beginning of the previous reign. Cardinal Charles, as abbot of St Denis, presided over the interment. Another Guise brother, René of Elboeuf, held the hand of justice, Henry of Guise held the crown, Grand Prior Francis of Guise the sceptre, and the duke of Guise the royal banner of France. By making the young king, as one historian at the Guise family has put it, 'their nephew by alliance, their pupil by necessity',[32] Mary Stuart had fulfilled the ultimate expectations of her family.

CHAPTER SIX

The White Lily of France

'Alba rosis albis nunc insere lilia...'
Nuptial song on the marriage of Francis and Mary,
referring to the union of the white lilies of France
and the white roses of the Yorkists

On 18th September, 1559, the young Francis was solemnly crowned king of France at Rheims: his consort Mary had already been crowned queen of Scotland in baby-hood and unlike previous queens of France had thus no need of further coronation to confirm her royal state. The weather was wet and windy. Nor was there any great display of pageantry on this occasion, owing to the recent and shocking death of Henry II: Throckmorton noted savagely that the city was scarcely decorated at all 'save that the arms of England, France and Scotland quartered were brimly set out in the show over the gate'.[1] Francis himself wore a coat of black velvet and Mary alone of the ladies who attended the coronation was not dressed in dark colours. The day after the ceremony, court mourning was resumed for a year to mark the late king's death. Although the ancient crown of St Denis had been placed on his head, the real power in France was very far from lying within the puny grasp of Francis II. The English ambassador Throckmorton analysed the situation as follows – the old French queen (Catherine) had the authority of regent, although she was not in fact regent in name; in the meantime the state was governed by the cardinal of Lorraine and the duke of Guise jointly, the duke having charge of the war, and the cardinal the ordering of all other affairs including finance and foreign affairs. The Venetian ambassador noted that the Guises now conducted secret inner discussions on matters of policy, just before official meetings of the Grand Council: these conferences took place either in Francis's chamber or in that of Queen Catherine.[2]

This political ascendancy had its parallel in the domestic arrangements of the new king and queen of France: Guisards were made gentlemen of the bed-chamber to the king, and Mary's new list of domestic officers was headed by those ladies who were to receive 800 *livres* in wages, including Antoinette of Guise, Anne d'Esté, the duchess of Aumale and the marquise of Elboeuf – her grandmother and her three Guise aunts. One of Mary's first actions after the death of Henry II as a formal expression of her joy at coming to the throne was to make a donation to the grandmother who had contributed so much to her upbringing. The court of France, with Francis, Mary and Catherine at its head, now resumed the endless journeyings which characterized its way of life. These travels were prompted by a variety of motives, including the calls of the chase, domestic convenience and in certain cases the dictates of security or politics. In the first instance the entire court proceeded to Blois to wait for the signal of the departure of young Elisabeth to Spain; from Blois the royal cortège went to Varteuil, and from there to a snow-strewn Châtelherault, which they entered at the end of November. On 25th November Queen Catherine finally permitted her child to depart, with grief so extreme that even the Spanish ambassador was moved by it. Mary herself was equally distraught at the prospect of the departure of her friend: she entrusted Elisabeth with a touching letter to King Philip from his new sister-in-law, saying that she could hardly bear to part with Elisabeth, were it not for the fact that she knew Elisabeth would be happy and contented in her new life. Nevertheless for Mary herself the loss would be irreparable. She ended her letter by begging the Spanish king to receive it 'as from the person who loves her [Elisabeth] the most in the world, and who wishes always to be – *Vôtre bien bonne soeur Marie*'.[3]

With Mary and the royal family immersed in their personal sorrow, the Guise brothers were left to grapple with the internal government of France, which represented at this period a problem which other less bold spirits might, with considerable justification, have shrunk from tackling. The Peace of Cateau-Cambrésis had not come in time to save France from cruel inflation, induced by the economic demands of the Italian wars. It has been estimated that at the death of Henry II the treasury staggered under a war debt of forty million *livres*: the theoretical resources of the crown were ten million *livres*, but the actual income only amounted to about half this, and the interest on the royal debt consumed it. At the same time the kingdom was being rapidly dissected by the presence of two religions, as French Calvinism became the natural target for discontent with the central authority.[4] Even if the country had not been plunged in such grave economic problems, some sort of regency, *de facto* if not *de jure*, would have been necessary for the young Francis. At the age of fifteen and a half, when he ascended the throne, his intelligence was scarcely more developed than his physique. In youth, like many other boys he had loved to hunt more than he had loved to learn, but since he was the dauphin of France, not enough pressure had been exerted to redress the balance. The result was that his mind, without being actually feeble, as his body was, had never really developed to the point when the possibilities of power and government excited him. As a king he lacked the necessary self-restraint to attend to the business of government when pleasure offered, his tutors in youth having concentrated more on the importance of the actual role he would play than the importance of the duties which were attached to it. The enemies of the Guises accused them of encouraging their nephew in his pursuit of pleasure in order to have the government of the realm to themselves. But there was no need to carry out such a policy of corruption, their work had already been done for them by the over-protective upbringing of Catherine de Médicis, who had with all her loving, maternal care developed only self-importance, not self-discipline, in her son.

The nature of the king's character was fully appreciated by the watchful ambassadors at the French court. His routine was understood to be dominated by his frantic love of hawking: in December 1559 he was reported as having retired to Chambord till Christmas, to which the Chancellor of the Privy Council was obliged to repair in order 'to arrange his finances for the next year'. In March 1560 when the king refused to see the English ambassadors, giving out that he was ill, their immediate instinct was to suspect that he was merely playing truant 'as the king is wont to go abroad very often to amuse himself for several days without transacting business'. This was an age when monarchs were still expected to reproduce in themselves the personal qualities of greatness, to win the admiration of their subjects. Duke Francis of Guise owned much of his prestige to his physical courage: despite her frail health Mary Stuart was famed for being personally fearless. King Francis, on the other hand, was timid by nature. He had a certain pathetic dandyism, a love of display revealed by his personal accounts, where swords were made with hilts coloured to match his various costumes; but this was no substitute for the careless courage so attractive in princes.[5] He lived in fear for his personal safety, which made it natural for him to depute the government of the kingdom happily to those he felt best able to secure it.

Francis was demonstrably incapable of ruling without guidance. But the vital regency – as it was in practice but not in name – was not surrendered to his wife's uncles by the other great nobles of France without a struggle. The powerful family of Bourbon postulated strongly that the king was not, in fact, legally of age at all, being only fifteen. Not only had he no right to choose his own counsellors, but being still a minor, he should automatically accept the first prince of the blood as regent: this was of course none other than King Antoine of Navarre, head of the House of Bourbon. Behind this weak and indecisive figure-head stretched the shadow of his restless, ambitious and hot-headed younger brother Louis, prince of Condé, a recent

Huguenot convert, and the sworn enemy of the Guises. An anonymous memoir of October 1559, which detailed these points, not only accused the Guises of trying to cut off Francis from his friends, but of aiming at putting the crown on their own heads, by emphasizing their spurious descent from Charlemagne. A Guise reply *'Pour la majorité du Roy très chrestien François deuxième'* by Jean du Tillet, bishop of Saint-Brieul, concentrated on the use of texts, laws and customs to prove firstly that the king of France traditionally came of age at fifteen, and thus had the right to choose his own Council, secondly that the regency in the past had not always been given to a prince of the blood, but on occasions also had been given to queens of France, and to the abbots of St Denis.[6]

King Antoine, having failed to assert his claims, withdrew from the court; the prince of Condé on the other hand took refuge in the Huguenot counter-plots which were the origin of the conspiracy of Ambroise. The spring plans of Francis and Mary and their court included a visit to Blois, and then on to the ancient medieval fortress of Amboise, where it was planned that the court should pass the Lenten season. Although this schedule was known to the Spanish ambassador at Christmas, the knowledge somehow eluded the Huguenot rebels, who laid their plans on the basis of finding the king at Blois – an infinitely easier centre to attack than Amboise, where the king was surrounded by his army. Condé was only the 'silent captain' of the enterprise, and did not appear in public as its leader. The ostensible ringleader of these Huguenot anti-Guisards was one La Renaudie; their aim was to seize the person of the king, with the immediate object of freeing him from the tutelage of the Guises, and the ultimate intention of setting up a new and Bourbon regency.

Amboise withstood the siege of the conspirators, and at the instigation of the cardinal of Lorraine the insurrection was punished by hideous reprisals in the streets of the town itself, while the chief rebels, having been tortured, were hung publicly in front of the castle windows after dinner in order that the court might enjoy the edifying sight. La Renaudie died bravely, protesting his loyalty to the king, and maintaining to the last that his only quarrel had been with the Guises. The cardinal, however, adroitly took the opportunity to point out to Francis that the fact that La Renaudie died so defiantly only went to show how cruelly he would have treated Francis if he had succeeded in capturing him. The blood-stained sight from the castle windows did not please every member of the French court. The gentle and tender Anne of Guise was so appalled at what she saw that she wept aloud, and cried out (all too percipiently, as it turned out) what a wealth of vengeance and hatred would fall on the heads of her innocent young sons in consequence. Nor is there any evidence that Mary, who all her life was characterized by a remarkable horror of bloodshed and positive aversion to violence, actually witnessed the hangings. It would have been remarkable if this delicate girl, whose health was a source of constant concern to those around her, and whose swoonings were a feature of court life, should have been considered a suitable spectator for these gruesome scenes.*

Quite apart from natural affection, there was another special reason for the great concern which the Guises always showed over the health of their niece. Although the Guises were accused of wishing to establish a Guise dynasty on the throne of France, it was an infinitely more practical plan to uphold the existing semi-Guise dynasty on the throne of France, in the persons of Francis and Mary, who were not only currently dominated by Guise influence, but whose children with their share of Guise blood would one day rule after them. The only flaw in all this planning was that there was as yet no dynasty, no clutch of Valois-Guise children to lay up security for the future – only an adolescent boy and girl both of them cursed with precarious health. Whether these frail creatures could be relied on to produce any child at all was very much open to question.

The question of the consummation of the marriage of Francis

---

* The Spanish ambassador, who described how Queen Catherine and the principal nobles of the court were almost always present at the savage questioning of the prisoners, did not list Mary's name among them (although it has sometimes been added to the list inaccurately by popular historians).[7]

and Mary, owing to the delicate nature of the subject, rests in the sphere of probabilities rather than that of certainties. Yet it is of obvious importance in tracing the development of Mary's character not only in France, but later in Scotland in the course of her confrontation with Darnley. The true facts of the situation are somewhat obscured because contemporary commentators understandably concentrated their observations on the simple issue of whether Mary was likely to conceive a child by Francis or not; whereas in the history of Mary, it is of equal interest to consider whether she had any sort of physical relationship with her first husband, or whether at the time of her return to Scotland she was still in fact a virgin. There was never apparently any doubt in the minds of those observers at the French court who had watched the young king grow up, that the queen of France would not produce a child, or if she did, as the Spanish ambassador crudely put it, 'it will certainly not be the King's'. Regnier de la Planche's derisive comments on the king's withered anatomy have already been noted (see footnote on p. 83). Although, to the joy of the Guises, Francis started to grow up somewhat once he became king, La Planche's description of physical deformity suggests that there was no real hope of conception, even if in other respects he could be held to have attained puberty before he died. The fact that he was unable to conceive a child was also well known at court on the basis of his deformity, for this was an age when the public nature of royal life meant that problems, even of such an intimate nature, could not be kept altogether secret from the watchful ambassadors: when the Spanish ambassador in Brussels told the English ambassador categorically that it was out of the question that the Scottish queen should bear a child, he was probably acting on back-stairs palace gossip, reliable if scandalous.[8]

This does not altogether rule out the possibility that the marriage was in some fashion consummated. At the time of the wedding, the Venetian ambassador at the end of a long account of the ceremonies, reported that the marriage had in fact been consummated that night, indicating the respective ages of the young couple. In spite of the warnings of the doctors, Francis had not died in childhood, but had grown to the age of fifteen; the Guises presumably hoped that time would wreak a further miracle with his physique, and that he would one day be able to procreate the longed-for Valois and Guise heir. There is evidence to the effect that, despite the cynicism of the court, Mary herself believed that her marriage was a complete one. A month after the death of Henry II, when the Spanish ambassadors came to bid her adieu, they found her extremely pale, and she almost fainted.[9] She received the letters of credit of the duke of Alva swooning and, supported by the cardinal, was lifted on the bed of the king. Chantonay made haste to tell the Spanish king that the general rumour was that the French queen was pregnant. Mary herself assumed the floating tunic, the conventional garb at the time for pregnant women, and the court went to Saint-Germain for the sake of better air for her health. However, by the end of September, these interesting rumours perished for lack of further support. Mary abandoned her floating tunics. There was no further mention of a royal pregnancy, and it was in fact only three months later that Challoner was able to report back to England the information which he had received in Brussels from Count de Feria.

To what then do we attribute these summer vapours of the young queen? Logically speaking, if there was to be any question of Mary being pregnant, however mistaken, the marriage must have been consummated. Unfortunately this is not an area where logic can necessarily be said to obtain. The general hope of the court, and the passionate desire of the Guises, was that Mary should conceive a child. This desire, which she herself heartily shared, must have been communicated to her most strongly. In this case, it seems likely that Mary transformed in her mind the feeble passion of the king into a true consummation of her marriage – indeed at the age of sixteen, the natural ignorance of youth must have made it all the easier for her to do so. In the same way she transformed in her mind the symptoms of ill-health into the symptoms of pregnancy: in the November of the previous year the English ambassador had reported that Mary was 'very ill and looked very pale and on the 12th kept to

her chamber all day long'.[10] The following autumn, when Mary
was actually queen of France, and the need for an heir increasingly urgent, it was easy to persuade herself that these symptoms,
from which she had in fact suffered all her youth, had suddenly
become those of pregnancy. Yet the king's undeveloped and
probably deformed physique and generally infantile constitution
make it extremely unlikely that anything more than the most
awkward embraces took place between them; whether or not
Mary was technically a virgin when she arrived in Scotland, she
was certainly mentally one, in that her physical relation with
Francis can hardly have given her any real idea of the meaning
of physical love.

Troublesome as was the internal situation in France, the situation
in Scotland was not much better – and here again religious
differences mingled with those of civil policy. French troops
were sent in increasing numbers to the assistance of the queen
regent, and the expedition of La Brosse, authorized by Francis
and Mary in November 1559, included several doctors of the
Sorbonne who were sent with a view to taking part in theological
disputes with the Scottish Protestants if the occasion offered. In
their turn, the Scottish insurgents being Protestant lords of the
congregation, appealed for aid from Protestant England. When
in October 1559 the duke of Châtelherault (the former Arran)
joined the party of congregation, he presented them with a
titular leader who had a claim to the Scottish throne. In October
of that year the insurgents even occupied Edinburgh temporarily,
announcing that, since Mary of Guise had brought French
troops to conquer Scotland, it was now lawful to suspend her
from her authority. But the Scots rebels – or reformers – did
not make any true headway until a firmer alliance was concluded
with England in the following spring. By the Treaty of Berwick,
signed on 27th February, 1560, between Scotland as represented
by Lord James and the Scottish lords of the congregation on
behalf of Châtelherault in England represented by Norfolk,
lieutenant of the north, it was stated that the English were to
intervene for the preservation of the Scots 'in their old freedom

and liberties'. Under these auspices English troops now came into Scotland, and besieged Leith, occupied by the queen regent and her French troops: significantly, the campaign was known as 'the War of the Insignia' in England, because of Mary's use of the royal arms.

The Treaty of Berwick on the Scottish borders had virtually coincided with the Tumult of Amboise in France: since Francis was thus unable to provide further military help for his wife's dominions, it was decided to take the more sensible course of negotiation. By a commission dated April 1560 Francis and Mary authorized M. de Montluc, M. de Pelvé and M. de la Brosse to try to bring back their Scottish subjects to obedience by peaceful means, including a promise to forget past wrongs, and also authorized them to treat with the English queen if necessary. As a result of these negotiations, culminating in the Treaty of Edinburgh which was concluded on 6th July, 1560, it was agreed that both English troops and French troops (save sixty in Inchkeith and sixty in Dunbar) should withdraw from Scotland, and that Francis and Mary by giving up the use of the English arms should thus recognize Elizabeth's title. On 15th July the English army moved away, and the French troops also started to embark; Lord St John was sent to France to ask Francis and Mary to ratify the treaty. This ratification was, however, never destined to take place, since on 11th August the Scottish Parliament promulgated a Protestant confession of faith, and five days later abolished the Pope's jurisdiction, and prohibited the celebration of Mass under the pain of death for the third offence. In a historic gesture, the process now known as the Scottish Reformation was thus officially brought to birth. It was Parliament, not the queen, that had acted as the midwife: although constitutionally speaking, the enactment which produced the Reformation needed the queen's assent, in fact it never received it. The Scottish Reformation was a strictly parliamentary will, the whole image of the Scottish monarchy had been altered in the mind of the people.

This long-term effect, however, was certainly not visible to Mary at the time. From the distance of the French court, it was difficult to realize that Queen Elizabeth had been constituted the protector of Protestantism in Scotland, whether she liked it or not, and that logically the Protestant Scots would turn to England rather than France for help in the future. Still more difficult was it to envisage that if Mary ever returned to her native country, her French Catholic connections would inevitably go against her, that a country which had newly reformed its own religion by act of Parliament without assent of the sovereign would regard the combination of her monarchical power, French upbringing and religious convictions as threatening its *status quo.**

In the spring and summer of 1560, however, the Scottish insurgency made its chief impression on Mary as a series of appalling troubles which faced her mother, to whom she felt an almost pathetic devotion from a distance. She identified the religious rebels of Scotland with those of France, unaware that the temper of the Scottish people was changing towards the new religion, whereas in France religious opinion was sufficiently if tragically balanced to result in long and stultifying wars. A letter to her mother, describing the coming mission of M. de la Brosse and M. d'Amiens to Scotland, dating probably from the end of March 1560, is lavish in its promises of love and assistance, saying that she swears she will not let her mother down, since the king, she knows, has a passionate desire to succour her, and has given Mary his word that he will do so. Mary begs her mother to care for her health, and to trust in God to help her in her adversities – for God has already helped her so much in all her troubles that surely He will not abandon her now when she needs Him more than ever.[12]

Unhappily the health which Mary so passionately wished for her mother, eluded her. This gallant woman who faced an alien people, and attempted to do at least the best she could in the

* Already Mary was regarded as a foreigner by many of the people who were in fact her subjects; it is significant that an account of her magnificent wedding written by a Scotsman who was a member of the crowd makes absolutely no mention of the fact that Mary was herself Scottish. The writer proceeds as if Mary had actually been an Englishwoman.[11]

cause of peaceful administration, was severely stricken with dropsy. She was seriously ill before November 1559, and by April of the next year was far gone with the disease. On 11th June, only a few weeks before the final settlement of the Treaty of Edinburgh, she died, horribly swollen and in great pain. Knox rejoiced over her end; he saw in it the hand of God taking vengeance on her for her behaviour at the siege of Leith, when she was rumoured to have exulted over the corpses of the Protestant dead (although such behaviour is more characteristic of Knox himself than of the merciful Mary of Guise). 'And within a few days thereafter yea, some say that same day,' wrote Knox, 'began her belly and loathsome legs to swell, and so continued till that God did execute his judgment upon her.'

Previously, Knox had described Mary of Guise's assumption of the regency with equal contempt – 'A crown was put upon her head ... as seemly a sight ... as to put a saddle upon the back of an unruly cow.'[13] But in fact Knox, as often when writing with his pen dipped in acid, did Mary Guise an injustice as a ruler. In an extraordinarily difficult situation, she had tried to do her best, and carry out the advice of her brother the duke of Guise – 'To deal in Scotland in a spirit of conciliation, introducing much gentleness and moderation into the administration of justice.' On occasions she was even prepared to carry out these counsels against the advice of her Guise brothers who had given it to her: as Regnier de la Planche himself admitted, Mary of Guise's plans for Scotland had always included acting gently and slowly by the use of Parliament and it was the Guise males who rejected this course, saying that their sister might be a good woman, but she would wreck everything by her tender methods.[14] In her introduction of the French administrators Mary of Guise also genuinely believed she was benefiting the Scots, since she was frankly appalled at Scottish administrative methods. As for Scottish laws she wrote of them that they were the most unjust in the world, not so much in their provisions, as in the manner in which they were carried out, and when one considers the internal state of Scotland in the age in which she arrived there, particularly in areas like the borders, where administration was either non-existent or archaic in the extreme, it is easy to understand how she derived this impression.

Despite her own sincere Catholicism, Mary of Guise also possessed sufficient balance and political acumen not to identify the reformed religion immediately and totally with the forces of darkness. In 1555 D'Oysel's hopes for a good reception among the Scots were dashed by what he described as the totally selfish attitude of the nobility, who wanted each one to be their own petty tyrant. But it was not until the events of late 1557, when the nobility of Scotland refused to fight under her banner against England, that Mary of Guise herself gave way to feelings of angry distrust for these treacherous lords, Catholic and Protestant alike. Even in 1559, when Henry II instructed that heresy was to be stamped out in Scotland, according to Melville, Mary of Guise still protested against her orders: although committed to a policy of French domination, on Mary's behalf, by which she hoped to preserve Scotland for her daughter, Mary of Guise nevertheless attempted all along to implement this policy in the most humane manner. The English certainly both feared and admired her intellectual qualities: Thomas Randolph wrote apprehensively of 'the Dowager's craft and subtleties'. Throckmorton admired her 'queenly mind', and over the peace negotiations wrote to Cecil for the love of God 'to provide that she were rid from hence, for she hath the heart of a man of war'.[15] When she was on her deathbed, Mary of Guise summoned the lords of the Congregation to her side, and in an affecting interview asked them to believe that she had genuinely favoured the weal of Scotland as well as that of France. Whether the lords believed her or not, we can at least accept her word that by her own lights she had done so.

The news of the death of Mary of Guise was known in France on 18th June, but was kept from her daughter until 28th June – with good reason, as it turned out, for Mary Stuart's grief when she finally did receive the news was heart-rending, and she underwent one of the physical collapses which inordinate sorrow was apt to induce in her. Michiel, the Venetian ambassador, had already paid tribute to Mary's devotion to her mother, saying that 'she loved her mother incredibly, and much more than daughters usually love their mothers'. Now he reported: 'The death of the Queen Regent of Scotland was concealed from the most Christian Queen [Mary Stuart] till the day before yesterday, when it was at length told her by the Cardinal of Lorraine; for which her Majesty showed and still shows such signs of grief, that during the greater part of yesterday she passed from one agony to another.'*[16] Nor were poor Mary of Guise's earthly troubles entirely terminated by her death, for even her wretched dropsical corpse proved a source of dispute. A funeral oration was made for her in Notre Dame on 12th August, six weeks after her death, but it was not until October that her lead-lined coffin was allowed to be conveyed to France, because the Scottish preachers disapproved of the superstitious rites which they feared during her obsequies. In March 1561 her body was removed to Fécamp in Normandy and in July taken to Rheims, where it was finally buried in the church of the convent of St Pierre of which her sister Renée was abbess.

Mary's love for her mother spurred her forward in her knowledge of Scottish politics; her appreciation of French and English politics was spurred on by her own increasing estimation of her position as queen of France and heiress – or rightful possessor – of the English throne. A few days after Henry II's death, Throckmorton commented that everything was being done by the queen of Scotland, who took a great interest in all matters around her. Mary was also acute enough to send for an inventory of the crown jewels, many of which had passed into the hands of Diane de Poitiers, immediately after the death of her father-in-law, with a view to acquiring what were now her rightful property as queen of France. Throckmorton's view of Mary Stuart has a particular interest. As English ambassador he had a definite motive for noting the twists and turns of her

* A portrait of her mother, brought by Maitland to Scotland in 1563, was carried with her by Mary on all her travels throughout her captivity, and was finally found among her belongings at Fotheringhay.

character as it developed; not only did she claim the English crown for her own, but she was also more plausibly the heiress to the throne. Life was uncertain, and Elizabeth was childless and unmarried; if Mary did not actually acquire the English throne by force, she might easily do so by inheritance. It thus behoved Throckmorton to keep a watchful eye on the nature and qualities of this young girl, whom the random chance of fate might one day establish as his own mistress.

It is significant that the Mary Stuart of Throckmorton's dispatches is a more intelligent and mature girl than the beautiful wilful delicate creature of, for example, the Venetian ambassador's reports to his own Italian court. Mary showed a hint of imperiousness in her words to Throckmorton concerning her refusal, with Francis, to ratify the Treaty of Edinburgh. 'My subjects in Scotland do their duty in nothing,' she told him, 'nor have they performed their part in one thing that belongeth to them. I am their Queen and so they call me, but they use me not so ... They must be taught to know their duties.'[17] Earlier when Throckmorton was taken to have an interview with the royalties in February 1560 the preponderance of the conversation was had with the Queen Mother Catherine, but at the end of the interview when Catherine made an observation to the effect that she wished to be on good terms with Elizabeth, Mary did intervene. '"Yes," she said, "the Queen my good sister may be assured to have a better neighbour of me being her cousin, than of the rebels, and so I pray you signify." '[18] The point may not have been a good one in terms of power politics – since Elizabeth might well prefer rebels across the border to an active young queen, however friendly, however cousinly – but it was one worth making from Mary's point of view, and shows that her political intelligence was beginning to emerge from the cocoon of the cardinal's tutelage.

The cardinal had been the instructor of her youth, but as queen of France, Mary had a new mentor in the art of politics – her mother-in-law Catherine de Médicis. It was no coincidence that Throckmorton had found the two queens sitting beside each other in February 1560. The records show that during the seventeen months in which Francis II reigned as king of France, Queen Catherine and Queen Mary were constantly in each other's company, and in fact Queen Catherine, far from being excluded from the source of power by the death of her husband, formed a royal triumvirate at the top of the pyramid of the court; as the mother on whom the king depended emotionally, and as the queen dowager who had authorized the Guises to assume power, she was now of infinitely more account in the counsels of the kingdom than she had been during the reign of Henry II. There has been much speculation concerning the relations of Catherine de Médicis and Mary Stuart: it has been suggested that Catherine disliked her daughter-in-law so intensely that she was finally capable of poisoning her son Francis, in order to bring to an end Mary Stuart's reign as queen of France. A great deal has been made of the story that Mary openly despised Catherine for her lowly birth, and described her contemptuously as nothing but the daughter of a merchant, the story resting on the word of the Cardinal de Santa Croce, the papal nuncio in France.[19] Whether or not Mary, with the imprudence of youth, made this highly unwise remark, it is certainly easy enough to imagine that an unattractive older woman should be jealous of an exceptionally attractive younger one, with the additional complications of a throne to exacerbate their feelings, quite apart from the traditionally trying relationships of mother and daughter-in-law. Yet the fact is that whatever her private feelings, outwardly Catherine exhibited positively maternal kindness towards Mary during her period as queen of France, and gave Mary no reason to suppose that she was anything but most amicably inclined towards her.

In December 1559 the English envoys reported that Catherine and Mary listened daily to a sermon in the chapel, or in their mutual dining-chamber. The interviews which ambassadors held with the royalties throughout this period generally found both queens together, with Mary sitting on Catherine's right hand. Often Mary and Catherine would be installed in one palace while Francis was away hunting based in another. In April, Mary was deeply depressed by the bad news from Scotland and it was

Catherine who took it upon herself to comfort her, just as the previous year Mary had taken to heart Catherine's own grief over the death of Henry. When Throckmorton had an interview with Mary on 6th August, Catherine was present and Mary requested Throckmorton to speak to the queen mother first.[20] Catherine was also present at the interview which Francis and Mary granted to Throckmorton on 15th September at Saint-Germain, and she was together with the young couple when Condé was arrested on 31st October. The natural trend of court life was to throw the two queens together in conditions of extreme intimacy, a state which appeared to be accepted by both women with perfect satisfaction.

Catherine had indeed been so sternly schooled in the previous reign in the art of maintaining friendly relations with those in positions of power that it would have been inconceivable for her to have displayed any sort of jealousy of Mary in public, while Francis remained on the throne. But to understand the true feelings of Catherine de Médicis towards Mary, it is necessary to appreciate that despite all her cunning, Queen Catherine was fundamentally not a political woman but a mother. The instincts of motherhood, gratified at long last after a hideous period of infertility, remained her strongest emotions. Thus she judged every situation from the point of view of how it might affect the welfare of her children; her desire for political strength sprang from her conviction that the more power she possessed, the more help she could give them. Mary, as ally or rival, was judged primarily from the point of view of Francis. While Francis lived, while Mary was his wife and as such a necessary adjunct to his life and happiness, Catherine would treat her with all the warmth and consideration which was her due; but once Francis was dead, once Mary was no longer the helpmeet of one child but a potential threat to the happiness of another, the picture was liable to be very different. As Regnier de la Planche truly observed of Catherine after the death of Francis, when she finally became the official regent of France: for the past twenty-two years she had plenty of leisure to consider the humours and fashions of the whole French court, so that she understood very well how to play her hand so as to win the game at last.[21]

Mary in her turn did not fail to be influenced by the personality of her mother-in-law. Not only did she imbibe a thoroughly dynastic approach to the business of being a queen, but from Catherine she learnt also that intrigue was a necessary, even enjoyable part of politics. These two thoroughly feminine lessons – that the considerations of the child or unborn child, the continuance of the dynasty, should be placed above all others, and that the most effective weapons in a queen's hand were those of diplomatic intrigue – were impressed on Mary consciously or unconsciously during the seventeen months in which she virtually shared the throne of France with Catherine de Médicis. The second lesson did not fall on particularly fertile ground: Mary, unlike Catherine, was not by nature a talented or adept intriguer. Yet she was to become an enthusiastic one. The effect of Catherine's early lessons can certainly be discerned in Mary's later career in Scotland and England.

Despite the temporary victory of the Catholic party at Amboise, the internal situation in France remained riven with economic difficulty and religious crisis. In France's desperate financial situation, it was generally agreed by August, by Huguenots such as Coligny as well as Catholics such as the Guises, that the only hope lay in trying to establish some sort of civil unity. But it was easier to call for unity than to achieve it. Both sides had their own notions of what was necessary. At a meeting of the Grand Council, Coligny spoke out boldly in favour of the return of the Estates, and the diminution of the king's guard, which he claimed was dividing Francis from his people. On 26th August, the Estates were convoked for the following December, and a date in January was chosen for a national synod of the French Church, provided the Pope should not have already announced an ecumenical council. But the lost tranquillity of France was not so easily restored. Still fearing for his life, Francis left Fontainebleau and went first to St Germain-en-Laye for safety, and then on to Orléans, which, with his wife and mother, he reached on 18th October. Here, surrounded by his army, he felt his person to be more secure, unaware that in his case the ravages of disease were more to be feared than the cold steel of the assassin. As the Spanish ambassador reported gloomily to his master that the religious situation in France was going from bad to worse,[22] the prince of Condé decided to gamble on a personal appeal to King Francis, whom he trusted to wean from the side of the Guises by the magnetism of his own physical presence. His trust was misplaced. On Condé's arrival in Orléans, Francis, on the instructions of the Guises, reproached him tearfully with his enterprises against the government. The prince of Condé was arrested, and on 26th November condemned to death.

But as the Guises' own fortunes had been transformed by the sudden death of Henry II, so Condé in his turn was to be saved by the workings of providence. The danger of ambitious hopes founded on the frail life of a solitary human being was once more demonstrated. King Francis announced his intention of setting off from Orléans to a prolonged hunting expedition, in the forests of Chenonceaux and Chambord, which would last him until the end of the month. But on Saturday 16th November, while still at Orléans, he returned from a day's hunting in the country, and complained of violent ear-ache. On the Sunday he fell down in a faint while at vespers in the chapel of the Jacobins. The weather had turned unexpectedly icy that November, and the Guises were criticized by the Spanish ambassador for letting the king hunt when the weather was so cold. Nevertheless at first neither the watchful ambassadors, the vultures of the sixteenth-century court, nor the anguished adherents of Condé had any idea how serious the situation was.

Francis's health had always been the Achilles' heel of the Guises' plans: his breath was foetid; his physical appearance was so alarming, with red patches on his livid cheeks, that it actually gave birth to sinister rumours that he had leprosy; from this rumour spread the still more disgusting gossip that Francis needed to bathe in the blood of young children, in order to cure himself. The peasants thus hid their children from the king as he passed, convinced that otherwise this young Herod would avail himself of their bodies. Subsequently both Catholics and Protestants accused each other of having invented this nauseating calumny: the cardinal was said to have invented it in order to pave the way for the Guises to ascend the French throne, and the Huguenots were accused of trying to blacken the reputation of the Catholic king. The true explanation of Francis's facial condition was probably eczema, caused by the continual irritation of a purulent discharge from his ear; this originated from a chronic inflammation of the middle ear, arising from the constant respiratory infection of his childhood. When the king fell down in a faint on the Sunday, a large swelling appeared behind his left ear, caused by this inflammation spreading to the tissues above and below it.[23]

The Guises, whatever their private fears, were desperate to hide the gravity of his condition, and suspended the posts; they announced to the court merely that the fogs of the Loire had given the king a cold in the ear. The Venetian ambassador was sufficiently hoodwinked by the story to report that the two queens Mary and Catherine were fussing over the king, who was not actually ill. On 19th November the Spanish ambassador asked for, and got, an audience of the king, but was stopped at the door by the cardinal, who said that the king was suddenly worse. Chantonay immediately felt suspicious, and now noticed troubled glances among the Guises. Ridiculous rumours began to fly round the court: that a Huguenot valet had thrown a mortal powder into the king's nightcap, or that an Orléans barber had poured poison into his ear, while doing his hair. Once more the occult art of astrology was called into play to cast light on the situation, and it was recalled that it had been predicted that Francis should not live long – a prophecy, incidentally, which had been made by doctors as well as astrologers, on the grounds of Francis's health by the former, and of his horoscope by the latter. But the Venetian ambassador personally believed that much of Catherine's sorrow was caused by her recollection of these predictions.[24]

The intense interest of the court in the illness of their sovereign was heightened by the fact that the fate of Condé

hung in the balance. If Francis died, he would be succeeded by
his brother Charles. As Charles was only eleven, there could on
this occasion be no question of withholding the regency from
the man generally believed to have the best claim to it – the
first prince of the blood, King Antoine of Navarre – who was,
of course, Condé's elder brother. King Antoine's first act as
regent was certain to be the reprieve and release of Condé. If
Francis lived, Condé would die. If Francis died, Condé would
live. In face of such interest, it was impossible for the Guises
to continue to cast a cloud of obscurity over the nature of
the king's disease forever. By 20th November, the Venetian
ambassador was able to write off a full and accurate description
of the king's symptoms. On 27th November, Throckmorton
informed Elizabeth that the king's illness was now sufficiently
serious for his doctors to doubt his ability to survive it; in any
case it was thought that he could not expect to live very long,
having wrecked his health in the first place by too much riding
and exercise even before this 'evil accident'. The Venetian
ambassador now learnt from someone who had been in his
chamber that the king was almost delirious. Even so, there were
those who still believed that the illness was nothing more than
a device of the Guises to prevent the supplication of Condé
being put before Francis.[25]

Alas, the wretched little king, far from being the victim of a
Guise plot, was the infinitely more tragic victim of his own
constitution. He alternated between fevers and violent crises,
followed by bouts of speechlessness. In addition to the natural
sufferings of his condition, he also endured purgations and
bleedings. On 28th November, a massive dose of rhubarb
brought him some relief, but two days later the headaches and
sickness redoubled. The watch in his bedroom was maintained
ceaselessly by Mary and Catherine, whose joint role in his agony
was to act endlessly as nurse and comforters. On 3rd December,
it was reported to Venice by their ambassador that Queen Mary,
Queen Catherine and the king's brothers were taking part in
processions to the churches of Orléans, to solicit divine aid for
the king's health.[26] Otherwise Mary spent the last weeks of her

husband's life in patient, silent nursing in his darkened chamber. Unlike their niece the Guises bore the king's affliction with little patience: their mental agonies at the prospect opened before them by his illness seemed almost as acute as the king's physical sufferings. In their frenzy, they attacked the doctors for doing no more for the king than they would have done for a common beggar; and in their pursuit of remedies they even turned to the stone of alchemy.

Neither Mary's patient nursing, nor that of Catherine, nor the rages of the Guises, nor their manifold remedies, affected in any way the ineluctable process of the king's illness. The inflammation was now spreading upwards into the lobe of the brain, above the middle ear: on Monday 2nd December, there was an apparent improvement in his condition due to the temporary release of tension when the tumour was pierced. But the inflammation, having now reached the brain, formed an abscess within it. With the formation of the abscess, nothing could save the French king from death. By the evening of 3rd December, Francis was *in extremis*. On Thursday 5th December, he fell into a swoon. At some point in his agonies, he is said to have murmured a prayer taught to him by the cardinal: 'Lord, pardon my sins and impute not to me those which my ministers have committed in my name and in my authority.' But on the Thursday, at a time variously reported to be five, eleven or ten, by La Planche, Throckmorton and Chantonay, the king's ordeal was at an end. A month off his seventeenth birthday, Francis II was dead.

Calvin wrote triumphantly to Sturm: 'Did you ever read or hear of anything more timely than the death of the little King? There was no remedy for the worst evils when God suddenly revealed himself from Heaven, and He who had pierced the father's eye, struck off the ear of the son.'[27] Calvin's Knox-like exultation reflected the natural view of the French Huguenots who had seen their cause forever swallowed in the voracious Catholic maw of the Guises. Now with the likelihood of Navarre's regency, it seemed that the French Huguenot cause had indeed been presented with a renewed opportunity to

triumph through the death of the wretched Francis. The position
of Mary was equally transformed by her husband's death: at the
age of just eighteen, she was no longer queen but queen dowager
of France. Her entire position in Scotland, which had been
founded on the umbrella-like protection which the French crown
had extended to those Scots which it favoured, was likely to be
in jeopardy now that her husband no longer sat on the French
throne, and her uncles no longer directed French policy. Time
would show whether she would evolve a better Scottish policy,
or a worse one, but at all events on the death of Francis, Mary
Stuart was obliged to work out a different one.

It is doubtful whether these political considerations were
uppermost in the young queen's mind during the days before
her husband's death, and the days of mourning afterwards. On
the contrary, the evidence shows that, almost alone of the central
figures at the French court, Mary abandoned herself to passionate
grief at the death of the king, a grief founded on deep affection
which she had felt for him, rather than the possible upset of
her political plans. She had lost the companion of her childhood,
the boy-husband who had loved her, and who had shared with
her the happy intimacies of their charmed upbringing at the
French court. Elisabeth had departed for Spain, Claude for
Lorraine. Alone of her close royal companions of her youth,
Francis had remained part of her life, and to their childhood
intimacy had been added the natural intimacy of husband and
wife. Since the first moment of their meeting at St Germain in
October 1548, when the five-year-old Scottish queen had been
solemnly presented to the four-year-old dauphin of France, and
King Henry II had rejoiced over the immediate love which the
children felt for each other, Mary and Francis had never been
apart for longer than a few months at a time. They had thus
been united by over twelve years of continuous friendship and
companionship, and all that happy childhood memories can
signify in the mind of a romantic and affectionate young girl. It
was only six months since the death of her mother which had
induced in her such profound feelings of affliction: now she
found herself bereft of a husband, with whom indeed she had

led a far more prolonged and contented existence than the few short months she had spent with her mother since babyhood. It was small wonder that Mary gave herself up to transports of true grief.

The sincerity of her feelings was not doubted at the time. Throckmorton commented that Francis had left 'as heavy and dolorous a wife as of right she had good cause to be, who, by long watching with him during his sickness, and painful diligence about him' had worn herself out and made herself ill. The stanzas which Mary wrote on the death of Francis, which struck a chord in the heart of Ronsard, bear witness to the eloquent simplicity of her grief for the lost love of her childhood:

> Si en quelque séjour
> Soit en Bois ou en Prée
> Soit pour l'aube du jour
> Ou soit sur la Vesprée
> Sans cesse mon coeur sent
> Le regret d'un absent
> Si je suis en repos
> Sommeillant sur ma couche
> J'oy qu'il me tient propos
> Je le sens qui me touche
> En labeur et requoy
> Tousjours est prez de moy...'*

The political realities of the situation would appear to her later – although some of them may have begun to come home to her when Catherine asked for the return of the crown jewels, which the date on the order of release and the short, hurriedly

---

* Wherever I may be
In the woods or in the fields
Whatever the hour of day
Be it dawn or the eventide
My heart still feels it yet
The eternal regret...

As I sink into my sleep
The absent one is near
Alone upon my couch
I feel his beloved touch
In work or in repose
We are forever close...

Translated by the author.

prepared inventories shows to have been only one day after King Francis's death, in a ghastly parody of events after the death of King Henry, when Mary herself had demanded the return of the jewels from Diane de Poitiers. In the meantime Mary wore white and shut herself in a black room lit by torches to give herself up totally to her sorrow. As the Venetian ambassador commented: 'Soon the death of the late King will be forgotten by all except his little wife, who has been widowed, has lost France, and has little hope of Scotland ... her unhappiness and incessant tears call forth general compassion.'[28]

CHAPTER SEVEN

Mary the Widow

'Since her husband's death the Scottish Queen hath showed ... that she is both of great wisdom for her years, modesty and also of great judgment ... which, increasing with her years, cannot but turn greatly to her commendation, reputation, honour and great benefit of her and her country.'

Throckmorton to Queen Elizabeth, January 1561

By tradition the mourning period of a queen of France lasted for forty days. The obsequies of the young king ended when his heart, enclosed in a leaden vase, was taken to the cathedral of Saint-Denis, outside Paris, traditional resting-place of the kings of France: here amid the numerous tombs the vase was placed on a pillar surrounded by sculptured flames, to symbolize that Francis as king had been as a pillar of flame in the Hebrew desert – a reference to his stand against the heretics. Immediately after the death of Francis, Mary, as we have seen, was prostrated by grief, and kept herself solitary; in any case visitors during the first fifteen days of her widowhood were limited by convention to those whose rank was considered sufficiently elevated to justify their entrance – the new King Charles IX, the king of Navarre, her uncles of Guise and the constable of Montmorency. For more personal consolation Mary depended on her grandmother Duchess Antoinette. However, once the first fortnight was over, and Mary's storm of sorrow had abated, it was inevitable that she should consider her future in the world: more especially did the subject of her future come rapidly into prominence since ambassadors were permitted to visit her during the second period of her mourning, and whatever the private unhappiness of a girl of eighteen who had lost her husband, they at least were untroubled by such considerations and, like her uncles of Guise, eager to press on to the burning topic of her future.

There were two possible cornerstones on which such discussions could be founded: a theoretical second marriage, and Mary's prospective return to Scotland. The Scottish situation was, however, rendered extremely uncertain by the fact that any sort of royal government had been in virtual abeyance since the death of Mary of Guise: the country was now ruled by a Protestant régime containing both John Knox and the queen's half-brother Lord James Stewart, under the titular leadership of Hamilton duke of Châtelherault. Mary was virtually an unknown quantity in Scotland at the time of Francis's death, and what little was known of her was feared: she was regarded not only as a Catholic by a country newly Protestant, but also as a foreigner by reason of her French upbringing and marriage. It therefore seemed highly unlikely that Mary would be received back in Scotland unless some foreign army propelled her there; for this reason her return to Scotland was regarded as being bound up with and dependent on her second marriage. Consequently during the spring of 1561 it was this marriage which received the full force of diplomatic and courtly considerations.

The historian Froude, in a trenchant phrase, has accused Mary herself of speculating on her next choice of husband before her first husband's body was cold.[1] In fact the marriage of a queen was unavoidably a political issue in the sixteenth century; just as Mary's first marriage had been fervently discussed from the very moment of her birth, when she was far too young to take any effective interest in the subject, so now it was natural that the subject of her second marriage should obsess the conversation and correspondence of ambassadors and courtiers, to say nothing of her Guise relations, quite regardless of her own personal feelings. The English ambassador, Throckmorton, made the point with his usual clarity when he indicated to the Council three weeks after Francis's death, on the occasion of his first interview with Mary: 'Now that death had thus disposed of the late French king, whereby the Scottish queen is left a widow, one of the special things your lordships have to consider, and have an eye to, is the marriage of that Queen."[2] His letters are abundantly filled with rumours on this critical subject. A whole week before Francis's death when Mary was immured in her husband's sick-room, Throckmorton reported from Orléans that there were plenty of discourses to be heard already of the French queen's second marriage and he cited the names of Don Carlos of Spain, Philip II's heir, the Archduke Charles of Austria, and the earl of Arran, Châtelherault's heir. After the death of Francis, beside the three front-runners already cited by Throckmorton, who continued to lead the field of gossip, an increasing number of other names were mentioned, including the kings of Denmark and Sweden, the young Lord Darnley, with his desirable inheritance of English royal blood, even the recently widowed duke of Ferrera, who was thought to have a special affection for the Scottish queen. There was always the possibility, mentioned at the Spanish court, that Mary would eventually marry her own brother-in-law, Charles, with a papal dispensation: even the name of her own uncle, Grand Prior Francis of Guise, was canvassed. In short, by the time Mary emerged from her forty days of mourning, possible candidates could be said to include almost any currently unmarried male of roughly suitable age, whose own position could be held to benefit in any way that of the queen of Scots, either by establishing her own throne of Scotland, or by strengthening her claim to the throne of England, or even by re-establishing her on the throne of France.

The torrent of speculation made it inevitable that Mary herself would have to express some sort of personal predilection on the two subjects of re-marriage and Scotland, once she returned to the ways of ordinary life – unless, of course, she was content to leave her affairs and her future in the hands of her uncles as she had done in the past. This, however, she did not seem especially inclined to do, or at any rate, not to the extent which she had suffered herself to be guided during her time as dauphiness and queen of France. It has been suggested that the

Guises lost interest in their niece once she no longer occupied the throne from which she could advance their interests: but the evidence of Mary's widowhood in France shows that on the contrary, it was she who attempted to stretch her political wings, and to struggle free as a butterfly from the chrysalis in which the Guises had lovingly contained her. As she was careful to tell Throckmorton just before her departure for Scotland, her uncles did not advise her on Scottish matters 'being of the affairs of France'.[3] Yet in the negotiations for a second marriage, the cardinal showed himself as anxious as ever to guide his niece. It was Mary the widow who was making the first efforts to think for herself, in a way which impressed all those around her.

In the first instance she evidently used the period of her mourning for a serious consideration of her future problems once her first collapse had given way to a more philosophical mood of resignation. Throckmorton visited her on 31st December, and his account of the interview shows us the first glimpse of the new Mary Stuart. There is no question but that the young queen made an excellent impression upon the English ambassador.[4] He wrote back to England that no great account had been made of the queen during her husband's lifetime, seeing that she had been 'under band of marriage and subjection to her husband (who carried the burden and care of all her matters)', and there had thus been no great opportunity to get to know her. But, he continued, since her husband's death she had shown, and continued to do so, that she was 'both a great wisdom for her years, modesty, and also of great judgment in the wise handling herself and her matters, which, increasing with her years, cannot but turn greatly to her commendation, reputation, honour and great benefit of her and her country'. Mary further impressed Throckmorton by professing herself ready to be guided by suitable advisers; 'And for my part,' continued Throckmorton, 'I see her behaviour to be such and her wisdom and kingly modesty so great, in that she thinketh herself not too wise, but is content to be ruled by good counsel and wise men (which is a great virtue in a Prince or Princess, and which argueth a great judgment and wisdom in her).'

Throckmorton's last comment was of course not only intended to apprise the English Council as to the true nature of the Scottish queen with whom they had to deal, it was also intended as an acid reference to the somewhat less wise and modest conduct of their own Queen Elizabeth. The later reputations of Elizabeth and Mary have somewhat obscured the fact that in the early 1560s, when they were both young women, it was Elizabeth who was considered headstrong, extravagant and stubborn, whereas Mary was generally rated to be modest, intelligent and anxious to do her best as a ruler by taking wise advice. One contemporary described Elizabeth's court at this period as a by-word for frivolity: 'Nothing is treated earnestly, and though all things go wrong they jest, and he who invents most ways of wasting time is regarded as one worthy of honour.'

Only a few months before, in September 1560, Amy Robsart, wife of the English queen's favourite, Robert Dudley, had been found dead in mysterious circumstances. The scandal, which invites comparison with the Scottish court tragedy of Kirk o'Field, although it had a different outcome, was not allayed by Elizabeth's continued association with Dudley and profuse rumours throughout the following winter that she intended to marry him now that he was free. Throckmorton himself was so terrified that his hair stood on end at the very thought, and he declared that he would not wish to live should that day ever come. How different was the conduct of the young queen of Scots, and how infinitely more becoming! It was no coincidence that Throckmorton chose to write to Dudley in the same vein, praising Mary's youthful discretion.[6]

Mary's forty days of mourning were officially ended when she attended a memorial service for Francis in the convent of Grey Friars at Orléans on 18th January 1561. She now withdrew from the strict seclusion of her first *deuil* to a palace a few leagues outside the town of Orléans, which she occupied with her grandmother. By this date Mary had already written to Scotland a moderate temporizing letter, by which she broke the news of Francis's death formally to the Scottish Estates, and assured them that she intended to forget past troubles and differences; she went on to express her desire to return to Scotland as soon as possible, in token of which she asked for royal accounts since the death of her mother, and demanded from the Estates a list of candidates to fill the roles of treasurer and controller in Scotland.[7] The gentle, positively placating tone of this letter was thoroughly in tune with what Mary had also told Throckmorton on the subject of Scotland – that she wished to return home as soon as possible, and hoped it would be at the request and suit of her subjects.

But at this very moment, Mary was also the willing participant in marriage negotiations with Don Carlos of Spain; it is evident that her attitude towards Scotland in the spring, despite her soft words to Throckmorton, was very much one of 'wait and see'. Marriage to Don Carlos, heir to the great throne of the Spanish empire, was an infinitely more glorious prospect than a highly speculative return to a distant kingdom. Mary Stuart had been trained to believe herself a worthy incumbent of thrones, and the Guises had encouraged her in this belief. Don Carlos was a Catholic and could be expected to be supported by Spanish troops. The Spanish marriage was Mary's first choice for her future after Francis's death, and the return to Scotland only assumed its full importance once the prospect of the Spanish marriage faded from the scene for the time being. As has been seen, while Francis lay *in extremis*, there had been rumours at the French court of the possibility of such a match. When the Spanish ambassador visited Mary in the second stage of her mourning, he was thought to have lingered an unconscionably long time, 'above an hour together' – too long, thought Throckmorton, for a conventional visit of condolence. The cardinal told Chantonay that his niece only wished for a Spanish marriage. On 10th January Throckmorton reported that 'the house of Guise use all means to bring to pass the marriage between the prince of Spain and the Queen of Scotland'. At the end of January Don Juan Manrique arrived at the French court, and according to the Venetian ambassador 'went to visit the Queen of Scotland, with whom, in the presence of the Duke of

Guise and the Cardinal of Lorraine, he held very confidential communications and, I am assured that, besides his other concerns, Don Juan is also empowered to treat a marriage between her Majesty and the Prince of Spain'.[8]

Don Carlos himself had little to commend him personally as a husband, and indeed in many ways was merely a still feebler version of the wretched Francis, without the advantage of having been well known to Mary in childhood. He was physically undersized, weighing less than five and a half stone. One of his shoulders was higher than the other, he had a marked speech impediment and was also an epileptic. At the time of Mary's first widowhood, he was sixteen, a few months older than his young step-mother Elisabeth of Valois. At the age of seventeen he fell headlong down a staircase, supposedly pursuing a serving maid, and the resulting concussion did nothing to improve his mental state. He lay for a long time, blind and partially paralysed, until an Italian surgeon gave him partial relief by a trepanning operation to cut a triangular piece out of his skull. This relieved the paralysis, but left him in turn prone to fits of homicidal mania: he also subsequently developed a passionate attachment to his young step-mother and a corresponding hatred of his father, the king.* There was certainly nothing in Don Carlos to inspire any flight of fancy in the mind of a young, recently widowed queen: it is interesting to note that at this stage in her career, Mary Stuart's choice of husband was without hesitation one whose attractions were strictly political and dynastic. She thoroughly justified Throckmorton's shrewd estimate of her character in this respect – so commendably different from that of his own wayward mistress Elizabeth. 'As far as I can learn, she more esteemeth the continuation of her honour and to

---

* This passion, which has been enveloped in the mantle of romance by Schiller and Verdi, was in fact more the one-sided fixation of an idiot than the reciprocated grand passion of their imagination. One may prefer the notion of the romantic liberal-minded Don Carlos of the opera: but there is no historical evidence that Elisabeth of Valois ever returned the devotion of her feeble-minded step-son, and she seems indeed to have lived comparatively happily with her elderly husband, before her premature death.

marry one that may uphold her to be great than she passeth to please her fancy by taking one that is accompanied with such small benefit or alliance, as thereby her estimation and fame is not increased."⁹

Fortunately or unfortunately, Mary Stuart was not destined to become another Spanish bride, like her cousin Mary Tudor. The possible consequences of such an alliance to a strong Catholic power, early in her career, for Mary herself, for Scotland and indeed the whole British Isles, lead one down the pleasurable but irrelevant avenues of speculation. There was an implacable, if unseen, obstacle in the way of these early negotiations, in the shape of the hostility of Catherine de Médicis. The death of Francis had resulted in a real political triumph for the dowager queen: although it was confidently expected that the regency of the kingdom would fall into the hands of the king of Navarre, Catherine had, by a mixture of coercion and cajolery, cleverly persuaded him to leave it in her own hands. In return she allowed his brother Condé to be pardoned, and past misdemeanours on the part of the Bourbons to be forgotten, and further fobbed off the king with the title of lieutenant-general of the kingdom. It was a gesture of supreme political and personal intelligence, since by retaining the regency in her own hands Catherine both prevented the warring nobles of the court from tearing the kingdom in two, and also promoted the interests of her own family, in the way which was dearest to her heart. The Guises, who only eighteen days before Francis's death had been so confident of Catherine's support, found that their power was considerably and effectively diminished, although Catherine was once again too clever to go so far as to drive them into open hostility. Her ultimate object was, after all, the safe rule of her son over all nobles in the kingdom, rather than personal revenge.

Catherine's attitude to her son's widow showed the same judicious mixture of outward conciliation and inward rigidity on any subject where their interests might clash. In her letter to the Estates of Scotland, in January, Mary paid Catherine a warm tribute for her kindness, and said that she could not have expected more consolation in her sorrow from her own mother.

She also told the Estates that since France was now ruled by the queen mother, the Franco-Scottish alliance would be firmer than ever. Catherine's private letters to her daughter Elisabeth of Spain tell a very different story.[10] Mary is referred to by the code name of *le gentilhomme*, a figure of whom Elisabeth is to be extremely wary. Officially, Catherine was given no cognizance of Mary's negotiations for a Spanish marriage; but her hostility to the match was none the less effective for being devious and serpentine, since it allowed her to maintain a delusive mask of friendliness to her daughter-in-law. Catherine feared that the house of Valois would be twice threatened by Mary's return to glory, through her marriage to Don Carlos. First of all, the star of the Guises would inevitably rise again, and with their niece so close to the Spanish throne, who knew what new twists they might not give to the skein of their ambitions. Secondly, Catherine feared for the position of her own daughter Elisabeth on the throne of Spain if Philip should die and Carlos inherit, in which case Elisabeth might be pushed aside as she, Catherine, had once been. While Catherine gave Elisabeth precise instructions on how to frustrate the match from the Spanish end, Catherine herself complicated the issue by dangling the prospect of another royal bride for Don Carlos in front of Philip's eyes – her own daughter Marguerite.

France was not the only country where Mary's Spanish match was looked on with concern. In England the prospect of Mary Stuart's marriage to a foreign prince, especially a Spanish one, was regarded as scarcely less threatening to the maintenance of English power, and when in March Elizabeth's minister Cecil wrote a memorial to his agent in Scotland, Thomas Randolph, on Anglo-Scottish affairs, the third point on his draft was headed 'the menace of a foreign marriage by the Scottish Queen'.[11] To Philip, confronted with the firm hostility of Catherine and Elizabeth of England, and with the prospect of Marguerite held out before him, Mary no longer seemed so alluring as a future daughter-in-law. Not only did Philip believe he would have to establish Mary on her throne by force, but he would also have to sacrifice his present good relations with Elizabeth of England.

Hitherto Philip had supported her in calming down her English Catholics, in order to balance the opposing Franco-Scottish nexus. So long as Elizabeth did not marry Dudley – and the possibility was now slightly receding – a Catholic rising in England to put Mary on the throne was unlikely. Faced with these considerations Philip understandably preferred the substance of Elizabeth to the shadow of Mary; perhaps he also shrank somewhat from the prospect of introducing a Guise cuckoo into the Spanish nest. By the end of April, Elisabeth of Spain was able to inform her mother that the Spanish negotiations with Mary had foundered finally, for lack of interest on Philip's part.

In the meantime Mary naturally continued to be a focus of interest for other countries, other aspirants. In February, the earl of Bedford arrived on an official embassy of condolence from Queen Elizabeth of England. Queen Mary thanked him graciously for her fellow-queen's comfort in her distress and added in her most friendly manner 'considering that the Queen now shows the part of a good sister, whereof she has great need, she will endeavour to be even with her goodwill; and though she be not so able as another, yet she trust the Queen will take her goodwill in good part'. It was on this occasion that Mary also took the opportunity to remind Throckmorton that he had not sent her the portrait of Elizabeth, despite her fervent desire to exchange pictures.* Bedford's next two interviews with Queen Mary were, however, on a less gracious, more down-to-earth level, since he had been instructed to ask her yet again to ratify the Treaty of Edinburgh. This treaty, by which peace had been established the previous July between England, Scotland and France, provided for the withdrawal of French troops from Scotland and pledged both France and England to a policy of non-interference there; it had also laid down that Mary and Francis should abandon forever the bearing of the English royal arms. Mary politely but firmly declined to agree to the ratification

---

* Mary's picture for Elizabeth was completed and sent by 1st December 1561. The two queens also exchanged portraits again in the next year, 1562.[12]

on the grounds that she must first consult with her Council, in view of her changed status as a widow, but once again went out of her way to show friendliness. She hinted that 'if her Council were here she would give such an answer as would satisfy him', and expressed a strong desire to meet Elizabeth personally, to talk over their differences, for she felt that thus 'they would satisfy each other much better than they can do by messages and ministers'.[13] This desire on the part of Mary to meet Elizabeth face to face, whether prompted by friendship, political wisdom or sheer feminine curiosity, was perfectly understandable; it is also easy to sympathize with Mary's reluctance to ratify the Treaty of Edinburgh so long as Elizabeth declined to recognize her cousin as heiress-presumptive to the English throne. By ratifying the Treaty of Edinburgh immediately, Mary would be discarding a potentially valuable card, for in return for the ratification it was Mary's hope that Elizabeth would set aside the will of Henry VIII from the English succession.

While still at Orléans, Mary received another manifestation of the importance of her claim to the English throne. A young scion of both English and Scottish royal houses, Henry Stuart, Lord Darnley, appeared at the court on an official visit of condolence to his widowed cousin. Darnley, then a youth of only fifteen or sixteen, had not himself provided the impetus for the visit. He had in fact met Mary Stuart briefly once before at the time of Francis's coronation, when his mother Margaret, countess of Lennox, dispatched him with a letter to the French court, concerning the restoration of Lennox to the family estates in Scotland. Now his ambitious, striving mother propelled the good-looking boy yet again in the direction of France, with the clear intention of dangling him, royal blood and all, in the path of the newly marriageable young queen. Darnley's mother was a Catholic, and having been born in England, it could be argued that he was not debarred from the succession by the will of Henry VIII. The Spanish ambassador in England, de Quadra, told his master Philip that if anything happened to Elizabeth, it was understood that the English Catholics would raise Darnley to the throne of England. But in the convoluted world of royal claims and counter-claims, wavering rights were held to be generally strengthened if reinforced by marriage to someone with other wavering rights. The plan was to induce Mary to wed Darnley, with the lure of thus bolstering up her claim to the English throne; Margaret Lennox entered into negotiations with the Scottish nobles at the same time, to the same effect. But, on this occasion at least, the royal fish did not rise to the bait. Mary herself was still involved in her dreams of a glorious Spanish alliance: if Darnley's appearance did make any impression on her sensibilities, this impression was stored away for the future, since her sensibilities at this time were so acutely subordinated to her political activities.

In the middle of March Mary decided to leave the French court, and set off on a prolonged round of visits to her Guise relations. She went first of all to the Guise *château* of Nanteuil, and then on to Rheims, where she made a three-week stay in the convent of her Aunt Renée, abbess of St Pierre, breaking the journey for a brief visit to Paris on 20th March to check over her clothes and jewels. From Rheims, she planned to go to Nancy, in Lorraine, to visit the court of her kinsman, Duke Charles, and her sister-in-law, Duchess Claude; from Nancy she could proceed easily to Joinville, the most outlying of the Guise *châteaux*. Melville, in his memoirs, attributes the journey to the spite of Catherine, now openly displayed: 'Our Queen, then Dowager of France, retired herself by little and little farther and farther from the court of France; that it should not seem that she was in any sort compelled thereunto, as of truth she was by the Queen Mother's rigorous and vengeable dealing; who alleged that she was despised by her good daughter, during the short reign of King Francis her husband, by the instigation of the House of Guise.'[14] But Melville is not always strictly accurate in his recollections. Mary had plenty of motives to take such a journey, without the animus of Catherine to inspire her, while Catherine herself understood only too well that hostile intrigues were more easily conducted under the guise of friendship to the victim. Apart from her natural desire to pay a round of visits to the family of whom she had always been so fond, it seems likely that Mary was also anxious to take part in family conclaves on the subject of her future, which would be easier to arrange away from the confined atmosphere of the French court.

It so happened that while Mary Stuart was on the route from Rheims to Nancy, she received two rival embassies from Scotland, which at the moment when the Spanish negotiations were foundering, opened up new possibilities in terms of a Scottish future. To Vitry in Champagne came first of all John Leslie, bishop of Ross, Mary's future envoy and historian, representing the party of the Scottish Catholics, and secondly James Stewart her half-brother, on behalf of the self-constituted Scottish Protestant government. Leslie's suggestions were bold enough: he believed that Mary should detain Lord James in France, and herself disembark at Aberdeen, where he swore she would find 20,000 men levied by her friends in the north of Scotland. She would then be in a position to take Scotland by storm. It is to Mary's credit that she rejected such extremist counsels immediately. The advice was of doubtful value in any case since even the strongest Catholic noble Huntly showed uncertain loyalties at this moment. However, one of the side-effects of Leslie's embassy was to confirm Mary's own view that she would be personally popular once she reached Scotland. (Had she not confidently told Throckmorton that the common people would be glad to see their queen come home?) Leslie told the queen that he expected her to 'over-shadow' her subjects with her presence when she returned like a newly-risen sun to scatter the clouds of all tumult shortly from the minds of her subjects.[15] In her interview with her half-brother the next day, Mary retained the bishop's image, while rejecting his advice.

The new emissary with whom Mary had to deal was her half-brother the Lord James. James Stewart was now a man of thirty, some twelve years older than his half-sister. His mother, Margaret Erskine, was that royal mistress who had served for the model of 'Lady Sensualitie' in Sir David Lyndsay's *Satire of the Three Estates*; as the sister of the earl of Mar she ensured her son a place in the network of Scottish noble families surrounding the crown, in which the Erskines were honourably situated. From his father King James v, Lord James inherited the royal Stewart blood which placed him so close yet so tantalizingly far from the Scottish throne. One consequence of the importance of kinship in sixteenth-century Scotland was to endow the sovereign's illegitimate children with great natural importance, because they shared the royal Stewart blood. It was not quite impossible that a strong male ruler born out of wedlock might be preferred to a weak female of legitimate descent. Of the nine known bastards of James v, three sons – Lord James, Lord Robert and Lord John Stewart – occupied high positions at Mary's court; and a daughter, Jean Stewart, who married the earl of Argyll, became one of her closest friends, a friendship which originated in their shared blood. James v had even made some sporadic efforts in 1536, when Lord James was four years old, to obtain the papal dispensation which would have enabled him to marry the child's mother, Lady Margaret. However, the position of Lord James would not have been automatically clarified by the marriage of his parents: although by Scots law the subsequent marriage of parents legitimated their offspring, this only applied to parents who were free to marry at the time of the conception; Lady Margaret had been married to Robert Douglas in 1527, four years before the birth of her son in 1531. Lord James might also have found himself in a disadvantageous position compared to any subsequent children born to James v and Margaret, who would have begun life as royal princes, without the stain of bastardy.*

Lacking the charm of his father, Lord James was a man of solemn manner and appearance; yet this *gravitas*, so unlike the qualities of the contemporary French nobility, was to prove highly successful in impressing the English when he dealt with them. From his Stewart father, James had inherited at least a

---

* Lord James was legitimated in February 1551. But the importance of legitimation in this period was not so much to remove a social stigma as to correct the fact that bastards could neither leave nor inherit property. The estates of a bastard descended to the crown on his death, if he was never legitimated during his lifetime.

subtlety lacking in many of his contemporaries among the Scottish nobility, which to the English made him seem a distinct improvement on his peers – or perhaps this fortunate ability to deal with England could be attributed to the fact that he was also one quarter Tudor. The English were delighted to be able to discern in him what they supposed to be a type of new Scotsman, upright, serious-minded and full of conscious rectitude, frequently given public expression, who seemed to them a distinct advance on the self-seeking Scottish nobles of the previous generation. Although more gifted politically than the sons of his fellow-nobles, Lord James was in fact far from immune from that practical avarice so characteristic of the Scottish nobility of this period – nor did he lack the hypocrisy which so often accompanies frequent public statements on the subject of honour. But this temperament, and above all quality of his religious views, which fitted in so well with those of the English politicians of the period like Cecil, meant that he was always able to deal easily, if not honourably, with his English equivalents, and this was to give him a practical advantage in Anglo-Scottish affairs at a later stage in his half-sister's career.

On his way to France on this occasion, Lord James had stopped in England: he certainly conferred with Cecil, with whom he had an old friendship, and may even have stayed in his house. His interview with Mary, held at St Dizier, was not unsatisfactory to both the participants, despite their widely differing points of view. Lord James had been instructed to ask the queen to embrace the Scottish Protestant faith: this she steadily refused to do. But she did state with some courage that she was prepared to come home without any other restrictions, or a personal armed escort, provided she could have use of her own religion in private. This Lord James himself had already expressed publicly to the Scots as being an acceptable demand. When it was suggested to him that the celebration of any sort of Mass, public or private, within the realm of Scotland would be a betrayal of the cause of God, he replied reasonably enough that this might indeed apply to a public Mass – 'but to have it secretly in her (Mary's) bedchamber, who could stop her?'[16]

Mary also allowed herself to be convinced by Lord James that it was politically wise to give the Protestant party its head for the time being in Scotland, although James later told Throckmorton Mary had begun the interview by ordering him a cardinal's hat, and several rich benefices in France, if he in turn would forswear Protestantism. The sacrifice of the prospect of these rich benefices did not mean that Lord James's mind was altogether concentrated on Scottish affairs, on this occasion, to the exclusion of personal gain, since he almost certainly took the opportunity to ask his half-sister for the rich earldom of Moray. Apart from the general understanding which they had reached on the subject of her return, Mary must also have been impressed as a result of this meeting with the notion that Lord James would constitute her natural adviser in Scotland, by virtue of their blood connection, as the Guises had done in France. She had emphasized to Throckmorton that she was prepared to listen to advice and even if all Lord James's advice had not been to her liking, the basis for some tolerable *modus vivendi*, in the event of her return, had at least been reached between them.

Yet Lord James was very far from being a Scottish Guise, in any sense of the word; his next actions showed that in his order of loyalties he placed the interests of the Scottish Protestant party, as embodied in an English alliance, well above those of his sister's confidence. Returning to Paris, he went secretly to Throckmorton's lodgings, and, in Throckmorton's own words, 'declared unto me at good length all that passed between the Queen, his sister and him, and between the Cardinal of Lorraine and him'.[17] Throckmorton in turn passed the information on to Elizabeth. Although James did actually inform Mary that he had met Throckmorton, he presumably did not impart to her the full nature of their discourses. On his way back to Scotland, Lord James once again stopped in England, and conferred with Cecil: it has been suggested on the evidence of Camden's *Annales*, that during his two weeks in London, James suggested to Elizabeth that she should provide for her religion and her safety by intercepting Mary on her journey back to Scotland.[18] But in fact, he had little motive for doing so, so long as Mary showed herself so adaptable, and so amenable to his advice; his subsequent actions show that his real intentions were to keep in well with both queens, rather than secure the captivity of one by the other. The prospect of a Queen Mary on the throne of Scotland, dependent on his counsels, and Queen Elizabeth on the throne of England, favourable to his policies, opened up new and agreeable avenues of ambition to Lord James. In the meantime James certainly won golden opinions from Throckmorton as a result of his confidences, who despite their illicit nature, wrote ecstatically that he was 'one of the most virtuous noblemen, and one in whom religion, sincerity and magnanimity as much reign as ever he knew in any man in any nation'. He also took care to suggest that there should be a genuinely silver lining to this cloud of intrigue – in the shape of a distribution of £20,000 sterling, among the chief men of Scotland, to include Châtelherault and, of course, Lord James.

James's advice to his sister on the subject of the Scottish Protestants accorded well with what Mary had already been told from other sources about the Scottish situation. Throckmorton heard that even the king of Spain had advised her to be prepared to temporize in matters of religion, on her first arrival. Melville tells us that all the Frenchmen who had recently returned from Scotland advised her to be most familiar with James, Argyll, Maitland and Kirkcaldy of Grange, in short to learn to repose most upon the members of the reformed religion.[19] Such practical advice, coloured by tolerance, accorded well with Mary's own temperament and religious convictions. In religious matters, her leaning was towards the tolerance of her mother, rather than the fanaticism of a cardinal of Guise. As a born Catholic, who had known no other creed, her faith was to her like her everyday bread, something which she took for granted, and yet which was essential to her, and without which she could not imagine her existence; it was, however, in no sense an Old Testament faith, a fierce Moloch of a faith, which demanded the sacrifice of all other faiths to propitiate it, such as animated Philip II of Spain.

Mary's innate clemency in matters of religion has sometimes

been mistaken for lukewarm convictions. The truth was that she drew a clear distinction between private faith and public policy. She herself gave Throckmorton the most explicit avowal of her beliefs, on the eve of her departure for Scotland;[20] 'I will be plain with you,' she told him. 'The religion which I profess I take to be the most acceptable to God; and, indeed, neither do I know, nor desire to know any other. Constancy becometh all folks well, and none better than princes, and such as have rule over realms, and specially in matters of religion. I have been brought up in this religion; and who aught would credit me in anything if I should show myself lighter in this case.' This eloquent profession of faith can scarcely be bettered as the personal apologia of a ruler, who at the same time believed in toleration and mercy for those around her. Although Randolph wrote when she was in Scotland, 'She wishes that all men should live as they please,'[21] Knox was quick to realize that such permissiveness did not mean, as some suggested in October 1561, that the queen herself should ever be of their opinion. Mary's personal Catholicism was total, her attitude to a state religion inclined to be pragmatic.

Mary's pilgrimage among her Guise relations culminated in a visit to the court of Lorraine, where Duchess Claude, her erstwhile friend, reigned in state. Claude was not destined to atone in public for the private disloyalty of her sister Elisabeth. The princess had grown proud, and used to the adulation of her little court; the widowed queen found little feminine consolation in her company. Nevertheless the Lorrainers gave her a grandiose reception, and 'a magnificent triumph' was planned, with cannons discharged from the city walls of Nancy, in her honour. Bishop Leslie describes how Mary was further entertained with hunting in the fields, and pleasant farces and plays.[22] These diversions did not prevent her falling ill with one of those tertian fevers to which she was so subject. It is possible that the attack was induced by the mental stress of deciding about her future, now that the negotiations for the Spanish marriage were finally halted. The attack was certainly sufficiently severe and prolonged to prevent her arriving at Rheims in time for the coronation of the young Charles IX as she had planned. Instead her grandmother fetched her from Nancy to Joinville, and here even on 25th May, she was still in bed in the throes of a prolonged convalescence, and not allowed to speak to anyone except her doctors. However, by 28th May she had managed to reach Rheims, and was there entertained once again by her aunt the abbess and her uncle the cardinal. On 10th June, Mary finally returned once more to the environs of the French court, from which she had been absent for a critical three months. Her return was accompanied by the formal rejoicings which befitted her rank as a dowager queen of France. She was officially greeted a league outside Paris by the duke of Orléans, the king of Navarre, the prince of Condé and the other princes of the blood, who accompanied her in state into the town. Here she was conducted to her actual lodgings within the palace by the king, the queen mother and the entire court.

Whether Mary's illness was induced by indecision or not, by the time she returned to the court from her wanderings, her mind was evidently made up to return to Scotland. Although a number of factors induced her to reach this decision, it was not the only alternative open to her. Despite the secret hostility of Catherine, Mary's rank in France entitled her to an honourable position at the French court, from which it would have been difficult to dislodge her, if she had been determined to maintain it. Her marriage contract to Francis specifically stated that in the event of his death, she was to be allowed the choice of remaining in France or returning to Scotland. Her marriage portion had made her duchess of Touraine, and her estates there and in Poitou were sufficiently widespread and lucrative to have maintained her in an adequate state; the Guise family, although somewhat blighted, were not totally destitute of power; if she remained on the Continent, it was not likely to be long before some more ardent royal suitor than Don Carlos emerged. To Mary herself must be given the credit of having personally settled for a bold course of adventure, rather than the more placid, less demanding existence which it would still have been possible for her to lead in France. The truth was that even as a young girl, Mary showed signs of having a gambling streak, and she was certainly singularly unendowed with conservatism in her nature: the familiar path was never to her automatically the most attractive path while there was another more daring route to be explored. Life in France, as she had known it so gloriously, appeared to have come to an end; but on the horizon, Scotland beckoned, which might provide in time – who could tell, but Mary was an optimist – as many golden opportunities.

As it happened, at the same moment the Scots themselves were beginning to feel more warmly about their absent queen. Among the politicians, it was the quick-witted Maitland with his sense of international values who pointed out that Mary's dynastic claim to the English throne could now work to the advantage of Scotland, rather than France, if she returned to her own country. They suddenly realized that a malleable young ruler, with a strong personal claim to succeed to the neighbouring throne, and apparently prepared to behave reasonably over religion, was certainly not to be discarded in a hurry. As a result of these cogitations, Lord James wrote a letter on 10th June which constituted a virtual invitation on behalf of the Protestant lords to return. Maitland himself wrote to Mary promising to do all he could for her service. Scotland for Mary therefore was not a *pis aller*, but a hopeful venture, in which her Guise blood encouraged her to expect success.

Neither Moray nor Maitland was especially put out by the fact that Mary still declined to ratify the Treaty of Edinburgh: not unnaturally they shared Mary's view that it was a subject that could be best dealt with once she had returned to Scotland and could consult her Council. Throckmorton on the other hand was still desperately hoping to secure the ratification. He sent Somer to Nancy in April and to Rheims in May: both missions were fruitless. Now that Mary was returning to the French court, he begged her with renewed fervour to grant long-withheld ratification. At an audience of 18th June, Mary pointed out that her health was still too frail for serious consideration of such matters, but she went on to say that since in any case she intended to return to Scotland very shortly, she would defer her answer until she had the advice of the Estates and nobles of her own realm. She told Throckmorton that she intended to embark shortly at Calais, and to this effect d'Oysel was being sent to Elizabeth with a message asking for a safe-conduct on her route back to Scotland.[23]

But when d'Oysel had his interview with Elizabeth on 13th July requesting a passport for Mary, the English queen at once asked him whether he had brought the ratification of the Treaty of Edinburgh with him. D'Oysel replied that he had no instructions on the subject. At this he was greeted by such hostility from Elizabeth as well as a blank refusal to give the safe-conduct that when Mary next spoke with Throckmorton she ironically suggested they should draw apart, in case he angered her by his speech, as she herself did not wish to be witnessed giving such a display of 'choler and stomache' as Elizabeth had shown to d'Oysel.[24] Elizabeth's behaviour smacks of childish pique rather than statecraft, and it was not well regarded at the time, even by her own ambassador. Throckmorton was frankly amazed at the refusal and said so to Cecil: in his opinion, the sooner Mary was plucked out of the tangled web of continental intrigue, into the comparative safety of distant Scotland, the better it would be for England. The Scots were appalled, since their avowed aim in the words of Maitland was to see both queens 'as near friends, as they were tender cousins', with a view to getting Elizabeth to recognize Mary as her heir; now here was one tender cousin treating the other in a way more likely to lead to distant enmity than near friendship. The Venetian ambassador, a more impartial judge of the situation, described the refusal as contrary to expectation and humanity.[25]

Elizabeth's refusal gave Mary Stuart her first public opportunity of rising magnificently to a crisis. She now displayed for the first time that quality of cool courage, when in the public eye, which was to be a feature of her later career. It was courage which owed nothing to physical well-being. At the beginning of July Mary had a renewed attack of the tertian fever, and when Throckmorton saw her on 9th July he noted that it had 'somewhat appaired her cheer', although Mary herself dismissed it lightly and said that the worst was over. Now, when she received Throckmorton on 20th July at Saint-Germain, having heard the news of the denied passport, she was infinitely composed; in a series of speeches to the English ambassador of fine histrionic power, she showed herself to be not only brave, but also reasonable and even charitable towards the woman who had thus rejected her – as well as incidentally having an eloquent command of language.[26] Like an actress before an audience, the eighteen-year-old queen seemed to derive strength from the fact that the eyes of Europe were upon her. Her interviews with Throckmorton lead one to the conclusion that Mary, far from being daunted by the drama of the situation, was positively inspired by it.

She began by expressing in polite terms her regrets that she should have bothered Throckmorton by demanding a passport which she did not in fact require. She had reached France in safety, she pointed out proudly, in spite of the efforts of the king of England to intercept her. Thirteen years later, she would surely once more reach her own country with her own people to help her. Mary also told Throckmorton that she had no intention of ratifying the treaty until she reached her own land, where she would have the benefit of the advice of the Estates, since she was bound neither in honour nor in conscience to perform what her late husband had commanded. But as a proof that she wished to live in amity with the English queen, Mary also pointed out on the vexed point of the English arms that since the death of both her father-in-law and husband she had borne neither arms nor title.

The next day Throckmorton came to see her again, and Mary spoke to him with renewed oratorical fervour: 'Monsieur l'Ambassadeur, if my preparations were not so much advanced as they are, peradventure the Queen, your Mistress' unkindness might stay my voyage; but now I am determined to adventure the matter, whatsoever come of it; I trust the wind will be so favourable as I shall not need to come on the coast of England; and if I do, Monsieur l'Ambassadeur, the Queen your Mistress shall have me in her hands to do her will of me; and if she be so hard-hearted as to desire my end, she may then do her pleasure, and make sacrifice of me; peradventure that casualty might be better for me than to live,' added Mary dramatically, although one suspects her real expectations were somewhat less pessimistic. 'In this matter, God's will be fulfilled,' she concluded and, in a final superb gesture, embraced the attendant Throckmorton.[27]

Mary followed up the interview with a friendly letter to Elizabeth to see if the safe-conduct could still be obtained, but without awaiting the answer, she forthwith made her preparations to leave France, passport or no passport. On 25th July, she departed from the court of Saint-Germain, here bidding adieu to King Charles, Queen Catherine and the majority of the nobility who had known her throughout childhood, youth and marriage. According to Leslie, the ancient Franco-Scottish alliance was not forgotten at this final moment and confirmation was made of 'a perpetual friendship to stand among them, as it had been between their predecessors, by most ancient band and league, inviolably in all times past'.[28] When the grand farewell *fête*, which was held in her honour at Saint-Germain, and lasted for four days, was over, the young queen set out for Calais, accompanied by her six uncles and other members of the court. The train stopped at Merly, the constable's house, on their way, where both the cardinal and duke of Guise fell ill overnight – although in this case the proverbial rumours of poison which greeted the incident were made less realistic by the fact that the king of Navarre was also stricken. On 3rd August, Mary was still at Beauvais, and Throckmorton then followed her on to Abbeville, where on 7th August, he had a final interview with the queen, at which both reiterated their former arguments, Mary laying special emphasis on the fact that since she was acting without the advice of her uncles, she genuinely needed to obtain the advice of the Scots before she proceeded further – 'I do so much know mine own infirmity that I will do nothing ... without counsel.'[29]

On 8th August Throckmorton bid the queen a last goodbye.

The admiration which the ambassador felt for the queen seems to have been reciprocated. Always generous to those who served her, Mary wrote to Lady Throckmorton the day before she sailed from Calais, saying that she had charged her *maître d'hôtel* to visit her and give her a present as a remembrance of her affection, and a token of the regard which she felt for her husband. Lady Throckmorton subsequently received two basins, two ewers, two salts and a standing cup, all of gilt. A zealous Protestant, whose career in England had been under a cloud during the reign of the Catholic Mary Tudor, when he was tried for complicity in the Wyatt rebellion, in France Throckmorton openly hated the Catholic Guises and admired the Huguenots. Yet he was clearly fascinated by the Catholic queen of Scots, as were so many of Queen Elizabeth's servitors who were to come into personal contact with her. As Mary was beginning to expand in her mind the possibilities of meeting the queen of England face to face, perhaps Elizabeth at the same moment was already digesting the fact that personal contact with the queen of Scots was apt to have an alarmingly seductive effect on the listener.

On the evening of 8th August, Mary rode to the abbey of Forest Monstrier, where she decided to send the lord of St Colme Inch and Alexander Erskine to England, accompanied by Throckmorton's servant Tremaine, for a final appeal for the passport. Before the effects of this letter could be felt – once again its tone was extremely friendly – the preparations for Mary's journey had been completed. The queen and her party were to travel in two galleys, accompanied by two ships. The preparations were not left entirely in the hands of the French. The hereditary Lord High Admiral of Scotland was also involved – this was none other than James Hepburn, earl of Bothwell. This spirited border lord had already swum into the ken of the Scottish queen during the previous autumn, when he had arrived at the French court for the first time. He did so characteristically, out of financial necessity, abandoning his Norwegian mistress, Anna Throndsen, in Flanders, while he made the expedition to seek further funds. Bothwell had been kindly received by Mary and Francis, and as he put it himself,

'The Queen recompensed me more liberally and honourably than I had deserved'[30] – these particular benefits being a present of 600 crowns as well as the post and salary of gentleman of the king's chamber. On this occasion Throckmorton had suspected some political coup and warned his correspondents in London that Bothwell needed watching, for he was a 'glorious [i.e. vainglorious], rash and hazardous young man'.[31] He paid a further visit to France in the spring, and by 5th July was back in Paris for the third time;* this time he was accompanied by the bishop of Orkney, himself a seaman of distinction, and Lord Eglinton, no stranger to nautical enterprise in the sense that he was generally suspected of piracy. As for Elizabeth, too late she relaxed her fury; by the time she wrote back to Mary denying any intention of 'impeaching' her passage, and saying that she had no ships at sea except for two or three small barks to apprehend pirates who were attacking the North Sea fishermen, Mary was no longer in France to receive the letter.

Mary's departure was not without its tragi-comic elements. The cardinal, for example, suggested that she should for prudence's sake leave her jewels behind in France, to which Mary, with a flash of wry humour, observed that if she herself were safe to go to sea, why then so were her jewels. She atoned for this, however, by giving her aunt the duchess of Guise, with characteristic generosity the day before she finally sailed, a magnificent necklace of rubies, emeralds and diamonds from her own collection, as a token of regard. The company of her own galley was planned to provide a galaxy of glamour and entertainment to beguile the young queen on her journey; it included three of her uncles, René of Elboeuf, the duke of Aumale and the Grand Prior Francis, as well as the four Maries, Mary Seton, Mary Beaton, Mary Livingston and Mary Fleming, whose French education was completed and were now to

* Although Bothwell did not travel back to Scotland on Mary's own galley, it does not seem fanciful to suppose that his return to France was connected with arrangements for her journey, not only on grounds of his hereditary office, but also because the contemporary Birrel's Diary specifically states that the queen was 'stolen out of France by sertain Lords'.[32]

accompany their mistress back to Scotland, as they had accompanied her to France so many years ago. On Mary's own galley were also to travel the young poet Châtelard and her admiring chronicler Brantôme.[33]

The day of embarkation dawned dull and misty, despite the fact that it was high August. Mary's wavering spirits were not lifted by the fact that a fishing boat in the harbour foundered and went down before the eyes of her watching party, with all its hands drowned. 'What a sad augury for a journey!' she exclaimed aloud. On Thursday, 14th August about noon, the servant of ambassador Throckmorton, passing by Calais, saw a stirring spectacle 'haling' out of the haven: two great galleys and two ships. He hastened to give the news to his master. It was news which Throckmorton had been expecting to hear and it cannot have been unwelcome to him. It was a brave sight which the English servant glimpsed at Calais, for it was the queen of Scotland setting forth across the North Sea on the 600-mile journey to her kingdom, unblessed by any passport of safe-conduct from the English queen, whose ships patrolled these seas. As the ambassador faithfully commenced the dispatch which would break this piece of news to England,[34] he imagined only the bravado of the gesture which he must have applauded. Even if his watchful eyes had been able to spy into the great white galley and discern the tragic weeping figure on its poop, he might scarcely have recognized this tormented being for his modest self-controlled young queen.

Up till this moment Mary had shown admirable courage and resolution, both in her dealings with Throckmorton, and more profoundly in her decision to 'hazard all she had' by returning to Scotland. But now that the die was cast, now that the ships were actually lying in the harbour of Calais, ready to take her away from all she had known and loved and held dear for that last thirteen years of what seemed to her like her whole life, Mary Stuart's steadfast spirit temporarily deserted her. There was now no great challenge to call forth the resources of her nature, only the prospect of bidding farewell as it might be forever, to her family, her friends and above all France, France the beloved land of her adoption.

As the galleys surged forward towards the unknown coast of Scotland, Mary herself gazed again and again on the fast-receding coast of France; clinging pathetically to that part of the ship which was still nearest to the French shores she murmured over and over again in a voice broken with tears: '*Adieu France! Adieu France!*'; again and again she repeated the words, and as the shoreline gradually faded from her sight, her laments only increased in fervour. Still mingling with the sound of the wind and the roars of the sea, her tragic young voice could be heard, eternally uttering its farewell, melancholy and prophetic. '*Adieu France! Adieu France! Adieu donc, ma chère France. . . . Je pense ne vous revoir jamais plus.*'

PART TWO

The Personal Rule

CHAPTER EIGHT

The State of the Realm

'Assez fins, astutes et inconstans d'affection'
*A judgement on the Scottish people
from an anonymous French memoir of 1558*

Although Ronsard, in a farewell ode to the queen, expressed the romantic wish that Scotland should fly before her ship, like the floating island of Delos, so that she would never be able to overtake it, in fact the fog-bound Scottish coast loomed out of the mist towards the queen's galleys in a prosaically short time. Queen Catherine wrote coolly to her daughter Elisabeth of Spain on the subject of her daughter-in-law's departure: 'She has set sail ... and if the winds are favourable, should be in Scotland within the week.'[1] As it happened the journey which had begun under such dramatic auspices turned out to be comparatively uneventful and only lasted five days. Throughout much of its span, Mary's mood of deep depression persisted; her soft heart led her to forbid the customary whipping of the oarsmen, as though in her own state of pain she could not bear to see further unnecessary suffering inflicted on others.[2]

The encounter with the English ships on the high seas provided the main excitement of the voyage. The English queen had at last dispatched a friendly message, in answer to the Commendator of Inchcolm's mission – too late for Mary to receive it in France. Elizabeth now stated that she had no intention of stopping the Scottish queen's passage; in any case she had no fleet in the North Sea, only a few barks who were positioned there to discourage piracy. Cecil subsequently described to Throckmorton how the English ships had found the Scottish queen on the high seas with a tiny brave little train 'not exceeding sixty persons of meaner sort'.[3] Mary, unaware of Elizabeth's volte-face, must have expected a more melodramatic meeting than that which actually took place. The English ships merely saluted the queen's galleys, and allowed them to proceed; they examined the rest of the ships for pirates, and finally detained Lord Eglinton, on suspicion; not long afterwards, however, he too was released and permitted to return to Scotland. The only true casualty of the embargo which Elizabeth had attempted to put on the journey was Mary's own stable of horses and mules which, having landed at Tynemouth, was prevented from proceeding further by the warden for a full month on the grounds that it lacked a proper passport.

There was a quality of anti-climax about this tame encounter, when so much had been threatened by Elizabeth, so much courage shown by Mary. But it was certainly believed at the time that Elizabeth had intended to capture Mary if she could, and even the English officials in the north of England seemed to be under the same impression that her capture was desirable: on Sunday, 17th August, the earl of Rutland wrote to Cecil that Mary had been seen off Flamborough head, with a great fleet surrounding the royal galleys, including eight galleys and sixteen ships, and boasted that if they came ashore Cecil would 'hear good news of their stay'. The next day or two great galleys were observed at Flamborough within a furlong of the pier, one all white, the other red, 'well trimmed and appointed', having two flags, a blue one with the arms of France and a white one in the stern glistening like silver. Having let their anchors fall, the galleys each put forth one naked man to swim (what bold spirit of the French party thus tested the bracing pleasure of swimming in the North Sea waters?). All the time at a good distance away, there was apparently visible a large fleet of ships;[4] but as all the contemporary evidence agrees that Mary landed at Leith with only two galleys, it seems likely that this phantom fleet off Flamborough head, far from being Mary's own entourage, was the English fleet hovering round the Scottish queen, uncertain how to proceed as they had no precise commands to intercept her. As for the true intentions of Elizabeth in London, probably she herself was not utterly sure how she would react if an English captain took the law into his own hands and captured the queen of Scots.

Such perplexities of motive and behaviour did not trouble Mary Queen of Scots. The only obscurity which surrounded the journey, from her point of view, once she had determined on it, was the physical obscurity induced by the weather. It had been hazy when the galleys left France, and it continued misty throughout the voyage. On the morning of the day the galleys were due to land at Leith, thick fog descended. A thick fog on the coast of Scotland was not an unexpected hazard, even in the middle of August; yet according to Brantôme the royal party seized on it as another unfortunate omen for the queen's arrival, while John Knox from the vantage point of Scottish *terra firma*, but with equal pessimism, saw in the fog a symbol of the fact that the queen was bringing with her to Scotland 'sorrow, dolour, darkness and impiety'.⁵ Only Mary herself seemed blithely unaware of these gloomy auguries, and determined to put on a smiling face come what might. Her natural buoyancy had helped to restore her spirits towards the end of the journey; now the prospect of meeting her subjects for what was in effect the first time on Scottish soil (discounting childhood memories when she had been queen in name only) presented her with the sort of challenge she especially appreciated – since all her life the sphere of personal encounter represented for her the most probable arena of victory. On Tuesday 19th August Mary Queen of Scots set foot once more on her native soil at the port of Leith, after an absence of just on thirteen years: her head was held high regardless of any melancholy portents.

Her arrival was unexpectedly early – at about nine o'clock in the morning – as favourable winds had also carried the royal party from France more swiftly than had been anticipated.

Nevertheless, by all accounts, her reception was enthusiastic and joyful, even if curiosity played at least as strong a part in it as loyalty. Since Holyrood Palace was not yet made ready for her arrival, the queen was taken first of all to the house of one Andrew Lamb at Leith; here she had a short rest and took her midday dinner, before being conveyed from Leith to Holyrood, on the outskirts of Edinburgh itself. She was conveyed on this short journey by a noble escort of Scottish lords including the earl of Argyll (one of the leading Protestant lords), the Lord Erskine and the Lord James, her half-brother. The memoirs of Lord Herries give further corroboration of the rejoicings which greeted her arrival, and even Knox admits that 'fires of joy' were lit at night.[6] The nobility might be bound in loyalty to greet their sovereign; they might be fired with the intention of creating a favourable first impression, which would lead to personal advancement later; but the common people were excited by the spectacle in front of their eyes – the 'beauty, youth and stately carriage' of their queen, Herries's phrase, despite the fact that Mary and her ladies were still in black or black-grey mourning for King Francis, who had been dead less than a year. Mary herself at the age of eighteen, tall, graceful, commanding, was everything in appearance that the popular imagination would have conjured up to fill the role of its newly arrived queen, if it had been allowed to choose.

Brantôme had an acid word to say about the cortège provided for the queen. He looked with contempt on the miserable Scottish horses which were brought to convey her from Leith to Holyrood, saying that these nags were a sorry comedown for a queen who had been used to the finest horses of France. But no doubt the sweet sound of popular acclaim in Mary's ears more than atoned for these deficiencies of transport; at all events she professed herself to be delighted with all she saw. What was more, Mary was able to express her pleasure to her subjects in their own language, for she had not lost her Scots despite the thirteen years spent in France. On her arrival in France as a child, she had indeed been able to speak nothing else, but she soon, by all accounts, learnt to speak French as well as a

Frenchwoman, and it was the language which she habitually wrote and presumably thought in. Nevertheless the presence of Scots attendants such as Lady Fleming, her nurse Jean Sinclair or even the Maries must have enabled Mary to practise her Scots: for in August 1560, when she gave Throckmorton an interview, he particularly stated that Mary spoke to him in Scots, and later the papal envoy related how the queen 'began to answer him in Scots',* which she preferred to use to Latin. Although Mary's Scots letters show that she never became fluent in the written language, Knox's history confirms the fact that she was able to converse freely and colloquially in Scots from the time of her first arrival in the country.[8]

At Holyrood Mary was installed in the magnificent towered and turreted palace which had been extended from an earlier tower in the reign of her father in the manner of the Scottish Renaissance; here not only the debt which the style owed to French architecture, as a whole, but also the fact that a number of French masons had been employed in the works, must have commended the whole building to critical French eyes. Lying on the outskirts of the city of Edinburgh, outside the actual town walls, Holyrood also enjoyed the amenities of wild country just beyond its very windows, as well as the convenience of having the capital city so close at hand – the ideal palace for a Stuart sovereign who could combine the pleasures of sport and politics to an ideal degree. The palace, then as now, was dominated by the bulk of Arthur's seat: as Fynes Morison described it at the end of the century, over Holyrood 'in a park of Hares, Conies and Deare, an high mountain hangs, called the chaire of Arthur'.[9] Joined to the palace was the abbey of

---

* In the sixteenth century the Scots language (as opposed to the Highland Gaelic, which Mary did not speak, since there was no way for her to have learnt it) was generally thought of as being about as different from English as two dialects of the same language: the difference was variously compared to that between Aragonese and Castilian, or the respective dialects spoken in Normandy and Picardy. As one authority puts it, 'any intercepted letter [in Scots] ... could be read by an educated Englishman'[7] (although today of course the transcription of documents in this language presents considerable difficulties). Mary only spoke English very limpingly before the period of her captivity, but was able to learn it quickly then.

Holyrood; both abbey and palace had been burnt by the English at the time of Hertford's invasion, seventeen years before, but had since been repaired.

Queen Mary now took possession of those royal apartments in the north-west corner of the palace which were to play such a significant role in her story. By the standards of Scotland of the day, they were extremely magnificent: there was a private chapel, and the ante-room had a fine heraldic painted ceiling, put up two or three years previously.[10] Security was, however, in no sense neglected at the expense of elegance: Holyrood in the time of Queen Mary was reached over an iron drawbridge, and the windows of the state rooms had iron gratings. Mary's first night at Holyrood was scarcely restful: although for once nobody seems to have thought of interpreting the disturbances as omens of what was to come. Having retired to sleep for the night, the queen was awoken by a night chorus of five or six hundred amateur musicians, playing what Brantôme feelingly described as wretched fiddles, and rebecs,* and singing psalms out of tune. The result was a series of appalling discords, which must have grated at least as much on the ears of the music-loving queen as they did on those of the outraged Brantôme. However, the next morning, Mary with her usual charm in such small matters, when she wished to please, assured the nocturnal serenaders that it had been a delightful experience, and even went so far, in the words of the critical Knox, as to 'will the same to be continued some nights after'.[12]

Despite all Mary's tact, despite her evident resolution to accept any manifestations of her subjects' strange national character with heroic enthusiasm, there is no doubt that the land of Scotland as Mary first saw it represented something very alien to the land in which she had been brought up. It was not that Scotland lacked links with France – indeed the two French marriages of James V and the subsequent French marriage of

---

* It is sometimes suggested that Mary's first night's sleep in Scotland was disturbed by the startlingly Scottish sound of the bagpipes. In fact a rebec is a stringed instrument played with a bow. The fault, if any, was in the unskilled nature of the playing, rather than the primitive character of the instrument.[11]

his daughter Mary could hardly have failed to forge such bonds: not only the French servitors of Queen Madeleine and Queen Mary of Guise, but also the French administrators introduced by the latter such as de Rubay, who acted as chancellor, de Bouton, governor of the Orkneys, de Villemore, and d'Oysel existed to prove it. Mary's own marriage, preceded by the two-way naturalization of Scots and Frenchmen in 1557, also meant that the titular ruler of Scotland lived in France, bringing a growing stream of Scots thither, on matters of administration or, as in the case of Bothwell, of petition.

While a great lord like Lord Seton emulated his master and made a French marriage to Marie Pieris, one of Mary of Guise's ladies-in-waiting, even before this outbreak of Franco-Scottish nuptials, there were links between the universities of Paris and Orléans and the Scots universities – a great prelate like Cardinal David Beaton had completed his education in Paris. The Scottish Reformation did not break these links but strengthened them since 'earnest and brotherly' relationships developed between the French scholars at universities and Scottish Protestant scholars: it was even thought worthwhile to publish the works of Sir David Lyndsay in France. The education of the sons of the leading Scots lords abroad was not an unheard-of phenomenon: the son of the Lord Lovat of the day slain at the Field of Shirts in 1544 was described as a 'well learned young gentleman, and brought up with great civility and knowledge in the realm of France'.[13] James Melville went to France with Mary Stuart at the age of fourteen to be educated as a page. Maitland of Lethington was educated abroad after the university of St Andrews. It is likely that Alexander Scott, the leading poet of the court of Queen Mary, went to Paris as a student of music.[14] Monks were often educated abroad or in turn came from abroad. The monastery of St James of the Scots at Ratisbon, said to be founded by Prince William of Scotland, brother of King Achaeus, adopted the lively John Leslie, bishop of Ross, as their patron in this period. Such centres provided a natural interchange of news and views between Scotland and the Continent.

In the same way, the trade of the east Scottish seaports with

France provided a more materialistic version of the interchange – as the merchants of the Scottish burghs exported linen and wool cloth, skins, and smoked and salted fish to France, in order to bring back such necessary luxuries as wine and salt. The courage of the average Scots as fighters gained them sufficient reputation abroad to make them in demand as fighters, demonstrated by the presence of the Scots archers and guards at the French court, even before the first marriage of James v. The Register of the Privy Seal shows that young Scotsmen went abroad for military service with enough regularity during this period to make it a definite feature of Scottish contemporary life. Leslie's comment on the whole subject in his *History* was that primogeniture often caused sons to seek their fortune out of Scotland – 'Of this comes, that so many of our countrymen, have such good success amongst strange Nations, some in the Wars, some in professing of Sciences, and some in merchandise'[15] – admirable enterprise which time has only confirmed as being an essential part of the Scottish character.

Unfortunately the adventurous success of the Scots abroad did not prevent them from being regarded by their European contemporaries as an extremely primitive, not to say uncouth, race when at home. An anonymous memoir on the state of Scotland, written by a Frenchman in 1558, the year of Mary's marriage, makes this point quite clear.[16] Scotland is described as a poor and infertile land, ill-disposed to strangers, and obsessed with family honour and family disputes. The Scottish manner of living is described as rustic, and the people themselves as '*assez fins, astutes et inconstans d'affection*'. Henri Estienne described the Scots as a simple people 'who consider themselves all to be cousins of the King'. André Thevet, almoner to Queen Catherine, painted a blacker picture: he described them as a lazy, proud, boastful people who, despite their poverty, were swollen with quite unjustifiable pride about their lineage.[17] When Riccio was stabbed to death by over fifty dagger-wounds, Castelnau de Mauvissière, who knew the Scots, commented that such ferocious behaviour was only to be expected from such a nation – he called it 'an extraordinary exhibition indeed, but one often enough to be seen among the Scots, when their spirits came under some sinister influence'.[18] A current French phrase *'poignarder a l'Écossais'* (stabbing through and through) carried the same connotation of violence. It has been pointed out already that the French took a patronizing view of the question of the government of Scotland, and believed that the Scots could only benefit from good sound French administration. Whatever her good intentions, Mary Stuart could not fail to be affected by the prevailing attitude of the land of her upbringing towards the land of her birth – one of condescension not unmixed with scorn.

How far was this picture of a savage primitive people justified, and how far did Scotland in the mid-sixteenth century merit the description *'lourde Écosse'*? The terrain itself must certainly have seemed somewhat dreary to one nurtured in the Loire valley of France, human beings perennially judging beauty by the standards they have known in childhood. Surprising as it may seem to later travellers, Scotland was on the whole a treeless country in the sixteenth century: the great forests of earlier times had disappeared save in the Highlands, and constant legislation on the subject shows that the need of planting trees was considered to be urgent. Although there were still extensive forests round Loch Ness and Loch Maree, the Lowland forests were more in the nature of groups of trees and clearings, and tracts of open country dotted with trees, used for hunting; in the meantime the government endeavoured to force smallholders to plant woods or orchards to cover three acres round their domiciles. Even so, when Sir Anthony Weldon visited Scotland with James VI in 1617, he wrote that Judas himself could not have found a tree on which to hang himself. Scotland was also dissected to a far greater extent than at the present day by endless and immense watery tracts in the shape of countless lochs and lochans, many of which have now disappeared – in Fife at this period there were for example twenty lochs or lochans as big as Lochleven.[19]

To add to this impression of bleakness, the climate was not only demonstrably colder, windier and wetter than that of France, for obvious reasons of latitude, but it also so happened that the period of Mary Stuart's personal rule in Scotland coincided with a marked change on the whole weather graph of Europe;* in Scotland this resulted in a series of exceptionally cold winters and stormy wet summers, and a sharp decline in the entire pattern of Scottish weather after 1560. The fact that 1563 and 1564 saw winters of outstanding severity with great loss of stock, 1565 an appalling harvest, and 1567 another unremittingly wet harvest time, can hardly have leavened the rigours of the Scottish climate to those unused to it. Even Bishop Leslie, in his account of the climate of Scotland, although he loyally denied that it was a cold place, admitted that 'the winds which are North, blow often very vehement swift and with a horrible sound'.[20]

There were of course tracts of Scotland which were exquisitely cultivated: Mary of Guise had admired Fife. Leslie and Buchanan both joined in giving the palm to Lothian, but in Tweeddale Leslie was dramatically excited by the numbers of sheep, and Lithgow described Clydesdale as the paradise of Scotland. However, even the fertile areas of the Merse and Teviotdale were possibly more wonderful to a native-born Scot than to one accustomed to the fertility of France, and since in any case many of the most theoretically cultivated areas in Scotland lay within the border area, where they might be devastated at any moment by English aggression, or straightforward free-booting, they did not always present the most luxuriant panorama of growth. Obvious symbols of civilization, such as fruit and flowers, were certainly in much shorter supply in Scotland than in France. Scottish villages and dwellings had always struck outside observers by their meanness: there were no enclosures, no fences or dykes or hedges, for the simple reason, as John Major explained, that the tenants had no permanent holdings, but hired or leased their land for four or five years, and thus

---

* The 'Little Ice Age' period of cold climate from 1550–1700 is now established by copious evidence from almost all parts of the northern hemisphere. See H. H. Lamb, *Trees and Climatic History in Scotland*, 1964. In human terms, the first years of the cold period must have been more onerous to endure than the last, when the cold weather was an established, if unpleasant, phenomenon.

had no motive to enclose their land.[21] Even the towns and burghs, whose political power was increasing, lacked stone walls to surround them, and life within them was still essentially medieval. Of the Scottish towns, although Edinburgh with its fair High Street extending the whole length of the town aroused universal admiration even amongst those who had travelled on the continent of Europe, few others could have compared with the French towns of Mary's youth. At the moment of her return, Scotland was in fact on the eve of a population explosion – by the end of the sixteenth century numbers had doubled. But in 1550 the population of Scotland was between five and six hundred thousand, a figure not much greater than it had been in the time before Robert the Bruce, since intervening wars had periodically decimated the nation. The population of France at the end of the 1570s, on the other hand, was between thirteen and fifteen million.[22]

Communications within Scotland were exceptionally difficult at this period: roads were poor and ill-maintained, as a result of which journeys were considered hazardous and amazing if they were completed without incident. Randolph wrote of his journey from Stirling to Inverness in 1562 – 'A terrible journey both for horse and man, the countries are so poor, the victuals so scarce.'[23] Norfolk complained of the 'deep and foul ways' even between Berwick and Leith, so that the artillery for the siege of Leith had to go by sea. Coaches were unknown until 1561, when the first one was introduced from France for the royal use. Bridges, like roads, were supposed to be kept up by the people nearest to them, but this was seldom done satisfactorily; ferries played an important part in the kingdom, but again ferrymen were notoriously knavish, as the frequent statutes against them showed. Communications were further threatened by the prevalence of vagabonds on land – whom statutes tried in vain to exterminate – and of pirates on the sea. There were plenty of taverns, but inns or hostels with quarters for travellers were almost unknown, as the nobles journeyed from their own houses to those of their kin, and there was therefore no call for them; a stranger was an object of wonder, if not actual animal hostility.

It was hardly surprising that the different sectors of a country so ill-served by its communications should be very cut off, one from the other. The border peoples, who were comparatively easy to reach, were extraordinarily difficult to subdue for any length of time; as Leslie said, their lives were torn between war and theft, and their own feuds were far more important to them than any dictates of the central government. The Highlands were considered virtually a separate area: John Major drew a stern distinction between the wild Scots of the north and east, and the 'householding Scots' of the Lowlands. Of the so-called wild Scots, half the population only spoke Gaelic, 'The language of savages' Ayala called it;[24] their main contact with the Lowlands was the moving down of cattle to Stirling and the Lowland cattle markets. The Western Isles were so distant that they could, when they chose, opt out of central politics altogether, in favour of local feuds, and play no part in Scottish national affairs. This occurred during the reign of Queen Mary; she never visited them at all personally, and there was no peer of Parliament at this period north of the earl of Argyll at Inveraray. In short, Scotland was a country still struggling painfully within the confines of a medieval framework: it had hardly begun to emerge from this restrictive cocoon at the date when Mary first arrived from France – a country in which, whatever its other faults of civil strife, this process at least was considerably more advanced.

Parallel with the primitive state of the countryside itself was the stratification of Scottish society in which notions of kinship were still held to be of paramount importance. It was the great lords, as the heads of clans or the tenants-in-chief of land, who received the true allegiance of the people who were their clansmen and their tenants based either on kinship or on formal bonds of 'manrent' made to them, which promised services in return for protection. These Scottish lords considered themselves to be virtually autonomous in their lands since the system of land tenure gave the crown practically no right to intervene between the tenant-in-chief and his inferiors. The growth of the lairds, who held their land directly from the monarch, was a political phenomenon whose importance was not apparent at the moment when Mary landed in Scotland. It was true that the lairds had demanded representation during the Reformation Parliament of 1560, having played a part in the revolution of 1559, but to the queen the nobles still appeared to block the way for any real contact between monarch and people. It was therefore with that complex but fascinating body, the Scottish nobility, that Mary had to deal if she was to deal with Scotland at all. And, in 1561, the great majority of their body were scarcely more advanced than the territories over which they held sway.

This is not to underestimate the power and splendour of the great magnates, who were just beginning to appreciate the value of display in a civilized society. Many of them had their own private *poursuivants*. In 1543 the then earl of Moray gave a banquet to the patriarch of Venice, at which he caused much fine crystal to be put on the table, as well as his silver. In order to make the point that Scotland was overflowing with such wares, at a given signal he had one of his servants tug the cloth, so that all the crystal fell to the ground and was smashed. As the patriarch was busy murmuring his regrets for this untoward occurrence, the earl casually had a further store of crystal brought in of still finer quality. The patriarch was duly impressed and exclaimed that he had seen nothing like it in Venice (where crystal was perhaps treated with greater consideration).[25] In 1529 John, 3rd earl of Atholl, a great feudal magnate with vast dominions, gave King James and the papal nuncio a magnificent entertainment in the shape of a hunt, at which the king was 'as well served and eased, with all things necessary to his Estate, as if he had been in his own palace in Edinburgh'; the earl had a special woodland palace constructed of green timber, the floor strewn with rushes and flowers, and the walls hung with tapestry and arrases of silk, with actual glass in the windows. The banquet held within this rustic folly, twenty miles from any dwelling (and which was destroyed when the banquet was finished, according to Highland custom), included ale, beer, wine, both white and claret, and *aqua vitae*, and for food, every kind of meat from beef, mutton and venison to swan and peacock, fish including

salmon, pike and eels, and even gingerbread. The whole entertainment was supposed to have cost Atholl £1000 a day, and
the nuncio summed up his reaction in outspoken terms: he
thought it a 'great marvel that such a thing could be in Scotland,
considering that it was named the arse of the world in other
countries'.[26]

Both these anecdotes tell us as much about the swaggering
character of the magnates concerned as they do about the state
of Scottish civilization. The list of the belongings of the earl of
Huntly, taken from the castle of Strathbogie after his defeat and
forfeiture in 1562, gives an interesting glimpse of the furnishings
and trappings to be found in the home of a great lord: the
forfeited goods included elaborate tapestries, beds covered with
velvet and hung with fringes of gold and silverwork, vessels of
gilded and coloured glass, and figures of animals.[27] The Regent
Châtelherault had his castle decorated with painted ceilings.
James Stewart, earl of Moray had an excellent library. The great
Lord Seton had gardens and orchards surrounding his castle
which the English vengefully sacked in their invasion of 1544;
he enjoyed the sport of horse-racing and, as recorded in the
annals of the burgh of Haddington, in May 1552 his horse won
a silver bell which he himself had presented. But as a class, the
magnates with their continental affiliations – men such as Lennox
and Glencairn who spoke French – must be distinguished from
the mass of the nobility, who were far from appreciating such
refinements. Leslie describes how nobles and commoners alike
wore the same clothes: the chiefs would dress themselves up
elegantly in grand clothes to go to court, and then change back
again. The horse was all-important in the need for show: 'If
therefore they have speedy horses, and wherewith they may
dress themselves and their wives,' wrote Leslie, 'they are not
mickle careful for the rest of their household gear.'[28]

The rough nature of the education which the preponderance
of them received may be judged from the fact that in 1559 it
was thought worth delivering considerations to Parliament that
the nobility should be better educated, so that the ruler should
not be forced to advance new men in their place. Lennox

apologized for his 'evil hand'; Huntly and Douglas were scarcely able to write, although they could do so in times of special crisis, for secrecy; Lady Huntly and Lady Erroll apparently wrote better than their husbands. The helpmeets of these men, as Ayala had noticed half a century earlier, were indeed a remarkable race and very often more estimable than their husbands, or perhaps the unbridled spirit is simply more attractive when manifested in the female than in the male sex. Ayala had called them 'really honest though very bold'.[29] The two Lady Huntlys, old and young, of this period, showed a mettle which outstripped their husbands. Despite the almost total lack of education granted to women – it was noteworthy that at the Reformation, nuns were almost illiterate, a much higher proportion than of the monks and friars – the wives of the Scottish nobility were from time to time capable of throwing up a figure of genuine intelligence and spirit, such as Jean, countess of Argyll, Jean Gordon, countess of Bothwell, or Agnes, countess of Moray, who put many of their male contemporaries in the shade.

The fortresses which these lords inhabited were in most cases as unpolished as their inmates. They were certainly very different from the fortresses of France to which Mary Stuart had been accustomed. Here she had known the magnificent newly constructed palaces of the French Renaissance, whose size alone dominated the eye. In Scotland she found a few royal palaces of only moderate size, by these standards, some few proper castles, and a plethora of strongholds, which were in effect only domesticated towers. These castles looked more like the elongated castle-houses in a German fairy-story than heavily castellated dwellings of Arthurian imagination. As for the squat tower dwellings, Lethington Tower, the home of Maitland (transformed by the work of later centuries into romantic Lennoxlove), provides an example of this sort of fortified pillar, with its heavily barred door on the ground floor, and nothing but slit windows as high as assailants could reach. When trouble came, women, children and cattle could be driven into the safety of this ground-floor chamber. Normally the house proper began on the upper floors; turrets and dormer windows, corbels and other decorative features could ornament these pillars, but basically they were merely intended for defence; and they represented an obviously stark way of life.

In every sense (except that of unity for a given cause) the Scottish nobility formed a tightly knit body, where feudal and family relationships were interwoven like the steps of a complicated Highland reel. Intermarriage was a feature of the situation, making it often as difficult for the historian to unravel their relationships and loyalties as it must have been for themselves. Patrick Hepburn, the fair earl of Bothwell, married Agnes Sinclair, whose mother Lady Sinclair was born a Hepburn. George, 5th earl of Huntly, married a Hamilton – Anne, daughter of the duke of Châtelherault; his sister Lady Jean Gordon was married to James, earl of Bothwell; his father the 4th earl was married to Elizabeth, sister of the Earl Marischal; the Regent Moray was married to Agnes, daughter of the same Earl Marischal; Patrick, Lord Lindsay of the Byres, was married to Euphemia Douglas, the Regent Moray's half-sister; Patrick, 3rd Lord Ruthven, was married first to Janet Douglas, natural daughter of the earl of Douglas, and second to Jane Stewart, daughter of the earl of Atholl, who had herself been married three times before. Apropos of another Ruthven–Atholl marriage, an English emissary wrote to Cecil in 1579, with a mystification which we may feel we share: 'The Earl of Atholl doth marry the Lord Ruthven's daughter. It is a question whether by that marriage the Lord Ruthven will draw the Earl to the devotion of Morton, or the Earl will draw the Lord Ruthven to his devotion, who is yet an enemy of Morton.'[30] Into this spider's web of relationships, it was especially hard for a foreign-bred queen to infiltrate, in order to command any sort of pre-eminent loyalty. At the same time Mary's Stewart blood meant that the nobles did not necessarily regard her, when it did not suit them, as more than *primus inter pares*.*

As a class the nobles had been decimated by Flodden in 1513,

---

* Sir James Fergusson has pointed out that the saying 'every Stewart's na sib to the king' gained its relevance from the fact that so many of them were.[31]

and again a generation later at Solway Moss and Pinkie Cleugh, in a manner reminiscent of the two generations of Europe depleted in the world wars of the first half of the twentieth century. The nobles with whom Mary had to deal had in many cases succeeded early to their estates, through the deaths of their fathers, and had grown up without the curb of parental discipline. Their broad lands were generally accompanied by a singular lack of cash, which left them a prey for the sort of venal considerations most prone to rob the character of any outstanding loyalties. Lack of money meant that morality was all too often a question of cash rewards, and not necessarily large ones. As de Silva wrote to Philip II, an expenditure of 8000 crowns brought Queen Elizabeth not only the good will but also secret information from the principal people of Scotland although many of them were Catholics.[32] In other ways than venality, the fibre of the nobles was undeniably coarse. Lyric poets such as Dunbar in an earlier period, and Fethy and Alexander Scott in a later one, spoke with clear and appealing voices where their private inspiration was concerned. Their poetry, closely mingled with the musical traditions of the time, was neither primitive nor cut off from other cultures, often showing direct connections with English courtly lyrics of earlier centuries. But in order to entertain the court in the age before Mary highly lewd verses like the 'Twa Mariit Wemen and the Wedo', containing sentiments of extreme crudity, were produced. In order to please the nobility, the poets had, in the words of C. S. Lewis, to 'lavish their skill on humours now confined to the preparatory school or the barrack-room'.[33] In this respect the court of the French Renaissance at which Mary had been reared cast at least a mantle of elegance over its corrupt morals.

The Scottish nobility included among its number many who were lawless and some who were violent. If the lawlessness merely reflected the general insecurity of an age of transition,*

* The Register of the Privy Council from the quantity of its enactments against violence, robbery, murder, etc. reveals the generally lawless state of Scotland in the 1550s, a legacy of the English invasions and the consequent breakdown of civil government.

this fact did not make it any more acceptable to their young ruler, or easier to deal with, to one hitherto cut off from such matters in France. As for the violence, there is a natural code of human decency which even insecurity does not excuse men from breaking, and this code was too often set aside by the Scottish nobility of this period, when it suited their convenience. Deeds of villainy were common. The nobles included in their ranks men like Patrick, Lord Lindsay of the Byres, ever prone to use physical assault as a weapon, whether storming the queen's chapel at Mass, or obtaining her signature to her abdication by threatening to cut her throat; or there were the two Lord Ruthvens of the age, one of whom was an alleged warlock, a macabre but bloodthirsty spectre at the feast of Riccio's death, and the other behaved with equal ruffianism towards Mary at Lochleven. The Regent Morton was a man of the most boorish calibre: the small greedy eyes in his florid face covered a cruel mind; his pudgy hands grasped avariciously all his life for what rewards and benefits were to be accrued; his slow speech concealed an unpleasant ability to revenge himself swiftly on those who had offended him. His atrocities in his time as regent included the hanging of women still holding their babies in their arms, and the driving of prisoners to the gallows like so many sheep, being pierced through by spears as they ran. Against such a background, the butchery of Riccio and the explosion at Kirk o'Field can easily be explained, if not condoned.

These lawless nobles were immensely preoccupied with superstition – not the complicated astrological arts of Catherine de Médicis, but the cruder form of witchcraft. Witchcraft first made its appearance in the Scottish criminal code in 1543 when the reformed religion aroused a passionate new desire for purity in such matters. Long before this date, witchcraft played its part in the fabric of Scottish society. There was also a persistent rumour about Bothwell and witchcraft, and he was often accused of having 'enchanted' Mary by her defenders. Janet Beaton, the lady of Buccleuch, and an ex-mistress of Bothwell, was also accused in placards in the streets of having used witchcraft to 'breed Bothwell's greatness with the Queen'. Margaret Lady Atholl was thought to have the power of casting spells, having diligently studied the subject with a magician, and it was she who was rumoured to have cast Queen Mary's pains of childbirth on Lady Reres. One ballad, 'Northumberland betrayed by Douglas', describing the incident when Sir William Douglas handed over the fugitive Northumberland to the English in 1570, even gives the regent Moray's mother, Lady Margaret Douglas,* as a witch.

But the main characteristic of the nobles, which applied to the greater magnates as to the lesser, was that they had absolutely no sense of the grand design. It was true that a revolution in religion had been accomplished beneath their gaze, in which many of them joined, but here the laurels for purity of spirit and intensity of theological vision seem to belong mainly to a lower social class than theirs. Even the cause of Protestantism did not bind together those Scottish nobles who were divided by the potent interests of family ambition. The Scottish nobles were given over to 'particularity' as every commentator at every level in this period pointed out:

> Neither for king, nor queen's authority
> They strive, but for particularity.

This is how Sir Richard Maitland, father of the politician Maitland, made the point in a bitter verse, written during the civil wars of the 1570s.

When Fontenay went to investigate Scotland in 1584 on Mary's behalf, he commented that money and family ambition were the only two things the Scottish nobles really understood; in his view, it was mere folly and a waste of time to preach to them their duty towards princes, the honour to be found in just

---

* Child, in his edition of Scottish ballads, thinks that this slur on the regent's mother is unjustified, and that she had been confused with that Lady Janet Douglas, sister of the earl of Angus and wife of Lord Glamis, who was burnt in 1537 on Castle Hill, for meditating the death of James v by witchcraft.[34]

and virtuous actions, and the desirability of leaving a memorial to posterity in the shape of good deeds done – when the only two things capable of charming the nobility with any degree of permanency were '*de biens et de grandeur*'. He felt that it was the misfortune of Scotland that the majority of the lords were incapable of taking anything approaching the long or altruistic view of any situation – they had, in his view, no wish to extend their view further than the end of their own toes, cast not the faintest thought over the past, and still less towards the future.[35]

Twenty years earlier, it is difficult to avoid the impression that the same combination of goods and grandeur was already what appealed irresistibly to the Scottish lords. They were a difficult, intractable, and above all highly unstable class to deal with, since it was impossible to anticipate with any certainty in which direction the weathercock of their purposes would blow from one minute to the next. They presented an especial problem to a young queen, brought up in a foreign country, and lacking the knowledge and intuition of how to deal with such men, which might have been inculcated naturally in childhood had she been brought up in Scotland. After all, Argyll, Glencairn and Cassillis were so very unlike Montmorency, Condé and the king of Navarre, although the former might be said to have occupied roughly in Scotland the position which the latter filled in France – a point made by the French memoir of 1558 which directly compared them.[36] Let us not paint the picture of the Scottish nobility too blackly at the cost of whitening the aristocracies of other countries. Ambition and intrigue were certainly not the monopoly of the Scottish nobility in sixteenth-century Europe. England had her Seymours, and France, as we have seen, her Guises. In so far as ambition could be held to constitute a vice, the cardinal of Lorraine and the earl of Morton, in both of whom its fires burnt brightly, would be judged equally for it, before the last Judgement Seat of heaven. Mary Stuart, on the other hand, was not gifted with such divine enlightenment. To her, accustomed to the cardinal with his eloquence, his literary tastes, his designs by Primaticcio, men of the type of Morton, 'unlettered and unskilful' in Maitland's phrase, presented a very different aspect. She could not fail to find them secretly distasteful as well as baffling because they were so unfamiliar. The Scottish nobles may not have been impossible by some absolute standard taking into account all the factors involved, but they were certainly fatally different to the nobles amongst whom Mary had been brought up.

CHAPTER NINE

Conciliation and Reconciliation

Let all thy realm be now in readiness
With costly clothing to decoir thy court.
Alexander Scott: 'A New Year Gift to the Queen Mary,
when she first came home', 1562

Exactly how different her new kingdom was from her old one, the young queen was speedily to discover on her very first Sabbath in Scotland. Up till that morning there had been, in Knox's phrase, nothing but 'mirth and quietness', but on the Sunday Mary, who had been assured by Lord James of the private practice of her religion, ordered Mass to be said in the chapel royal at Holyrood.* The preparations for the service were all too familiar to a country which had only been officially Protestant for one year. The onlookers exclaimed furiously: 'Shall the idol be suffered again to take place within this realm?' and speedily resolved: 'It shall not!' Patrick Lindsay, the future Lord Lindsay of the Byres, went so far as to shout out in the courtyard that the idolatrous priest should be put to death. The servant carrying the altar candles was put into a state of terror when his candles were seized by one of the crowd, and together with some of the altar ornaments, either broken or trodden into the mud. The reformers did not actually penetrate

---

* The chapel in which Mary had her Mass said was the private chapel royal, to be distinguished from the church attached to the abbey of Holyrood; this became known as the chapel royal in the reign of Charles II, but at this date was used as the parish church of the Canongate.

the chapel itself; here at the very threshold they found the person of the Lord James, barring their entry: not only had he given his word to Mary that the private Mass should be respected, but he also had a devout horror of such extremism. Inside the chapel the queen, her Guise uncles and her French servants attended a Mass which was understandably fraught with tension – the English ambassador reported that the priest was in such a state of mortal fear that he could hardly lift the Host at the Elevation.[1]

If the queen received a rude shock from the incident, she did not allow it to affect her determinedly tolerant religious policy. The next day, Monday 25th August, she issued a proclamation in which she announced that she intended with the aid of her Estates to take a final order, which she hoped would please everyone, to pacify the differences in religion. In the meantime, she charged the whole world, in order to prevent tumult or sedition, to make no alteration or innovation in the state of religion, or to attempt anything against the form of public worship which she had found standing on her arrival in Scotland – under pain of death. She further commanded that no one should molest any of her domestic servants or those who had come with her out of France in the practice of their religion – equally under pain of death.

This proclamation may seem to us, from a modern standpoint, comparatively wise, and certainly singularly free from Catholic bigotry. It aroused, however, the venomous ire of many of the extremist Protestants, and especially that of their leading evangelist, John Knox. The next Sunday Knox took the opportunity of preaching a great denunciation of the Mass from the pulpit: one Mass, he declaimed, was more fearful to him than ten thousand armed enemies being landed in any part of the realm. While still in France, Mary had already formed the most unfavourable impression of Knox, and she told Throckmorton that she believed him to be the most dangerous man in her kingdom. Now she determined to grasp the nettle. She sent for Knox to come to Holyrood, and here took place the first of those dramatic interviews, which as recounted by Knox himself in his *History* have a positively Biblical flavour.

Knox was now a man of forty-seven. Having been rescued from 'the puddle of papistry', as he put it,[2] by George Wishart in the 1540s, he had joined the murderers of Cardinal Beaton in the castle of St Andrews, and after its fall, had done a spell in the galleys. On release he went to England, and from there, on the accession of Mary Tudor, to the Continent where his travels brought him finally to Geneva, where he became a disciple of Calvin. He returned temporarily to Scotland in 1555: the strength of his character and the force of his convictions enabled him to win over many of the greater men to Protestantism by his evangelism when the lesser men had long been interested in it. His main contribution to the Scottish Reformation had thus been made before Mary Stuart's arrival in Scotland, and indeed before the death of Mary of Guise, but his personality ensured that he remained a potent force on the Scottish scene, and it was an unlucky hazard for Mary Stuart that he happened to be living in Edinburgh, the first year of her residence there, to act as a demoniac chorus for all her actions, which good or bad, he presented in the most malevolent light.

Knox's character was compounded of many contradictions. He saw himself as a heaven-sent preacher, whereas in fact he was a bold earthly revolutionary who openly preached violence and notoriously considered the death of an unjust ruler absolutely justified. He was a good summarizer of the accepted truth; but he was a savage hater, and obstinate defender of a position once he had adopted it. Lord Eustace Percy in his life of Knox made a sympathetic examination of the reformer's true nature and decided that his real spiritual bent was that of the mystic who was compelled by events to adopt the role of preacher and interpreter: 'In the whole sweep of the Old Testament and the New, what first caught his ear was a voice which almost passes the range of human hearing: neither the words of God to man, nor the words of man to God, but a fragment of the huge soliloquy of God himself.'[3] Knox was an egoist, but his egoism led him to be a cunning politician and excellent lawyer, with an eye to the essentials in any argument. He was not born to the nobility, yet he was immensely brave in his confrontations with the nobles and the queen: as Morton said at his tomb, 'Here lies one who never feared the face of man.' His virtues included a ferocious, rather coarse sense of humour, seen in his writings, very different from Mary's own light ironic sense of humour, it is true, but something which might have enabled them to strike better accord if circumstances had been different; he was also genuinely patriotic when few men even knew the meaning of the word. Above all, he loved to dominate, as with so many egoists, and it was this need for domination which doomed his relations with Mary from the start. Scotland, and especially Edinburgh, was his stage: he the great preacher, the victor of the Scottish Reformation, was not going to surrender the front of the stage to the young queen, newly come from France. In his imagination he saw even his first encounter with her as a battle, from which he must emerge victorious if the whole Scottish Reformation was not to be imperilled. Knox thus braced himself for the meeting, like an ancient Catholic saint about to wrestle with the devil, not a mature Protestant politician about to meet a young girl who had so far shown herself to be remarkably tolerant in both word and deed. In short, Knox, in his preconceived notions about Mary, was quite as determinedly misguided, if not in such a romantic spirit, as many of her partisans have been since.

Mary's very sex was against her in Knox's opinion: whereas in the sixteenth century it was theoretically considered to be against the natural law for women to rule men, nevertheless most people were content to regard an actual woman ruler as a necessary evil which might have to be endured from time to time. Knox, however, went much further than his contemporaries and in his *First Blast of the Trumpet against the Monstrous Regiment of Women*, published in 1558 against Mary Tudor, declared roundly that to promote any woman – those 'weak, frail, impatient feeble and foolish creatures' – to any form of rule was the 'subversion of good order, of all equity and justice', as well as being contrary to God and repugnant to nature.[4] Now on 4th September he was confronted in a personal interview with one of these feeble and foolish creatures sitting on the throne of his own country of Scotland.

Lord James was also present at the interview, but tactfully stayed in the background. Mary began by attacking Knox for raising her subjects against her mother and herself, and also for writing *The Monstrous Regiment*. Knox conceded the point about her sex, and said that if she behaved well, and the realm was not brought to disaster by her femininity, he personally would not disallow her rule, on those grounds alone. When Mary struggled with him over the religious issue, however, she found him much less accommodating. Finally Knox agreed to tolerate her for the time being – his phrase, which owed little to courtly flattery, was 'to be as well content to live under your Grace as Paul was to live under Nero' – provided that she did not defile her hands by dipping them in the blood of the saints of God. But he still firmly asserted the rights of the subject to rise up against the unworthy ruler, who opposed God's word. Mary was quite clever enough to see the dangers in this, and quite bold enough to say so: 'Well then,' she exclaimed, 'I perceive that my subjects shall obey you, and not me; and shall do what they list and not what I command; and so must I be subject to them and not they to me.' When Knox replied that this subjection to God, as represented by his Church, would carry her to everlasting glory, Mary pointed out: 'Yea ... but ye are not the Kirk that I will nurse. I will defend the Kirk of Rome, for, I think, it is the true Kirk of God.' But Knox refused to admit Mary's ability to judge on such matters: 'Conscience requireth knowledge,' he said, 'and I fear right knowledge ye have none.' Mary said quickly: 'But I have both heard and read.'[5]

The result of this interview was an *impasse* in terms of human relations. Knox has been accused of speaking churlishly to the queen: he certainly spoke to her in a manner to which she was scarcely accustomed from her life in France, but she on the other hand seems to have been stimulated rather than otherwise by his abruptness. It is true that she relapsed into tears at one moment, but Randolph thought they were tears of anger rather than grief. All her life Mary Stuart had a feminine ability to give herself suddenly up to tears when her sensibilities were affronted; she seems to have used it as a useful method of relieving her feelings; it never prevented her actions from being extremely hard-headed once she had recovered her composure. Knox himself quickly realized that Mary was far from being a feeble puppet, which her career in France might have led him to expect. He told his friends: 'If there be not in her a proud mind, a crafty wit and an indurate heart against God and his truth, my judgement faileth me.' In the same vein, he reported to Cecil in London that on communication with her he had spied such craft as he had not found in such an age.[6]

Mary was still being so enthusiastically greeted by her subjects that an incident in the chapel royal, a rude sermon from Knox, and one brusque interview were not enough to damp her spirits. She had been received with elaborate rejoicings on her ceremonial entry into Edinburgh: here were to be seen fifty townsmen dressed up as moors, in yellow taffeta costumes, their arms and legs blackened, and black visors on their faces, and on a stage at the Tolbooth four fair virgins representing the virtues, while at the Cross, there were four more virgins in 'most heavenly clothing', and from the spouts of the Cross wine poured forth abundantly. Some of the sights had undercurrents of Protestantism – a child who appeared at the Butter Tron, descending out of a painted cloud from a temporary wooden gateway, presented her pointedly with a Bible and a Psalter, and when she reached Holyrood once more, another child made a speech suggesting she should put away the Mass. But a scheme for burning an effigy of a priest saying Mass had been abandoned at the instance of the Catholic Huntly in favour of merely burning effigies of Coron, Nathan and Abiron, the sons of Izhar and Eliab, to represent the evil of false sacrifices – a message which it was a great deal easier for the queen politely to ignore. Indeed Knox thought the welcome given to Queen Mary so irritatingly lavish, that he remarked indignantly that in their farces, masks and other prodigalities 'fain would the fools have counterfeited France'.[7]

After three weeks at Holyrood, Mary set out for a short progress round her kingdom: here again she was met with the same combination of enthusiasm, marred by occasional incidents where the truth of the Protestant religion was suddenly felt to need public demonstration. She went first to Linlithgow, the palace of her birth, and after two days on to Stirling. Here she was endangered by human rather than the divine fire with which Knox had threatened her: a candle accidentally set light to her bed curtains while she was asleep. Although the fire was quickly put out, Randolph took the opportunity to record an old prophecy that a queen should be burnt alive in Stirling, which, he said, apparently with some regret, had proved just about as successful as Lady Huntly's prophecy that Mary would never reach Scotland.[8] On Sunday there was some sort of incident when her chaplains tried to sing High Mass in the chapel royal, and it was said that the earl of Argyll, a leading Protestant, and Lord James disturbed them; after a fracas some of the priests and clerks left their places with bloody heads and broken ears but the most part of the congregation seem to have taken the incident calmly. At Perth, although the pageants once more had a sternly anti-Catholic slant, the queen herself was greeted extremely honourably, and presented with a golden heart, filled with more pieces of gold.

Despite Mary's determined optimism, and gracious behaviour towards her subjects, whatever their religious opinions, the events of her journey, her arrival and her reception had clearly subjected her to considerable strain. Now that strain inevitably began to tell on her health. The Diurnal of Occurrents relates that in the streets of Perth she fell sick and was carried from her horse into a lodging not far off, with the sort of nervous collapse 'she is often troubled with, after any great unkindness of grief of mind'.[9] However, as always, she was quick to recover, and at Dundee was once more greeted enthusiastically and given a princely reception. At St Andrews on Sunday 21st September there may have been a religious squabble of some sort, since a rumour reached Randolph in Edinburgh that a priest had been slain. Certainly at some point in the journey Lord James and Huntly had a violent quarrel about Mass, when the Catholic Huntly said that if the queen commanded it, he would set up the Mass in three shires. But the point was that the queen did not command it: instead she merely continued on her way for a quick visit to Falkland Palace, and so back to Holyrood, where she was once more safely installed on 29th September.

Knox reported that Mary remained steadfast in her 'devilish opinions' at the end of her journey, despite the evidence she had received that most people found them repugnant; but he had, in his prejudiced attitude to the queen, missed the point about her attitude to the reformed religion. It was not a question of her private beliefs, which were, as she herself had told Throckmorton a few months previously, steadfastly Catholic. It was a question of the administration and good government of Scotland. Here the sights she saw during her progress can only have confirmed her in the conviction which she had already expressed in her proclamation of 25th August – that it was in the best interests of peace and stability in Scotland that the Protestant *status quo* should be preserved, so long as she herself could worship in private in the way she pleased. When she first arrived, Mary found herself in a curious situation administratively speaking apropos the structure of the Protestant Church. In the years leading up to the Reformation, the power of the Scottish crown over its native Church had increased with every decade, as royal control close at hand gradually replaced that of the far-off papacy. In 1535, the Pope conceded the right of King James not only to recommend to but also to nominate to vacant prelacies. Since the income from benefices could now be granted if the king so wished to others than its spiritual incumbent, the whole system developed into a useful method of royal patronage. The process expanded so rapidly that by 1560, in the words of Professor Donaldson, 'There was no financial temptation for the Scottish crown to proceed to a formal breach with Rome because it was already exploiting the Church's wealth with sufficient success'.[10]

But this exploitation of the Church by the monarchy was not brought to an end when the religion of Scotland was officially changed by edict of Parliament in August 1560. This edict was never confirmed by the sovereign, which made it technically illegal. But in any case no provision was made at the time for linking the new religion to the old ecclesiastical régime. By 1561 no financial arrangements had been made for the new ministers. Queen Mary was as free as her predecessors to proceed with the presentation of livings and benefices: there was absolutely no incumbency upon her to present them to the ministers of the reformed Church.* Thus the Scottish crown in the 1560s, freed by the Reformation from the last vestige of papal control, had enormous potential powers of patronage within its grasp. There was an excellent opportunity in this respect for a competent sovereign, well advised, to increase his own strength, since circumstances had conspired to play into the hands of the crown. This applied to a Catholic sovereign as much as to a Protestant one – so long as the Catholic sovereign showed no signs of wishing to restore the Catholic religion to the country. Catholicism as a spiritual force had temporarily retreated into the mists by the time Mary reached the shores of Scotland. One of the factors in this retreat was the remarkable lack of Catholic leadership at the time, which meant that too little was done to rally the Catholics at the moments of crisis. Archbishop James Beaton, for example, who might have constituted a Catholic leader, went to France in 1560 and never returned. Huntly was markedly unreliable as events were to prove. The Protestants, on the other hand, felt a crusading spirit concerning their newly achieved Reformation. When Alexander Scott presented to Mary his 'New Year Gift' of a long poem at the beginning of 1562, his courtly connections encouraged him to address dulcet phrases towards his young queen:

---

* There is hardly a single example of a minister being appointed to a benefice before the autumn of 1566.

> Let all thy realm be now in readiness
> With costly clothing to decoir thy court.

These same connections did not prevent him warning Mary
solemnly that papist idolatry had been newly engraved in certain
hearts as a result of her arrival – a development which was to
be thoroughly deplored. Yet all the evidence shows that Mary
herself was perfectly content to accept the facts of the situation,
and had no wish to engrave idolatry anew on any heart, so long
as that heart beat loyally towards its sovereign. Very far from
being set on re-establishing the Catholic religion in Scotland,
she seems to have seen herself as the powerful Catholic sovereign
who rules at peace her Protestant people.

In the meantime she was also able to benefit from the breach
between Knox and the less extreme members of the reformed
Church, those for example who strongly doubted whether it
was lawful to resist an ungodly prince as Knox suggested. Knox,
strident as his voice might be, did not by any means speak for
all members of the reformed religion. As Knox himself angrily
reported, the Protestant lords were apt to be seduced from
extremism by contact with the gentle and civilizing influence of
the court.[11] When the town council of Edinburgh issued an
insulting proclamation on 2nd October, putting Catholic priests
in the same category as prostitutes and whoremongers, Mary
managed to get the proclamation suppressed and the council
deprived of its privileges, with the full co-operation of both
Maitland and Lord James, whom indeed Knox furiously blamed
for the whole episode. Then when Queen Mary had a sung
Mass in her private chapel on All Hallows Day (1st November),
it was finally decided after a conference among the Protestant
leaders that the queen should be able to behave as she wished
with her household in private. But the actual singing of the
Mass caused considerable commotion.

The English ambassador Randolph not only paid tribute to
Mary's cleverness throughout her first autumn in Scotland, but
indicated that those who had imagined Mary was without wisdom
were liable to be surprised, since he himself had detected in her

the fruit of the 'best-practised' cunning of France combined with the subtle brains of Scotland.[12] Part of this cleverness on the part of the young queen was to take the financial situation of the ministers of the new Church sufficiently seriously to make provision for them: in February 1562 it was decided that the monetary situation of these ministers was sufficiently desperate for it to be necessary for the crown to take some action. It was therefore decided that while two thirds of the revenues of the benefices were to remain with the existing holders for their lifetimes (probably neither ecclesiastics nor members of the reformed Church), the other third was to be collected by the government, and divided between it and the reformed Church. It was a perfectly acceptable compromise, which showed once again that Mary drew a sharp distinction between the private Mass in her chapel and the public weal in Scotland; and it also helped on the interests of the crown.

As the editor of the Register of the Privy Council at this period has observed, one looks in vain through its pages for any evidence that Mary was a rabid Catholic intent on establishing her own religion in Scotland, and intent on destroying the reformed religion which had replaced it.[13] Both Melville and Castelnau confirm Randolph's opinion that on her first arrival in Scotland Mary's behaviour was designedly accommodating and tactful, never more so than on the subject of religion, as a result of which she was rewarded with considerable personal popularity. Melville wrote that she conducted herself 'so princely, so honourably and so discreetly, that her reputation spread in all countries'; Castelnau indicated that the Scots were delighted with their beautiful young queen and, thanks to her efforts to make herself agreeable to them, they counted themselves lucky to be ruled by one of the most perfect princesses of her time.[14] The Pope wrote to Mary anxiously in December, suggesting that on the subject of Scottish Catholicism she should take Queen Mary Tudor as her model, who 'surely did not defend the cause of God timidly',[15] but Mary Stuart was very far from adopting the methods of her Catholic cousin in England. Her energies at this point were absorbed in an infinitely more worldly design – to get herself recognized by Queen Elizabeth as her legitimate successor to the English throne – and in this plan fervently expressed Catholicism could only work to her disadvantage.

The conciliation of her Scottish subjects was only one half of Mary's plan: reconciliation with Elizabeth was the other. Once she was assured that Elizabeth had actually dispatched the safe-conduct – it arrived back in Scotland four days after she landed – Mary's mood towards her cousin was as purposely friendly as her mood towards the Scots had been. Only thirteen days after her arrival, she commissioned Maitland to go to England and try to treat with the English queen on the subject of the succession; Maitland duly set off in September. William Maitland was the obvious choice for the mission. He had been Mary of Guise's envoy to London in February 1558, and to Paris in March 1559, and envoy for the Protestants to London again in 1560: he was thus by far the most experienced diplomatist out of the rather limited selection offered by the Scottish nobility. Maitland can fairly claim to be the most interesting character in Scotland in the time of Queen Mary because he represented a type of new man: aged thirty-three when Mary arrived, roughly the same age as Lord James, and fifteen years older than the queen herself, he had been converted to Protestantism by Knox in 1555. But it was politics not religion which interested him. His grandmother had been a Seton, and his grandfather died at Flodden, but he himself, one of the seven children of Sir Richard Maitland, belonged to the new highly political class of lairds surrounding the capital, who had been considerably affected by the English occupation of Haddington in the late 1540s. Maitland had been Secretary of State to Mary of Guise, but did not allow this fact to prevent him from joining the Protestant insurgents under Châtelherault in the autumn of 1559.

His father, himself in public service of one sort and another for over sixty years, gave Maitland some Polonius-like advice at the beginning of his career, *Counsel to my son being in the court*, in which he admonished him to be neither a flatterer nor a scorner, to remember the instability of fortune even in the highest position of government, and in short not to be over-confident in a world as changeable as the moon or the sea. But as it turned out, Maitland was not the sort of character to be easily caught in a fixed position, while the moon and the sea changed round him. His very political abilities led him to exercise a certain pragmatism – did not Buchanan term him the Chameleon? – and his relations with Mary of Guise had already shown that, like a modern civil servant, he did not feel bound to go down with the minister. Yet Maitland was regarded by his contemporaries as having a finesse lacking in others, and an ability which made him 'subtle to draw out the secrets of every man's minds'.[16] as Buchanan put it. He was excellently educated and his correspondence is garnished with classical allusions and wit. In other ways, in his lack of ascetic fervour and his emphasis on the practical in politics, Maitland's spirit matched Mary's own. He was even supposed to have carried his cynicism as far as to observe that 'God is a bogle of the nursery'.* In theory at least, he was the ideal adviser for Mary out of the limited selection available in Scotland, and he was certainly the ideal envoy to send to London.

Maitland's interview with Elizabeth took place in London, in the presence of both Cecil, Elizabeth's adviser, and Dudley, her favourite. The Scottish point of view on the subject of the succession had already been put to Elizabeth in a humble letter from Lord James, before Mary even arrived in Scotland. Ratification of the Treaty of Edinburgh was to be given in exchange for Elizabeth's acknowledgement that Mary stood next in line to the throne, after herself and her lawful issue. Maitland pointed out on behalf of Mary that this meant that she could not ratify the Treaty of Edinburgh as it now stood, because the terms of the Treaty called on Mary to surrender not only her present claim to the English throne, but also all further claims after the death of Elizabeth and her problematic offspring. In

* His biographer Sir John Skelton could, however, find no contemporary sources for this saying.[17]

reply, Elizabeth showed herself nothing if not friendly towards the queen of Scots; although her first impulse was to concentrate on the vexed subject of the treaty ('I looked for another message from the Queen your sovereign'), once she realized that the Scots lords, as well as Mary, were in earnest on the subject of succession, she gave herself over to a frank discussion of the whole question.

In the course of this, Elizabeth even went so far as to vouchsafe the information that she herself preferred Mary to all her rivals: she knew of no better right than Mary's, and no one who was strong enough to keep Mary from the throne. At the same time she positively declined to give Mary the acknowledgement she desired. The reason she gave was the impossible burden which it would lay on her own relations with Mary. 'The desire is without example,' said Elizabeth, 'to require me in mine own life, to set my winding sheet before my eyes. Think you that I could love my own winding sheet? Princes cannot like their own children, those that should succeed unto them ... How then shall I, think you, like my cousin, being declared my Heir Apparent?' She also put forward a more practical, less personal reason of her own safety: 'I know the inconstancy of the people of England, how they ever mislike the present government and have their eyes fixed upon that person that is next to succeed.' And she quoted in Latin: 'They are more prone to worship the rising than the setting sun.' Elizabeth went on to describe her own experiences as a focus of opposition during the reign of Mary Tudor. With these personal revelations, and an unresolved situation, Maitland had to be content. However, Elizabeth made one concession in that she agreed to accept a certain modification of the treaty, so that Mary should not have to sign away her claim, beyond the period of Elizabeth's life and that of her lawful offspring. Elizabeth also suggested that Maitland and Cecil should correspond privately on the subject, although under the supervision of the two queens; the situation, if fluid, seemed also full of promise. In this auspicious atmosphere Maitland returned to Scotland at the end of September.

The truth was that Elizabeth was in a more complicated

situation apropros her successor than might appear from a first glance at the Tudor family tree. Mary Stuart, the obvious successor, had as we have seen been theoretically debarred by the will of Henry VIII, which precluded foreigners from succeeding. Maitland, in the course of his mission, did not enter into controversy concerning the will of Henry VIII, but merely made the point that Henry VII, in wedding Margaret Tudor to James IV, had not intended to deny her the succession; Elizabeth herself, by saying that she knew of no better right than Mary's, showed that she was not allowing her father's will to enter her calculations. But in 1561 Mary was extremely unpopular in England, being considered virtually a Frenchwoman and a Guise, as well as a Catholic, and she was especially disliked by the English Parliament, which was strongly Puritan in tone; Elizabeth, in her personal favour towards Mary, was certainly in contradiction to the majority of her subjects at this period. There were other claimants, whom the English as a body might be thought to prefer: Margaret, countess of Lennox, mother of Darnley, was a granddaughter of Henry VII; although her claim was inferior to Mary's as she descended from Margaret Tudor's second marriage, yet she was an English subject, which gave her an advantage in some English eyes. On the other hand her legitimacy could be questioned, since her father Archibald Angus had divorced her mother on grounds of precontract. Then there was the twenty-five-year-old Henry Hastings, earl of Huntingdon, who descended from the countess of Salisbury, niece of Edward IV, and last representative of the Plantagenets. His strength was in his sex – in 1560 the Spanish ambassador de Quadra reported, 'the cry is that they do not want any women rulers'.[18] He was also Dudley's brother-in-law, he was a Protestant, and was lieutenant for Leicestershire where he had strong connections.

By far the most serious counter-claimant was Lady Catherine Grey, the twenty-three-year-old sister of the ill-fated Lady Jane Grey. Catherine Grey, like Mary Stuart, was a great-grand-daughter of Henry VII, but she descended from his young daughter Mary Tudor who had married the Duke of Suffolk. By 1561 Lady Catherine had already led a checkered matrimonial career, by which she had incurred the spiteful enmity and personal dislike of Queen Elizabeth. Her first marriage to Lord Pembroke's son was dissolved. She then secretly married Lord Hertford in late 1560, but without the queen's permission, which had been made necessary by an act of 1536. In the summer of 1561, her obvious pregnancy forced her to admit to the marriage, as a result of which both she and Hertford were clapped in the Tower. On 24th September, at roughly the same moment as Maitland's mission to Elizabeth on behalf of Mary, she gave birth to a son, Edward Seymour. This piece of unwelcome parturition roused Elizabeth to a pitch of vindictive fury. She referred to the unpleasant subject bitterly to Maitland when she alluded to those who, by showing themselves not to be barren, had declared to the world that they were more worthy of the throne than herself or Mary. Elizabeth had both mother and father cross-examined, and as they could provide no witnesses of their wedding or find the priest involved, the marriage was finally declared invalid in May 1562. Despite this stern lesson in the unwisdom of illicit romance, the unhappy Lady Catherine managed to have sufficient contact with her husband within the confines of the Tower to give birth to a second son Thomas in February 1563. By the finding of Elizabeth's commission, both these sons were of course illegitimate, somewhat reducing Lady Catherine's desirability as a candidate for the throne.

Nevertheless in the 1560s it was Lady Catherine who was regarded as the most likely successor to Elizabeth by the English Parliament, on the grounds that she was Protestant and she was English. So strong were her claims thought to be that Philip II of Spain is even supposed to have worked out a scheme by which he would have abducted her, in 1560, and married her off to that famous putative bridegroom Don Carlos, in order to establish her immediately on the throne of England, on the grounds that she was legitimate, and Elizabeth was not.[19] However, when Lady Catherine was revealed to be a Protestant, Philip lost interest in her. Mary Stuart on the other hand was the subject of various English attacks at this period. 'Garboduc' attacked her right to succeed as an alien; in the Parliament of

January 1563 Sadler made a speech against Mary the foreigner succeeding to the throne: 'Our common people and the very stones in the streets should rebel against it.' In October 1562, when Elizabeth was gravely ill with smallpox, de Quadra reported that there was absolutely no certainty about the succession, the Protestants being divided between Catherine Grey and Huntingdon, and the Catholics between Mary and Margaret Lennox. Under the circumstances it is easy to understand why Mary believed that the personal favour of Elizabeth constituted her best hope of being recognized. Mary believed that Elizabeth could and would override the will of Henry VIII. Elizabeth's dislike of Catherine was blighting her chances. Elizabeth's love of Mary – if it was sufficiently stimulated – might be the making of her fortunes. Throughout the autumn and spring, Mary devoted all her efforts to bringing about the personal meeting between the two queens, by which she felt certain she could win the all-important affections of Elizabeth.

Mary was not deluding herself on the subject. In the opinion of one of Elizabeth's modern biographers, Sir John Neale, 'There is no resisting the conclusion that Elizabeth was prepared virtually to assure Mary of the succession, assure her of it on conditions that are easy to guess: no league with France, friendship with England, an acceptable marriage, and probably ultimate conversion to Protestantism.'[20] The first three of these conditions would not have been difficult to fulfil for a Mary so set on being acknowledged as heiress, and the last one lay only in the sphere of possibilities. The important point, which Mary had ably grasped, was that she herself should inspire Elizabeth with confidence, so that she would be armoured by Elizabeth's favour against the hostility of the English Parliament, and presumably many of the English Protestants. By far the best way of inspiring this confidence was to meet the English queen face to face: had she not won the golden opinions of Throckmorton? Surely it would be no more difficult to win the affections of Elizabeth, with whom she had in common not only their cousinly relationship, but also the mutual problems of government in the hands of the weaker sex. As she had told

Bedford, when she was first widowed: 'We are both in one isle, both of one language, both the nearest kinswoman that each other hath, and both Queens.'[21] In view of Mary's known success in the sphere of personal contact, her steady aim to meet Elizabeth must be regarded not as the caprice of an inquisitive woman, but as a sound piece of political reasoning.

Once Maitland was back in Scotland, he corresponded with Cecil for the rest of the autumn and winter, according to Queen Elizabeth's suggestion. At the same time Elizabeth herself sent Sir Peter Mewtas to Scotland, officially to greet Mary on her arrival in Scotland, unofficially to demand ratification of the treaty. Mary diplomatically suggested in reply that as so many matters in the treaty had concerned her late husband, the whole subject should be considered anew: in November she put forward the names of new commissioners. All Mary's letters to Elizabeth throughout this period have the same attitude of friendliness which would seem positively sugary to our ears, were it not for the high stakes which were to be won by cajolery. Mary means 'nothing more earnestly than continuance of tender amity and good intelligence' between the two of them; she finds that Mewtas has 'so wisely and discreetly uttered and expressed the sincerity of your [Elizabeth's] affection towards us'.[22]

Elizabeth still evinced a personal desire that the whole affair should be conducted secretly, or through the medium of Randolph; thus on 23rd November she replied to Mary's gracious letter, turning down the idea of new commissioners. Maitland now tried in vain to discover privately from Cecil what the next approach should be from the Scottish queen. But as Cecil did not take the hint, Mary's answer had to be framed without any secret advice from England. Mary's letter of 5th January is skilful, and once again tolerant and loving; she cannot imagine what lack Elizabeth has found in her letter and her answer to Mewtas, she now fully accepts Elizabeth's own suggestion that she should communicate 'privily' to Elizabeth's envoy Randolph instead of relying on a new set of commissioners, 'Or rather' – and here once again Mary is hammering on her favourite theme of personal contact – 'by our own letters to you.' 'We will deal frankly with you,' cried Mary to Elizabeth, 'and wish that you deal friendly with us; we will have at this present no judge of the equity of our demand but yourself.'[23] Mary was well aware of the value of flattery. If Mary was dealing with some other prince on the whole question, there is no one whose advice she would rather take than Elizabeth's – 'such opinion have we conceived of your unrightness in judgment'. She injects a note of appeal: 'We will require nothing of you, but that which we could well find in our heart to grant unto you, if the like case were ours.' Once again Mary suggested that she would ratify the treaty immediately, if only her ultimate right could be recognized, but she ended by proposing her pet objective, a personal interview: 'If God will grant a good occasion that we may meet together, which we wish may be soon, we trust you shall more clearly perceive the sincerity of our good meaning than we can express by writing.' It was a masterly letter, a tribute to the political cunning of Maitland, and the propitiatory temperament of Mary.

Mary did not rely only on the seductive quality of her letter: she also wooed the English queen with gifts and even verse. Randolph reported in February that Mary intended to send Elizabeth a fair ring with a diamond in it, made like a heart, and this ring seems to have been finally conveyed to England by du Croc in the summer.[24] According to Bishop Jewel the ring was further enhanced by 'flattering and elegant verses'; these may have been in French in which case they were by Mary herself, who was fond of saluting such occasions with poems of her own composition, or alternatively they were Latin epigrams composed by George Buchanan, who included two such in his works, suitably inscribed from the queen of Scotland to the queen of England. It was in return for this gift that Elizabeth sent a fine ring to Mary the next year via Randolph, which was by his account 'marvellously esteemed, oftentimes looked upon, and many times kissed'.

The effect of these advances upon the English queen was just as Mary hoped. Elizabeth rose to the bait. In late December Cecil wrote to Throckmorton that he found a great desire in both queens to have an interview, although he gloomily feared the worst from two such different women meeting.[25] When Elizabeth finally replied to Mary's letter of 5th January, she certainly did not object to the proposed interview. Mary and Maitland took this lack of negative for a positive acquiescence in their plans; although Maitland had hoped to get some of the outstanding issues settled first, it was decided that he should return once more to London, to negotiate for the meeting, the prime impulse being still the urgent desire of Mary that it should take place. Her relations with Elizabeth were indeed a subject on which she allowed herself to dwell with fantasy as well as affection; one of her favourite jokes at this period was the notion that if the queen of England had been a man, she would have willingly married her. 'This Queen wished that one of the two were a man, to make an end of all debates,' reported Randolph, adding perhaps rather unnecessarily, 'This ... I trowe was spoken in her merrie mood.' This little pleasantry of the volatile queen of Scots had, however, already occurred a year earlier to the serious-minded Sir Nicholas Throckmorton. Then in the full flush of his admiration for Mary Stuart as widow of France, he wrote: 'Methinketh it were to be wished of all wise men and her Majestie's good subjects, that one of these two Queens of the Ile of Britain were transformed into the shape of a man to make so happy a marriage, as thereby there might be an unitie of the whole and their appendances.'[26]

In the absence of any signs of such a miraculous transformation, however, the negotiations for the interview continued. On 19th May Mary persuaded the Scottish Council to agree to it in principle, although they were understandably worried about the safety of her person, in view of the fact that it was less than a year since the English queen had been threatening to imprison her if she landed on English soil. There were other considerations to dampen the ardour of the Scottish Protestants: such meetings were notoriously expensive, and the Scots did not especially wish to send so much money into England and leave it there. Not only that, but they feared that if Elizabeth was seduced by Mary's charm she might cease to keep them under her protective wing. The Scottish Catholic party were concerned that their queen, who had shown a disappointing lack of interest in their case, should be further corrupted by a meeting with the Protestant Elizabeth and were correspondingly opposed to the whole project. But Mary's will prevailed. Maitland was sent to London on 25th May and reached it on 31st May. Her enterprise bore dividends. Elizabeth now showed herself positively favourable to the whole project of the meeting and Maitland brought Cecil round to his way of thinking that on balance a meeting of the two ladies would be advantageous to their respective countries. The English Council were less enthusiastic and, like their Scottish counterpart, pleaded the expense – they reckoned that the whole undertaking would cost at least £40,000. Not only the two councils but the face of heaven itself seemed set against the meeting, since the summer of 1562 was so wet as to make many of the roads between the two countries virtually impassable.

Despite these setbacks, articles for the proposed meeting were agreed on, and duly ratified by Elizabeth. In the articles, York was suggested as the best venue, and the dates mentioned were between 20th August and 20th September. Later, Sheffield House, which was to feature again in the years of Mary's captivity, was put forward as a possible site, before Nottingham was fixed upon in the preliminary arrangements. Maitland optimistically termed Elizabeth to be 'earnest bent' on the project; on 10th June she wrote a letter to this effect to Mary, which pleased the Scottish queen so much that she placed it sentimentally in her bosom, next to her skin. When Maitland returned to Mary in Scotland with the good news, he brought with him Elizabeth's portrait. Mary, with typical female curiosity, asked Randolph whether the likeness was a good one, to which Randolph replied that soon she would be able to judge for herself. Mary exclaimed that this was what she most desired – she hoped that they would strike such deep accord at the meeting, that afterwards the most painful thing which could happen to either of them would be that they had to take leave of each other.[27] In London the prospect of the encounter was considered sufficiently certain for the actual masques to be devised which were to entertain the two queens, the chosen allegorical theme being the punishment of False Report and Discord by Jupiter at the request of Prudence and Temperance. The detailed and long-winded plans for the masques – three nights of them – were vetted personally by Cecil and much courtly care was exercised in the delicate task of balancing the allegorical compliments to both royal ladies.[28]

Unfortunately False Report and Discord were in the end never destined to be consigned to the prison of Extreme Oblivion at the instance of Prudence and Temperance. At the very last minute, with that element of unhappy fatality which never seems far absent from the story of Mary Stuart, the meeting had to be put off – through no lack of keenness on the part of Elizabeth, or the objections of the English Council, but owing to the explosive situation in the rest of Europe. It was to be France, the country for which Mary felt such poignant affection, the country she still secretly thought of as her native land, whose chaotic affairs proved a sudden stumbling-block in the way of the long-desired meeting. On 1st March, 1562 the duke of Guise ordered his followers to fire on a Protestant prayer-meeting at Vassy; the next month Catholics and Huguenots in France were at war with each other. The natural sympathies of Mary would have been supposed to lie with her Guise uncles and the Catholics; the natural sympathies of Elizabeth with the Huguenots. It was a point Throckmorton made from France, when he instantly urged Elizabeth to back the Huguenots, as Spain was likely to intervene on behalf of the Catholics. But although Mary might weep, torn between anxiety for her uncles and fear for her English negotiations, throughout the summer she had not allowed her sympathies with France to override her political designs on England. Elizabeth answered her Council personally when they tried to use the urgency of the French situation to dissuade her from meeting the half-French Catholic queen of Scotland at such a juncture. Cecil continued to hope very practically that the interview might at least lead to a number of benefits for England – the confirmation of the Treaty of Edinburgh, the breaking off of the Franco-

Scottish alliance, or even the conversion of Mary from the 'Roman Religion'.[29] On 25th June peace was agreed in France and on 6th July Elizabeth finally settled that she should set out for the meeting as arranged. On 8th July Cecil prepared a safe-conduct for Mary. But on 12th July the French peace collapsed, the war was renewed; Elizabeth had to admit that it was no longer possible for her to set out for the distant north of England with civil strife raging so closely just across the Channel, in which at any moment England might have to intervene, if Spain did likewise.

Mary first heard the news of the sudden débâcle of her plans from Maitland. She took refuge in a violent flood of tears, and kept to her bed for the rest of the day, nursing the cruel and unexpected disappointment. The next day she received Elizabeth's envoy, Sir Henry Sidney, who had been dispatched to Scotland on 15th July to acquaint her with the course of events. Sir Henry brought with him a more consoling piece of intelligence: Elizabeth offered to plan the interview for the next year, 1563, between 20th May and 31st August, at York, Pomfret, Nottingham, or some other place nominated by Mary. Mary allowed herself to be comforted by the thought that the meeting was only postponed, not cancelled, and her spirits revived. After all, her personal energy and enthusiasm, aided by the skills of Maitland, had been within an ace of achieving this great diplomatic coup, and only circumstances, not Elizabeth's own intentions, had prevented it. With the natural optimism of her nature, she convinced herself that in the mirror of the future, that dark and cloudy surface, she could see reflected the image of success, only a year away. Little did she know that this image was merely an illusion – that the meeting between Elizabeth and Mary, which has been so often fabled by poets and dramatists, the possible consequences of which are incalculable, but must surely have been immensely favourable to Mary, was destined never to take place.

CHAPTER TEN
Governor Good and Gracious

Be governor both good and gracious
Be loyal and loving to thy lieges all
Lord Darnley to Mary Queen of Scots

Whille Mary negotiated for the throne of distant England, the boisterous spirits of her Scottish nobles presented her with certain very different problems at home, involving not only the public peace but her own physical safety. While Lord James, whom Mary considered to be her natural protector, was away on the borders dispensing justice, there was a sudden alarm that Châtelherault's eldest son, the eccentric earl of Arran, intended to abduct the queen. Although the court sprang to the alarm, it subsequently turned out that rumours of the plot had originated in a chance remark of Arran's; in fact the only true stability that the nervous and highly-strung man showed in his wavering career was in his neurotic fixation on his cousin Mary. The next crisis had more substance to it. A mutual hatred existed between James Hepburn, earl of Bothwell, and the Hamiltons, and Bothwell decided to win the favours of an Edinburgh girl Alison Craik ('a good handsome wench' said Randolph)[1] in order to practise a crude revenge on Arran 'whose whore the said Alison was suspected to have been'. Bothwell, Mary's half-brother Lord John Stewart and her Uncle René of Elboeuf (who lingered on in Scotland after the departure of her other Guise relations) gained entry to the house of Alison's step-father, an Edinburgh merchant, on the first night wearing masks; the second night, they were denied admittance, either because Alison did not choose to betray Arran with his political enemies or because she simply did not care to repeat the experience. Whereupon Elboeuf and Bothwell forced their way in. The result was an uproar. The Church Assembly presented a horrified petition to the queen and the Protestants seized the opportunity to suggest that such conduct was typical of a Catholic degenerate like Elboeuf. Mary herself had a prudish horror of such bawdy behaviour: it ill accorded with her own refined interpretation of court life and she administered a stern rebuke to Elboeuf and Bothwell.

Undismayed by this rebuke, Bothwell and Lord John boldly threatened to repeat the offence the next night, and defied anyone to stop them. At this the Hamiltons took furious umbrage and assembled aggressively in the market-place armed with spears and jacks. It was now Bothwell's turn to gather up a muster of his own adherents. At the prospect of what looked like being an ugly affray, the townsmen were summoned by the common bell, and Elboeuf's Gallic spirits were so roused that he declared ten men would not be able to hold him back from the battle (but as he was within the royal gates of Holyrood, and the main action was centred between the Cross and the Salt Tron, in the city itself, the prospect of his intervention was somewhat limited). At the last minute it was Lord James, Argyll and Huntly, rushing down from the court, who managed to disperse the assailants. The whole incident illustrated the swift rough passions which ran so high in Mary's nobles; in these disputes, animated by long-held family hatreds, the queen appeared in the role of an outsider.

The third incident once again involved Arran and Bothwell. At Christmas Mary had been unable to reconcile them, and Bothwell had been obliged to leave the court in the general interests of peace. Towards the end of March, these two contentious nobles were once more on amicable terms, largely as a result of the good offices of John Knox. No sooner had the reconciliation taken place than Arran went to Knox with a disreputable story about Bothwell.² Bothwell, he said, had suggested to him that they should join together in a conspiracy, by which James and Maitland would be slain, and the queen herself abducted by force to Dumbarton Castle. After that, he, Bothwell, would share the rule of the kingdom with Arran. Not content with his revelation to Knox, Arran wrote a full account of the matter to Mary and James, who were then at Falkland, saying that Bothwell's true motive in the matter was to bring about the ruin of the House of Hamilton by devious means. Arran's sanity had long been a matter of common speculation and family concern; as Randolph put it, the earl was 'so drowned in dreams and so feedeth himself with fantasies, that either men fear that he will turn into some dangerous and incurable sickness or play some day some mad part that will bring him into mischief'.³ To his distracted father, it now seemed that he had finally opted for this latter alternative, and had well and truly involved himself in a most dangerous piece of mischief; Châtelherault forthwith shut up the wretched Arran. However, with the determination of lunacy, Arran managed to smuggle out a second letter in code to Randolph, which Randolph duly passed on to the queen.

Just as Queen Mary was digesting the news of the plot, which at best must have greatly perplexed her, at worst alarmed her for her own safety, Gavin Hamilton, Arran's kinsman, panted up with the news that Mary must not credit anything that Arran might have written or would report, for it was all false. Lord James acted with dispatch on Mary's behalf: making short work of Hamilton's excuses, and those of Bothwell, he had them both arrested on suspicion of conspiracy. Arran proved the more slippery to hold of the two: half-naked, he managed to escape out of his window from his confinement in his father's castle, 'with cords made out of the sheets of his bed'.⁴ He then made his way to the home of Kirkcaldy of the Grange at Stirling. Here he gave himself to the ravings of madness, howling and shrieking of devils and witches, and protesting that everyone wanted to kill him. His passion for Mary was transformed by his addled brain into a series of delusions, in which he believed himself to be her husband, and lying in her bed. From Stirling, he was brought to St Andrews, and kept in close confinement, until he was finally confronted with Bothwell, in the presence of Mary and the Privy Council. Here, obsessed by fantasies, he charged Bothwell with high treason; Bothwell, characteristically, wanted the matter settled by single combat, but since this was obviously impossible under the circumstances, suggested a court of law. This suggestion was ignored. Instead Arran, still refusing to withdraw his accusations, was taken back to St Andrews and almost immediately to Edinburgh Castle, where he was put into the charge of James Stewart. It was certainly no age to be mad in: he does not seem to have been kindly treated, even by the low standards of the times towards lunatics, since Stewart was later 'ill-bruited for the rigorous entertainment' he gave to him. He never fully recovered his sanity; in 1564 he was described by Randolph as mad, jaundiced, lying eating little and desiring only solitude, suspicious of all around him. And in May 1566, he was liberated on a caution of £12,000, and was allowed to reside quietly with his mother.*

Although there was no proof of his guilt except the word of a madman, Bothwell was sternly treated. He was left to languish a prisoner in Edinburgh Castle without trial, Mary being persuaded by James that it would be highly politically embarrassing to bring the incident out into the open, since if Arran was shown to have borne false witness, he would have to be executed, and he was too near the throne for this to be desirable. It was also put to Mary that Bothwell had been intriguing with the English. Mary had the keen dislike of ingratitude sometimes found in those who themselves have generous natures, and therefore particularly hate to feel themselves treated any differently by other people. She was annoyed that the man to whom she felt she had been so good should show himself so false, and she quoted pointedly to Buchanan in Latin a maxim from

* Arran plays no further part in the story of Mary Queen of Scots. Yet he lived on, unhappy invalid, for nearly half a century, and did not die until 1609, when all the actors in his story were long since dead, and the son of the woman he had once loved with the obstinate passion of an idiot was securely established on the throne of England.

Livy: 'It is safer not to accuse an evil man, than to pardon him'. Châtelherault was in a pathetic state over the whole incident: Mary was moved to see the tears pouring down the old man's cheeks like those of a child who had been beaten. Nevertheless he had to surrender the castle of Dumbarton, as the price for his supposed political treachery.

The episode, with its mixture of pathos and brutality, has a twofold interest. Firstly it shows that the abduction of Mary's person was a subject of comparatively common discussion – since it arose twice within the first six months of her arrival in Scotland – and certainly not a novel idea in April 1567 when it was finally achieved. It is true that there is absolutely no tenable evidence against Bothwell except the babblings of a lunatic, but it is just possible that there was something more sinister at the back of it all, and that Bothwell did make some chance remark to Arran, which acted on Arran's mad passion for Mary, and set him off on the whole disastrous train of thought. One must bear in mind the possibility that Bothwell was at least toying with the idea of an abduction so early in the period of Mary's personal rule. Secondly, the episode reveals how closely Mary's lot was joined with that of Lord James. At this point, she was making no attempt to rule the Scottish nobles by balancing them against each other, now advancing one faction, now promoting another. On the contrary, she was clearly backing Lord James in whatever he chose to do. This policy would be perfectly satisfactory so long as the interests of Lord James and Queen Mary coincided; should they ever diverge, the queen might find that she would need the other strong nobles in the kingdom to support her, whom she was now allowing her half-brother to put down as he willed.

Shortly after her arrival Mary had chosen her Privy Council, the chief nobles of the kingdom, six of whom were to be in constant attendance on her, to help her dispatch routine business. The Privy Council was vested with full executive powers, sat in the royal palace, and its members were traditionally chosen by the sovereign. However, the true direction of affairs was firmly vested in the hands of Lord James and Maitland; Randolph described them as being above all others in credit with the queen, and contrasted their two techniques of dealing with her: Lord James treated her according to his nature in a homely and blunt fashion, whereas Maitland approached his young mistress more delicately and finely. The practice of having the six nobles in attendance soon lapsed. Since the Acts of the Privy Council had the same force as Acts of Parliament, it was on the Privy Council and its directors that the full administrative business devolved. The role played by Parliament in this period on the other hand was comparatively remote: this was more especially true since between Parliament and the sovereign stood a committee called the Lords of the Articles, to which was delegated its actual business. The Lords of the Articles were an expedient which had grown up out of the remissness of some members of Parliament in attending sessions, as well as the difficulties of prolonging their attendance. Parliament only assembled in practice to vote approval or disapproval of the acts presented to it for sanction by this committee.[5]

As the Lords of the Articles in their turn tended to be amenable to whatever ruler or strong faction was in power, it will be seen that the potential powers of the Scottish crown within the constitution at this period were widespread. The problem was the implementation of these powers in a backward country, rather than the nature of these powers themselves. There were some hopeful signs for the monarchy for the future: although the great magnates held the great offices of state, transmitted by a more or less hereditary title from father to son, there were other lesser posts such as advocate, justice-clerk, treasurer and secretary to be filled by the lesser gentry – the secretaryship for example was Maitland's post; these positions could be personally attached to the sovereign. Against the strength of local justice administered by the lords could now be balanced the endless officials attached to civil and consistorial tribunals, belonging to the central legal order, at the head of which stood the supreme court. The lesser burgesses and lairds who were first called into life at the time of the Reformation Parliament would grow to challenge the great magnates, and the crown might expect to benefit from their challenge.

It will be seen in the civil government, as in the ecclesiastical structure, that the possibilities of the crown under Queen Mary were extensive, if the potentialities of her royal position were ever converted into actualities. But apart from the obvious disadvantage of the strength of the nobles, the crown had two other great weaknesses. It had no standing army – and bitterly had the Scottish nobles resented it when Mary of Guise tried to establish such a thing; the crown, should it be involved in action necessitating war, had to depend on the locally raised hosts of other loyal nobles, with the consequent dangers of personal vendettas being involved in royal policy. Secondly, the financial resources of the Scottish crown were cripplingly restricted. Mary Stuart received an annual income of 40,000 *livres* as her jointure as queen dowager of France, although there were constant troubles over the payment and administration of this sum, which became acute during the years of her captivity. But the lands and properties of her father had been largely squandered by the expensive English wars during her minority.* Other royal lands had been apportioned to the nobles during Mary's minority, although by the ancient law of minority of lesion, she would have a right to resume these on her twenty-fifth birthday, in six years' time. The royal income therefore depended, apart from the lease on its own lands, on wardships or minors and heiresses, export dues derived from duties on trade at the burghs† and ecclesiastical revenues. The entire income from the collectory of crown property amounted to about £18,000 Scots.[7]

Apart from her personal resources, the resources of the crown were meagre indeed and economic organization correspondingly backward. The method of collecting taxes in Scotland in the

---

* At this point the finances of the crown had become so critical that the most intimate royal treasures had to be sold, including the gold and crimson coat worn by James v in Paris during his courtship of his first wife Madeleine, the crystal and agate cup which had been made for Queen Madeleine as a child, and the dresses left behind by the summer queen; even the cap sent by Pope Paul III to James v vanished, as did the historic cup from which Robert Bruce used to drink.[6]

† Fiscal business had of course been greatly interrupted by the English wars, with consequent loss of revenue to the crown.

sixteenth century has been compared unfavourably with that of twelfth-century England, taxes being farmed out for collection to sheriffs whose offices had become hereditary. In any case, the only instance of national taxation during the six years of Mary's personal rule was a levy of £12,000 for the baptism of Prince James. The total royal revenue in 1560 was around £40,000 Scots or about £10,000 sterling.[8] Compared to this, that of Queen Elizabeth was £200,000, rising to £300,000 in the last ten years of her reign:[9] yet Elizabeth was always notoriously conscious of poverty. It is hardly surprising that in Scotland the treasurer's deficit amounted to £33,000 in 1564, and was up to £61,000 in 1569.[10] Indeed, Queen Mary would have been hard put to it to pay a standing army had she been endowed with one. In short, one problem Mary Queen of Scots faced throughout her personal rule was that of frustrating royal poverty. It was no wonder that the French memoir of 1558 on the state of the country dwelt vividly on the poverty of the Scottish monarchy, which it ascribed to the lack of a proper royal domain, and the absence of any means of imposing taxation. Mary, like her grandfather James IV, could fairly be described as 'in want of nothing ... but not able to put money into his strongboxes'.[11]

At the same time, during the second half of the sixteenth century prices were rising fast all over Europe due to the influx of silver from the New World. From this desperate need for money resulted the strange 'treasure-hunter's' economics of the period[12] – the persistent searchings for gold and silver deposits, which unfortunately lay in Scotland only in small and scattered pockets and involved high working and transport costs. For much of her reign Mary was also too poor to issue a coinage, although this had been done yearly from 1529 to 1542. At the same time the Register of the Privy Council shows that it was the policy of Mary's government to try and make French currency legal tender, and to discourage the entry of currency from England, which was made treasonable – although the English currency was getting a reputation for purity from the developing commerce with the Hanse towns and the Low

Countries. Another economic expedient was developed when the government realized that considerable profit could be derived from the issue of a silver coinage, at a considerably greater face value than its true value in silver: ryals began to be issued with a nominal value of thirty, twenty and ten shillings, but costing much less to mint. Naturally, such debasements had the effect of only encouraging hoarding and speculation. During the period of Mary Stuart's personal rule, it would be true to say that just as the crown suffered from straitened finances it was incapable of curing, so the country suffered from economic difficulties for which the government also could supply no certain remedy.

Despite these gloomy considerations, for the first years of her life in Scotland Mary Stuart made a fair attempt to recreate the conditions of the French court and to enjoy the native resources of Scotland. Fortunately she had a natural appetite for pleasures of many different types, as well as being blessed with youthful high spirits and enthusiasm, which enabled her to create pastimes where she did not find them; in particular she had a positive mania for outdoor pursuits – all her life her physical constitution demanded a daily ration of fresh air and exercise if she was to feel herself well. Although later in her life, this was to mean that she suffered cruelly from the conditions of close confinement, it meant that now she was well suited to the conditions of life in Scotland, where she was destined to spend nearly half her life in the saddle, progressing about her dominions. In the Scottish countryside she also had endless opportunities for the hawking and hunting which she loved, as had her father James v, and later her father-in-law and husband. Falkland Palace in Fife was a favourite centre for royal sport, having been rebuilt for this purpose by James v, with new stables built in 1531, so that it occupied rather the same role as Balmoral Castle in the life of Queen Victoria as a holiday and hunting retreat. It was surrounded with parkland and to the north lay the Forest of Falkland. It was not left to chance that the royalties should enjoy good sport: roebucks and stags were actually brought in litters along with the court, from their last stopping place; they were then temporarily released for the chase. When the court moved on again to Edinburgh, the deer were rounded up, and brought on to be released once more in the royal park at Holyrood. Wild boar, to be hunted among the oaks of the forest, were specially imported from France. Hawks commanded good prices: James IV had paid £189 for a trained bird, Mary herself acquired hawks from as far as Orkney and Zetland, and in 1562 hawks were among the presents she sent to Elizabeth, £80 being paid for conveying them to London.

To Mary, a fearless rider who loved the excitement of the chase, not only hawking but deer-hunting was a popular pastime; anti-poaching laws had to be made to preserve the deer for the royal delectation, since on one occasion it was found that 'the deer [were] so destroyed that our Sovereigns can get no pastime of hunting' when they had repaired to a special piece of forest on purpose for the chase. Deer-hunting was far from being the solitary hardy stalking of modern times: the deer were actually beaten in to where the lords would be lying, their heads and antlers appearing over the hill 'making a show like a wood', as Taylor described it in his *Penniless Pilgrimage*.[13] It was a primitive sport by our standards, the cries of the men, with their arrows, javelins and clubs, mingling with the barking of the dogs, often Irish wolf-hounds, who were used to catch the beasts. In 1564 an especially magnificent deer-hunt was organized for Mary by the 4th earl of Atholl; Mary camped for the occasion on the shores of Loch Locky, on the east side of Beinn a' Ghlo, on a spot now traditionally known as Tom na Banrigh, or the queen's hillock. One of Queen Mary's retainers described how 2000 Highlanders (or 'Wild Scots' as he noted that they were called) were employed for two months to drive all the deer from the woods and hills of Atholl, Badenoch, Moray and all the counties about, into a special area – 'As these Highlanders use a light dress, and are very swift of foot, they went up and down so nimbly that ... they brought together 2,000 red deer, besides roes and fallow deer.' The queen and the other great men waited in the glen as the deer thundered towards them, led by one magnificent leader who thrilled Mary's heart, until Atholl warned her that if this leader, either in fear or in rage, turned in their direction, the entire herd would follow and they might be stampeded. This did in fact happen to some of the Highlanders, when Mary let her dog loose on a wolf and the stag bolted; in spite of throwing themselves flat in the heather, two or three Highlanders were killed, and others injured.[14]

In his *History of Scotland*, Leslie emphasizes the importance of hunting to the Scots as a national pastime: in her enthusiasm for it, Mary certainly met with the full accord of her subjects. Archery – for which she would wear a velvet glove – also appealed to her, and she had butts set up in her private gardens at Holyrood, where one spring day she was surprised by Randolph shooting with the vigorously Protestant Master of Lindsay against Lord James and one of her ladies, showing that it was easier to be friendly with the turbulent Lindsay on the common basis of sports than on that of religion.[15] She played at golf and pall-mall (croquet). With her penchant for fresh air, she loved to walk in the gardens surrounding her palaces, and frequently held audiences of her ambassadors there – Randolph even mentions one interview taking place in the garden of Holyrood in February. Here there were two gardens, a north and a south, into which Mary is said to have introduced on her own initiative a young sycamore from France, which was to become the parent of all the groves celebrated in Scottish songs. The other palaces of Linlithgow, Stirling and Falkland also had their estates and parks, the gardens of Stirling lying far below the castle on the level ground, so that the butts could be surveyed from the castle walls.

Mary Stuart had her resplendent side, when she appeared to her subjects as Diana the goddess of the chase; but she also had another charming and touchingly domesticated side to her character in marked contrast to this dazzling public *persona*. This paradox is stamped on many of her actions, which hover between the imperious deeds of the woman born a queen, who loved to shine in the eyes of her people, and the more clinging reactions of a woman, who was after all markedly feminine, in temperament as well as in sex. She adored small dogs, as well as the great hounds of the chase, and this trait did not wait for the cramped conditions of her captivity to manifest itself: there is mention in her inventories of pretty blue velvet colours for the queen's little dogs; a daily ration of two loaves of bread was set apart for them; payment was made to the boys who looked after them, and occasionally they were sent to France. She loved to embroider, and is described as sitting at her Council, placidly plying her needle, a model of the compliant female. Mary Stuart was also marked all her life, in its early no less than in its later stages, by extreme attachment to her servants, particularly her own personal attendants, with whom she felt she could share her joys and woes without fear either of their presumption or of their disloyalty. Mary's court therefore had an agreeably intimate character, which spread outwards from the feminine side of its queen's own nature. There were certainly indoor pleasures enough to be enjoyed. The queen had a gambling streak, as her mother had had before her, and loved to play at cards or at dice, losing a jewel of crystal set in gold to her father-in-law Lennox on one occasion. She enjoyed biles or billiards, and in Lent 1565, before they were married, Mary and Darnley together lost an agate ring and brooch worth 50 crowns to Mary Beaton and Randolph, a debt which Darnley gallantly paid. Mary enjoyed backgammon, and also chess, her library including *The Rules of Chesse* translated from French by William Caxton in 1474. She loved to watch the plays of puppets, a new fashion which had lately spread out of Italy.[16]

Mary was also a considerable linguist, and the number of languages which she had learned as a child in France was reflected in her reading-matter. Besides French, Latin, Scots books, and a few English volumes, there were books in Italian and Spanish — while the presence of books in the original Greek suggested that the queen either understood a smattering of Greek herself, or else had at least an interest in the culture of the Greeks. At all events her library was extensive: from the two incomplete lists of it made at Holyrood in 1569 for the Regent Moray, after she had fled to England, and in 1578 at Edinburgh Castle, it is possible to form at least some impression of her literary tastes.*[17] Her library was kept at Holyrood in a green-carpeted room, and by 1566 her collection of Greek and Latin books had grown sufficiently large to be left by her in her will to the university of St Andrews. There were a quantity of medieval and modern Latin prose, including the famous copy of Buchanan's translation of the Psalms. This was dedicated by him to Queen Mary in Latin in lines which are strangely poignant when one recalls that it was later Buchanan who was to be Mary's chief traducer:

> Lady, whose sceptre (yours by long descent)
> Gives Scotland now a happy government,
> By beauty, virtue, merit and sweet grace
> Queen of your sex, star of our age, our race —
> Accept (light task) done in the Latin tongue,
> The glorious Psalms the prophet-king once sung...†

Greek authors represented included Homer, Herodotus, Sophocles, Euripides and Plato, and there were French translations of the classics such as Suetonius, Plutarch, Ovid and Cicero. Italian books numbered the *Decameron*, Aristo's *Orlando Furioso*, Petrarch, and Marcus Aurelius translated into Italian.

By far the greatest proportion of the books is, of course, in French. English books are rare, but include the Acts of Parliament of Queen Mary Tudor, less frequently browsed over one feels than the volumes of history and French poetry, which seem to have been Mary Stuart's real loves. Brantôme bore witness to her genuine passion for poetry – her library includes the works of Clément Marot, du Bellay and Ronsard, all poets she had known and loved in France. Mary seems to have had a preference also for medieval romances either of the Arthurian legends or the story of Roland. Melville reports that when she

---

* The libraries of her ancestors had been destroyed at the time of the sack of Holyrood in 1544, so that previous kings cannot be credited with the listed books. On the other hand, the Edinburgh Castle list does include the childhood books of James VI.

† Translated by James Michie.

had leisure from the affairs of the state 'she read upon good books, the history of diverse countries'[18] – books such as the chronicles of the emperors and kings of Austria, found in the list of Edinburgh Castle, and histories of the medieval kings of France. The colourful mixture of event and character to be found in history evidently appealed to her – it is obvious from her answers at her trial in England, and her conversations with Paulet at the end of her life, that she had read and pondered on English history. In short, her library shows the typical all-round tastes of what might be termed an educated Renaissance woman who enjoyed reading widely as her fancy listed – as well as the individual touches to be found in any library, such as *The Book of Hunting* (the sort of book which might also be found in the fine library of any eighteenth-century English gentleman), a book on astronomy, and dutifully enough the bound sermons and prayers of her uncle the cardinal of Lorraine.

There are three books on music listed: for music Mary Stuart would seem to have had a profound feeling which, like her love of poetry, appealed to the romantic, rather than the inquisitive, side of her nature. She herself played on both the lute and virginals, and as she plucked her lute strings she loved to display those long white fingers, which Brantôme and Ronsard admired. Although Melville in his famous interview with Queen Elizabeth described Mary as playing only 'reasonably well' for a queen, the verdict of Mary's contemporaries who did not have to discuss the matter with her jealous rival is more generous.[19] Mary had a charming, soft singing voice which, like her speaking voice, won the admiration of her listeners, and on whose natural ability Conaeus commented. Musical talent played its part in the selection of her valets of the bed-chamber – later it influenced the choice of Riccio; in 1561 she had five violas and three players on the lute, and some of the valets of the bed-chamber also played and sang, so that Mary could beguile the long dark Scottish winter evenings with the sort of little musical supper parties which she had enjoyed in France. The queen also loved to have music to accompany her Mass; at first this presented a problem, since the chapel organs had been destroyed at the time of the Reformation as being profane instruments, with the exception of that at Stirling which the mob could not reach. In 1562 Randolph reported her as being desolate because no one would play at her Mass on Christmas Day;[20] however, by April 1565 she had a band of musicians, and at Easter High Mass Randolph furiously noticed that 'she wanted now neither trumpets, drum, nor fife, bagpipe or tabor'.[21]

The skill of Mary, for which Knox had a particular loathing, which summed up to him everything he detested about her character, education and upbringing, was her dancing. There was a genuine and irreconcilable difference of attitude. To Knox, dancing seemed truly an invention of the devil, something which good women never practised; in his opinion, the activities which Mary got up to whenever she was alone with her 'French fillocks, fiddlers and others of that band' made the whole atmosphere more like a brothel than a place for honest women. If we are to believe Knox, in December 1562 Mary danced excessively 'beyond midnight' out of glee, because she had received the news that the persecution of the Huguenots had begun again in France.[22] He immediately resorted to his favourite weapon of the denunciation of the pulpit, as a result of which Mary summoned him to their second interview, some eighteen months after the first.

She received him in her chamber, attended by Lord James, Maitland and Morton. Knox proceeded to qualify his condemnation of dancing with certain provisos – he said that he was prepared to tolerate dancing if the principal vocation of the dancer was not neglected, and that the dancers took care not to dance as the Philistines did, for the pleasure they took in the displeasure of God's people. If they did fall into either of these two heinous errors, they should 'receive the reward of dancers, and that will be drunk in hell, unless they speedily repented'. Mary Stuart on the other hand had been brought up in France to dance, and she danced well and elegantly; in the words of Melville, once more jealously cross-examined by the queen of England, she danced 'not so high and disposedly' as Elizabeth, but in Conaeus's less inhibited phrase she danced most 'gracefully and becomingly'. With Mary Stuart, dancing was a natural expression of her pleasure in life, as well as an artistic performance; it is small wonder therefore if the young queen, just nineteen, dancing with the ladies of her court in a carefree but hardly unseemly fashion, should have felt that of the two of them it was Knox, and not her, who was the Philistine.

In her dress, at least, Mary Stuart was able to give the femininity of her nature full reign, because to be magnificently attired was expected of a sixteenth-century queen, by all except the most bigoted and puritanical. Even in childhood, she had been distinguished by a keen interest in clothes when she teased her governess into letting her have as splendid gowns as the princesses of France. When she grew up, and had what virtually amounted to a constitutional duty to dress herself elegantly, she did so with innate good taste – lacking her cousin Elizabeth's inclination to bedizen herself ostentatiously, possibly because she was conscious that unlike Elizabeth she had the sort of beauty which was best set off by rich simplicity. Of course a large proportion of her time as a young woman was spent in mourning – for her mother, her father-in-law, and finally for her husband. The outward signs of grief were taken extremely seriously at this period – it has been noted that she was wearing black when she first arrived in Scotland. After Francis had been dead a year, in December 1561, the court went into half-mourning but Mary herself did not totally cast off her mourning until she married Darnley four years later. Perhaps she understood how to make her many black accoutrements a dramatic foil for her red-golden hair, white skin and golden eyes; for the same reason, white appears and reappears throughout the list of dresses in her wardrobe, there being perhaps no better setting for a glowing complexion than a white dress: the list of her robes, with their descriptions and colours, fully explains how she came to be known as '*la reine blanche*' in France. Indeed her detailed wardrobe books show the intense interest which Mary Stuart took in every detail of her clothes: there are lists of all the articles delivered from the wardrobe at Holyrood each month from the beginning of 2nd September, 1561 to June 1567 when the nobles took arms against her.[23] Ordinarily, she wore dresses of camlet (a sort of mohair), damask or serge, stiffened in the neck with buckram, and mounted with lace and ribbons; the queen was also fond of loose dresses ('*à l'Espagnole*'); her riding skirts and cloaks were of Florentine serge, often edged with black velvet or fur. Beneath her gowns were '*vasquines*', stiffened petticoats or farthingales to hold out her skirts, expanded with hoops of whale bones to give a crinoline effect. Her underwear included silk doublets, and there is mention of '*brassières*' of both black and white silk. Her 'woven hose' often were made of gold and silver, and it is specifically mentioned that they were of silk. Her hats and caps were of black velvet and taffetas – her veils of white.

On state and ceremonial occasions, the queen's clothes were universally glittering. The inventory of the queen's dresses made at Holyrood in February 1562[24] lists 131 entries, including sixty gowns, of cloth of gold, cloth of silver, velvet, satin and silk. There are fourteen cloaks, five of which are in the Spanish fashion, and two royal mantles, one purple velvet and the other furred in ermine. There are thirty-four *vasquines* and sixteen *devants* or fronts (stomachers), mainly of cloth of gold, silver and satin. The dresses themselves ranged from the favourite white – often with silver fringes and embroidery – and preponderant black, to crimson velvet, orange damask embroidered in silver; the embroidery was so rich and detailed that it was often passed from dress to dress, and listed separately among the jewellery.

Not only Mary's dresses, but also her jewels were of enormous importance to her: these of course represented something more than adornment, since by being treated as solid financial assets, they could be given as presents, held for security, or sold to pay troops, if necessary. In her childhood, Mary Stuart was decked by her attendants in those jewels considered fit for an infant queen; in Scotland she enjoyed the enhancement of a series of romantic gems; later in her life, her jewels were to enjoy a career as checkered as her own, as they were stolen, seized, sold to Elizabeth, or pawned, all to her violently expressed anguish. The inventory of her jewellery, made also in 1562,[25] contains 180 entries, an increase of twenty-one over the inventory of the queen's jewels made at the time of her departure from France – new acquisitions include a cross of gold set with diamonds and rubies which Mary had just redeemed for £1000 from the hands into which it had been pledged by Mary of Guise. She had also acquired some new Scottish pearls from an Edinburgh goldsmith, for Scottish pearls were held to share with Bohemian pearls the honour of being the finest in Europe, although still rated as inferior to the pearls of the Orient. As she loved white, so the queen seems to have had an especial affection for pearls – it was noted that she was wearing two of a group of twenty-three pearls in her ears at the actual moment when the inventory was taken. But rubies she also seems to have admired, as she loved to wear crimson velvet; and among her profusion of rings, necklaces and earrings, there is mention of enamel, cornelian and turquoise, as well as, of course, gold and diamonds.

The queen paid fashionable attention to the care of her hair, and the elaborate dressing of it, according to the caprices of the time. We know that among her Maries, Mary Seton was an especially skilled hairdresser, having learnt the art in France. Even in her youth, when she had lovely thick glistening hair – those tresses '*si beaux, si blonds, si cendrés*' wrote Brantôme – the dictates of the mode led her to use perukes or false hairpieces. Later in her life her glorious hair darkened, and the sorrows and illnesses of her captivity caused it to thin and go grey prematurely. Then, false pieces of hair were to be essential, but now in her heyday, she made use of them equally: there is repeated reference to her perukes or the bags to keep them in, in her wardrobe lists. By 1569 Nicholas White mentions that she had them of all different colours, and Sir Francis Knollys was impressed by the pretty fashions created on her head by Mary Seton when she first arrived in England (he considered the art a novelty although Queen Elizabeth herself had no less then eighty perukes). Queen Mary's perukes were among the first necessities which she sent for from Lochleven, and as can be seen by the awe of Knollys, these much-travelled handmaidens of beauty were dispatched to Mary at Carlisle by her wardrobe master Servais de Condé only a month after she reached it herself.[26]

The queen of Scots had a childish love of fancy dress and dressing-up which she preserved throughout her life. It has already been mentioned that she loved to adopt Scottish national dress in France, and even had herself painted in it, according to Brantôme, although the portrait does not survive. In Scotland, with a romantic love of the Highlands, reminiscent of her descendant and admirer Queen Victoria, Mary adopted the costume of wearing the so-called 'Highland mantles' – these were not plaid, but loose cloaks reaching to the ground, and generally embroidered. In this she followed her father, who had had himself made a Highland suit in 1538, including 'variant coloured' velvet to be a short Highland coat, and 'Highland tartan' to be hose – trews and a belted plaid being the contemporary form of Highland dress rather than the later kilt.* Queen Mary had three cloaks, one white, one blue and one black embroidered in gold.[27] In Scotland also, Mary loved to adopt male costume, and wander about the streets, enjoying the sort of romantic incognito among her subjects which has always been considered the perquisite of adventurous royalties. With her height and long legs, she must have made an engaging picture, and would surely have earned the admiration of Brantôme, who wrote that only a lady of perfect beauty with perfect legs should attempt such a disguise, in order that no man should be able to tell 'to which sex she really belonged, whether she was a handsome boy or the beautiful woman she was in reality'.[28] At one banquet given to the French ambassador, the queen appeared with her Maries, all dressed as men; riding against the rebels in 1565, she dressed up as a man to ride at the head of her army, the cynosure of every loyal eye. On Easter Monday 1565, Mary and her women dressed themselves up like burgesses' wives, in

---

* Tartan is also not to be understood in the modern sense: it was the name given to a certain material, which in the sixteenth century was not necessarily checkered. During his visit to the Highlands at the beginning of the next century, John Taylor still did not describe tartan more specifically than as a 'warm stuff of divers colours'.[27]

Stirling, and ran up and down the streets, according to Randolph, gathering money for the banquets; later they all banqueted where Randolph himself was lodging, to the wonder of the common spectators.[29] Three weeks before she married Darnley, they both sauntered about the streets of Edinburgh in disguise until supper-time, and did the same thing again the next day, causing a certain amount of gossip.

In all these pranks and escapades, of the type in which royalty have always indulged to escape the gilded bird-cage of their existence, it is unnecessary to discern more than natural high spirits and youthful love of pleasure. Certainly there were no sexual scandals surrounding the sovereign, as there had been in the time of Mary's father, and in so many monarchs before and since. Mary, who throughout her first years in Scotland was an unattached and beautiful girl, with no restraints except those of prudence to hold her back from the wildest excesses had she wished to indulge in them, was as clearly *sans reproche* in her court life as she was *sans peur* in the hunting field. The only scandal to be seen was the scandal, in the eyes of Knox at least, of the spectacle of human enjoyment. Mary conducted herself in a thoroughly innocent, somewhat hoydenish fashion, some-what like the Shakespearian heroines whom she so much resembles — like Rosalind, rejoicing in her boy's attire in the Forest of Arden, but fainting at the sight of Orlando's blood on a handkerchief. Certainly, like Rosalind, although caparisoned like a man, she did not have a doublet and hose in her disposition, but retained all her female impulsiveness.

Mary Stuart's simple sense of fun, what Randolph called her 'merry mood', fitted in well with the boisterous sense of humour of her Scottish subjects at this time, although this was certainly more bawdy in its most outspoken manifestations. The sixteenth-century Scots did not necessarily see the reformation of their religion as leading to the end of those hearty, crude, bucolic games and sports which they had long enjoyed; they loved the favourite May game of Robin Hood, with its Abbot of Unreason and its Queen of the May. When these games were forbidden by the magistrates in May 1561, for the disturbance they caused, the ban caused public riots, and Robin and his men patrolled the streets all the same in defiance. One of Robin's companions was arrested, condemned to death and carried to the gibbet, until he was rescued on the verge of the hanging by his fellow-rioters. The people who enjoyed this sort of entertainment naturally loved the pageantry brought to the country by Mary and her court. On Sunday 30th November, a few months after Mary's arrival, her uncle Elboeuf and her half-brothers Robert and John Stewart took part in 'running at the ring', two teams of six, one disguised as women and the other as strangers in fancy dress. Elboeuf did well but the 'women', led by Lord Robert, won; the queen watched it all with great enjoyment. A week later, on Saturday 5th December, the anniversary of Francis's death was marked by the solemn presentation of a huge wax candle draped in black velvet; the next day, possibly because it was two days off Mary's own nineteenth birthday, there was 'mirth and pastimes' upon the seashore at Leith, a romantic, if chilly, prospect upon the winter sands, at which the queen was present.[30] Court life was enlivened by numbers of paid jesters, often female. One, known as 'La Jardinière', had her own keeper or *gouvernante*, Jacqueline; La Jardinière was given a green plaiding coat, handkerchiefs, and linen for underclothing. Another favourite of the queen, Jane Colquhoun, received a red and yellow coat in 1566. A special canvas bed was made for another of Mary's female fools, Nichola, 'La Folle', whom she brought from France, and who stayed with the queen until her imprisonment in England, when Lennox paid generously for the 'fool's' return to her native land.[31]

Among the special features of the social life of the time were the weddings of the nobility, which were nearly always the occasion for banquets and masques. Mary seems to have had a wistful love of weddings, and loved to give not only feasts but also bridal dresses to her favourites. Two significant weddings took place in her first year in Scotland. In January 1562 Lady Janet Hepburn, Bothwell's sister, married Mary's half-brother, Lord John, at Bothwell's own castle of Crichton; both Queen Mary and Lord James came to the castle, with Bothwell acting as host, and the English ambassador was duly impressed by the sports and pastimes which were indulged in. Four weeks later Lord James's own nuptials to Lady Agnes Keith were celebrated in Edinburgh with great splendour. He was created earl of Mar the day before the marriage, which was held in St Giles Cathedral, with Knox preaching the sermon. A long train of nobles witnessed the rites and then went to Holyrood, for the first instalment of three days' banqueting – on which Knox commented sourly that 'the vanity used thereat offended many godly'.[32]

The series of masques included that held after the wedding of Argyll's sister at Castle Campbell in midwinter 1563, at which shepherds appeared wearing white damask and playing sweetly upon the lute. Perhaps the most splendid of all the banquets was that which Mary herself gave at Shrovetide in 1564 when she was just recovering from an illness. It was reported by Randolph that no Scotsman had ever seen anything like it except at the marriage of a prince: it lasted for three days and all the attendants, as well as the queen herself, her ladies and her gentlemen, wore classical black and white. Randolph himself echoed the prevailing mood of carefree enjoyment when he told Cecil that until the arrival of the French ambassador, du Croc, in May 1563, who brought in the sterner atmosphere of outside affairs, all those at the Scottish court 'did nothing but pass our time in feasts, banqueting, masking and running at the ring and such like'.[33]

Through all this tapestry of court life ran the bright threads represented by the four Maries. Knox, ever eager to repeat scandals about the court if he could learn them, concentrated much of his attention on the Maries and the queen's women in general, presumably because scandal about them could be held to smear the queen. For example, he repeated one actual case which had come to public knowledge at the beginning of Mary's rule; of a 'heinous murder' committed in the court – 'yea, not far from the Queen's own lap'. A French woman who had served in the queen's chamber was said to have 'played the whore' with the queen's apothecary and in the course of the liaison unwisely conceived a child. Father and mother then conspired together to murder the infant: 'Yet,' to continue Knox's account of it all, 'were the cries of the newborn bairn heard; search was made, the child and mother both deprehended, and so were both the man and the woman damned to be hanged upon the public street of Edinburgh.' But Knox did not mention what Randolph reported, that it was the queen herself, with her profound disgust of immorality in sexual matters, who insisted on the death sentence being carried out. Instead he went on to add that it had been well known that 'shame' hastened the marriage between John Semple, called the Dancer, and Mary Livingston, surnamed the Lusty. Having delivered this Parthian shot, he still could not resist saying it was well known what shocking reputations the Maries and the rest of the dancers at the court enjoyed: 'The ballads of the age did witness, which we for modesty's sake omit.'*[34]

But *pace* Knox, the four Maries had in truth simple natures: like their mistress they were easily pleased by court festivities and enjoyments, and their reputations certainly did not deserve to be besmirched by his slurs. Their faults, if any, sprang from the natural light-heartedness and frivolity of youth, rather than anything more vicious. Mary Livingston owed her nickname of

---

* From this anecdote of Knox it used to be deduced, notably by Sir Walter Scott, that the beautiful and melancholy ballad of the *Queen's Maries* with its haunting refrain

> Last night the Queen had four Maries
> Tonight there'll be but three
> There's Mary Seton and Mary Beaton
> And Mary Carmichael and me.

applied to the court of Mary Stuart, despite the fact that the Maries of the ballad were named Mary Beaton, Mary Seton, Mary Carmichael and 'me' (Mary Hamilton) whereas Queen Mary's last two maids were of course named Mary Fleming and Mary Livingston. The ballad has subsequently been traced to a scandal at the court of Peter the Great in early eighteenth-century Russia, where one of his wife Catherine's maids of honour of Scottish origin, Mary Hamilton, was executed for the murder of an illegitimate child, after having had a love affair with the Tsar Peter. The ballad, which Child dated between 1719 and 1764, evidently made use of the well-known fact that Queen Mary in the sixteenth century had employed four girls named Mary to serve her, and grafted it on to the tragedy of Mary Hamilton in Russia.[35]

the Lusty to her energetic habit of dancing rather than to any raging physical appetites: there is no other contemporary evidence other than the venomous suggestion of Knox that her marriage was hastened by pregnancy, and her eldest child was indeed born a year after her marriage. Mary Livingston was considered reliable enough to be given special charge of the queen's jewels, and her nuptials in fact at her family home at Falkirk seem to have been the occasion for special and long-planned rejoicings, which do not accord with the notion of a shameful union. The truth was that Mary Livingston was a girl of high spirits and exceptional vivacity, two qualities which were scarcely likely to commend her to Knox.

Although the first to marry, Mary Livingston was not the *belle* of the quartet: this honour was always accorded to Mary Fleming. Originally it was her royal blood which set her apart from the other Maries: later, as her beauty bloomed, her remarkable combination of looks and vitality made her, in the opinion of Leslie, 'the flower of the flock'. At the Twelfth Night festivities of 1564 Mary Fleming, dressed as Queen of the Bean in cloth of silver, her neck, shoulders and what seemed like the whole of her body set with jewels, so dazzled the gaze of Thomas Randolph that, although Mary Beaton was his acknowledged favourite among the four, he expressed the opinion that 'the fair Fleming' was surely chosen by Fortune to be a queen, and not for Twelfth Night only: assuming the mantle of Paris, he compared her in lyrical terms to Venus in beauty, Minerva in wit and Juno in worldly wealth – the two former being given her by nature, and the third he assumed to be at her command within the kingdom of Scotland. Buchanan too extolled the praises of this queen-for-the-night in Latin verse, terming her Queen 'Flaminia', to whom virtue itself had already supplied a sceptre.[36]

Mary Beaton seems to have been the most classically beautiful of the four,* but she lacked the flowering fascination of Mary

---

* There are no contemporary portraits of the four Maries to be seen. One picture once thought to be that of Mary Beaton showing her with fair hair and dark eyes is now thought to date from the late seventeenth or early eighteenth century.

Fleming, which the fair Fleming owed perhaps to her share of Stuart blood. Like Mary Fleming, Mary Beaton's beauty and worth were praised by Buchanan in verse, but her character was cast in a less flamboyant mould. The meekest of the four, Mary Seton, a daughter of one of the grandest houses in Scotland, was naturally pious and more devoted to the service of her mistress than to the pleasures to be derived at the court, as her subsequent history showed.

Whatever Knox's feelings about the Maries, and whatever his strictures on masques and similar diversions, we may be sure that Mary's subjects themselves thoroughly enjoyed such display since it was twenty years since there had been anything in Scotland approaching proper court life. Randolph described what a pretty sight the Maries made as they rode with their mistress to Parliament in 1563 – 'virgins, maids, Maries, demoiselles of honour, or the Queen's *mignons*, call them as you please, your Honour' wrote the English ambassador;[37] the effect was the same: they made a pleasing spectacle. The burgesses' wives who were reported to find the queen's dresses too rich were probably nonetheless happy to be able to watch them go by. To the argument that Mary was extravagant, it may be answered that she was considerably less extravagant than her cousin Elizabeth in both her dress and her progresses. Not only was Mary used to infinitely more prodigal expenditure at the court of France, but also much of her glamour consisted in her personal charm. In any case, such display on the part of a sovereign was an essential part of personal and monarchical government, as one Elizabethan contemporary observed: 'in such ceremonies, does the art of good government much consist'.[38] The result, as even Buchanan, later to be her harshest critic, admitted, was that this pretty, high-spirited creature, with her hunting, her hawking, her masques, her clothes, her jewels, was able to charm those members of the Scots nation who were there to be charmed. She indeed 'fleet the time carelessly, as they did in the golden world' in her own particular Forest of Arden. Buchanan himself wrote of this period in her life:[39] 'Apart from the fascination of her varied and perilous history, she was graced with surpassing loveliness of form, the vigour of maturing youth, and fine qualities of mind which a court education had increased or at least made more attractive by a surface gloss of virtue.'

CHAPTER ELEVEN
The Fall of Huntly

Far o'er the crashing forest
The giant arms lie spread:
And the pale augurs murmuring low
Gaze on the blasted head

Lord Macaulay

On 11th August, 1562, Mary Queen of Scots rode north on her first visit to her Highland dominions. She had long intended to visit these wild and individual territories: a ceremonial visit to Aberdeen had been planned for Easter-tide as early as January, but had apparently been delayed by the English negotiations. Now that the interview with Queen Elizabeth was temporarily postponed, the queen of Scots was free to resume the plan; but in the interval since the progress was first mooted, it seemed that her purpose had altered. Her primary intention was no longer to extend her knowledge of her kingdom, nor merely sporting (as the date might suggest to modern eyes); it had now become distinctly punitive. The might of the Gordons, under their magnificent but unpredictable head, George, 4th earl of Huntly, had long loomed over the north-east of Scotland like the shadow of a great eagle which might at any moment swoop on its prey. This fact in itself, however disquieting, would not have inspired a martial expedition – quite apart from the fact that Huntly's state approached that of an independent monarch, he was in any case the leading Catholic magnate. Firstly, it might be dangerous to attack him, and secondly, it might be unwise. But in the course of the summer,

Huntly's third son, Sir John Gordon, became involved in an unsavoury scandal, and provided the queen with a *casus belli* against one Gordon at least, if she needed one.

In June Sir John severely wounded Lord Ogilvie in a street brawl in Edinburgh as a result of which he was thrown into prison. The feud with the Ogilvies had arisen because the Ogilvie of Findlater had disinherited his own son James Ogilvie of Cardell and left his lands, including the castle of Findlater, to Sir John in his place. The disinheritance was at the instance of Ogilvie's second wife, who persuaded Ogilvie that his son had made amorous advances to her, and thus deserved punishment. The step-mother herself now became the mistress or 'pretended spouse' of John Gordon, who was not only a bold cavalier but good-looking also, and as Buchanan put it 'in the very flower of youth'. Public opinion was outraged and the scandalous alliance did the poor woman little good in the end, for when Sir John could not secure from her all the lands he wanted, he shut her up in a 'close chamber' and both discarded her as a mistress and disowned her as a wife.¹ But matrimony was much on the mind of the ebullient Sir John: as a scion of the Catholic Gordons, he had been suggested as a possible husband for the queen herself. He himself seems to have been confident (on little foundation) that his dashing good looks had already caught her eye. Now his volatile temperament could not long endure the incarceration of prison. He escaped, and fled northwards to the safety of his father's domains.

Mary did not view his offence with either a merciful or an indulgent eye. He had escaped justice, and he had also possessed himself of the lands of her own master of the household – none other than that James Ogilvie of Cardell who had been so cruelly dispossessed by the accusations of his step-mother. Mary now determined to pursue Sir John in the course of her northern progress, and James Ogilvie was among the courtiers who accompanied her on the journey. Scandal apart, Mary also intended to demonstrate that the Gordons could not behave as they pleased with impunity. Huntly had been out of favour with the queen since January, since he had made no secret of his disapproval of her cool policy towards the Scottish Catholics. Not only had Mary rejected his plan of a Catholic rising at Aberdeen, when she was still in France, but ever since she had refused such provocative offers as 'setting up the Mass in three shires'. The untrustworthy temperament of the 4th earl made him indeed a delicate subject to handle either in conflict or alliance – as Randolph observed unpleasantly, were it not for the fact that 'no man will trust him either in word or deed', he would have been capable of doing a great deal of mischief.[2]

The character of the 4th earl belongs to that great tradition of independent Highland lords who throughout history have posed such problems for the central government – since their policies, which have seemed so strangely inconsistent from the viewpoint of the centre, have in fact been consistently bent towards the aggrandizement of their own clans. Huntly had powerful royal connections: as the grandson of James IV by his natural daughter Margaret Stewart, he was, although thirty years older, Mary Stuart's first cousin (she always addressed both him and his son as 'cousin' in her letters), and since his own father died when he was a baby, he was actually brought up with King James V. Two of his nine sons were married to two daughters of the duke of Châtelherault. His power extended across the north-east of Scotland in a formidable array of tangible castles, and intangible but effective family alliances. Not only did he hold the royal castles of Inverness and Inverlochy, but he was further supported by his own castles of Strathbogie, Bog of Gight, Aboyne, Ruthven in Badenoch and Drummin in Glenlivat; from 1549 onwards, he was allowed to hold the large and profitable earldom of Moray under the crown. At different dates, the local Fraser lords of Saltoun and Lovat had made bonds of manrent to him, as had the captains of Clan Cameron and Clan Chattan. The grandeur of his household impressed even Mary of Guise's French court when they came north. Now, at fifty, grown corpulent with age, like a great northern bear, he seemed the very pattern of the Highland patriarch.

The past career of this patriarchal figure had, however, been somewhat chequered. As one of the leaders of the Scots army at Pinkie Cleugh (where his white and gilt armour dazzled the eye) he had been captured by the English; although Leslie tells the story of his romantic escape from Morpeth while his jailers were playing cards, in fact he procured his release by the more down-to-earth method of signing an indenture with Somerset to pursue the cause of King Edward VI in Scotland. He was imprisoned by Mary of Guise in 1555, but restored to favour to become lieutenant-general of the kingdom two years later. Yet her favour and his Catholicism did not prevent him defecting to the reformers briefly in April 1560: his motives seem to have been his notorious 'doubleness and covetousness' since he was careful to stipulate that he should continue in supreme authority in the north as before. When his castle of Strathbogie was sacked, among its contents was found a large proportion of the ecclesiastical ornaments of Aberdeen Cathedral which Huntly was said to have stored away for use when Catholicism was restored.[3] Yet his defection at this critical moment virtually wrecked the Catholic cause. Now Huntly was once more openly professing the faith of his fathers, but Mary's caution towards this unstable character can readily be imagined, since not only she but all his contemporaries generally reckoned him to be totally untrustworthy in the final analysis, in all except that which intimately concerned his own clan.

There was a further complication between Huntly and the central government: although Huntly, free from interference in the north, had profited from the revenues of the lands of the earldom of Moray ever since 1549, the title itself had been given secretly to Lord James at the end of January 1562 by the queen. At his wedding in February Lord James had actually been invested earl of Mar, but when Lord Erskine protested that this earldom was an Erskine perquisite, Lord James resigned it a few months later, retaining only the secret Moray earldom; nevertheless despite this private assurance of Moray from the queen to Lord James, the news was not broken to Huntly. It has been suggested that the prospect of the formal acquisition of the earldom of Moray provided a sinister motive for Lord James to drag his sister northwards, and persuade her to strike down the overmighty Huntly. It was true that Lord James was quite as avaricious as most of his contemporaries: certainly his best chance of publicly acquiring the earldom which he had already acquired secretly was to proceed north with an adequate force, and possess himself of it. In this, he clearly needed the assistance of the queen. But it is equally certain that when Mary and James set forth for the north in August 1562 they were perfectly united in their aims. For the last year James had been Mary's chief adviser and she had accepted all his lessons. James did not need to drag Mary north: she herself was anxious to make her progress and in doing so restore the errant Sir John to the arms of justice. As for the earldom of Moray, one of the points of the gift was intended to be the curtailment of Huntly's expanding powers. With regard to Mary's ultimate intentions towards Huntly, the evidence suggests that in August the queen had made no positive decision, but was content to see how Huntly would react to her northern progress before judging whether he was indeed an over-mighty subject, or merely a convenient Catholic viceroy. The focus was therefore for better or for worse on the behaviour of Huntly.

Queen Mary arrived at Aberdeen, via Stirling, Coupar Angus, Perth and Glamis, on 27th August. Here in this Huntly-dominated town, she paid a visit to the university (although it was to St Andrews she left a bequest of Greek and Latin books to its library in her will of 1566). At Aberdeen she was also greeted by the countess of Huntly, who was surrounded by a splendid train of attendants. This remarkable and vigorous woman had been born at Keith, a sister of the Earl Marischal, and was incidentally aunt to that Lady Agnes Keith whom Lord James had recently married. Clearly the strain provided a series of redoubtable helpmeets, for Elizabeth, countess of Huntly, not only provided the decision which her husband often lacked, but was also not above turning to the aid of her tame 'familiars' or witches, when inspiration from any other source was lacking. Now she pleaded as a mother with the queen to overlook Sir John Gordon's indiscretion and pardon him. Queen Mary, with the strictness with which she seems to have regarded all scandalous misdemeanours, insisted that Sir John must return to ward at Stirling before he could be pardoned. The gallant Sir John was thus temporarily induced to surrender himself – but shortly afterwards his turbulent nature reasserted itself, and escaping once more, he gathered a force of 1000 horse about him.

The Gordons were traditionally skilful horsemen. With this force, Sir John now proceeded impudently to harry the queen's train as she proceeded north. He later admitted that this was done with the deliberate intention of abducting her and, unlike Arran, he seems to have been gaily certain that the queen would accede to the arrangement. His confidence in his powers of physical attraction was unfortunately misplaced. This flagrant defiance of her royal authority enraged the queen, who promptly refused to visit the Huntly stronghold of Strathbogie, on her road to Inverness. Caution as well as anger may have played its part in the decision: for it was highly uncertain what might befall her once inside the Gordon stronghold, in the grasp of the unstable Huntly, to say nothing of the mercurial Sir John. It was afterwards suggested that had Mary stopped at Strathbogie, Huntly would have had Lord James, Maitland and Morton killed and established a Catholic coup. He would most likely have completed the operation by marrying off Mary – to be 'kept at the devotion of the said Earl of Huntly' – to his son. Mary certainly told Randolph indignantly later that among Huntly's crimes had been the fact that he would have married her off 'where he would'.[4]

In the meantime Huntly was given no chance to put these dastardly plans, if indeed he held them, into effect. Queen Mary by-passed Strathbogie, and taking a more western route to Inverness, she stopped instead at Darnaway Castle. Here in this stronghold a few miles from the sea, set aloft amid surrounding forests in the centre of the earldom of Moray ('very ruinous' complained Randolph, except for the hall which was 'fair and large') she took the opportunity to announce that Lord James had been granted the earldom in place of that of Mar. She also issued an order against John Gordon for his efforts to 'break the whole country, so far as is in his power', as well as failing to return to ward.' When Mary finally reached Inverness on 11th September, she had brusque confirmation of Huntly's attitude towards her. The keeper of the castle, Alexander Gordon, another of Huntly's numerous offspring (he had nine sons and three daughters), refused her entrance, although it was a royal, not a Gordon, castle, being only committed into Huntly's charge by virtue of his position as sheriff of Inverness. This was not so much insolence as actual treason, whether by Huntly's specific orders or not, and in the queen's mind certainly lent colour to what he would have done if Mary had stopped at Strathbogie. Huntly, on hearing that the rest of the Highlanders were rallying behind the queen, took alarm at the situation, and sent orders to his son to admit the queen. Mary Stuart then entered Inverness Castle, and its captain was promptly hanged over the battlements for his defiance.[6]

Installed at Inverness Castle, Mary was now able to taste the sweets of Highland life, which has commended itself to so many royalties since: the sport, the freedom, the beauty of the scenery all appealed to her romantic temperament. She felt a childish happiness to feel herself among this strange people dressed in their skins (half of whom only spoke Gaelic, a language she could not speak), so tough that they habitually slept out in the heather, said Leslie, but now came down from their distant glens to gaze on this beautiful young creature they were told was their queen. In order to please them, not only did the queen herself adopt Highland dress, some of it acquired hastily in Inverness according to the royal accounts, but plaids were also purchased locally for several of her courtiers. To Inverness came the local lords: the young gentlemen of the Fraser clan were presented to her, at their head their seventeen-year-old chief Lord Hugh of Lovat, nephew of that Lord Lovat who had perished with his eldest son and so many of the Fraser men eighteen years before in a clan battle on the Field of Shirts at Loch Lochy. The newly be-plaided courtiers were impressed by this muster of Highlanders, having never seen such an abundance of them before, and the queen showed particular favour to the good-looking young boy. As a result young Lord Hugh, 'not a little vain' of the dash which he had cut, offered the services of his Frasers to the queen against the Gordons, in order to avenge the deaths of his forebears at the Field of Shirts. The queen tactfully replied, however, that she was loath to give cause for a further quarrel between the clans. When Queen Mary departed from Inverness, Lord Hugh and his Frasers merely conveyed her to the banks of the Spey – and sad to relate for the self-confidence of youth, a number of Frasers ended by fighting against the queen for the Gordons.[7]

Although Randolph grumbled dreadfully at the appalling journey from Stirling to Inverness, and though the surrounding power of the Gordons was to say the least of it menacing, all in all Mary Stuart had never seemed more blithe. She evidently looked on the Highlanders as noble savages, a category she found more sympathetic than their opposite numbers, the savage nobles, in the south. Randolph was amazed at her happiness and her health: 'In all these garbullies,' he wrote, 'I never saw her merrier, nor dismayed, nor never thought that stomache to be in her that I find! She repenteth but, when the lardes and other at Inverness came in the mornings from the watch, that she was not a man to know what life it was to lie all night in the fields, or to walk upon the causeway with a jack and knapscall [helmet] a Glasgow buckler and a broad sword.'[8] In short, Rosalind was in her element: the very spice of danger, provided by the fact that Sir John still hovered impudently in her wake, far from upsetting, merely stimulated the queen.*

From Inverness, Mary, still dogged by Sir John, proceeded to the seat of the Catholic bishop of Moray at Spynie. It was

---

* In all Queen Mary made two expeditions to the Highlands: it was on the second occasion, in the summer of 1564, that she made her way north to Ross-shire once more through Inverness. *En route* to Dingwall, the chief town of the earldom of Ross, Mary stopped at the priory of Beauly, founded in the thirteenth century by monks of the Valliscaulian order, and taking its name from the beauty of the place, commemorated in its Latin charter – *Monasterium de Bello Loco*. The name seemed apt also to the queen three hundred years later, and inspired her to a royal play upon the words: '*Oui, c'est un beau lieu*' she is said to have exclaimed, with gracious good humour.[9]

suspected that Sir John might finally choose to attack as the royal party crossed the Spey, and Mary's scouts reported that up to 1000 Gordon horsemen were concealed in the woods. But no attack came. As the queen passed the castle of Findlater, the former Ogilvie stronghold, she called on it to surrender; but since there was no response, and the castle could not be captured without cannon, owing to its sea-girt position, she abandoned the effort, and passed on back to Aberdeen. Here, on 22nd September, she was received with a rapturous and loyal welcome, whatever intrigues Huntly might be meditating at nearby Strathbogie. The great question which now faced the queen and the new earl of Moray* was how next to proceed against Huntly: was he to be allowed to maintain this mighty sway over the north of Scotland, so complete that his son temeritously dared to defy the queen outside her own castle of Inverness, and another son, an escaped criminal, harried the queen's troops, with impunity, while he himself apparently planned a state of near-independence? Mary, spurred on by Moray, now sent for 120 harquebusiers and experienced soldiers such as Lord Lindsay, Kirkcaldy of the Grange and Cockburn of Ormiston (all incidentally keen Protestants), as well as some cannon. She also forwarded a message to Huntly asking him to surrender his own formidable cannon, which stood in the courtyard at Strathbogie, in order to menace the Highlanders into subjection.

A prolonged game of cat-and-mouse now ensued with Huntly; the earl himself, drawn two ways, was clearly not yet quite sure in his own mind whether he was engaged in a rebellion or not; 'letting I dare not wait upon I would', he temporized by sending his eldest surviving son Lord Gordon to consult Gordon's father-in-law Châtelherault in the south. Knox wrote later that Gordon actually tried to raise the south to the same effect as his father was raising the north, and to this effect even contacted Bothwell, who had just escaped from his own imprisonment in Edinburgh Castle. But in the meantime Huntly offered to join

---

* As Lord James will be referred to in the future to distinguish him from Mary's son James.

with the queen to pursue his errant son John Gordon, provided he could appear with an armed force to support him. The queen understandably did not trust the appearance of Huntly surrounded by his Gordons, and Huntly equally declined to appear alone. Frightened of being captured, the great earl now took humiliatingly to sleeping every night under a different roof (easy enough in Gordon territory) but spending his days at Strathbogie. When the queen's army got to hear of this, Kirkcaldy set out from Aberdeen with a small party of twelve men in order to surprise Huntly at his midday dinner and hold the entrance to Strathbogie until reinforcements arrived. Unfortunately the reinforcements proceeded both too quickly and too noisily, and Kirkcaldy was still parleying with the porter for an entrance to the castle when the clatter of their approach alerted the watchmen. Huntly had time to abandon his half-eaten meal, rush through the castle to the back and escape over a wall on to a waiting horse, without boots and without sword, but nevertheless still free. And on his fresh horse he soon outdistanced his pursuers.

Lady Huntly was now compelled to welcome the royal emissaries in Strathbogie at last: they found it stripped bare, except, rather touchingly, for the chapel, which had been left completely furnished with all its candles, ornaments and altarbooks, in readiness for the queen's visit, when it had been expected that she would use it. But as Huntly and John Gordon had both now disappeared, and the latter had recently captured fifty-six harquebusiers from a company near Findlater, which rendered him still more dangerous, it was considered by the government that the final stage of rebellion had been reached. On 16th October, by orders of the Privy Council, both Huntly and John Gordon were 'put to the horn' or outlawed; although the keys of both Findlater and Auchendown were sent, the queen was not to be placated. In a grim mood, she commented that she had other means to open the Gordon doors; in the meantime she demanded the surrender of Strathbogie itself, which was refused. The 4th earl promptly retired to the hills, in his fastness in the wilds of Badenoch, and might have tasted the pleasures of guerrilla warfare indefinitely, had he remained there.

Lady Huntly, however, was not content to leave the situation in this unsatisfactory state. First of all she attempted to have a further interview with the queen outside Aberdeen, which was denied to her. She then returned to Huntly's side, and persuaded him that in his present critical state the best defence was attack. She seems to have been encouraged in her advice by the prophecy of her tame witches that by nightfall Huntly would be lying in the Tolbooth at Aberdeen, without any wound in his body. Egged on by his martial and optimistic wife, the earl now abandoned his stronghold, and marched militantly towards Aberdeen. Randolph at any rate was in no doubt as to his intentions: he believed that Huntly intended to 'apprehend the Queen, and do with the rest of his will'. Knox put Huntly's force at seven or eight hundred men, although other estimates made it over a thousand.[10] Clearly, from the speech which he made to his men before battle, Huntly believed that many of the queen's host would desert to his cause when the fighting began. In any case, he was able to take up a commanding position on the Hill of Fare, above the field of Corrichie.

Even at this stage, Huntly's fatal indecision struck him again: according to Knox, when he saw the determined numbers falling thin, he intended to retire from the scene before the battle could begin the next morning. However, his ill-health and corpulence prevented him from rising before ten o'clock in the morning, by which time it was too late. By now Maitland had made 'a vehement orison' to the queen's troops, urging them to remember their duty and not to fear the multitudes before them. Huntly addressed his vehement orison, on the other hand, to God; falling on his knees, he addressed Him in the following prayer, which he considered appropriate to the occasion: 'O Lord I have been a bloodthirsty man, and by my means has mekle innocent blood been spilt; but thou give me victory this day and I shall serve Thee all the days of my life ...'[11] But the prayer was not granted. As the days went on, the royal harquebus fire raked Huntly's troops on the hill, forcing them off their eminence, and as a swamp lay at the bottom they found themselves virtually cut off in a trap. Moray and his men hacked down the Gordons, and Huntly and two of his sons, Sir John and seventeen-year-old Adam Gordon, were captured and brought before him. At this dramatic moment in his fortunes, the great northern earl finally found the strain of the situation too much for him. There and then he dropped down off his horse in front of his captors, stone dead from either heart failure or apoplexy, brought on by strain and overweight – or as the Diurnal of Occurrents vividly put it, 'he burst and swelled'.[12]

The sudden departure of Huntly's wayward spirit from his all too solid flesh did not prevent his lifeless body from undergoing prolonged indignities. Immediately after the battle his unmarked body was thrown roughly over a pair of 'crealles' (fish baskets), and as it was late, taken to the Tolbooth at Aberdeen to lie there for the night – thus fulfilling the witches' prophecy in true ironical and Delphic fashion. His corpse was then disembowelled and shipped south from Aberdeen to Edinburgh, £50 having been spent on a French doctor in Aberdeen and a surgeon in Edinburgh, together with spices, vinegar, *aqua vitae* and other necessities for the embalming of the body.[13] It was all the more important to guard against the putrefaction of the late Huntly since the corpse itself was destined to be brought to trial by an ancient law, which provided for the presence of the offender, living or dead, for trial in front of Parliament, in cases of treason against the queen.*

In May 1563, seven months after his death on the field of Corrichie, the embalmed corpse of Huntly was set up in front of the full session of Parliament, with Queen Mary sitting on the royal throne. The grisly relic was then solemnly declared guilty of treason, and sentence of forfeiture passed upon it and its erstwhile belongings, with the title of the earldom of Huntly declared to be attainted. The body, still unburied, was then

---

* This ghoulish procedure has been traced back to the days when Parliament was a ceremonial sitting of the court of the lists for trial by battle, and the importance of the presence of the corpse was a reminder of the personal element in trial by combat.[14]

deposited in the Blackfriars Priory in Edinburgh, and it was not until April 1566 that it was allowed to be carried back to the north, to be laid in the family tomb of the Gordons in Elgin Cathedral. The fate of the gay young Sir John Gordon was shorter and sharper. On 2nd November he was executed, in the presence of the queen herself, who was compelled to attend in order to give the lie to stories that she had encouraged him in his affections and his wild matrimonial schemes. Having a horror of bloodshed, she was extremely reluctant to do so, and as it turned out the reality was even worse than her imaginings. Sir John cried out that the presence of the queen solaced him, since he was about to suffer for love of her. But the executioner was clumsy at his task and the spectacle reduced the queen to passionate weeping; she was indeed so horrified by her ordeal that she ended by breaking down completely, and had to be carried to her chamber, where she remained all the next day, in a state of nervous collapse.

Two of Huntly's sons, Alexander and John, having been sacrificed in the general holocaust of his family's fall from grace, Mary proceeded to spare the life of the eldest son George, Lord Gordon; he had not been involved in the final battle, having been away in the south consulting Châtelherault, and after being officially condemned with his father, he was pardoned and merely put into free ward at Dunbar. Huntly's youngest son, Adam Gordon, was also spared. The rich vestments from Aberdeen Cathedral stored at Strathbogie since 1559 were taken down to Holyrood, where it seems the queen treated them more as Gordon spoils rather than as the ecclesiastical heritage they were, for they were probably among the gilded vestments in her belongings turned to secular uses in the spring of 1567 making a rich bed for Darnley and a doublet for Bothwell. The spoils of Strathbogie Castle were either taken by the queen or given to Moray for his new castle of Darnaway. Besides the earldom of Moray, whose revenues were estimated by Randolph at 1000 merks a year, Moray also received the sheriffdoms of Elgin, Forres and Inverness. Hence the tumbling-down of Huntly's power in the north left an empty space which Moray, rather than the crown, was able to fill; while the disappearance of the leading Catholic magnate from the Scottish scene could not fail to weaken the Catholic cause there, and in turn benefit the reformed religion.

It has sometimes been argued that Mary made a fundamental mistake in allowing the balance of power to be upset in this way. The north of Scotland, which conceivably could have been a Catholic *bloc* under a friendly Huntly, to play off against a Protestant south, was now broken up into different units; and when the attainder was removed three years later for Huntly's son, the properties were too dissipated for him to become the magnate his father had been. But even before 1562 Mary had never shown any signs of supporting Huntly either as a magnate or as a Catholic, and had repeatedly snubbed his overtures in favour of the Protestants. Her attitude towards Huntly was very much affected by her general policy since her arrival in Scotland, of leaning upon the advice of Moray and Maitland; her aim was to quieten down all possible Catholic insurrections, in favour of general peace, the maintenance of the royal authority and the *status quo*. It may well be argued that Mary's policy was unwise, compared to the more serpentine procedure of backing each noble in turn, and luring them in some fashion to destroy each other, until the crown should be left triumphant. By this reasoning Huntly should have been skilfully built up, rather than bloodily laid low. Certainly the 'pale augurs' might well murmur low over his 'blasted head', when they reflected how critical Mary's situation could be if Moray's loyalty faltered. There was, however, an obvious difficulty in the way of pursuing this policy of checks and balances, quite apart from Mary's own inexperience of Scottish affairs; this was the character of Huntly — so manifestly unreliable.

Mary herself was in no doubt afterwards that Huntly's treachery had been proved by the evidence discovered after his death, and the confessions of Sir John and Huntly's servants (one of them made before the battle of Corrichie): all of which suggested that in his last moments Huntly did have some wild ill-conceived plan of seizing Mary's person, and upsetting the Protestant régime in favour of a Catholic one. Mary continued to regard Huntly as a double-dyed traitor, and when she wrote to her uncle in France and to the Pope in January 1563, protesting her continued devotion to the Catholic faith, she clearly felt no regret that circumstances had compelled her to lay low her greatest Catholic subject – it had been an unpleasant duty which it would have been dangerous not to have carried out.[15] By denying her entrance at Inverness, refusing to join her in the hunt against his son, and finally in taking up arms against her with the possible object of abducting her, he had certainly made it extremely difficult for her to support him against Moray, even if she had so wished. Thus Moray was easily able to gratify his natural avariciousness, and acquire the rich spoils in the north, having no need to work out any more subtle conspiracy. It is significant that Maitland himself, on his way back to southern Scotland, revealed that he was finally convinced of Huntly's treachery: 'I am sorry that the soil of my native country did ever produce so unnatural a subject as the Earl of Huntly hath proved in the end against his Sovereign,' he wrote. 'Being a Princess so gentle and benign ... Well, the event hath made manifest his iniquity, and the innocence as well of her Majestie as of her ministers towards him.'[16] In short, it was the character and temperament of Huntly which made it impossible in the final analysis for any dependence to be put upon him.

Chastened in spirit by her experiences, and by the chilling fate of Sir John Gordon, Mary made her way southwards again and was back in Edinburgh by November: here, along with Maitland, she fell victim to the fashionable new disease, influenza, lightly dubbed 'the New Acquaintance', but was otherwise not directly threatened by any personal danger for the next few months, at least. In the spring of 1563, however, she was to be the subject of a more intimate assault than the projected abduction plans of either Arran, Bothwell or Sir John Gordon. Among the train of French courtiers who accompanied the queen to Scotland from France in 1561 was a certain Pierre de Châtelard: well-born, charming-looking and gallant, Châtelard was also a poet, a fact which naturally commended itself to

Mary. He was attached to the suite of the son of the Constable de Montmorency, Damville, who was also counted among Mary's admirers, to the extent that he was supposed to have desired to abandon his wife, still in France, out of love for the Scottish queen. Mary certainly wrote to the constable when he departed that she found his son the most agreeable company.[17] Châtelard himself speedily followed suit by professing the sort of wild lyrical passion suitable in a chivalrous man of literary aspirations for a lovely young queen. It was the sort of admiration – light, courtly and elaborately meaningless – which Mary Stuart particularly enjoyed, because it committed her to nothing (unlike the more vigorous proposals of a John Gordon) and it was something to which she had long and agreeably been accustomed at the court of France. It was after all much more to her taste to be celebrated in verses than dragged into a Highland fastness and forcibly married. There was no suggestion at the time of anything at all scandalous in her attitude to Châtelard, and Knox's insinuations (written after the event) that she had been over-familiar with him can safely be attributed to his vicious desire to put everything the queen did in the most evil light – he was also incidentally probably unaware of the gallant licence allowed to poets at the French court, and if he had been aware of it, would have regarded it as a further proof of French devilry. Châtelard ended his visit to Scotland with his master Damville, and returned to France.

In the autumn of 1562, however, he decided to revisit the Scottish court; on his way through London, he confided that he was about to visit 'his lady love', and soon he was back with Mary's court at Aberdeen, with a letter from Damville, and a book of his own poems. Mary received him in her usual friendly way, and with the compulsive generosity which she showed to those who pleased her, presented him with a sorrel gelding which had been given her by her half-brother Lord Robert, as well as some money to dress himself as befitted a young gallant: these favours were still absolutely no more than she showed at many times in her life to those around her, nor was there even now the faintest suggestion of impropriety in this conventional relationship of beautiful queen and platonic admiring poet. All this made Châtelard's next move particularly incomprehensible. On the night when Maitland was about to set forth again for England, at the queen's request, Mary, Moray and Maitland all conferred together until past midnight. Châtelard seized the opportunity to dash into her bed-chamber unobserved, and hide under the bed. Luckily he was discovered by two of her grooms of the chamber, making their routine search of her tapestries and bed, and thrown out. The queen was not told of the incident until the morning, but immediately the news reached her, she ordered Châtelard to leave the court.

Châtelard, however, was either self-confident enough or crazy enough to follow the queen to St Andrews. The next night he proceeded to burst in on her, when she was alone with only one or two of her women, and according to what Randolph first heard, made such audacious advances to her that the unfortunate queen cried out for help. Her brother Moray rushed in, and Mary, in a state of near-hysteria, begged him to run his dagger through the man to save her. Moray, with greater calm and prudence, soothed his sister, and persuaded her that it would be better if Châtelard's life were temporarily spared, so that he could face a public trial. Randolph later heard that Châtelard's intentions in making this second foray into the royal apartments had been merely to explain away his first intrusion, on the grounds that he had been overcome by sleep, and had sought the first convenient resting-place.[18] Whether he attempted to advance this implausible explanation or not, Mary's reaction to the whole incident was highly hysterical, and no spinster ever reacted with more horrified indignation to the presence of a man in her bed-chamber than the already once married queen of Scots.

Châtelard was sent to the dungeons of St Andrews, and after a public trial sentenced to execution on 22nd February. Romantic to the last, just before his execution, he read aloud Ronsard's Hymn to Death there and then in the market square of St Andrews. The beautiful last lines of the poem must have seemed strangely ironical to those of the bystanders who understood enough French to appreciate them:

> Je te salue, heureuse et profitable mort...
> ...puisqu'il faut mourir
> Donne-moi que soudain je te puisse encourir
> Ou pour l'honneur de Dieu, ou pour servir mon Prince...*

In fact it was far from clear for whose honour, or in whose service, Châtelard was dying. Just before he died, his last words echoed out, 'Adieu, the most beautiful and the most cruel princess of the world' – words which are given slightly differently by Knox: 'In the end, he concluded looking unto the heavens, with these words "O cruel Dame".' The sense, however, is in both cases the same, despite Knox's efforts to give the common French word *dame* a more sinister import: 'That is,' he wrote, 'Cruel mistress. What that complaint imported, lovers may divine."[9] Châtelard's general behaviour and these rhetorical last words all lead one to suppose that the young poet was a victim of one of those unbalanced passions for a royal personage, to which princesses have been subject all through history, royalty being notoriously a great aphrodisiac to an unstable mind. Châtelard had mistaken Mary's gracious reception for something more humanly passionate, and died for his error. The queen's outraged withdrawal from his advances makes it quite clear that she never reciprocated them in her own mind – as indeed does the method by which Châtelard chose to approach her, since if they had been lovers already or intending to become so, she would presumably have arranged a more convenient rendezvous and one which was less likely to be interrupted.

But it is possible that there was a more sinister explanation for Châtelard's advances. Publicity seems to have been one of

---

* I salute you, happy and profitable Death...
...since I must die
Grant that I may suddenly encounter you
Either for the honour of God, or in the service of my Prince.

the main features of his attempt on the queen's virtue: if Châtelard's wits were not actually wandering, he must have realized that he was all too likely to be discovered in her bed-chamber by her attendants. The ugly speculation arises whether this was not in fact Châtelard's intention, and whether his ultimate aim was to blacken Mary's reputation rather than win her love. According to Maitland, Châtelard had confessed to Mary that he had been dispatched by persons in a high position in France expressly to compromise her honour, and the duchess of Guise hinted at the same thing to the Venetian ambassador. Mary mentioned the name of Coligny's first wife, and told Maitland there were other names involved she could not trust to paper. The nuncio at the French court heard that the incident had been arranged to give Mary a bad name.[20] In the circumstances, it is significant that Châtelard himself turned out to be a Huguenot. Even his casual remark in London about his lady love may have been intended to draw attention to his relationship with the queen. Whether Châtelard was an emissary of the French Huguenots or a lovesick fool, the one certain piece of evidence which emerges from the whole affair is that Mary's reaction to the escapade was markedly severe. Death was after all a high price for Châtelard to pay for an amorous adventure. It is true that Mary may have justified his subsequent execution in her mind by the knowledge of the plot which had been woven around her, yet both Randolph and Knox confirm that her first reaction to his entry had been to demand for him to be killed by Moray. There was no hint here of the loose easy-going morals of the French court, which it has sometimes been suggested that she acquired along with her education.

It was a sad spring for the young queen. Two or three days after Châtelard's execution, her uncle Duke Francis of Guise was shot down by a Huguenot assassin, Poltrot, who knew him by the white plume in his hat, and attacked him from behind – thus fulfilling the prophecy of Luc Gauric that he would die from a wound in his back, which the duke had once angrily repudiated as being a slur on his courage. On 15th March came the news that he had died. Mary was overcome with grief and her ladies shed tears 'like showers of rain'.[21] Only a few weeks later another uncle, the Grand Prior Francis, also died. Mary, upset by these repeated sorrows in the only family she had really known, melancholy after the Châtelard episode, so distasteful to her nature, exhausted in health by the long Scottish winter and bouts of illness, burst out to Randolph that she was really almost destitute of friends; she outlined her many adventures and vicissitudes since her husband's death, and confessed that the burden suddenly seemed too much for her to bear. In an access of feminine weakness, she read Queen Elizabeth's letter of sympathy with tears in her eyes, and exclaimed to Randolph that neither of them could afford to turn down a possible support – how much better everything would be if the two queens were indeed friends! 'For I see now that the world is not that that we do make of it, nor yet are they most happy that continue longest in it.'[22] These were gloomy sentiments for a young girl just turned twenty-one. Mary Stuart had now been a widow for over two years. Since the Châtelard incident Mary Fleming had been taken to sleep in her room for company and protection. But it was high time that she made a serious attempt to share the load of her responsibilities with a proper partner, especially since her naturally dependent nature inevitably turned to a masculine adviser, as a sunflower turns to the sun. Neither James Stewart, earl of Moray, in her counsels, nor Mary Fleming in her bed-chamber were adequate substitutes for the wise, strong, loyal husband whom she now more than ever needed to support her.

CHAPTER TWELVE

A Husband for a Girl

'... The case was different for an heiress to a kingdom, who by the same act took a husband to herself and gave a King to the people. Many were of the opinion that it was more equitable that the people should choose a husband for a girl, than that a girl should choose a King for a whole people.'

Buchanan on the marriage of queens

Mary Stuart was young, beautiful and attractive: she was also a queen, and she could offer an independent kingdom as a dowry to any husband. On the surface, it would seem that it should not have been too difficult for her to find a suitable candidate, since she had none of the psychological problems of an Elizabeth Tudor, and was sufficiently conventionally feminine to long for a male partner on whom to depend. In theory therefore she had a wide choice of possible husbands: but, in practice, so many considerations had to be taken into account, that while the field was not exactly reduced – since many candidates met one or other of the requirements – it was impossible to declare a clear winner, since none of them met them all. This was true if only because many of the requirements were actually contradictory. The only point on which everyone agreed was that the choice was an important one, not in terms of Mary Stuart's happiness, but because whomever she married would inevitably expect to become king of Scotland – not merely a titular consort in the more modern sense. Francis had always been known as king of Scotland, and had also been granted the crown matrimonial: any future consort might expect to enjoy the former privilege and hope to enjoy the latter. Under the circumstances, Buchanan's views on the subject of an heiress to a kingdom may be appreciated: by the same act she 'took a husband to herself and gave a King to the people. Many were of the opinion that it was more equitable that the people should choose a husband for a girl, than that a girl should choose a King for a whole people." However, Mary had no intention of consulting her people on this subject, which she considered to be essentially a matter of royal prerogative: it was now the subject of anxious consultation between herself and Moray and Maitland, in Scotland, while her French relations the Guises held and acted on views of their own in France.

The first problem was that of religion: was Mary to marry a Catholic like herself, as was generally assumed to be her intention, an Archduke Charles of Austria for example, or even her cousin Henry of Guise? Or would she perhaps attempt the more daring policy of binding together her subjects by wedding someone of their own religion – even the name of the prince of Condé was put forward at one point. Both courses had obvious dangers: a Catholic marriage would inevitably upset the balance she was so carefully maintaining between her private religion and the public religion of her country, by emphasizing that she was very much a Catholic at heart whatever her outward tolerance to the Protestants; a Protestant marriage on the other hand would be difficult to explain to her Catholic relations and allies on the Continent, on whom she still depended.

Apart from the religious question there was the question of status: was she to marry an independent prince with a kingdom of his own, a king of Denmark or Sweden, or even her ex-brother-in-law the twelve-year-old King Charles of France, whose name was mentioned in this connection despite his youth and their previous relationship? Don Carlos, as sole heir to the mighty Spanish dominions of Philip II, also came into this category. Or was she to marry a subject within a kingdom: an Englishman such as her cousin, Henry, Lord Darnley, or even the duke of Norfolk, a Scot – a Hamilton, a Gordon or some other scion of a powerful clan – or a Frenchman such as the duke of Nemours? Once again there were obvious disadvantages to both courses: an independent ruler with a kingdom of his own could not fail to treat Scotland as a satellite, and could scarcely be expected to put Scottish interests above those of his own country; the raising-up of a mere subject to royal rank, on the other hand, would certainly arouse jealousy and dissension among the Scottish nobles, who scarcely allowed their actual sovereign the prerogatives of monarchy, and would certainly view the elevation of one of their own rank most unfavourably. As Archibald Douglas had noted long ago, when the queen was a baby, the ideal thing might seem to be a second son of 'France, Denmark, or England if such a thing existed ... that one of the second sons might thereby be King of Scots, and dwell among them keeping the Estate of Scotland which evermore hath been a realm of itself'.[2] The trouble with this solution, quite apart from the comparative shortage of second sons among the European royal families at this date – none in England or Spain, and those in France still mere children in 1563 – was that such a candidate might easily combine the disadvantages of both the foreign prince and an inferior subject: his foreign nationality would inevitably involve Scotland in certain alliances and commitments in which her own interests might not be paramount, and his own status might not be sufficiently impressive to cow the Scots.

Among all these imponderables, there was the matter of the views of Queen Elizabeth on the subject. So far, while Mary's domestic policy had been towards the maintenance of peace and order, and the religious *status quo*, her foreign policy had been directed towards getting herself recognized as Queen Elizabeth's successor on the throne of England. In this endeavour, in which so far no real progress had been made, Mary's putative husband was obviously a trump card: yet once more how was this card to be played? Was Elizabeth to be asked to nominate a husband of her own choice, which Mary would meekly accept in order to show herself satisfactorily pliant to Elizabeth's wishes, and thus worthy of the recognition which she desired? Or was the prospect of a foreign Catholic husband hostile to England to be held over Elizabeth's head, to blackmail her into granting the recognition, lest her own problems with her English Catholics should be thus increased? Again there were drawbacks to both courses: if Elizabeth nominated the husband, but still refused to give formal recognition until after the marriage, Mary would have surrendered her advantage, with no certainty of gain; if Mary carried through her threat and married a strong Catholic, then Elizabeth might understandably announce that Mary by her actions had excluded herself forever. Still on the tack of the English royal succession, might it not be more to the point if Mary attempted to bolster up her English claim (still strongly rebutted at this date by the English Parliament, and with the shadow of Henry VIII's will lying across it) by marrying someone else in whose veins also ran the vital blood which brought them within the English royal family tree. It could be argued that marriage to a Darnley, for example, or even one of Geoffrey Pole's sons, would reinforce Mary's own claim by a sort of royal osmosis. But here again, Elizabeth's attitude to the subject would clearly be vital, for although such a marriage might impress the English Parliament, Elizabeth herself might feel that her actual throne, rather than the succession to it, was being threatened.

In the face of so many unknown or unknowable elements, so many possible avenues of action, each one barred by some sort of obstacle, so many diplomatic negotiations, both secret and open, some merely the reported rumours of ambassadors, others the declared (but not necessarily sincere) intentions of monarchs, the marriage of Mary Stuart took on a very different appearance from the simple matching of a nubile and beautiful young girl with an excellent worldly position to offer her husband. In face of the chaos and tragedy in which these negotiations ended, it is legitimate to question whether there was indeed *any* happy solution to the marriage problems of Mary Queen of Scots: one may perhaps return to the 'merry' wish of Mary and the devout wish of Throckmorton – how much simpler if one of the queens had been a man, so that they could have married each other.* The consort was indeed the perennial problem of the female ruler in this century: it is significant that the one queen who emerged in the eyes of the people as having never made a mistaken match was Queen Elizabeth – who made no match at all, despite negotiations which lasted for three-quarters of her reign.

The first negotiations on the subject which Maitland undertook in the spring of 1563 revealed that Mary's personal attitude to marriage had not changed since the early days of her widowhood as queen of France: Don Carlos was still the object of her desire, and as it was Spanish prestige – backed up by troops and Spanish money – which made him so desirable, it is evident that Mary saw marriage at this point very much in terms of power politics. Just after the Châtelard incident, Maitland was sent again to London, on the ostensible excuse of offering Mary's meditation between Queen Elizabeth and the warring French; his instructions also bade him pursue the subject of Mary's claim to the English throne after Elizabeth, but secretly he was commissioned to reopen the negotiations for a Spanish marriage with de Quadra, Philip II's ambassador in London, by hinting that the alternative might be a match with the young French king. The mere mention of this prospect was enough to terrify Philip sufficiently to start up discussions of the subject once more – although he did stipulate that the utmost secrecy should be preserved if the negotiations were to have any chance of success. The true attitude of Moray and Maitland towards this Spanish marriage can only be guessed at: it is impossible to be certain whether they actually approved of a Catholic bride-groom for the queen, hoping to be able to rule an independent Protestant Scotland for themselves once more, with Mary safely installed on the throne of Spain as she had once been installed on the throne of France; or whether they were merely attempting to bluff Queen Elizabeth into showing her own hand over

---

* Confronted with such a problem, it was perhaps regrettable that the solution of the royal family of Egypt was not open to that of Scotland: Dr A. L. Rowse once suggested that if Mary had been able to marry her half-brother Moray, as Cleopatra married Ptolemy, she might have fared much better.

Mary's projected marriage. In any case the Spanish negotiations now went forward once more.

Despite Philip's plea for secrecy, the news of these discussions began to leak out in France: here they naturally caused the same apprehension in the breast of Catherine de Médicis as the prospect of a French marriage had caused in that of Philip of Spain. The Guisards themselves with the traditional French jealousy of Spain would have infinitely preferred the prospect of the Archduke Charles, brother of the emperor, and Mary's uncle the cardinal took it upon himself to enter negotiations for his hand, of his own accord, parallel with the Spanish negotiations. But there is no reason to suppose that Mary herself ever seriously considered the archduke – at one point the queen grew quite angry with her uncle for thus embroiling her with definite authority. Archduke Charles had one important defect, in that he was generally thought in Scotland to be too poor to maintain the state of consort, especially for a queen who was hard put to it to manage her own finances; even if his brother gave him a large allowance, as was suggested, he still would not have the army behind him, which his cousin Don Carlos could command as heir to the Spanish throne.

Naturally the news of these negotiations also came to the ears of Queen Elizabeth herself – Maitland was after all conducting them under her nose in London, and Throckmorton took care to repeat all the gossip from France. Before Maitland returned to Scotland, Elizabeth took the opportunity to inform him that if Mary married either Don Carlos or the Archduke Charles, or indeed any other imperial candidate, she could not avoid becoming her enemy; if on the other hand Mary married to her satisfaction, Elizabeth sweetly added, she would surely be a good friend and sister to her, and in the course of time, make her her heir. This was the crux of the problem: how was Mary to marry to Elizabeth's satisfaction, if Elizabeth did not express any definite choice? Now, from the autumn of 1563 onwards, Elizabeth began to drop broad hints as to who her personal choice might be. The only trouble was that Elizabeth's choice of candidate was sufficiently eccentric to arouse serious doubts as to whether it was a genuine suggestion, or whether on the contrary she was merely trying to prevent Mary in the end making any marriage at all.

The husband whom Elizabeth apparently had in mind was her own favourite Lord Robert Dudley. She had first mentioned his name to Maitland in the spring of 1563, when he arrived in London: jokingly, as it seemed to Maitland, she observed that Lord Robert Dudley would make a good husband for the queen of Scots. Maitland could indeed hardly fail to treat the suggestion as a pleasantry since at first sight Dudley had absolutely no obvious advantages as a husband, and a great many obvious disadvantages. His stock, far from being royal, was actually tainted by treason, his father the duke of Northumberland having been beheaded, and the title put under attainder; he himself was generally considered to be Queen Elizabeth's paramour, and whatever the truth of their relationship, her familiarity with him had certainly caused scandal throughout Europe, and continued to do so; thirdly, his first wife Amy Robsart had died under the most suspicious circumstances, which, it was generally believed, left him free to marry Queen Elizabeth, if she would have him, and the country would accept it. Now Maitland was asked to consider this controversial figure as a husband for his own mistress, a born queen, the widow of another king, and herself highly conscious of her own position, as well as being the bearer of an unblemished character. Maitland showed himself at his diplomatic best when he answered Queen Elizabeth that it was a great proof of the love she bore to the Scottish queen 'as she was willing to give her a thing so dearly prized by herself', but that Queen Mary would hardly wish to deprive Queen Elizabeth of the joy and solace of Lord Robert's companionship. In a further vein of witty invention, he suggested that Elizabeth herself should marry Dudley, and then bequeath both her husband and her kingdom to Mary when she died.[3]

In September 1563, the Scots had perforce to take the suggestion more seriously: Randolph was instructed to approach Queen Mary, newly arrived at the castle of Craigmillar near Edinburgh, after a western progress, and hint broadly at Queen

Elizabeth's own wishes on the subject of Mary's marriage; he was to indicate a husband, the English queen added in her own hand to the instructions, 'perchance as she would hardly think we would agree to'.[4] Randolph of course mentioned no actual name of an English noble, but he did confirm to Mary that the continuance of friendship with Elizabeth was impossible if she married into either imperial family. In November Randolph was given further instructions on the subject – but still he did not officially name Lord Robert Dudley, contenting himself with pouring cold water on 'the children of France, Spain or Austria', and telling Mary that her late husband, the king of France, had been a perfect example of whom *not* to marry.[5] Mary replied that she could only give a vague answer to such vague propositions; she needed after all to know the names of suitable bridegrooms, not unsuitable ones. It was not until the end of March 1564 that Randolph was authorized officially to offer Lord Robert Dudley, as most suitable among the English nobles, a year after Elizabeth's first hint to Maitland. Mary's outward reaction was meek: she listened graciously once more, and suggested as she had done previously in the autumn that a conference should be held at Berwick between English and Scots. Inwardly, however, she can hardly have regarded the notorious Lord Robert as an acceptable husband – she who still longed for the heir of the Spanish empire – unless of course he brought with him a definite recognition of her title to succeed Elizabeth as a dowry.

While Mary pursued a Catholic marriage abroad, her policy at home continued to favour the reformed religion as it had done ever since her arrival. She herself certainly felt that she had absolutely no choice in the matter. At an interview with the papal nuncio Gouda in the summer of 1562, Mary told him that she could not even promise him a safe conduct while he was in Scotland, and advised him to stay indoors as much as possible and not attempt to deliver the Pope's briefs – unless he wished to die violently. She herself, explained Mary patiently, would be quite powerless to help him if anything untoward occurred. Nor did Gouda feel that Mary's apprehensions were unjustified: she made an excellent personal impression on him, and he accepted her word that she intended privately to live and die a Catholic, whatever the ways of her kingdom. Mary also refused quite flatly to consider sending Scottish priests to the Council of Trent: once again she protested her personal devotion to the Catholic cause, but said that the dispatching of a Scottish deputation would be quite out of the question under the present circumstances. Equally, when a college for training Catholic priests was suggested to her, Mary dismissed it in one word as 'impracticable'.[6] The truth was that Mary, from the vantage point of Scotland, could perceive realities about the religious situation there not readily understandable by the distant papacy or even by her uncle in France, the cardinal. Her continual aim in her letters abroad was to explain this dichotomy she was obliged to practise in order to preserve the peace – devotion to Catholicism in private, tolerance towards Protestantism in public. But, of course, it was a dichotomy which it was not easy to convey in letter to those who had never visited the country.

In 1563, Parliament, with the queen's agreement, provided that Protestant ministers should have the use of manses and glebes and that churches should be repaired. Symbolical of Mary's desire to preserve religious amity and peace in her country (at the expense of those zealous Catholics who still hoped she would fight for their cause) was her renewed attempt to win the friendship or at least the approval of John Knox. In the middle of April 1563 the queen was staying on the island of Lochleven with Moray's mother Lady Margaret Douglas and his half-brother, Sir William Douglas. Here, in this ill-omened fortress which was to play such a significant part in her future story, she sent for Knox. Together queen and reformer took part in a long and fairly friendly dispute in the great hall of the castle. Mary asked Knox to abate the persecution of the Catholics, especially in the western regions of Scotland, where it was fierce, and Knox in return asked her to administer the laws of her kingdom, which had made Catholicism illegal. The next morning, as she was hawking near Kinross, the queen sent for

Knox again, and among other topics she raised were the fearful quarrels between the earl of Argyll and his wife – Mary's beloved but wayward half-sister, Jean Stewart, who was, as the queen herself admitted, 'not so circumspect in all things as that she wished her to be', and much preferred the delights of Holyrood life to a quieter existence in the west of Scotland with her husband. Now Mary attempted to charm Knox by asking him to mediate in this domestic dispute, which was becoming a scandal of court life: and although Knox said later that the whole conversation showed how deeply Mary Stuart was able to dissemble, in fact he did write a stern letter to Argyll on his matrimonial problems.*[7]

The news of Mary's Spanish negotiations, however, provoked a sterner reaction from Knox. A Catholic match was the very last thing he could be expected to countenance and he thundered forth from the pulpit on the subject in Edinburgh, in front of a large congregaton of the nobility, assembled in the city for Parliament, despite Maitland's somewhat disingenuous assertion that 'such thing never entered in her (the Queen's) heart'. The public rebuke was too much for Mary. She sent for Knox to come to Holyrood and in 'vehement fume' exclaimed that no prince had ever been so treated – had she not borne with him more patiently than any other ruler 'in all your rigorous manner of speaking both against my self and my uncles; yea,' she continued indignantly, 'I have sought your favours by all possible means. I offered unto you presence and audience whensoever it pleased you to admonish me; and yet I cannot be quit of you.' She added in a voice choked with 'howling', in Knox's immortal trenchant phrase, and tears (so many tears that the chamber boy, Knox says, could scarcely find enough napkins to mop them up) that she would be revenged upon him.[8]

Knox tried to justify himself by saying that it was his duty to speak plainly but Mary burst out again and again: 'What have you to do with my marriage?' and finally in a surge of irritation:

---

* The earl and his countess were never permanently reconciled despite the good offices of Knox and the queen: they were finally divorced and Argyll married again.

'What are you within this commonwealth?' which gave Knox the opportunity for the crushing reply: 'A subject born within the same, madam.' He proceeded to speak again at length on the horrors of a Catholic marriage, which only brought forth further floods of angry tears from the queen. Erskine of Dun tried to calm her by tactfully praising her beauty and charms and suggesting that any prince in Europe would be glad to marry her, but Mary was not to be smoothed with fair words; furiously she requested Knox to leave her presence, regardless of the fact that he solemnly assured her how much he disliked tears, since even the tears of corrected children wounded him. Knox departed, characteristically taking the opportunity on his way out to point out to the maids of honour in attendance that their 'gay gear' would little avail them at the impending coming of the Knave Death.

That summer the queen made her progresses in west and south-west Scotland, visting the local castles, seeing and being seen by her subjects and last but not least enjoying the pleasures of the chase. The court made ready their 'highland apparel' for the tour and the English ambassador Randolph, not to be outdone, fitted himself out 'in outer shape ... like unto the rest'.[9] In July, Mary was actually guest of the earl of Argyll, the warring husband of Jean Stewart, at Inveraray; in August she toured the south-west, staying first with Lord Eglinton, on to Dunure Castle at St Mary's Isle by mid-August, then to Dumfries and so to Drumlanrig; by 27th August she was at Peebles. As the queen hunted and harmlessly enjoyed the sight of some of the most beautiful scenery of her dominions, back in Edinburgh Knox was enraged to hear that she was having the Mass said constantly on her route. Nothing daunted by the interview in the spring, Knox took the opportunity to preach energetically against Mary once more: 'Deliver us, O Lord, from idolatry.' Such defiance could not pass forever unchecked. But as the year wore on, Knox dared to go even further. Two militant Protestants forced their way into the chapel royal in Mary's absence and broke up the Mass of her household. They were arrested but Knox took the line that their trial should be an occasion when the congregation showed its solidarity in favour of the accused, in order to protect them from condemnation. To this effect, he wrote round Scotland, urging the members of the congregation to attend the trial. It was a flagrant insult to the authorities and to the queen. As a result, in December, Knox was summoned before the Council on a charge of treason. He arrived with an enormous following, and when the queen saw him sitting there bareheaded at the end of the table, she burst out laughing, and in an access of high spirits, her angry tears dismissed but not apparently forgotten, she exclaimed in her broad Scots: 'Yon man gart me greit (make me weep) and grat never tear himself. I will see if I can gar him greit.' However, although Knox admitted having written the offending letter, the Council voted that he had not committed treason; so far from being made to weep by Mary, the following spring Knox merely succeeded in angering her further – and pleasing himself. As the burgesses of Edinburgh gossiped, the fifty-year-old reformer married, as his second wife, the seventeen-year-old Margaret Stewart, daughter of Lord Ochiltree, and as such one of Mary's own kin – 'of her own blood and name'.[10]

It was hardly surprising that throughout the autumn of 1563 the courtiers noted that the poor queen frequently succumbed to fits of weeping and depression, alternating with bursts of merriment. Her French physician attempted to cure her by putting her on a diet. But the death of her uncle, the slow progress of her marriage plans, her own loneliness, to say nothing of the loquacious hostility of the uncharmable Knox, were all enough to produce a pattern of nervous ill-health. In December she took to her bed with an unidentified pain in her right side – which was to recur for the rest of her life; Randolph suggested that her collapse might have been due to exhaustion after dancing too long on her twenty-first birthday, and she herself put it down to praying too long in an icy chapel after Mass, in a bitterly cold winter.[11] By mid-January she had recovered. The whole attack may well have been exacerbated by Mary's tension at the lack of conclusion over her marriage plans.

Although Elizabeth's nomination of Lord Robert had come

to Mary's attention in spring 1564, she continued to hope rather for success in the direction of Spain until August: then Philip II, changing his mind once more on the subject, and having procrastinated once again for nearly eighteen months, indicated to his ambassador that the negotiations were once more closed (a decision in which the growing insanity of his son must have played some part). Even so, in the autumn of 1564 Mary dispatched James Melville to London, with the vain hope of revivifying the plan of the Spanish match: in fact Melville's main occupation was to charm Queen Elizabeth with his courtly manners and enjoy in return a prolonged display of her accomplishments, in order that he should thus estimate her more highly than her rival queen of Scots. Melville was, however, also called upon to witness a significant rite by which Dudley was created earl of Leicester and baron of Denbigh, which honours were specifically intended to fit him to wed Queen Mary, although one unrehearsed detail of the rite – by which Elizabeth tickled her favourite's neck in the midst of the ceremony – may have been considered by Melville to have had the opposite effect.[12]

Nevertheless the Dudley negotiations still wound on, and in November 1564 a conference was finally held at Berwick on the subject between Moray and Maitland on one side, and Randolph and Bedford on the other, without, however, anything definite being promised by the English with regard to the recognition of Mary's title in return for the Leicester marriage. As the Scots naturally regarded this recognition as the vital *quid pro quo* for a match which they had no other reason to desire, by December, as Randolph reported to Cecil, they were beginning to clamour for some sort of frankness on the subject from the English. But in reply Cecil was far from frank; on the contrary, he took refuge in phrases of much obscurity more suitable for an oracle than a statesman: let their negotiations, so full of promise, not 'be converted to a matter of bargain or purchase' he wrote, since the English crown 'if it be sort for, may sooner be lost than got, and not being craved, may be as soon offered as reason can require'.[13]

This sort of riddle was all very well, but it was now nearly two years since Mary had started her second serious round of marriage negotiations, and still the English party were taking refuge in saws and sayings and making no definite commitment. In short, Mary was no nearer getting either a husband or the succession to the English throne, although she had been a childless widow over four years, as a result of which there was still no direct heir to the Scottish throne closer than the Hamiltons. Under the circumstances, the impatience of the Scottish party who wrote to Cecil of his 'many obscure words and dark sentences' is understandable; Maitland and Moray pointed out to him quite plainly that if Elizabeth would not establish 'the succession of her crown' it would be quite impossible for them to induce Mary to marry an Englishman, and she would then make her own choice.[14] Yet still no promise came. Not only that, but the next emanation from England – the appearance of young Lord Darnley himself, mysteriously granted permission to travel to Scotland in early February 1565 – cast serious doubts over the whole straight-forwardness of the English point of view.

It was an interesting enigma why Darnley, young, eligible and handsome, with the royal blood of England and Scotland in his veins, should be suddenly allowed to return to Scotland at this very moment, by permission of Queen Elizabeth. The name of Darnley had always played a minor part in any discussion of Mary's possible suitors because of his position in both the Tudor and Stuart family tree, and because he was roughly the right age to be Mary's bridegroom. The match had certainly always been in the mind of Darnley's ambitious striving mother Margaret, countess of Lennox, and it was not for nothing that she had sent him hotfoot to France to condole with Mary on the death of Francis.* In September 1564 the earl of Lennox, who

---

* Dr Strong has pointed out that the double portrait of Darnley and his brother, from which Eworth copied his own picture, is in the unusual medium of tempera painted on linen, which suggests that it was designed for travelling: it may therefore have formed part of the ambitious countess's plans for bringing her handsome son to the notice of the queen of Scots.[15]

had long been banished from Scotland for trying to capture Dumbarton Castle in 1544 with English troops, was allowed to return to Scotland ostensibly to look to his estates. None other than Queen Elizabeth herself pleaded with Queen Mary to receive him. According to Melville, Elizabeth's motive in thus smoothing Lennox's way was quite definitely to promote the Darnley marriage: Elizabeth told Melville Darnley was one of the two that she had in her head to offer unto the queen, as born within the realm of England.[16] In the course of the ceremony by which Leicester was invested with his titles, Elizabeth also teased Melville that he would prefer to see Darnley, who was standing by, as a husband for his queen rather than Leicester. The presence of her husband in the rival camp did not dim the ardour of Margaret Lennox in forwarding the claims of her son: the Lennox Jewel, for example, once thought to commemorate Lennox's death in 1571, is not thought on grounds of style to date from this earlier period, and in any case contains no memorial details of Lennox's life, such as might be expected in a commemorative piece. Margaret Lennox certainly took advantage of the return of Melville to Scotland to send jewels to her husband in 1564: she may have taken the opportunity to create an elaborately emblematic *objet d'art*, whose complicated symbolism would convey messages to her husband on the subject of her matrimonial schemes, too dangerous to commit to paper.* When Mary wrote to Elizabeth in December 1564 asking that Darnley might be allowed to come north to join his father, neither Elizabeth nor her advisers can have been in any doubts that Darnley was now a strongly fancied runner in the Scottish queen's matrimonial stakes. The Spanish contender had recently vanished from the race, and in view of Elizabeth's behaviour Leicester was still not a certain starter: the odds on Darnley, who was Catholic, semi-royal, and apparently approved of by Elizabeth, now dramatically shortened.

It was popularly believed at the time by the Scots that Elizabeth herself had launched Darnley, in order to trap Mary

---

* See G. H. Tait, FSA, 'Historiated Tudor Jewellery', *Antiquaries Journal*, 1962.

into a demeaning marriage, although, as Randolph indicated in his letter of 12th February, it seems to have been Leicester and Cecil who combined together to get the boy his licence to come north.[17] Elizabeth's part seems to have been a passive one: having an extraordinary inability to make up her mind on matters of emotion, she probably did not know herself whether she desired the marriage of the beloved Leicester and Mary. This inability nearly always turned out fortunately for her, since it allowed others to take the action, and in doing so, it was they who made the mistakes. In this particular case, it is likely that Leicester and Cecil, encouraged by the indecisive passivity of Elizabeth, launched Darnley as a sort of Trojan horse into the Scottish queen's kingdom. Queen Mary could not fail to be interested in such an obvious candidate for marriage: as Melville put it, she might prefer Darnley 'being present' to Leicester 'who was absent'; and of Leicester and Cecil it was of course Leicester who had a further personal motive to embroil the negotiations – he may well have been anxious not to have them concluded while Elizabeth herself still remained unmarried. Elizabeth later told de Silva that it was Leicester who had refused to consent to the match, and thus wrecked it.[18] The Scots, who were becoming obstreperous in their desire for some sort of concrete result, would become confused between Leicester and Darnley. Mary herself would dither between the two claimants and continue to remain unwed. The English therefore would be able to continue in that policy of masterly inactivity which best suited their own interests over the marriage of the Scottish queen; as for Elizabeth, she could continue to use the unmarried and therefore uncommitted state of Mary as an argument for not recognizing her place in the English succession. This seems to have been the tortuous reasoning of the English at the beginning of February when Henry Stuart, Lord Darnley, left London, by specific permission of the English queen.

Darnley was on the borders of Scotland by 10th February, and at Dunbar the next day, whence he went on to Haddington, finally reaching Edinburgh on 13th February. Here he spent three days, in the course of which he was most warmly received by Elizabeth's envoy Randolph, who lent him his own horses, as Darnley's had not arrived. Darnley was entertained by Lord Robert Stewart at Holyrood where, according to Randolph, his pleasant social manner made an agreeable impression. Mary was away hunting in Fife. Here on Saturday, 17th February, at the house of the Laird of Wemyss, the first meeting for four years between the ill-starred couple took place. The young man whom Mary saw before her was eminently handsome. Although Melville had assured Queen Elizabeth that he found him almost too effeminate – 'beardless and lady-faced' were the words he used – this was more evidence of Melville's wish to please Elizabeth, than of Darnley's lack of attraction.[19] The contemporary portraits by Eworth, standing with his younger brother, or painted alone three-quarter length, show that Darnley at the age of eighteen* was nothing if not outwardly good-looking. In these portraits Darnley appears at first sight like a young god, with his golden hair, his perfectly shaped face with its short straight nose, the neat oval chin, and above all the magnificent legs stretching forth endlessly in their black hose. But on closer inspection the god appears to be more Pan than Apollo: there is something faun-like about his pointed ears, the beautiful slanting hazel eyes with their unreadable expression, and even a hint of cruelty in the exquisitely formed mouth with its full rosy lips. It was Darnley's height which was considered at the time to be his main physical characteristic – had not Elizabeth called him 'yon long lad' when she pointed him out to Melville – and he was fortunate in being slender with it, or as Melville put it, 'long and small, even and straight'. His elegant physique could hardly fail to commend itself to Mary for two reasons. Firstly, beautiful

---

* Hay Fleming pointed out that there is mystery about the actual date of Darnley's birth. This is usually given as 7th December, 1545. But Knox's Continuator states that Darnley was not yet twenty-one at the time of his death (10th February, 1567). In March 1566 he was specifically stated by Mary's own messenger to the cardinal of Lorraine to be nineteen years old.[20] It seems that the earliest date he could have been born to fit with this evidence was 11th February, 1546. If the 7th December birthday is accepted however, Darnley must have been born on 7th December, 1546: he was thus four years younger than Mary, not three.

as she was, Mary was nevertheless tall enough to tower over most of her previous companions, including her first husband Francis. The psychological implications of this height can only be guessed at, but Darnley was certainly well over six feet one inch.* Mary for once could feel herself not only overtopped at dancing, but also physically protected by her admirer if she so wished; as a novel sensation it could hardly have failed to be pleasant. Secondly, as Mary was also a woman of strong aesthetic instincts, she would tend to appreciate the effeminate beauty of a Darnley more than the masculine vigour of some of her Scottish nobles.

The handsome youth had been well-trained in all the arts considered suitable for a gentleman – or princeling – of the period; he could ride a horse, hunt, dance gracefully and play the lute extremely well. In this respect he took after his father Mathew, earl of Lennox, who had been one of the most gallant figures at the Scottish court before his English marriage. The aim of his ambitious mother had been to make his courtly ways as winning as his outward appearance. To his internal qualities she had unfortunately paid less regard. It was true that his education was in the impressive mould of royalty at the time of the Renaissance: when he was only eight he was accomplished enough to send a letter to Queen Mary Tudor in which he asked her to accept 'a little plot of my own penning' which he termed Utopia Nova. He is traditionally supposed to have translated the works of Valerius Maximus into English. Better attested is the fact that he wrote some pleasant poems, a talent he must have inherited from his mother, herself a poetess;[21] the subjects Darnley chose for his verses included fittingly enough a long address 'to the Queen' on how to treat her subjects, in which he adjured her somewhat priggishly:

* His height has been calculated to have been between six foot one and six foot three inches on the evidence of his reputed thigh bone in the museum of the Royal College of Surgeons. See *Skull and Portraits of Henry Stuart Lord Darnley*, Karl Pearson, FRCS.

> Be governor both good and gracious
> Be loyal and loving to thy lieges all
> Be larger of freedom, and nothing desirous;
> Be just to the poor, for any thing may fall...

But whatever the veneer of education lovingly applied to his surface, it had in no sense left Darnley an intellectual. Throughout his short life he showed remarkably little interest in any matters of the mind, and a single-minded concern for the pursuit of pleasure. The truth was that Darnley was thoroughly spoilt: he was the product of a striving mother and a doting father, and even the most rigorous education would probably have left little impact on a personality which from his earliest years had been encouraged to regard himself as the important centre round which the world revolved.

As a character there was very little to commend him despite or more probably because of all the maternal solicitude which had been expended on him – on his first arrival in Scotland Randolph did not want 'a little cold' which he was suffering from to get to the ears of Lady Lennox, lest she should be alarmed.[22] Apart from being spoilt, he was headstrong and ambitious; but he was ambitious only in so far as his mind could hold any concept for long enough to pursue it, since above all he desired the palm and not the race. It was the outward manifestations of power, the crown, the sceptre and the orb, which appealed to him: the realities of its practice made no appeal to his indolent and pleasure-loving temperament. Vanity was by far the strongest motive which animated him. It was vanity which made him seek out evil companions, such as the profligate Lord Robert Stewart, even from the first moment of his arrival in Edinburgh, and seek solace in the admiration of low company. If the pursuit of pleasure led him inevitably on to fresh excitements, and thus to more vicious enjoyments as simpler pleasures failed, it was his vanity which brought about his quick touchy temper, and his fatally boastful nature; finally, his vanity was the fatal flaw which made Darnley incapable of assessing any person or situation at its true worth, since he could not help relating everything back to his own self-esteem. The kindest judgement made about him was that of the cardinal of Lorraine – *'un gentil huteaudeau'*[23] (a nice young cockerel) – but such lightweight figures had a way of becoming dangerous if they were inserted into serious situations.

None of this was apparent to Mary Queen of Scots at her first meeting with her cousin in Scotland, at Wemyss Castle. She merely saw and admired his charming exterior, which, like a delightful red shiny apple ready for the eating, gave no hint of the maggots which lay inside. Her reaction was instantaneously romantic: she told Melville that 'he was the properest and best proportioned long man that ever she had seen...'[24] Although the long man went on to see his father Lennox who was at Dunkeld with his kinsman Lord Atholl, he was back at the queen's side on the following Saturday, in order to cross over the queen's ferry with her towards the south. From now on, he was scarcely allowed to be away from her side. On Monday Darnley listened to Knox preach, dined with Moray and Randolph, and finally at Moray's instance danced a galliard with Mary – the tall graceful young couple looked so suitable together that at this point Randolph reported, 'A great number wish them well – others doubt him, and deeply consider what is fit for the state of their country, than, as he is called "a fair jolly young man".'[25] Yet the tide was running very strongly in favour of the fair jolly young man – more especially since in mid-March Randolph was finally instructed to tell Mary that the Leicester marriage would definitely not be exchanged for her succession rights. Mary was deeply depressed by the news, and wept bitter tears: but it had the inevitable effect of focusing her attention still more strongly on Darnley now physically present by her side, as Elizabeth and her advisers must surely have anticipated when they sent the final crushing message.

In the meantime marriage was in the air of Mary's little Scottish circle. During the previous autumn Mary's secretary Maitland had begun to court the dazzling Mary Fleming, he being a recently widowed man of forty, and she a girl of twenty-two. Maitland was clearly fascinated by her radiant youth and vitality, although Kirkcaldy scornfully described her as being about as suitable for him 'as I am to be pope'.[26] Maitland's passion became an open subject for discussion at the court, and in February Maitland confessed to Cecil that his passion brought him at least one 'merry hour' out of the four and twenty, whatever the troublesome affairs of the kingdom, even advising Cecil himself to turn to such amorous sport for relaxation since 'those that be in love, be ever set upon a merry pin'.[27] Randolph was scornful over Maitland's infatuation which he described in withering terms, but Randolph himself, a forty-five-year-old bachelor who observed the gambolling of the Mars with gallant approval, was himself an unsuccessful admirer of Mary Beaton, and his account was probably tinged with jealousy. In the end it was not the acknowledged *belle* Mary Fleming who was to be the first Marie to wed, but, as we have seen, her energetic agile companion, Mary Livingston, who chose as her bridegroom a younger son of Lord Sempill. The marriage took place on Shrove Tuesday, 6th March, 1565. The queen was not only party to the marriage contract and gave the bride a dowry of £500 a year in land, but also paid for the wedding gown and bridal banquet, as was her custom with her favourite ladies. As the first of the Maries to marry, the wedding of Mary Livingston naturally attracted a great deal of attention, and the French and English ambassadors give many details of the impending ceremonies for two months beforehand (the detailed preparations certainly give the lie to Knox's suggestion of a hurried ceremony). Randolph described Sempill as 'a happy Englishman' for winning the estimable Mary Livingston as a bride. Mary Stuart's own views on the subject were best expressed by the French ambassador in his report to Catherine de Médicis: 'She has begun to marry off her Maries, and says that she wished she herself were of the band.'[28]

Up to this point, however much Mary had enjoyed the company of Darnley, she had not shown any evidence of passion for him: Randolph weighed up the favour she had shown him as proceeding 'of her own courteous nature' rather than anything more serious. In March Mary still seems to have regarded

Darnley as a suitable candidate for marriage only because of his English and Scottish royal blood and his religion, and not for any more personal reason. But in April the situation dramatically changed. Darnley fell ill – an illness which was to transform his fortune and that of Mary Queen of Scots. The illness itself was of no great moment: it began with a cold, which Darnley attempted to cure by sweating it out, and then turned into measles. The young man was incarcerated in his room in Stirling Castle. It was the situation of his sick-room which was the crucial fact about his illness. Inevitably, within the confines of the enormous fortress, like a private town hanging above the plain of Stirling, the young queen found her way with increasing frequency to the bedside of her handsome young cousin. She began to visit him continually and at all hours, and she even took to staying past midnight. She constituted herself his nurse. When measles was succeeded by an ague, the distracted girl refused to ride forth to Perth until Darnley was recovered, and her care was redoubled. Under the influence of the proximity of the sick-room, and the tenderness brought forth by the care of the weak, the suffering – and the handsome – Mary had fallen violently, recklessly and totally in love.

There can be no doubt that whether Mary herself realized it or not, her feelings for Darnley were overwhelmingly physical. The demanding nature of her passion can easily be explained by pent-up longings which were the result of an inadequate first marriage, which had aroused few physical feelings in her and satisfied none. In the years since Francis's death she had led a life of celibacy, allowing herself courtly flirtations but nothing more, and had been seemingly horrified at any more crude confrontation with life, such as Châtelard presented to her. Her thoughts about marriage had been concentrated on the power it would bring her, for Don Carlos as a bridegroom could have offered few other consolations, and she had shown little interest in the prospect of that great lover Robert Dudley as a possible husband. Now at one touch of Darnley's hand, the caution, the concentration on the issue of her marriage in which Elizabeth's approval was so vital, the discretion and wisdom which all had praised in her during her four years as queen of Scotland – all were swept away in a tide of tumultuous feelings which Mary Stuart can scarcely have known she possessed.

CHAPTER THIRTEEN
The Carnal Marriage

~

Nuptiae carnales a laetitia incipiunt et in luctu terminantur
(Carnal marriages begin with happiness and end in strife)
Cecil's comment on the marriage of Amy Robsart and Leicester

In March 1565 Darnley had been one possible candidate among the many from whom the queen of Scots might choose her consort. In April he became the one man she was determined to have beside her as husband. From Stirling she took a keen interest in the intrigues on the subject in Edinburgh. The faithful Maitland was promptly dispatched to London to acquaint Elizabeth with the news and, as it was hoped, win her approval – this sanction being doubly necessary because Darnley was not only a member of the English royal family through his Tudor descent, but also held to be an English subject. At this point Mary genuinely believed that she would receive this approval. Her confidence was easy to understand: Darnley had come north with the official blessing of England, and he was an English noble of the type whom Elizabeth had often observed that she wished Mary would marry. From hearsay Mary had reason to suppose that Darnley was one of Elizabeth's own candidates, if the Leicester marriage failed. Maitland reached London on 15th April. But at this point the honeyed trap – as Darnley now turned out to be – was sprung. Mary to marry Darnley! Darnley, the great-grandson of Henry VII, with a claim of his own to the English throne! No indeed. Elizabeth, made newly aware of the disapproval of the Scottish Protestants for a Catholic bridegroom and anxious to dissociate herself from the project, now took the line that the whole idea of the marriage was preposterous, and represented a renewed attempt on Mary's part to acquire the English throne for herself. In London Margaret, countess of Lennox, was first commanded to keep to her room and later sent to the Tower. Regardless of the fact that Lennox and Darnley had gone north with her express permission, Elizabeth exploded with anger and demanded their instant return. When neither paid any attention to her angry bulletins, Throckmorton was sent north to dissuade Mary from the disastrous, nay, menacing course of marrying Darnley.

Mary in Scotland was in no state to listen to the advice of even the sagest counsellor. Love was rampant in her heart for the first time, and she could hear no other voice except the dictates of her own passionate feelings. In the words of a poem of the period, it was a case of 'O lusty May, with Flora Queen' at the court of Scotland.[1] Randolph wrote back to Leicester in anguish of his 'poor Queen whom ever before I esteemed so worthy, so wise, so honourable in all her doings', now so altered by love that he could hardly recognize her. To Cecil he described a queen seized with love, 'all care of common wealth set apart, to the utter contempt of her best subjects'.[2] Randolph was in a particular state of despair at the whole situation because it was being widely stated in Scotland that Darnley had been deliberately dispatched by Elizabeth to trap Mary into a mean marriage, and he only wished that there was not so much concrete evidence to back up these suspicions.

Darnley himself reacted predictably. In the same breath as he bewailed his once-honoured queen's infatuation, Randolph reported that Darnley was now grown so proud that he was intolerable to all honest men, and already almost forgetful of his duty to Mary – she who had adventured so much for his sake. Darnley's health had taken an unconscionably long time to recover, and even while on his sickbed he had struck the ageing duke of Châtelherault on his pate to avenge some fancied slight. By 21st May he had only been seen outside the four walls of his room once, and was still more or less confined to his bed. Well before Darnley's final emergence Throckmorton managed to see Mary at Stirling and put to her as strongly as possible Queen Elizabeth's dislike of what she considered to be a hasty manner of proceeding with Lord Darnley.

At this point Mary would surely have been wise to have taken serious thought. It was true that the approval of Philip II of Spain for the match was sought and won; Charles IX of France was approached through Castelnau and approved; her Guise relations were informed (although Mary's beloved Anne of Guise must have been somewhat surprised by the development since only in September she had given it as her opinion that Mary's innate pride was far too strong to permit her to wed a mere subject – 'her heart was too great to debase it').[5] All these approvals were as nothing compared to the approval of Elizabeth, for after all Elizabeth could offer Mary what none of these other potentates had it in their power to extend – the reversion of her own throne. Over the question of Mary's marriage, hypocritically as she might behave, maddeningly as she might procrastinate, Elizabeth was still in the position of paying the piper and therefore calling the tune. Only the rashest and most impetuous of women would have proceeded now on the same determined course without taking heed of Elizabeth's declared disapproval – but this was what love had apparently made Mary Stuart. She and Throckmorton argued fruitlessly, while Mary tried to put her own point of view; finally Throckmorton concluded that the queen was so far committed in this matter with Lord Darnley, as it was irrevocable, and 'that there was no point in exercising any persuasion and reasonable means any further'. Gloomily the courtier who had once so much admired Mary for her discretion in her first widowhood in France, and had wished that Elizabeth could behave more like her, concluded that she had been captivated, either by love or cunning, or rather, 'to say truly, by boasting or folly'.[4]

Darnley's recovery did nothing to dim the queen's love. Now she was so infatuated that many began to suggest that Darnley had actually bewitched her, looking for a supernatural explanation of her great love when a natural one was only too obvious. At the beginning of June Randolph moaned again to Leicester that Mary and Darnley were still exchanging great tokens of love every day, and Mary seemed to have laid aside all shame in her behaviour. He even suggested that passion had caused the queen to lose her looks somewhat – but perhaps he merely meant that her dignity had been laid aside in favour of the reckless glowing aspect of a woman in love.[5] Darnley's pride waxed with the queen's affection: to show his virility, he launched out characteristically with blows towards those who he knew would not dare to retaliate. On the day in May on which he was created earl of Ross, he drew his dagger on the wretched justice clerk who brought him the message, because he was not also made duke of Albany as he had expected. It was the typical gesture of the spoilt and vindictive child. By the beginning of July, Darnley was held in such general contempt that even those who had been his chief friends could no longer find words to defend him. Randolph made the gloomy, but as it proved singularly accurate, prophecy: 'I know not, but it is greatly to be feared that he can have no long life among these people.'

The truth was that even if Darnley had spoke with the tongues of men and of angels, Mary Stuart would have had sufficient problems in persuading her court to accept him as her bridegroom. In the course of the summer Darnley wooed Mary with a light and courtly love poem:[6]

> If langour makes men light
> I am for evermore
> In joy, both even and morrow...
> The turtle-dove for her mate
> More dolour may not endure
> Than I do for her sake...

If such felicitous pleadings recalled to Mary pleasantly the far-off days of the French court, her advisers were singularly unimpressed by them. To the Scots now around the queen, whatever Darnley's poetic talent, his arrogant nature was merely the final disaster in a long train of possible disadvantages. Firstly there was the attitude of England, crystallized in the discussion of the English Privy Council on 4th June, where the two great perils of Mary's marriage were laid down as firstly the plain intention of Mary by such a match to occupy Elizabeth's throne now rather than later, and secondly 'the increase and credit of the Romish religion in England'. The avowed hostility of England was naturally fuel to the smouldering flames of Scottish hostility: Moray, for example, had viewed the match with great gloom from the start, since he had little desire to see the rival Lennoxes raised up, and his own credit and influence with his sister, built up over four years, debased. Added to which, Darnley had made it clear that he regarded Moray's spreading dominions in Scotland as surprisingly and disagreeably extensive, and even passed unpleasant remarks on the subject to Moray's brother, Lord Robert Stewart, an unwise choice of confidant.

Moray withdrew from the court at the beginning of April, on the ostensible excuse that he did not wish to witness the popish ceremonies at Easter. The whole benefit of his advice and approval which Mary had enjoyed for so long was thus removed from her, at one swoop, as Moray now proceeded to indulge in a series of confused but hostile manoeuvres, whose intention was to demonstrate his opposition to Darnley, without breaking into open rebellion, until he should be assured of English support for his cause. But there were other Scottish nobles, quite apart from Moray, who had ancient, feudal or hereditary reasons for disliking and fearing the Lennoxes: to many Scots Darnley seemed to combine the disadvantages of both the subject and the royal prince as a husband. The Hamilton faction was newly united with Knox in their disapproval of the marriage.* Even the Maries were said to be against the match –

* An unpublished letter in the Register House, Edinburgh, from Mary to John Spens, her advocate, on a legal matter, dated from Stirling on 9th April, contains a passionately scribbled postscript in the queen's own hand, in which she directs the advocate to find out more concerning certain 'secret gatherings' said to be held in the evenings in Edinburgh between Knox and Gavin Hamilton: 'I pray you endeavour to learn what is done or said and inform me thereof, using all the

and to be out of credit with the queen in consequence. The only name mentioned as encouraging it was that of David Riccio, the queen's new secretary for her French correspondence, and Darnley's boon companion.

All the while Mary was caught fast in the tangled bonds of passion. So vehement did her love seem, and so overweening the pride of Darnley, that it was even rumoured that they had been secretly married in early July. It is very probable that the queen had gone through some betrothal ceremony with Darnley at the beginning of May, in the very first ecstasies of love, betrothals then resembling marriages in the sense that much greater liberties were allowed between the betrothed pair. But an actual secret marriage is rendered unlikely by the fact that Mary deliberately and impetuously married Darnley before the arrival of the papal dispensation from Rome. The dispensation was necessary because they were step-first cousins, and Mary was acting on the presumption that the dispensation had already been granted in Rome even if it had not yet arrived in Scotland. She was certainly in no mood for hole-in-the-corner ceremonies.* On 22nd July Darnley was at last given the coveted title of duke of Albany. On 29th July the heralds proclaimed that Darnley (or Prince Henry as he was termed) should henceforth be named and styled 'King of this our Kingdom'. This was Mary's ultimate proud pursuit of her own desires, since rightly she should have asked Parliament to give Darnley the coveted title of king. By bestowing it herself, she was pledging her full authority in the cause of her future husband. Finally, on Sunday morning 29th July, between five and six o'clock in the morning, a radiant Mary

diligence you can, but take good care that no one learns that I have written anything to you on this matter..."
* But Mary was wrong in supposing that the dispensation had already been granted. The dispensation was granted in Rome some time after 1st September and before 25th September; it arrived in Scotland several weeks after that – but was not of course published, since the marriage had already taken place on the assumption of its existence, and to publish its actual date would have been embarrassing to the queen.⁸ Unless Mary and Darnley went through a further marriage ceremony after the date of its granting (of which there is no record) their marriage was technically invalid.

was conveyed to the chapel royal at Holyrood, on the arm of her future father-in-law the earl of Lennox, and the earl of Argyll, there to await her chosen consort, once the young Lord Darnley, now King Henry of Scotland.

For this wedding, however, there was to be no dazzling white marriage robe for Mary Stuart, whatever the romantic passion which inspired her: she wore on the contrary a great mourning gown of black, with a wide mourning hood attached to it, which apparently much resembled the costume which she had worn on the burial day of Francis. This was to indicate that she came to her new husband not as a young and virgin girl, but as a widow, a queen dowager of France. Having been led into the chapel, she remained there until her future husband was brought in by the same lords. They exchanged the vows of the marriage service according to the Catholic rite and three rings were put on Mary's finger, the middle one a gleaming diamond. Darnley then left Mary alone to hear Mass, abandoning her with a kiss, and himself going straight to her chamber to await her. With the marriage completed, Mary was now at last by custom required to cast off her mourning garments, and signify that she was about to embark upon 'a pleasanter life'. In Randolph's words, after 'some pretty refusal'[9] which with some reason he believed was more for form's sake than from any genuine reluctance to abandon her widowed state, she allowed everyone standing round to take out one pin; then, giving herself into the hands of her ladies, she changed out of her black clothes.

There then followed the usual dancing and festivities of a nuptial celebration; if they did not compare with the grandiose ceremonies which had accompanied Mary's marriage to Francis, they were at least considered magnificent by Scottish standards, and seven years was perhaps long enough for the memories of such far-off grandeurs to have faded in Mary's mind. There was a banquet for the full court of nobles, the sound of trumpets, largesse scattered among the crowd and money thrown about the palace in abundance. After the dinner there was some dancing, and a brief respite for recovery, before the supper, as magnificent as had been the dinner. Finally, as Randolph reported, 'and so they go to bed'. It is to be hoped that Mary Stuart, who had sacrificed so much for this match, found at least this part of the ceremony to her satisfaction: there is no evidence to prove that she had anticipated the marriage ceremony and become Darnley's mistress in the course of the summer, beyond the bawdy rumours of their enemies, who said that they had lain together at Seton. It is significant that Randolph, who had had every opportunity of observing the young couple throughout the summer, specifically advised the English Council to the contrary:[10] 'Suspicious men,' he wrote, 'or such as are given of all things to make the worse, would that it should be believed that they knew each other before that they came there [to bed]. I would not that your Lordships should so believe the likelihoods are so greatly to the contrary.' Certainly the wildness of Mary's infatuation seems to point to tormenting and unslaked physical feelings rather than the comparative satisfaction of a liaison. Throughout her four and a half years of widowhood, Mary Stuart had displayed a strong sense of her own 'majesty' where the attentions of young gallants were concerned; in the course of the last year she had seemed in addition obsessed by the subject of marriage. Darnley had long been one of those on her list of possible husbands. Therefore when she finally fell in love with him in the Easter of 1565, she had no reason to surrender herself to him outside the bonds of marriage, when there was the prospect of connubial bliss with him in the future.

Knox wrote of the prolonged rejoicing after the marriage ceremony: 'During the space of three or four days, there was nothing but balling, and dancing, and banqueting.'[11] The pen of Buchanan, who owed feudal allegiance to the earl of Lennox, was pressed into service for the many masques which followed; in one Diana complained that the foremost of her bright band of five Maries had been taken from her by the envious powers of love and marriage, and in another the four remaining Maries offered oblations to the goddess of Health.[12] To many, the most significant ceremony which followed was that which took place the next day. On Monday, 30th July, Mary deliberately had the fact of Darnley's new title of King Henry* announced once more by the heralds, with the further proclamation that henceforward all documents and proclamations would be signed by them jointly in the two names MARIE and HENRY, that is, 'set forth in the names of both their Majesties as King and Queen of Scotland conjunctly'. At this news, there was a heavy ominous silence among the nobles of Scotland. Not one as much as said 'Amen'. Only the happy doting father, Lennox, at seeing his darling thus glorified, cried aloud: 'God save his Grace!'

Cecil had commented on the ill-fated marriage of Leicester and Amy Robsart that *Nuptiae carnales a laetitia incipiunt et in luctu terminantur* – Carnal marriages begin with happiness and end in strife.[15] Mary was allowed little enough time to enjoy the happiness of her own 'carnal marriage' before the first presages of strife were made apparent. Already, before her wedding, Moray had indulged in behaviour which was at best menacing, at worst plainly rebellious; he declined to attend the convention of the nobility called at Perth at the end of June on the grounds that he was ill, and lurked at Lochleven; from here he spread a rumour that the Lennox faction was planning to assassinate him. It was a time when rumours were spreading freely – the Lennox party in their turn suggested that Moray intended to kidnap Lennox and Darnley and ship them back to England, but the existence of this plot has never been concretely proved. Moray was also involved in more practical schemes: on 1st July he asked Randolph for a subsidy of £3000 from Elizabeth to support the Protestant religion in Scotland, and the English

---

* The title of Lord Darnley was a courtesy title, which he bore as the elder surviving son of the earl of Lennox, according to the English custom (in Scotland at this period Darnley would have been known as the master of Lennox). Darnley was created earl of Ross in May and duke of Albany in July, before being proclaimed as 'King Henry' by the queen. In the present work, however, which already contains three King Henrys – Henry VIII of England, and Henry II and III of France – he will still be referred to as Darnley for the sake of clarity. But it is important to realize that Darnley was universally referred to as 'the king' in Scotland at the time.

alliance. Furious with Mary for her choice of Darnley as a husband, Moray's intention was to show that she was endangering the Protestant religion. But in her desire to win support for the Darnley marriage, Mary had on the contrary taken the trouble to court the favour of the reformers. Nor was Darnley himself, although now a professed Catholic, a shining example to the other members of his faith: in England he had acted as a Protestant, and once back in Scotland, he had happily listened to the sermon of John Knox in St Giles Church, as well as avoiding the nuptial Mass to his own wedding, which Mary had attended: Darnley's faith appeared to have a chameleon quality about it, which enabled it to assume whatever colour seemed convenient at the time. Mary's conciliatory attitude on the subject of religion showed up Moray's rebellion for what it was – jealous disaffection springing from feudally inspired hatred of the Lennoxes, with religious overtones introduced for the sake of English subsidies, rather than a genuine revolt of conscience.

On 6th August Moray was put to the horn or outlawed, having refused to put in any appearance before his sister to explain his behaviour, despite promises of safe-conduct for himself and eighty of his followers. His two most powerful allies, Châtelherault and Argyll, were informed that they would be outlawed in their turn if they gave him any further assistance. Mary now acted with admirable promptness. The properties of Moray, Rothes and Kirkcaldy were seized on 14th August; on 22nd August Mary announced that she intended to march against the rebels, and ordered a muster of troops (to pay for which she pledged her jewels). In order that Moray's rebellion should be seen for what it was – the foray of a rebellious noble rather than a religious crusade – Mary once more announced that no religious change was intended. Atholl was made lieutenant in the north, in order to hold Argyll at bay. On 26th August Mary rode out of Edinburgh towards the west of Scotland, with Darnley swaggering at her side in gilt armour: she was swearing revenge on Moray, but the vivid emotion brought such a sparkle into her spirits that in the course of the campaign even Knox's narrative expressed admiration of her as she rode at the head of her troops: 'Albeit the most part waxed weary, yet the Queen's courage increased man-like, so much that she was ever with the foremost.'[14]

In her absence, Moray, Châtelherault, Glencairn and Rothes entered the city; but they discovered that there was little support for them there from Protestants and Catholics alike, Mary having by now made herself extremely popular with the ordinary people – who in the course of her four years in Scotland had seen no evidence that she intended to deprive them of the practice of their new religion, and their minds set at rest on this subject positively enjoyed the acquisition of a young and beautiful queen, who understood better how to reach the hearts of her humbler subjects than those of her nobility. Threatened by the guns of Edinburgh Castle, manned by Lord Erskine, now earl of Mar, Moray departed. In Glasgow, Mary decided to wait until her northern levies should reach her at Stirling at the end of September before finally attacking Moray. In the meantime she issued another proclamation promising a definite settlement of the religious question. Randolph heard that Mary was putting such enthusiasm into her cause that she frequently rode with a pistol at her saddle, outriding all her ladies and gentlemen except 'one stout lady'.[15]

It was left for Moray and his associates to appeal endlessly for the help from England which they believed had been promised to them by Elizabeth, but by the end of September the most Moray had got out of Elizabeth was the promise of an asylum in England, if he should need it. Meanwhile the English Council dithered and finally came down against him. Early in October, Moray realized his cause was hopeless, and on 6th October fled across the border from the southwest of Scotland, as Mary prepared to attack him. In London he underwent the humiliating experience of being told by Elizabeth, in the course of a personal audience, duly witnessed by the French ambassador, that he had done very wrong in rebelling against Mary. Having publicly exculpated herself from the charge of abetting the Scottish rebels, Elizabeth, in a triumph of double-talk, said that she would intercede with Mary for the return of Moray. Moray now settled down at Newcastle, to brood on the possibility of more favourable developments in Scotland.

It is difficult to explain Moray's conduct in terms of statesmanship: not only was Mary not threatening the Protestant religion at the end of July, but it was actually his rebellion which enabled Mary to send an emissary to Rome in September asking for a papal subsidy to assist her in the conflict. Mary had understandably been experiencing some difficulty in the past two years in convincing the Pope that she truly had the cause of Scottish Catholicism at heart. Yet papal money continued to be a golden lure as was papal approval to one who might at any moment need foreign Catholic support: now Moray's rebellion, so publicly stated to be in the cause of Protestantism, presented the Scottish queen with a perfect opportunity to present herself in Rome as a champion of the Catholic faith. But the truth was that Moray, in his revolt, was no more championing Protestantism than Mary was championing Catholicism by attacking him. The composition of their respective parties shows how strongly feudal and family alliances still acted in Scottish politics.

Moray had Châtelherault on his side, because the Hamiltons were perennially opposed to the Lennox Stewarts, who contested their claim to be the next heirs to the Scottish throne; Mary in turn reacted to Moray's revolt by pardoning young Lord Gordon, Huntly's son, who was released from ward and restored to his father's title on 3rd August, for the very good reason that the Huntlys were now the sworn enemies of Moray. Even Bothwell was now allowed back into royal favour because his enmity against the Hamiltons could be relied on keeping him loyal to the queen: the crude insults which he was said to have bestowed on Mary after her escape to France (she was the 'cardinal's whore', and she and Elizabeth between them did not add up to one honest woman)[16] were conveniently forgotten in the need to suppress Moray. The presence of the keen Protestant and traditional Hamilton ally, Argyll, on the opposing side meant that Atholl could be relied on to act against him on Mary's side to preserve the balance of power in the north of Scotland.

Indeed during the Chaseabout Raid, Argyll took the opportunity to despoil Lennox and Atholl, which he considered evidently a more important task than supporting Moray against the queen. Lastly the 'slow and greedy' earl of Morton, head of the Douglas clan, supported the queen, because Lennox's wife Margaret had been a Douglas, and Darnley was thus 'mother's kin' to the Douglases.

The Chaseabout Raid, as Moray's abortive rebellion was called, marked a significant change in Mary's attitude to her Scottish nobles, which may not have been politically wise, but whose genesis was certainly easy to trace. She certainly did not despair of the Scottish people – indeed her experiences during the raid only confirmed her in her prognostication to Throckmorton when still in France, that she would manage to appeal to 'the common people' of Scotland. But in the course of four years, her two major subjects had both revolted against her, in the interests of their own power, as it seemed to her. She had defeated them both, married the man of her choice, and had been able to reestablish herself as a champion of the Scottish Catholic cause abroad, without in fact making as yet any significant concessions to the Catholics in Scotland – in short, she was riding high. None of these experiences had taught her to trust her own nobility at any point where her interest might conflict with theirs: she therefore took the natural step of relying more and more on those who had no mighty Scottish lands and clans to back them up, no family feuds to sway them, and who did not belong to the spider's web of Scottish family relationships. In her newly important relations with the papacy, her vast correspondence with her French relations, and even with Spain, Mary began to make use of a sort of middle-class secretariat. These rising stars were not even lairds as Maitland had been but, in Randolph's term, 'crafty vile strangers'[17] – although Mary saw them as loyal and discreet servants. It was a move which was passionately resented by the nobles who saw themselves about to be edged out of the centre of a stage they had occupied so tempestuously and for so long.

Randolph, in his discussion of the subject, mentioned two

Italians, Davy and Francisco (Francisco de Busso), and an Englishman called Fowler. Others who were complained of were Sebastian Danelourt and the Scottish lawyer James Balfour. In his criticism of Mary, Moray had mentioned that she relied on such men, rather than take what he chose to term 'the wholesome advice and counsel' of her barons. Of these men, Davy or David Riccio* was the most interesting character. He had first arrived in Scotland in 1561 in the train of the ambassador from Savoy, and he came of a good but imp- overished Savoyard family; he was of course a Catholic, although no evidence has ever been found in the Vatican to confirm the suggestion of his enemies that he was at any time a papal agent. He was now aged about thirty-five; but otherwise the only fact on which everyone agreed about this cuckoo in the royal nest – which appears in every contemporary record whether of friend or foe – was that Riccio seemed extremely ugly by the standards of the time,† his face being considered 'illfavoured' and his stature small and hunched. Although he had a Latin love of fine clothing – after his death an extravagant peacock's wardrobe was discovered – Buchanan commented spitefully 'indeed his appearance disfigured his elegance'.[18] Riccio also seems to have been avaricious, since a cache of £2000 was discovered among his effects, which would have been difficult to amass out of his yearly pay of £80 and lends colour to the accusations of his enemies that he took bribes. Riccio, however, first came into Mary's service on a more spiritual level.

Ugly as he might be, avaricious as he might be suspected to be, Riccio was generally conceded to be a fine musician. Music as we have seen was Mary's private passion. Riccio entered Mary's employ when she needed a bass singer to make up a

---

* The correct spelling of his name. Rizzio seems to have originated from Rizio in the first printing of Knox's *History* in 1644.

† The portrait usually given as that of Riccio, from which many engravings have been made, showing a soulful gentleman fingering a lute, with fine eyes, a chiselled mouth, a neat beard, certainly does not depict him as ugly; but it is an imaginary portrait, dating from the late seventeenth or eighteenth century, and has no connection with his true appearance.

quartet with the valet of her household. Although Riccio was clearly a talented performer, there is no concrete evidence to prove that he combined these talents with those of a composer.* Riccio, apart from his musical talent, was also an amusing conversationalist; to a queen who was in Melville's phrase 'of quick spirit, curious to know, and get intelligence of the estate of other countries and would be sometimes sad when she was solitary, and glad of the company of them that had travelled in other parts',[19] Riccio provided an agreeable opportunity to discuss the Europe they had both once known.

When Mary's French secretary Raullet died at the end of 1564 Riccio was appointed in his place; this meant that he was nominally responsible for her French correspondence, as opposed to Maitland, who was her secretary of state and responsible for all her affairs. But by the autumn of 1565 Randolph was able to observe spitefully about Maitland that he had been sufficiently pushed out of the centre of affairs to have the leisure to make love – to his coy mistress, Mary Fleming.[20] Melville paints a picture of Riccio standing at the entrance to Mary's chamber, smiling at the nobles as they went by, and being glowered on in return.[21] Certainly Maitland, in terms of power politics, had reason to resent the advancement of Riccio, since it had led to his own decline. But to Mary the loyalty of Riccio at least was beyond reproach, and she had a natural horror of disloyalty, especially when it was accompanied by ingratitude. As Mary wrote to de Foix, the French ambassador in London, in November 1565, in a long letter pleading with him to get her mother-in-law Lady Lennox released from the

---

* He was credited with the composition of the music for seven Scottish songs – *The Lass of Patie's Mill, Bessie Bell, The Bush Aboon Traquair, The Bonnie Boatman, And Thou were my Ain Thing, Auld Rob Morris* and *Down the Burn David*, in the 1725 edition of *Orpheus Caledonius*; later James Oswald attached his name to certain songs in the *Caledonian Companion*, and was accused of having done so for the sake of publicity. In fact the legend of Riccio the composer rests on tradition only, and as such can be neither proved nor disproved – although it seems infinitely more likely that a native Italian would be interested by, collect and play rather than actually compose such characteristically Scottish melodies. See John Glen, *Early Scottish Melodies*, for a balanced discussion of the whole subject.

Tower, the ingratitude of Moray seemed to her fantastic: here was a mere subject on whom she had showered honours and goods, trying to prevent her marrying whom she pleased. Again and again she reverted to the topic as she utterly refused to allow the release of Lady Lennox to be made conditional on her pardoning Moray and his fellow-rebels.[22] In a memorandum on the reasons for her second marriage, she bitterly related how Moray had deliberately agreed to the idea of Darnley at first, in order to spite the pretensions of the Hamiltons, under the impression that he could scotch the match whenever he wished.[23]

Mary had *au fond* an unhypocritical and undissembling nature: in this respect she was curiously unlike her contemporary queens, Elizabeth Tudor and Catherine de Médicis, who had after all been brought up from childhood in far harder schools of learning than the idolized young queen of Scotland. Although Mary enjoyed the prospect and motions of intrigue, and took a keen interest in letters, schemes and news, she lacked the disposition of the true intriguer: the born double-agent, by not knowing which interest he really wants to come out on top, except his own survival, is able to take advantage of every new twist of the situation and thus in the end always survive – both Elizabeth and Cecil had something of this temperament. Mary on the other hand was by nature frank and open, as she knew herself; she was also passionate, quick to love, quick to hate, easy to weep, easy to laugh. This meant inevitably that she had a love of being committed: she preferred action, whatever the cost, to inaction, whatever the gain. Her fluctuating health may well have played some part in this; it was infinitely easier for one of her nervous energies to galvanize herself to spring forward than to rally her strength for a debilitating period of waiting. But such tendencies marked Mary off from the real plotters. Her love of commitment meant that in turn she felt bitterly betrayed when those around her seemed to neglect her interests for their own, showing no equivalent commitment to her. Her fiercest hatreds were always reserved for those whom she had raised up and who now let her down – Moray was now in this category and Darnley was shortly to enter into it.

Unfortunately this July marriage, begun in the high summer of love, did not preserve its warmth into the cooler temperatures of autumn and winter. At first, as Melville said, Mary was so delighted with her new acquisition, Darnley, that she did him great honour herself, and willed everyone who desired her favour to do the like and wait upon him. But after the honeymoon was over – a honeymoon spent as it happened virtually on the field of battle, defending Darnley as a choice of husband – Mary was ready to return to the more serious business of ruling Scotland. In her work, she was only too happy to have Darnley beside her – for his signature, that of 'King Henry', was together with hers on every document, as she had promised, and even the summons to serve in the field at the time of rebellion was sent out jointly in their two names. It was true that Mary signed on the left (the position of honour because it was read first) and Darnley on the right* (unlike Francis who had occupied the left). But his signature was nevertheless always present with one exception – that of a safe-conduct to England; Elizabeth refused to accept it on grounds that she did not acknowledge Darnley as king but on the contrary as 'a subject and an offender', and after a debate in Council, Randolph did manage to get Darnley's signature left off ('notwithstanding all the former promises made to him').²⁴ Apart from this single victory of expediency over principles, Mary throughout the autumn continued to bolster up the power of 'King Henry'.

Yet Darnley was obviously not much interested in the process of government. He continued sulkily to demand the crown matrimonial (egged on by his father Lennox), and wished to spend more money than Mary, perpetually embarrassed in this respect as we have seen, could easily provide: the crown matrimonial, which Francis had enjoyed, could only be granted by Parliament, at the instance of Mary, but it would have ensured

---

* The six documents among the state papers in the Register House at Edinburgh dated from July 1565 to May 1566 signed by Queen Mary and Darnley after their marriage invariably show their signatures in this position; on at least two occasions, however, Darnley asserted himself by making his signature considerably larger than that of the queen.

that Darnley's power was equal with Mary's while she lived, and continued after her death, if Darnley survived her. Darnley's way of showing himself worthy for this high honour was a strange one: Knox's Continuator summed it up neatly: 'As for the King, he past his time in hunting and hawking and such other pleasures as were agreeable to his appetites, having in his company gentlemen willing to satisfy his will and affections.'[25] Darnley's continued love of the chase and sport in particular meant that governmental measures were often held up by his absence, since they demanded the joint signature. In the second half of November, when the queen was seriously ill with the recurring pain in her side, Darnley spent about nine days hunting in Fife: this was the occasion when an iron stamp or seal was made of his signature to prevent delays. Even Darnley's partisan, Buchanan, admitted that Darnley raised no objection to the practice: the queen told Darnley that while he was busy hawking or hunting, matters of importance were unseasonably delayed, and 'he consented to this proposal as he did not wish to offend her in anything ...'[26] The seal was duly given into the custody of David Riccio. At all events, to those accustomed to the double signature at the end of a document a stamp of one of the signatures would hardly have been noticed.*

At the beginning of December, Mary went to the palace of Linlithgow to convalesce after her recent indisposition. Perhaps her illness had been exacerbated by other more fruitful symptoms: she must by now have been about two and a half months pregnant with the future James VI.† The birth of an heir –

---

* In England signatures by wooden stamp were used from the reign of Henry VI onwards.

† James was born on 19th June 1566. By the law of averages, he was therefore conceived on or about 19th September 1565. The circumstances of his birth might seem to suggest that he was premature, since his mother had endured such hardships during the pregnancy. But after the murder of Riccio, Mary specifically declared in her letter to Archbishop James Beaton of 2nd April 1566,[27] that she had been nearly *seven* months pregnant at the time of the assassination (9th March 1566). Yet a calculation based on James's birth shows that she was in fact only approaching *six* months pregnant. This seems to show that Mary in April believed her pregnancy to be more advanced than it was. It certainly disposes of the notion that James was premature, since by Mary's calculations James was born late rather

preferably male – was of vital importance to Mary's plans; if she gave birth to a son, she would automatically be placed in a much stronger position with regard to the English succession than a mere childless queen. Randolph, in the manner of courtiers, watched the queen eagerly for signs of pregnancy, and was avid to pick up court gossip on the subject. By 31st October, he was reporting to London: 'It is given out by some of her own that she is with child, it is argued upon tokens I know not what, annexed to the kind of them that are in that case.' By 12th November Randolph wrote that it was now commonly said that 'she is with child, and the nurse already chosen. There can be no doubt and she herself thinks so.' Mary's November illness temporarily persuaded Randolph that the rumours of pregnancy were false, especially as on 1st December, he reported her as being up once more, and 'taking as much exercise as her body can endure': although she herself believed she was pregnant, those around thought it to be 'something worse'. However, when Mary set out for Linlithgow, it was not on horseback but on a litter, in Randolph's words 'being with child, as the rumour is again common among us'.[28] By 19th December Lady Lennox in the Tower in London knew the happy news of her impending grandchild and by the spring the queen's pregnancy was an undeniable fact.

The prospect of motherhood – much as she must have desired it for dynastic reasons – did not increase Mary's affection for Darnley. In view of the four-year gap in their ages, there may originally have been something quasi-maternal in Mary's feeling for the beautiful young Darnley, which she was now able to satisfy more conventionally in the prospect of impending motherhood. It is significant that her confidant Leslie, in his *Defence of her Honour*, deliberately chose to refer later to her 'very motherly care' for her husband – 'for besides all other respects, though they were not very different in years, she was to him not only a loyal Prince, a loving and dear wife, but a most

than early. One therefore returns to the most likely date of on or a little before 19th September 1565 for conception.

careful and tender Mother withal'.[29] In addition ill-health was obviously causing her discomfort which may in turn have caused distaste for the more physical aspects of married love. Certainly her violent infatuation for Darnley had not survived the onsets of pregnancy, and she could after all no longer share the pleasures of hunting and hawking which both had once enjoyed so keenly. On 20th December, Bedford from Berwick reported that, 'The Lord Darnley followeth his pastimes more than the Queen is content withal; what it will breed hereafter I cannot say, but in the meantime there is some misliking between them.' On 25th December Randolph noted that 'a while ago there was nothing but King and Queen, now the Queen's husband is the common word. He was wont in all writings to be first named: now he is placed second.' The relative placing of the two names Henry and Mary was at the heart of the mysterious matter of the silver 'ryal', a new denomination of coin introduced shortly after their marriage at a nominal value of thirty shillings. This 'ryal' showed the heads of Mary and Darnley facing each other on one side, and on the other in Latin a reference to their marriage – 'Whom God has joined together, let no man put asunder'. In December Randolph also reported that this coin had been withdrawn from circulation in Scotland, because the names of the royal pair were engraved on it in an unusual order as HENRICUS & MARIA D. GRA. R. & R. SCOTORUM. Randolph represented Mary as now regretting the prominence given to Darnley's name, which for once preceded that of the queen.[30]

The best summary of the points of difference between Mary and her husband is provided in the memoirs of Lord Herries: Mary believed 'all the honour and majesty he had came from her: that she had made choice of him for her husband by her own affection only, and against the will of many of the nobility'. Darnley, on the other hand, was complacently convinced that 'the marriage was done with the consent of the nobility who thought him worthy of the place; that the whole kingdom had their eyes upon him; they would follow and serve him upon the fields, where it was a shame a woman should command'. And as the memoirs added: 'These conceits [were] being continuously buzzed in the young man's head."[31] It was, however, quite one thing for Mary to get on badly with her husband, and for Darnley's young head to buzz, and quite another for this disagreement to be put to savage use by Mary's enemies. Darnley by himself was powerless, whatever his posturings. Darnley as the tool of Mary's opponents could have a cutting edge. For it was a regrettable fact that by the beginning of 1566 there were quite a number of Scottish nobles who were inclining to put themselves in the category of the queen's enemies. Their disputes with the queen had quite different origins from those of Darnley, and formed very different patterns. But the combination of two forces of disaffection was capable of proving very dangerous for Mary – and fatal for her servant David Riccio.

CHAPTER FOURTEEN

Our Most Special Servant

'Some of our subjects and council by their proceedings
have declared manifestly what men they are ... slain
our most special servant in our own presence and
thereafter held our proper person captive treasonably.'
Mary Queen of Scots to Queen Elizabeth of England,
15th March 1566

In January 1566 Mary Queen of Scots was in her own
estimation riding high, with her courage unimpaired and her
resolution only strengthened by the recent ordeal through
which she had passed with such success; the future, bringing
with it the prospect of the birth of an heir, looked bright to
a woman whose nature combined spirit and optimism with
tenderness. But there was no denying that the opposition which
was building up against her both within and without Scotland
had an ugly aspect to it: if she had appreciated its real extent,
even Mary in her most buoyant mood might have experienced
some unquiet moments while she speculated just how and when
such thunder clouds would break into the fury of the storm.
First of all there were set steadily against her those Protestant
lords temporarily in exile, such as Moray; their primary desire
was to return to Scotland, but their hostility to Mary was given
a new edge when she threatened, in addition to banishment,
to attaint them and declare their properties forfeited at the
forthcoming session of Parliament, to be held in the spring.

Then there were the Kirk and Knox who feared to see Mary
take advantage of her new strength since the defeat of Moray
to advance the claims of the Catholic Church; this they also

suspected she might try to accomplish at the coming parliamentary session. As it happens, the contemporary rumours
that Mary was about to join a Catholic League with other foreign
Catholic powers have been shown to be groundless – no record
having been found of such a League, let alone Mary's intended
participation in it* – and what plans if any Mary had for helping
the Catholics at the forthcoming Parliament will never be known.
At most she would probably have asked for toleration of the
Mass for Scottish Catholics, rather than the rabid attacks to
which the Mass and priests were subjected when detected; Mary
was certainly modern enough in thought to wonder why the
Catholics should not enjoy the free practice of their own religion,
which she had so unquestioningly granted to the Protestants
from the first moment of her arrival in Scotland. But of course
Knox, like all those who have accomplished a revolution, was
hysterically fearful to see its effects undone, and any ideas of
mutual tolerance would have fallen on very deaf ears indeed. In
January an emissary came from the new Pope Pius v, with an
extremely friendly if somewhat over optimistic message for the
queen on the subject of the recent revolt: 'Most dear daughter –
We have heard with the utmost joy that you and His Highness,
your husband, have lately given a brilliant proof of your zeal by
restoring the due worship of God throughout your whole realm.
Truly, dearest daughter, you understand the duties of devout
kings and queens ...' The Pope went on to encourage her to
weed out completely 'the thorns and tares of heretical depravity
...',¹ and promised all the help possible in this worthwhile task.
Although Pius v seemed to have but little idea of the true state
of affairs in Scotland, Mary was quite acute enough to send her
own emissary, the bishop of Dunblane, for the second time to
ask for a papal subsidy – since the Pope's mention of 'all the
kind offices that paternal love can suggest' certainly spelled
financial aid to Mary, always extremely conscious of this problem.

* See Pollen, *Papal Negotiations*, p. xxviii, where Mary's involvement in a Catholic
League, as a result of the meeting of the Catholic sovereigns at Bayonne in July
1565, has been shown to be a chimera of the Protestant imagination, just as any
Protestant league in Europe was equally a figment of Catholic fancy.

Added to these two groups were those other Protestant nobles within the confines of Scotland, such as Morton and Maitland, who hated to see Mary's other 'base-born' advisers advanced to the detriment of their own position. It will be seen that Riccio, as chief representative of this despised and hated class, was the natural scapegoat for all the sections of the community opposed to the queen. He was also of course the obvious suspect on which Darnley could pour his rage and jealousy against his wife – if such a jealousy could be focused on the hunched figure of the little Italian. It was now the work of Mary's opponents at court to incite the foolish bombastic Darnley into such a state of frenzy that he might be persuaded to join in their own more serious enterprises. In order to do so it was necessary to present to Darnley that in the opinion of many Scottish nobles he, not Mary, would make the most suitable ruler of Scotland. This was the notion which was now 'buzzed' in Darnley's excitable brain.

The extreme cynicism of such behaviour should not be overlooked – the Scottish nobles, including Moray, were now proposing a scheme which involved the coronation of Darnley, the very man against whose elevation they had rebelled in August. Darnley was still nominally a Catholic, and since Christmas 1565, when he ostentatiously went to Mass to score a point over his wife, he had been flaunting his faith in the face of his compatriots for some reason of his own. On the Feast of the Purification, he processed through the streets of Edinburgh with lighted tapers, a notably Catholic gesture; on another occasion he asked Lords Fleming, Livingston and Lindsay whether they would be content to go to Mass with him 'which they refusing, he gave them all evil words'.[2] Bedford reported that Darnley would have liked to shut up the noblemen in their chambers and force them to go to Mass. Yet this Catholicism was apparently of no account to the Protestant Lords Moray, Ochiltree, Boyd and Rothes now that their persons and properties were threatened by the oncoming session of Parliament: Darnley's qualities and religion, so distasteful in July that he could not be tolerated as a royal consort, were in February apparently sufficiently worthy to make a candidate for supreme power, with the backing of the Protestant lords.

It was now plainly suggested to Darnley that his wife was Riccio's mistress, and the waning of his own power was due to the machinations of the Italian. It was not difficult to arouse the jealousy of a man of Darnley's vain temperament, and Darnley's cousin Morton seems to have done much of the trouble-making. Mary, conscious of her innocence, added fuel to the flames by openly finding pleasure in Riccio's counsels and his company. Could there have been any truth in the story? Neither Riccio's age, height nor his ugliness would have been any certain bar against a woman finding him desirable, since attraction follows its own rules. It is true that Mary Stuart herself did not appear to find men of this sort appealing – Darnley, young, elegantly beautiful and outwardly romantic, was the type she apparently admired; all we know of her relations with Riccio, including her behaviour at his death, seems to fit into the pattern of ruler and confidant, rather than mistress and lover. But what really militates against the possibility of Mary having had a love affair with David Riccio is the timing of it. Later the reproach was to be flung in the face of James VI that he was actually 'Davy's son'.* In January Randolph wrote dolefully to Leicester: 'Woe is me for you, when Davy's son shall be a King of England',[3] but as this was only a few weeks before he was asked to leave Scotland by Mary, and as ever since her marriage to Darnley his reports on her behaviour had been openly laced with spite, too much attention should not be paid to the scandalous prophecy. In order for the accusation to be true the queen would have to have been indulging in a secret love affair with Riccio throughout that same summer in which she was so obviously infatuated with Darnley; she would then have had to conceive a child by Riccio less than two months after her marriage to Darnley, when to outward observers she was still deeply in love with her husband. It seems that the worst that

---

* In later years King Henry IV of France (Henry of Navarre) observed that James could indeed claim to be the modern Solomon, since he was the son of David.

Mary can be accused of, with Riccio, as with Châtelard, is a certain lack of prudence which was very much part of her character, rather than some more positive indiscretion.

The character of Darnley was like a tinderbox, on which it was all too easy for the disaffected nobles to strike a flame, using Riccio as a flint. Early in 1566 the Order of St Michel was brought by a French envoy M. Rambouillet to Edinburgh, to bestow upon Darnley on behalf of the king of France. When asked what arms should be placed upon Darnley's shield, Mary coldly 'bade them give him his due',[4] as Knox's narrative has it: the fact that she did not specify the royal arms was a further unwelcome indication that she did not intend to bestow the crown matrimonial upon Darnley in the coming Parliament. Darnley retaliated with a series of debauched and roistering parties, which caused considerable scandal in Edinburgh; in the course of them, he made several of Rambouillet's suite hopelessly drunk. Quite apart from the intoxication he spread about him, Darnley's own drunkenness was beginning to constitute a public problem. At the home of an Edinburgh merchant, he became so wild in Mary's presence that she tried to halt his drinking, at which he insulted her, and she left the house in floods of tears. Nor was his drunkenness his only weakness: he searched for his pleasures in many different corners of human experience. On the one hand there were rumours of love affairs with court ladies; on the other, in a letter to Cecil in February, Sir William Drury hinted at something so vicious which had taken place at a festivity at Inch-Keith, too disgraceful to be named in a letter, that Mary now slept apart from her husband.[5]

Despite the anxiety caused by Darnley's behaviour, Mary persisted in her plan to hold a Parliament in March at which the Protestant lords who had rebelled would be attainted and their properties forfeited. She turned a deaf ear to any suggestion that they should be pardoned, with the exception of Châtelherault, who had been forgiven on condition he went into banishment for five years. Under these circumstances the two-pronged conspiracy to restore these lords and give Darnley the crown matrimonial went forward. On 9th February Maitland, who now clearly despaired of the pardoning of Moray, and feared for his whole Anglo-Scottish policy, wrote to Cecil that since the rebels were not to be readmitted, there was nothing for it but 'to chop at the very root'.[6] This sinister phrase seemed to hint at least at the possibility of removing Mary from her throne – and it might of course mean something more violent directed towards her actual life. On 13th February Randolph sent a communication to Leicester on the whole subject, which casts an even more lurid light on the secret intentions of the conspirators: 'I know for certain that this Queen repenteth her marriage, that she hateth Darnley and all his kin,' he wrote. 'I know there are practices in hand contrived between father and son to come by the crown against her will. I know that if that take effect which is intended, David, with the consent of the King [Darnley], shall have his throat cut within these ten days. Many things grievouser and worse than these are brought to my ears, yes, of things intended against her own person.'[7] Let us not forget, what was surely ever-present in the minds of Lennox and Darnley, that if Mary vanished from the scene, and her unborn child never saw the light of day, Darnley had an excellent chance of becoming king of Scotland in his own right. It was a propitious moment for the Lennox Stewarts, since the head of the Hamiltons was abroad in disgrace; this might prove the ideal opportunity for them to stigmatize the Hamilton claim to the throne as illegal once and for all.

A bond was now drawn up by those conspirators active in Scotland; these included Morton, George Douglas the Postulate, his illegitimate half-brother, Ruthven and Lindsay, both married to Douglas wives. The former Protestant rebel lords who signed included Ochiltree, Boyd, Glencairn, Argyll and Rothes, as well as Moray, who signed it at Newcastle on 2nd March. Maitland did not actually sign the bond, from whatever motives of caution or self-preservation, although Randolph listed his name among the conspirators. In this bond, the declared intentions were to be the acquisition of the crown matrimonial for Darnley, and the upholding of the Protestant religion, and the return of the exiles. The lords were careful to obtain Darnley's signature, in order that he should be as thoroughly implicated as themselves; but in all the clauses of the bond there was no mention of any sort of violence or of David Riccio – only Item Five had a faintly menacing ring: 'So shall they not spare life or limb in setting forward all that may bend to the advancement of his [Darnley's] honour.'[8] One aspect of the conspiracy which seemed to rob it still further of any possible content of idealism was the fact that it was known about in London beforehand. In February Randolph's known agent had been caught *flagrante* supplying money to the rebels; Mary had sent for Randolph, furiously upbraided him, and then ordered him to leave Scotland; from Berwick, however, he still remained thoroughly in touch with the seething atmosphere of Edinburgh. On 25th February he was able to write a full report of the conspiracy and its known adherents to London; Elizabeth reacted characteristically to a situation which she saw was about to put Mary at a new disadvantage: on 3rd March she wrote her a threatening letter, criticizing Mary's treatment of both Moray and Randolph, although one was an ambassador caught bribing rebels, and another a Scottish subject who had rebelled against his queen.[9] Elizabeth also sent £1000 to Moray at Newcastle.

Yet Mary herself seemed to have no inkling of what was about to happen – or else she had gained sufficient self-confidence in the past year to believe that she would weather the storm. The spreading panoply of court life continued to flower on majestically, ignorant of the fact that its roots were threatened. On 24th February the marriage of Bothwell and Lady Jean Gordon, sister to Huntly, was celebrated with considerable pomp. The significance of the match was the dynastic union of two of Mary's firmest adherents. In token of her approval, Mary herself supplied the eleven ells of cloth of silver for Lady Jean's wedding-dress, although Bothwell firmly insisted on the marriage taking place according to the Protestant rite. Love does not seem to have played much part in the match: Lady Jean had a cool detached character, warmed by a masculine intelligence – 'a great understanding above the capacity of her sex' as her son later put it.[10] Her long clever face with its firm nose and rather bulbous eyes lacked beauty and softness: she was hardly the type to appeal to Bothwell, judged from the standard of those women with whom he had been involved up to the present. She did, however, possess one definite attraction in her solid dowry, provided by her brother Huntly, and Lady Jean herself proved to have an excellent appreciation of the values of the property – later she managed to hold on to her lands through thick and thin despite Bothwell's attainder. The real love of her life, the man for whom she reserved affections which Bothwell never touched, seems to have been Alexander Ogilvy of Boyne: two months after Lady Jean's own marriage, he was wedded to the beautiful Mary Beaton.*

In the meantime the behaviour of Riccio, like that of Darnley, played into the hands of the conspirators. Froude has given the most sympathetic interpretation of Darnley's fatal incursion into Scottish politics – he was 'like a child who has drifted from the shore in a tiny pleasure boat, his sails puffed out with vanity . . .'.[11] But if Darnley was a child, Riccio was like the bullfrog in Aesop's fable, inflated by his own arrogance. The astrologer Damiot tried to warn him of the dangers of his situation, and told him to 'Beware of the Bastard'; Riccio assumed this referred to Moray and replied confidently: 'I will take good care that he never sets foot in Scotland again' – forgetting that the description could apply to a number of other people in sixteenth-century Scotland. Damiot talked of his unpopularity, Riccio said grandly: '*Parole, parole*, nothing but words. The Scots will boast but rarely perform their brags.' Mary took the same line. Melville tried to warn her also of what was going on, saying he had heard 'dark speeches', and that there were rumours current that they should hear some unpleasant news before Parliament was ended. Mary replied that something of the sort had also come to her own ears, but she had paid no attention since 'our countrymen were well-wordy'.[12]

---

* It is pleasant to relate that this relationship had a happy ending rare in the annals of the time: Lady Jean and her lover were finally united in marriage over thirty years later when both Mary Beaton and Lady Jean's second husband, the earl of Sutherland, were dead.

On Thursday 7th March Parliament assembled. Mary went personally to the tollbooth for the election of the Lords of the Articles, glittering in a silver head-dress. Bothwell bore the sceptre, Huntly the crown and Crawford the sword. Darnley pointedly did not accompany her, in token of his displeasure at not being granted the crown matrimonial. Parliament was put under considerable pressure by Mary to draw up a bill of attainder against Moray, and Tuesday 12th March was fixed as the date at which the bill was to be passed. The fixing of this date automatically induced the climax of the conspirators' plans. On the evening of Saturday 9th March, the queen was holding a small supper party in her own apartments at the palace of Holyrood; advancing pregnancy and ill-health had made her increasingly disinclined to go about in Edinburgh, preferring the company of her intimates at home. Those present with her all fell into this cosy category – her half-brother Lord Robert Stewart, her half-sister and confidante Jean, countess of Argyll, her equerry Arthur Erskine, her page Anthony Standen, and of course her secretary and musician, David Riccio himself. Perhaps there was to be music later, or perhaps this was to be one of those evenings, which Darnley said he so much resented, when the queen and Riccio played at cards until one or two in the morning. At any rate, the atmosphere was innocuous and domestic rather than exciting. At the time of his death, Randolph reported that the dandyish Riccio was wearing 'a night-gown of damask furred, with a satin doublet and a hose of russet velvet'.[13] It used to be suggested by critics that the fact that Riccio was in his 'night-gown' proved an unlawful degree of intimacy with the queen, but in the sixteenth century the word 'night-gown' was used in its literal sense to denote informal evening dress, the sort that might be expected to be worn on this sort of occasion.*

The true story of the dramatic events which interrupted this

---

* Ruthven suggested that Riccio was also wearing his cap in the presence of the queen – which does seem to denote remarkable familiarity. But it is significant that Randolph, who was at pains to find out the most suggestive details possible, does not mention this one. Ruthven is the only source which mentions the subject of the cap.

supper party has to be pieced together from the many differing accounts of it. Two people among those present wrote their own eye-witness accounts of what happened, within a few weeks of the murder: Queen Mary wrote a letter to James Beaton, archbishop of Glasgow, her ambassador in Paris, on 2nd April giving her version of the affair, and Ruthven, one of the murderers, wrote an account of it with Bedford at the end of March for English consumption.[14] Although both accounts must be expected to suffer from partiality, the queen to accuse and Ruthven to excuse, at least these letters represent fairly instantaneous reactions. Mary's later account of it all, to be found in Nau's *Memorials of Mary Stuart*, was told by her to her secretary when she was in captivity, long after the death of both Riccio and Darnley; although valuable for narrative detail, the motives it sometimes attributes to the participants must be regarded with reserve, since Mary's emotion, recollected in tranquillity, has by no means decreased in fervour.* Of all other accounts it must be remembered that the writers concerned were not present (although Melville was in the precincts of Holyrood) and therefore dependent on secondhand information.

One of the most important aspects of the affair is the scene in which it was set. Mary's apartments in Holyrood lay in the north-west corner of the palace, on the second floor; the rooms were four in number – a large presence chamber at the head of the main staircase, draped in black velvet, with the arms of Mary of Guise on the ceiling, a bed-chamber of considerable size lying directly off it, and off that again two very small rooms in each corner, not more than twelve foot square, one a type of dressing-room, the other a supper-room hung in crimson and green. Beneath these apartments, on the first floor of the palace, lay Darnley's rooms, which were roughly equivalent to the queen's. The two sets of apartments were connected by a narrow privy staircase which came out in the queen's bedroom, close to the entrance to the supper-chamber. The intimacy of the

---

* Claude Nau did not join the queen's service until 1575; his *Memorials* were written in 1578.

occasion has already been stressed. But although in one sense the supper-room was totally cut off from the outside world, except for the privy staircase, in another sense it was not a very secure place to choose to perform a murder.* The heart of Mary's apartment was indeed a curious place from which to choose to pluck one of her own servants, since there were the guards surrounding the queen's person to be taken into account. How much simpler it would have been to kill a mere servant in some other less public place. After all Riccio went normally and unguardedly about his business in Holyrood. Earlier there had been some story that George Douglas had offered to Darnley to throw him over the side of the boat while they were fishing at Castle Douglas,¹³ but Darnley had jibbed at the idea; such a scheme, quick, secret and unprovable, would certainly have made more sense as regards the elimination of a mere servant. The question arises why the choice of the queen's own rooms was deliberately made instead. Ruthven, in his narrative, attributed the choice of location to Darnley, who, he said, wanted to avenge the public insult to his honour by a public coup. But this time Ruthven was busy piling all the blame possible on Darnley. The king was after all a weak character, notoriously easy to sway. The fact that the murder was deliberately planned to take place in the presence of the queen when she was nearly six months pregnant points to some malevolent intentions towards her own person (as Randolph prophesied in February), as well as the elimination of a presumptuous servant.

Although it was Lent, meat was served at the queen's supper party, since her condition permitted her to ignore the fast. As the supper was being served, to the great surprise of all those present, the figure of Darnley suddenly appeared up the privy

---

* Although Holyrood was restored and extended in the reign of Charles II, Queen Mary's apartments can still be seen in much of their original state, as they were at the time of the murder: indeed, they form the most dramatic visual link to be found today with her life story, so many of the buildings connected with her now lying in ruins. But the staircase which can now be seen connecting the king's apartments with the queen's has no connection with the sixteenth-century privy staircase. This is still in existence, but concealed behind the Charles II panelling.

staircase; although he was by now a comparative stranger to these domestic occasions, preferring to go his own way in pursuit of pleasure in the streets of Edinburgh, he was still welcomed as the king. But a few minutes later there was a far more astonishing apparition up the staircase – Patrick Lord Ruthven, with a steel cap on, and with his armour showing through his gown, burning-eyed and pale from the illness of which he was generally thought to be dying on his sick-bed in a house close to Holyrood. So amazing was his emergence at the queen's supper party that the first reaction of those present was that he was actually delirious, and had somehow felt himself pursued, in his fever, by the spectre of one of his victims. Ruthven – who did in fact die three months after these events took place – was a highly unsavoury character, popularly supposed to be a warlock or male witch, or at any rate in Knox's phrase to 'use enchantment'. However, his first words left the queen in no doubt as to what had brought this death's head to her feast. 'Let it please your Majesty,' said Ruthven, 'that yonder man David come forth of your privy-chamber where he hath been overlong.' Mary replied with astonishment that Riccio was there at her own royal wish, and asked Ruthven whether he had taken leave of his senses. To this Ruthven merely answered that Riccio had offended against the queen's honour. On hearing these words, the queen turned quickly and angrily to her husband, realizing the Judas-like quality of his visit. She asked him if this was his doing. Darnley gave an embarrassed reply. Ruthven, by his own account, launched into a long and rambling denunciation of Mary's relations with Riccio, reproaching her for her favour to him, and for her banishment of the Protestant lords. Riccio had shrunk back into the large window at the end of the little room, but when Ruthven made a lunge towards him Mary's attendants, who seem to have been stunned into inaction, at last made some sort of protest. 'Lay not hands on me, for I will not be handled,' cried Ruthven, with his hand on his dagger: this was the signal for his followers, Andrew Ker of Fawdonside, Patrick Bellenden, George Douglas, Thomas Scott and Henry Yair, to rush into the room, also from the privy staircase. In the ensuing confusion the table was knocked over and Lady Argyll was just able to save the last candle from being extinguished by snatching it up as it fell (although presumably the flickering light from the large fireplace still filled the little room). While Riccio clung to the queen's skirts, Ker and Bellenden produced pistols, and others wielded daggers. Finally the fingers of the little Italian were wrenched out of the queen's skirts, and he was dragged, screaming and kicking, out of the supper-room, across the bedroom through the presence-chamber to the head of the stairs. His pathetic voice could be heard calling as he went: *'Justizia, justizia! Sauvez ma vie, madame, sauvez ma vie!'*[16]

Here he was done to death by dagger-wounds variously estimated at between fifty-three and sixty: a savage butchery for a small body. Mary was convinced later that the first blow had been struck over her shoulder: at all events, the first knife-wound was made by George Douglas the Postulate, Morton's illegitimate brother, thus fulfilling the prophecy of Damiot concerning the Bastard; he carefully used Darnley's own dagger for the bloody deed in order to involve him still further in the crime. Riccio's serrated and bleeding corpse was now dragged down the winding main staircase. Here as it lay on a chest it was stripped of its belongings by a porter, who moralized as he did so in truly Shakespearian fashion: 'This was his destiny,' he soliloquized, 'for upon this chest was his first bed when he came to this place, and there he lieth a very niggard and misknown knave.' By now such commotion, such screams and cries had alerted the rest of the palace. Mary's own domestics came rushing to her assistance from the outside, with their own weapons of sticks and staves, without knowing exactly what peril threatened her. At the same time, up the wider outside staircase could be heard cries of 'A Douglas, a Douglas' as the rest of the clan rushed to support the inner conspirators. Ruthven later blamed the ensuing commotion for the death of Riccio, saying that the assassins feared he would otherwise be rescued; he stated that their original intention had been to bring him before Parliament. But the excuse seems thin, in view of the violent nature of the attack. Mary herself, by her own account, originally offered in the supper-room to let Riccio appear in Parliament, if he had done wrong, yet Ruthven dismissed the notion as worthless.

For the rest of her life, Mary Stuart was to believe that her own life also had been threatened in the course of the tumult in the supper-room and that Darnley, her own husband, had intended to compass her own destruction, and that of her unborn child. It is indeed impossible to understand her later attitude to Darnley without taking into account this steadfast inner conviction on the queen's part. After the birth of James, she burst out angrily to him: 'I have forgiven, but will never forget! What if Fawdonside's pistol had shot, what would become of him and me both? Or what estate would you have been in? God only knows, but we may suspect.'[7] In her account of events, she laid great stress on the violence which had been shown to her personally. This violence she laid at the door of Darnley, believing that she and her child had been about to be sacrificed at the altar of his ambition to become king of Scotland. In her mind she obviously believed that she had only escaped this fate through her own resolution and because her will was stronger than Darnley's – a conviction backed up by the fact that she was now to escape entirely through her own courage and daring. It was only too natural for a woman six months pregnant, having undergone such a traumatic experience of a pistol pointed at her stomach, to be imbued with these feelings. Even for us, the desperate circumstances of the murder make it hard to believe that something violent if unspecific was not meditated against her – perhaps it was hoped that the shock of the murder would cause her to miscarry and die (the death of the mother was then the end of most late miscarriages).

But at the time the quality of Mary Stuart's spirit was proof even against such an appalling experience, despite her condition. Far from shrinking from the danger, she turned furiously on Darnley, now left with her in the supper-chamber, and upbraided him. Then Ruthven returned from the carnage and, sinking on to a chair, called for wine to revive him; although the queen herself was still standing she still did not lose her poise and defiance. Gazing at the wine, she inquired acidly: 'Is this your sickness, Lord Ruthven?' In the course of a three-cornered wrangle between herself, Ruthven and Darnley, in which Ruthven called in question once more her behaviour as a wife, the queen refused to be cowed in any way; if one report is to be believed, she even told Ruthven that she had 'that within in her belly' which would one day be revenged upon him.*[18] In the course of the conversation, she had to deal with still further threats to her person: the disturbance at Holyrood had alerted the people of Edinburgh and the alarm bell of the city had been sounded. In order to quiet the townspeople, Darnley went to the window and spoke to them reassuringly in his familiar voice. When Mary strained to make her own voice heard, Lindsay brutally threatened to 'cut her in collops' if she made another move in the direction of the window. Finally Ruthven left and Darnley too departed. Mary sent one of her ladies for news of Riccio's fate. When she was told that he was dead, she wept for a moment; but a moment later drying her tears, observed calmly: 'No more tears now; I will think upon revenge.'[19] She also retained her composure sufficiently to send a lady to Riccio's room to recover a black coffer, with her ciphers and writings in it.

As Ruthven informed those left in Holyrood that the former Protestant rebels were now on their way back to Edinburgh, Mary was left to spend the night alone, without any sort of medical attention or a midwife, which might have been thought necessary, and only old Lady Huntly, widow of the 4th earl, to keep her company. So far, the conspirators seemed to be in complete outward command of the situation, except for the annoying fact that of their other intended victims, Bothwell and Huntly had escaped by jumping out of the back windows of the palace, past the lion pit. It had originally been projected to slay these two and Lords Livingston and Fleming as well as Riccio,

---

* If true, it was certainly an accurate prediction. It fell to the future James VI to put to death both Ruthven's son and his grandson, the 1st earl of Gowrie, in 1548, and the 2nd earl in 1600, at the time of the Gowrie conspiracy.

and hang Sir James Balfour as being all adherents of the queen. Now they contented themselves merely with the death of a Dominican priest, Father Adam Black. This very night, when the conspirators' triumph seemed certain, was crucial in the history of Mary Stuart. At some point in the course of it she took the bold decision to choke down her feelings of revulsion for Darnley and win him over on to her side, reasoning that the character of Darnley might now be the weakness of the conspirators' cause, as it had once been the weakness of her own. Since she had survived the slaughter, it will never be known exactly what plans the lords now had for the queen. She herself, presumably getting the news from Darnley, afterwards said in her letter – and amplified it to Nau[20] – that they intended to hold her in prison in Stirling until she gave birth to her child, and afterwards indefinitely; 'in the meantime the king could manage the affairs of state with the nobles'. Lord Lindsay was supposed to have remarked callously that she would find plenty of pastime there at Stirling in nursing her baby and singing it to sleep, shooting with her bow in the garden, and doing her fancy work. Although Lord Lindsay added that he happened to know that such things delighted her much, it was a tame prospect for one who had been queen of Scotland all her life, and thoroughly enjoyed the business of ruling.

Therefore when at daybreak the next morning, Sunday, Darnley went once more to her chamber, he found his wife calm rather than tearful, resolute rather than reproachful. Darnley himself seems to have been comparatively hysterical as a result of Riccio's death, and the queen told Nau that he pleaded with her with the old familiar endearments to forgive him for what had happened: 'Ah, my Mary,' he said (as he was wont to address her). In the meantime old Lady Huntly showed herself a resourceful companion of the first order, trained no doubt by the old days as the wife of the 4th earl. She offered to smuggle a rope ladder in between two plates and continued to suggest other schemes for escape until Lord Lindsay, breaking abruptly into the room (as the queen sat on her *chaise percée*), ordered her to depart. Even so Lady Huntly managed to take a letter to her son in her chemise (her outer clothing was searched), ordering him to stand by at Seton the following night. As escape by towels or ropes out of her window was clearly out of the question, because she was guarded above, Mary had a simpler and more intelligent plan. At some point in the course of Sunday she won back the facile Darnley by convincing him that his own prospects were as bleak as hers under the new régime, and that if he was not careful, they would both end up in ward in Stirling Castle. It was a triumph of a stronger character over a weaker one.

Armed with the knowledge of Darnley's new treachery, Mary was able to greet the conspirators the next day, Monday, with composure and even charm. She promised pardon, and that she would overlook recent hideous events: she even drank to the compact, although she could not quite bring herself to drink to Ruthven. Moray, apprised of what was about to take place, had set off from Newcastle: he arrived back in Edinburgh on the Monday, the day before his attainder had been due to be passed by Parliament. At this point Mary was unaware of Moray's complicity in the plot, and memories of their old intimacy, those early days in Scotland when the brother had seemed the natural loving protector of the younger sister, flooded back. Mary flung herself in his arms, crying: 'Oh my brother, if you had been here, they had not used me thus.' But when Moray in return chose to treat her to a sententious lecture on the virtues of clemency Mary not unnaturally fired up and pointed out tartly with reason that 'ever since her earliest youth, her nobility and others of her people, had given her frequently opportunities of practising that virtue and becoming familiar with it'.[21] As she felt her indignation overcoming her, she was compelled to feign the pangs of labour in order to preserve secrecy about her intentions, and she ordered the midwife to attend to her, whom the lords themselves had appointed on Sunday. This midwife unwittingly played her part in helping Mary's escape, for some of the lords remained suspicious of Mary's true feelings, despite her promise of pardon; however, the woman, who was their nominee, assured them of her own accord that the queen was extremely ill and in danger of her life, as a result of what she had been through. At eight o'clock on the Monday evening Mary carried the second stage of her plan into effect by sending for Stewart of Traquair, the captain of the royal guard, Erskine, her equerry, and Standen, one of her pages; she then begged them in the name of chivalry to assist her not only as a defenceless woman, but also as the mother of the future king of Scotland. These gallant gentlemen proved susceptible to her appeal, and promised to stand by her escape, in the manner she now outlined.

At midnight the queen and Darnley made their way down the privy staircase up which the assassins had filed only fifty-two hours before. Darnley's acquiescence meant that Mary could now use the staircase as an escape route; they then made their way through the back passages and servants' quarters of Holyrood, where Mary's French servants would not betray her escape, and finally past an outside cemetery, close to the abbey of Holyrood. Here, by Mary's account, Darnley gave an involuntary sigh at the sight of a newly dug grave, and confessed to his wife that she was practically treading on the burial ground of the wretched Riccio* – 'In him I have lost a good and faithful servant,' said Darnley, 'I have been miserably cheated.' These gloomy reflections were checked by the need for silence. Outside the abbey to meet the royal couple were Erskine, Traquair, Standen and two or three loyal soldiers with horses. Mary mounted pillion behind Erskine. Darnley took a horse of his own. In a short while, under the friendly cover of darkness, they were clear of the town.

The plan was to go to Dunbar Castle, pausing at Seton to pick up the nobles who had been alerted via Lady Huntly. The ride was of necessity fast, and as furious as possible. Even so,

---

* It seems inconceivable that Mary should then have told Darnley bluntly that he himself would go the same way before a year was out – as Lennox announced in his own narrative,¹¹ written after Darnley's death. Even if Mary nourished the thought, she would scarcely have chosen such a dangerous moment to give it expression, when she was still within the bounds of Holyrood, and still dependent on the goodwill of Darnley.

Darnley, in a panic of fear at being hunted down by the men he had so recently betrayed, kept spurring his own horse and flogging that of the queen, shouting: 'Come on! Come on! By God's blood, they will murder both you and me if they can catch us.' Mary pleaded with him to have regard to her condition, at which Darnley only flew into a rage and exclaimed brutally that if this baby died, they could have more.[23] By the time they reached Dunbar Castle, on the coast, twenty-five miles from Edinburgh as the crow flies, the long night was almost over. For a woman in an advanced state of pregnancy, a five-hour marathon of this nature must have been a gruelling ordeal. Even now, the queen's formidable courage did not desert her: she is said to have sent for eggs to cook breakfast. Here at Dunbar* Mary set herself about the task of consolidating the advantage which her liberty had given her.

On 15th March she dictated a long and passionate description of her experience, to be sent to Queen Elizabeth in London. She described the butchery of her secretary before her very eyes. 'Some of our subjects and council by their proceedings have declared manifestly what men they are ... slain our most special servant in our own presence and thereafter held our proper person captive treasonably ...'[24] She appealed to Elizabeth to beware of similar betrayals, which might lead to similar horrifying ordeals. She ended with the note that she had intended to write the letter in her own hand, to make it all seem more immediate, but 'of truth we are so tired and evil at ease, what through riding of 20 miles in five hours of the night, as with the frequent sickness and evil disposition by the occasion of our child' that the task had proved beyond her. Nevertheless, whatever physical reaction the queen was suffering after the event, she appeared to be once more triumphing over her enemies, as decisively as she had done in the previous August – and once more as a

---

* It was at this moment in history that the important wardship of Dunbar Castle was transferred from the laird of Craigmillar to the earl of Bothwell, to punish the one and to reward the other for their respective roles in the Riccio affair – this transfer led to the dramatic part played by Dunbar Castle in Mary's abduction by Bothwell in the following year.

result of her own boldness and promptitude. The escape of Bothwell and Huntly proved decisive. Atholl, Fleming and Seton also came to her at Dunbar. Men began to flock to the queen's side at Dunbar, stirred up by these loyal agents. Soon there were 4000 men at her command. On 17th March Mary issued a proclamation from Dunbar calling for the inhabitants of the surrounding districts to meet her at Haddington next day with eight days' provisions. On 18th March she was able to re-enter Edinburgh victoriously at the head of 8000 men, only nine days after the murder which had caused her to flee from the city so precipitately.

Darnley rode beside her, like a sulky page. At the news of his defection, his fellow-plotters had fled from Edinburgh on the morning of 17th March realizing that their rebellion no longer had any focal point. Morton, Lindsay, Ker of Fawdonside and Ruthven went to England; Maitland, who had certainly known of the plot, although he had not wielded a dagger, went to Dunkeld; John Knox, who may not have known in advance what was proposed, but certainly applauded Riccio's killing as a goodly deed, went to Ayrshire. Moray alone remained in Edinburgh since he had cunningly arrived in the city too late to be implicated in the bloody events of the night of 9th March, and the fact that he had signed the pre-murder bond was of course unknown to the queen. Mary was also reconciled to Glencairn and Argyll. In any case, in her new grim determination to avenge the butchery of Riccio and pursue his killers to the utmost limits of her power, Mary was now prepared to forgive the previous rebels of the Chaseabout Raid. Time's revolutions – and the treachery of Darnley – had combined to effect the pardon of Moray, which Mary had once strenuously refused to grant, despite the pleadings of her own nobles, and the admonitions of the queen of England.

CHAPTER FIFTEEN

Breakdown

'He misuses himself so far towards her that it is an
heartbreak for her to think that he should be her
husband.'

> *Maitland: On the relations between Mary and Darnley,*
> *October 1566*

It was easy enough, once Mary was back in Edinburgh, to
rescue the body of Riccio from its common grave and have
it reburied according to the Catholic rite he had professed,
in her own chapel royal.* Ten days later Riccio's brother, Joseph,
a boy of eighteen, was made French secretary in his place. Mary,
being anxious not to rule over a torn kingdom on the eve of
the birth of her child, also took the trouble to reconcile Moray,
Glencairn, and Argyll, recently allowed back into her favour,
with Huntly, Bothwell and Atholl; together these two groups
were now to make up the effective body of the Privy Council.
Mary's vengeance was thus officially reserved for the brutal
murderers of her servant who had actually burst into her
apartments – Morton, Ruthven, Lindsay and their minions. But
as they were now safely escaped to England, the only two lives
which were actually forfeited for the crime were those of two
of Ruthven's retainers: Tom Scott, under-sheriff of Perth, whose
official position of 'warding the Queen within Holyrood' made
his crime especially reprehensible, and Henry Yair who had

---

* Not, as Buchanan suggested, in the royal vault with Mary's father; this lie was
finally nailed in the seventeenth century when the king's tomb was opened.

killed the Dominican priest Father Black shortly after the murder of the Italian, and was executed the following August. Two other underlings, Mowbray and Harlaw, were released at the scaffold when the queen, characteristically moved by mercy, 'gave them their lives'.[1] Yet the murder of the Italian had marked a turning-point in the affairs of Mary Queen of Scots, and the memories of the affair were not so easily laid in peace and forgotten, as his poor lacerated corpse.

The most obvious result of the affair was Mary's abiding hatred of Darnley. She had either concealed this in order to escape from Holyrood or else she did not at this point realize the full extent of her husband's complicity. Although she told Nau that Darnley had admitted to her on the Sunday that he had signed a bond to procure the crown matrimonial, and Leslie repeats the story, she did not mention the fact in her letter to Beaton of 2nd April. Whether Mary knew beforehand or not, the conspirators now took the understandable if vindictive step of sending the bond to the queen, so that she should see for herself the full extent of her husband's treachery. Yet once more Mary was obliged to put a good face upon the situation for the time being, and issue a public statement of his innocence at the market cross. It was not within the compass of her thoughts to take any action against her husband before the birth of her child, since Darnley was quite capable of casting doubts upon the child's legitimacy, if it suited his purpose. Although there were already rumours of a divorce between the two by the end of April – Randolph said Thornton had gone to Rome to treat about it – Mary, like all the Scots, had heard far too many arguments over the legitimacy of heirs, as the result of the subsequent divorces of their parents, to risk considering the subject before her child was actually born. In May there was another rumour from Randolph that Darnley would leave Scotland after the birth of the baby, and go to Flanders. He described Darnley's new situation thus: 'He is neither accompanied for, nor looked for by any nobleman, attended by certain of his own servants, and six or eight of his guard, he is at liberty to do or go what or where he will.'[2] In his reflective moments Darnley must have realized that this aimless freedom might in fact be the deceptive liberty in Scotland – the queen, Moray and his associates, Bothwell and the loyalist nobles, he had betrayed them all or tried to attack them at one or other point in his career. Should these potential enemies flag, there was also a whole new ferocious band of them headed by Morton, now in England, who might not stay there forever.

Mary's relations with Darnley settled down into an uneasy truce until the birth of her child. Darnley had not reformed his behaviour: during her confinement he 'vagabondized every night'.[3] In these circumstances it was natural that Mary should come to rely increasingly for political advice on those nobles who had proved themselves loyal to her throughout the two crises which she had faced in the past year.* Into this category fell notably James Hepburn, earl of Bothwell, who as he leapt clear of the lion-pit at Holyrood, and rode off to summon Mary's subjects successfully to her assistance, seemed to display that combination of resource, loyalty and strength which Mary had so persistently sought among her Scottish nobles. Now that he was reconciled with Moray, and firmly allied by marriage to Huntly, he seemed set in Mary's estimation to form a useful loyal member of the Scottish polity. Yet Bothwell in his character seemed to sum up those very paradoxical contrasts which made it so difficult for anyone not brought up among them to understand the nature and behaviour of the Scottish nobles. For whereas Darnley by reason of his English royal blood and English upbringing was atypical of the Scottish nobility, Bothwell shared the turbulent contentious characteristics of his class – and it was this class whose motives and actions Queen Mary was never able to predict successfully. In the past she had been baffled and angered by Huntly, puzzled and hurt by Moray, appalled and shocked by Morton. Now she was once again, by the unwitting fault of her French upbringing, to make a mistake of judgement, and see in Bothwell the mirage – it was no more than

---

* Mary's well-known memoir in which she expressed a preference for the services of a loyal 'man of low estate' to those of the nobility is attributed by Prince Labanoff to the period directly after Riccio's death. But as it is in Nau's handwriting, it seems more likely that Mary dictated it to her secretary later during her captivity.[4]

that – of a strong wise protector, able to solve her problems by holding down the other nobles under his heel.

Bothwell was not a stupid man; he had been well educated by his kinsman the bishop of Moray, as his letters and writing show, and his books included volumes on both mathematics and the arts of war. He was well travelled: in Denmark he had picked up a Norwegian mistress, Anna Throndsen, whom he had seduced under promise of marriage; and it was seeking funds to support himself on this occasion that he had first met Queen Mary at the French court. He had made several expeditions to France, and spoke French himself. He was adventurous by nature, and his life (he was at this date about thirty) had already been full of ups and downs; apart from his imprisonment in Edinburgh Castle he had done a spell in the Tower of London in 1564 while trying to escape to France. When Mary sent for him at the time of the Chaseabout Raid, he arrived in a fishing boat from Flushing, eluding capture by the English. He came of the great border family of Hepburns, and in feudal terms his power stretched across the south-east of Scotland, with certain specifically family dominions, and the wardship of other royal castles (such as Hermitage and Dunbar) dependent on royal favour. Bothwell, like all his class, was keenly interested in the acquisition of such royal castles for the family interest, and official positions such as lieutenant of the borders had the natural corollary for him of the extension of his family's power. His family, and indeed he himself, suffered from the proverbial pennilessness of the contemporary nobles, and his marriage contract to Jean Gordon shows that he was heavily in debt at the time. In the past there had been something amounting to a family tradition for the Hepburns to attempt to improve their fortunes by favour of widowed queens. Bothwell's own father, Patrick, the Fair Earl, had courted Mary of Guise throughout the winter of 1543* in a ludicrous competition for her affections

---

* There is, however, no evidence that their relations were consummated, and still less reason to suppose that Earl Patrick had a liaison with Mary of Guise early in 1542; yet the scandalous rumour that Bothwell was 'near sib' to Mary Queen of Scots could, as Professor Donaldson points out,¹ only be explained if Earl Patrick

with Lennox (by a curious coincidence, to be Mary Stuart's father-in-law) in which fine clothes played an important part. An earlier Patrick Hepburn had been linked with the widow of James 1, and an Adam Hepburn with Mary of Guelders. After the battle of Pinkie Cleugh Bothwell's father even negotiated with the English to marry an English princess in return for handing over the castle of Hermitage. In their marriage projects Hepburns had tried without success to become the Habsburgs of Scotland.

Yet the effect of Bothwell's concentration on the possibilities of the main chance was in fact to give him a far better record of loyalty to the central government – in the shape of Mary of Guise and her daughter – than most of his contemporaries. In the same way his religious attitudes showed a real degree of consistency. He refused to marry Jean Gordon according to the Catholic rite, despite Queen Mary's pressure, and was described by Randolph as being one of those very strong against the Mass.[6] His critics retaliated by accusing him of being interested in the black arts which he was thought to have acquired during his education in France. La Mothe Fenélon told Charles IX that Bothwell had principally used his time at the schools in Paris to read and study sorcery and magic. At any rate his ambition was certainly boundless: as the memoirs of Lord Herries put it, he was a man 'high in his own conceit, proud, vicious and vain-glorious above measure, one who would attempt anything out of ambition'.[7] But his brain and methods were the reverse of Machiavellian, and to consider his political acumen in the same category as that of Cecil, in the sense that he now became the adviser on whom Mary relied, as Elizabeth relied on her secretary, is to demonstrate how very retarded sixteenth-century Scotland was, in political terms, compared to sixteenth-century England.

It was significant that at two crucial moments in his career – in November 1560 serving Mary of Guise against the insurgents

had been her natural father, making Bothwell her half-brother. In the absence of any other support for the theory, the rumour must surely be dismissed along with the many other scandalous rumours concerning the parentage of famous persons which abounded during this period.

under Châtelherault, and in June 1567 before Carberry Hill – Bothwell issued a challenge for personal combat with his enemies; as a feudal baron, and primarily a soldier, he was apt to choose the quick, if bloody, solution to any problem. It was true that during his brief spell as the queen's husband Bothwell showed signs of a certain administrative ability, as a soldier can sometimes make a successful politician in a crisis; in the same way the coarse-grained Morton made not a bad showing as regent from the administrative point of view. But Bothwell's personal qualities negated his usefulness in any delicate situation, and made him the last person to unite successfully that essentially disunited and suspicious body, the Scottish nobility. For one thing, Bothwell's violence and his boastfulness (when Throckmorton called him a 'glorious, rash and hazardous young man' he was of course using the word glorious in the derogatory sense of vainglorious) scarcely led to popularity. Violence in matters of policy was accompanied by a streak of roughness, verging on bullying in private life. His servant Paris testified that he had kicked him in the stomach when Paris tried to argue with him.[8] He was certainly not a man who was prepared to try using charm to gain his objectives: as Mary told Nau, 'he was a man whose natural disposition made him anything but agreeable or inclined to put himself to much trouble or inconvenience to gain the goodwill of those with whom he had been associated'.[9]

Bothwell's relations with women fell into the same adventurous but straightforward pattern as his career. Although interested in women, he drew a sharp and effective distinction between sex and marriage: Anna Throndsen never did secure the marriage contract she desired and departed disconsolately to her home some time in 1563. His name was also linked with that of the legendary Janet Beaton, aunt of the queen's Marie, made famous as Sir Walter Scott's Wizard Lady of Branxholm, who could bond to her bidding 'the viewless forms of air': this remarkable lady enjoyed five husbands – the last at the age of sixty-one – and a number of lovers in the course of a long and full life. When she became Bothwell's mistress, he was twenty-four and she many years older, her unfading beauty generally attributed to the practice of magic, a subject she may have had in common with her lover. Despite the difference in their ages, they may have gone through some sort of ceremony of 'hand-fasting', Bothwell being fascinated by her combination of audacity, determination and sexuality. But it was finally Jean Gordon, the comparatively rich sister of the powerful Huntly, whom Bothwell actually married, the marriage contract making it clear that it was the bride who was making the settlement on the groom rather than the other way round. Bothwell evidently regarded lust as a simple sensation to be quickly gratified. The deposition of Thomas Craigwallis at the time of his divorce gave an evocative picture of his relations with his mistress, pretty little black-eyed Bessie Crawford, the blacksmith's daughter – a fifteen-minute rendezvous in the steeple of the abbey at Haddington, and another tryst in a mid-chamber of the kitchen tower at Crichton (Thomas remaining at the door); a subsequent encounter took place 'in a chamber within the cloister' according to Pareis Sempill's evidence, 'and when my lord came forth his clothes were loose, and Patrick Wilson helped him up therewith'.[10] Marriage on the other hand was a more serious business to be undertaken for the positive motive of gain.

In appearance Bothwell lacked the hermaphrodite beauty of a Darnley; he was only of middle stature, compared to Darnley's slender height – his mummified corpse at Dragsholm measures five feet six inches. Although those who had reason to deplore his influence over Mary Stuart, like Brantôme and Buchanan, rather childishly described him as having been hideously ugly – 'like an ape in purple' said Buchanan – another of Mary's partisans, Leslie, said that he was of great bodily strength and beauty, although vicious and dissolute in his habits.[11] The only known portrait traditionally said to be of him – a miniature now in the Scottish National Portrait Gallery – shows a face which is certainly not conventionally handsome; there is even something simian here to confirm Buchanan's insults; the complexion is swarthy, the nose appears to have been broken, the ears large and slightly protruding, the lips under their carefully trained moustache with its curling ends are full and sensual, the eyes look suspiciously out of the picture like those of a watchful animal. It is the face of a man who might well prove attractive to certain types of women, because it is strong and vital, yet from another point of view it gives the impression of one to whom the defence of the rights of the weak would seem a thorough waste of time.

At the beginning of June Mary began to make detailed preparations for the birth of her child: at the wish of her Council, she had been lodged in Edinburgh Castle since early April, since the great castle frowning on its rock over the town below was evidently felt to be a safer locality for this important event than Holyrood, so recently demonstrated to have the flimsiest defences; it would also be understandable if Mary herself had been reluctant to give birth to her child in the same apartments where her servant had been butchered. In view of the hazards of the time towards any mother and child in the process of labour, let alone one who had been through the Scottish queen's experiences in March, it was particularly import-ant that Mary should make a will. This testament, of which she made three copies, one to keep, one for those who were to execute it in Scotland, and one to send to France, provides an interesting commentary on her state of mind on the eve of this critical occasion.[12] The lords also signed a document binding themselves to adhere to the queen's testament, in view of the fact that she was (through imminent childbirth) 'in peril and danger of her life': in this semi-governmental measure, which was presumably directed against Darnley, it is significant that Bothwell's signature was high up and prominent among the other loyal lords.[13]

Mary's first thought is for her child, to whom, if it survives her own death, everything is to be left without further dis-tinctions. But in the event of their joint death, she lays down minute provisions for the disposal of her jewels, in which her foremost concern is the establishment of a rich inheritance for the Scottish crown itself: her choicest gems, including the Great Harry, are to be annexed to the Scottish crown in perpetuity by Act of Parliament, in remembrance of herself, and the Scottish alliance with the house of Lorraine. Darnley is included in the will, as befits the queen's husband, and is left twenty-six bequests, among them a diamond ring enamelled in red of which the queen notes in her handwriting, 'It was with this that I was married; I leave it to the King who gave it to me'; although Buchanan later stated quite erroneously that Darnley had been totally ignored in the will, not only does Mary acknowledge the conventional claim of her husband to be remembered but she also leaves minor bequests to both Lord and Lady Lennox, as her father- and mother-in-law.

However, it is to her French relations, who seem to have possessed her true heart, that her most affectionate and detailed bequests are made: she still feels herself sufficiently a member of the house of Guise to outline a gift of rubies and pearls, to be handed down from generation to generation as the legacy of its first-born. The family of Duke Francis and Duchess Anne, whom she had known so well as little children, and who had grown to adolescence since her departure, are left rich jewels, the most precious going to the youngest son, Francis, namesake and godson of Mary's first husband,* Duchess Anne, Mary's beloved aunt and correspondent, herself receives splendid jewels and another aunt, the Abbess Renée, for whom the queen seems to have felt a daughter's affection after her mother's death, receives a number of bequests including a portrait of Queen Elizabeth in the frame of a mirror. Other Guise children, those of the Elboeuf and Aumale families, all now growing up, are remembered with Mary's own namesake and god-daughter, young Mary of Elboeuf, receiving again a specially large share. To the cardinal of Lorraine goes an emerald ring.

In Scotland, it is her illegitimate Stewart relations whom Mary treats as her own family; not only her confidante and half-sister Jean Argyll, but also Moray, his wife Agnes and their daughter are mentioned; Mary's godson Francis, son of her half-brother Lord John Stewart and Bothwell's sister, is given special con-

---

* It is interesting to note that the name Francis was introduced into Scotland by the god-children and namesakes of Queen Mary's first husband.

sideration. One of Mary's charming traits was a fondness for young children as this will shows. The queen seems always to show a particular affection for this boy, reminiscent of her later fondness of Arbella Stuart; owing to the early death of his father, he became her ward as well as her nephew and godson; she heaped him with honours and lands until in captivity she could do no more.* Other legatees included the two Lady Huntlys, young and old (young Lady Huntly being the only Hamilton to be mentioned in the will), and Privy Councillors then in favour including Argyll, Atholl, Huntly himself and of course Bothwell. Otherwise Mary's innate concern seems to have been for her servants – not only the four Maries, but also an endless string of other ladies-in-waiting, maids-of-honour, women of the bed-chamber, and equerries are remembered, including the faithful Arthur Erskine, behind whom she had ridden to Dunbar, Riccio's brother Joseph, to receive a ring to be delivered to a secret destination (perhaps some relation or dependent of David Riccio, of whose existence Mary knew), and Mary's favourite bed-chamber woman Margaret Carwood, who had entered her service in 1564. Like all servants at court, Mary's attendants tended to form a tight little circle who were both related to each other and who married each other – as Erskine had recently married Magdalene Livingston, a royal maid-of-honour who was also the sister of the grander 'Marie', Mary Livingston. Their intimate little world of service is here commemorated in the queen's will.

According to the custom of the time, the queen took to her lying-in chamber ceremoniously on 3rd June to await the confinement. Already in May the midwife Margaret Asteane had been provided with a special black velvet dress for the coming occasion; an enormous and sumptuous bed hung in blue taffeta and blue velvet had been prepared for Mary's use, and as much as ten ells of Holland cloth commissioned to cover the baby's

* This child whom Queen Mary befriended was to become the notorious Francis Stewart, earl of Bothwell, of the reign of James VI; being Bothwell's nephew through his mother Janet Hepburn, he was given his uncle's title in 1581 by James VI.

cradle.[14] The apartments Mary now inhabited in Edinburgh Castle were in the south-east corner, within the old palace, and thus overlooked the town; the actual room in which the birth took place was extremely small, like so many of the important rooms of this period, and lay off the chamber now known as Queen Mary's room. On 15th June a false alarm about the birth gave rise to premature rejoicings; but it was not until four days later that the labour actually began. This was long, painful and difficult, and the queen was 'so handled that she began to wish that she had never been married'. This was despite the efforts of Mary Fleming's sister Margaret, countess of Atholl, to cast the pangs of childbirth upon Margaret, Lady Reres, by witchcraft; Lady Reres lay in bed, suffering likewise with her mistress, but Mary's pangs do not appear to have been solaced in consequence. The baby prince was finally born between ten and eleven on the morning of Wednesday 19th June, with a thin, fine caul stretched over his face. Despite this hazard, and despite the length of the labour, he was an impressively healthy child, as Killigrew, the English ambassador noticed five days later when he was shown the naked infant. Killigrew first saw the baby sucking at the breast of his wet-nurse – Lady Reres, who was perhaps given the post as a consolation for her earlier ordeal – and the baby James was later unwrapped for his inspection, much as Mary herself had been displayed in infancy to Sir Ralph Sadler. Although Mary could only manage to speak to him faintly with a hollow cough, Killigrew concluded that her child was likely to prove 'a goodly prince'.*[15]

* This is the appropriate moment to dispose of, briefly, the imaginative notion that Mary's child died at birth, and another Erskine baby, child of the countess of Mar, was substituted. This tale is backed by no contemporary reference, and the present (13th) earl of Mar and Kellie has told the author that he can find nothing in his extensive family archives to support the theory of an Erskine family tradition. The story has arisen apparently as a result of two events – firstly, in 1830 a skeleton, rumoured to be that of a child, was found in the wall of a chamber in Edinburgh Castle by some workmen; the bones were wrapped in a woollen cloth (not cloth of gold with a royal cipher or a *fleur-de-lys* on it, as is sometimes stated); secondly, at the end of the last century, it was noticed that James VI, in the portraits of his maturity, bore an undoubted resemblance to the 2nd earl of Mar, who would, if the story were true, have been his full brother.[16]

The birth of a male heir was signalled with immense rejoicings in Edinburgh, and now five hundred bonfires were lit, to illuminate the city and the surrounding hills with their festive fire. The whole artillery of the castle was discharged, and lords, nobles and people gathered together in St Giles church, to thank God for the honour of having an heir to their kingdom, the fact that St Giles was the main Protestant church demonstrating the great legacy of goodwill which awaited any queen who gave birth to a healthy prince in this era. Sir James Melville, given the good news by Mary Beaton, rode off to London an hour later to break it to Queen Elizabeth. The English queen reacted with her famous outcry, the primitive complaint of the childless woman for a more favoured sister: 'Alack, the Queen of Scots is lighter of a bonny son, and I am but of barren stock.'[18] It was true that the birth of James duly enhanced Mary's merits as a candidate for the English throne. A strange little incident about the time of Mary's accouchement involved an English spy, Rokeby, who was supposed to have lured Mary in Edinburgh into unwise pronouncements concerning her future on the English throne – although even Rokeby admitted in his report to Cecil that Mary 'would be content that she would have it

These two slender threads have been woven into a tissue of fantasy, by which it is suggested that Mary arranged the substitution after the death of her own child, in order to prevent Darnley seizing the throne. It ignores the fact that Mary was a young woman, able to have more children, quite apart from the difficulties of arranging such a substitution within the confines of Edinburgh Castle, filled with nobles of conflicting loyalties, including the Archbishop Hamilton, who would scarcely have stood by while the claims of his own house were set aside. Nor can any special importance be attached to the fact that Lord Mar was shortly afterwards made the governor of Prince James, since this office was, as has been seen, hereditary in the Erskine family. This leaves the question of the resemblance of James and the 2nd Lord Mar, on which two points should be noted: firstly, the interrelation of the great Scottish families which was such a feature of this period meant that such a resemblance could emerge quite naturally, as such resemblances do not always descend directly from father to son – the grandmother of the 1st Lord Mar had in fact been a Lennox Stewart. Secondly, the portrait of James VI as a child by Honthorst is so strikingly like that of his legal father Darnley as a young man by Eworth as to make further arguments on the subject surely unnecessary. In short, the little skeleton in the wall – if child it truly was, and this point was never officially stated at the time of the discovery[17] – is far more likely to be the sad relic of a lady-in-waiting's peccadillo than a queen's conspiracy.

after …' Others were not so discreet as to wait for 'after'. In a poem of thanksgiving for James's birth, Patrick Adamson in Paris even went so far as to refer to him as *'Serenissimus princeps'* of Scotland, England, France and Ireland, a gesture which not only infuriated Elizabeth in London, who ordered her envoy Bedford to make a protest about it at James's christening, but also produced angry outbursts in the English House of Commons; Adamson finally underwent six months' imprisonment for his indiscretion.[19] The birth of a son, however, strengthened Mary's hand over the English succession for the future in a way which was obvious, and which even the English Commons could not obliterate by intemperate speeches.

The birth of an heir also inevitably moved the child's own father, Darnley, further down the line of succession for both English and Scottish thrones. Queen Mary, aware of the temperament with which she was dealing, took care to display the baby to him publicly and announce: 'My Lord, God has given you and me a son, begotten by none but you.' She went on, uncovering the child's face: 'Here I protest to God as I shall answer to him at the great day of Judgment, that this is your son and no other man's son. I am desirous that all here, with ladies and others bear witness.' She added, as though to clinch the matter by a note of contempt for her husband: 'For he is so much your own son, that I fear it will be the worse for him hereafter.'[20] Having thus, as she hoped, preserved her child from the stigma of illegitimacy, Mary devoted the rest of her time in Edinburgh Castle to his care, having the baby to sleep in her own room, and frequently watching over him at night. A few days after the birth, she sent for Anthony Standen, the faithful equerry who had helped her escape from Holyrood, and had him knighted by Darnley. Pointing to the child in its cradle, she announced in words which showed how far Mary was from forgetting the events after the murder of Riccio: 'For that you saved his life…'[21]

The birth of James had two dramatic effects upon Mary Stuart: she no longer had any pressing motive for demonstrating a public reconciliation with Darnley, and at the same time her own extremely precarious health had its balance finally destroyed. There is no evidence that she ever really recovered it before her extremely serious illness at Jedburgh four months later, and this illness in turn led to a prolonged phase of highly nervous, almost hysterical ill-health, which lasted right until her incarceration on Lochleven the following June. But for her actions and movements during the next eight months, the critical period from the birth of James in June 1566 until the death of Darnley in February 1567, it is extremely important to distinguish between information and reports written at the time – that is to say before the death had taken place – such as ambassadors' comparatively impartial reports on the state of Scotland, and Mary's own letters posted to France, which could not be altered by *arrière pensée*, and those accounts written long after the event, specifically to prove Mary's guilt with Bothwell. These later accounts include the *Book of the Articles* written by Buchanan as an accusatory brief at the time of her trial in England, two years later, and Buchanan's own *History*, and his *Detection of Mary Queen of Scots*. The point of Buchanan, who was bound by allegiance to Lennox, and therefore to Darnley, is to prove as salaciously as possible that Mary had enjoyed an adulterous liaison with Bothwell from the birth of her child, and even possibly before. But in the course of making his charge, Buchanan allowed himself the luxury of so many glaring inaccuracies that it is difficult to take his opinion on any aspect of the situation seriously – of these the comment on the queen's will is only a minor example: the tale of Bothwell hauled up by a rope unwilling and half-naked out of one mistress's bed directly into that of the queen by James's wet-nurse is probably the most ludicrous.[22]

It is a remarkable fact that there is no uncontested evidence among the letters or reports written *before* Darnley's death, whether French, English or Scottish, to show that Mary was involved in a sexual affair with Bothwell while her husband was still alive. There are on the other hand a number of pointers to the fact that she was not. The picture of the Scottish court through the autumn and winter of 1566, built by contemporary comments, is of a queen to whom her husband was becoming an increasingly distasteful problem, and a nobility to whom he was becoming an increasingly urgent one. Not one observer made any attempt during this period to connect the queen's growing scorn for Darnley with her growing affection for Bothwell, although the point would have been one which the ever-watchful ambassadors would have been delighted to make if they had felt it to be true. Of the couple, Mary and Bothwell, Mary was racked in health, not in itself very conducive to romance, and desperate to solve her marital problems; she was also well aware by now that she had created these problems for herself originally through her physical infatuation for Darnley; the very last intention in her mind was to tread so soon again down the treacherous paths of passion. Bothwell on the other hand was steadily bent on his own personal advancement in Scottish government affairs. It is questionable whether the one had the energy, and the second the inclination for the time-wasting business of an adulterous love affair when there were so many important matters to hand.

Before the end of July, Mary left Edinburgh for Newhaven, to see if a change of air would restore her lost health, and from there went on by sea to Alloa, the seat of Lord Mar. She particularly enjoyed the pleasure of sea travel – as Buchanan put it, she 'joyed to handle the boisterous cables' – but on this occasion she made the journey alone, unaccompanied by either Bothwell or Darnley. Darnley, having not been informed of her departure, later followed Mary to Alloa but stayed there only a few hours, as Bedford duly reported back to England. In the same letter Bedford also noted that Bothwell's arrogance was making him so unpopular with his fellow-nobles that he believed that there might be some plot in hand against him. A few days later Bedford reported again that Bothwell was now as much hated as Riccio had ever been, and also that the queen was not getting on well with her husband.[23] It was significant that Bedford made no attempt to connect the two facts; on the contrary, by mid-August it was Moray's influence over his half-sister which was said to be causing Darnley to sulk: Bedford wrote that his jealousy was such that 'he could not bear that the Queen should use familiarity with men or women, and especially the ladies of Argyll, Moray and Mar, who keep most company with her'.[24] Mary now went hunting in the extreme south of Peeblesshire, with Bothwell, Moray and Mar, but without Darnley.

Reunited in each other's company at the house of Traquair, home of John Stewart of Traquair, captain of the queen's guard, the royal couple apparently gave way to their most open and shocking disagreement. Romantic Traquair, said to be the oldest inhabited house in Scotland, guarding and guarded by the Tweed, lies amid rich park lands ideal for hunting. A stag hunt was planned for the next day, in which both Mary and Darnley were expected to take part. But at supper, the queen begged to excuse herself on the grounds that the exertion would be too much for her health. When Darnley refused to listen, she whispered in his ear that she suspected she was again *enceinte*. Darnley answered aloud, in roughly the same words he had used before, during the ride to Dunbar, 'Never mind, if we lose this one, we will make another,' at which Traquair rebuked him sharply for his un-Christian behaviour. Darnley (who was probably drunk) then exclaimed coarsely: 'What! ought not we to work a mare well when she is in foal?' The anecdote comes from Nau,[25] and in relating it to him the queen may perhaps have allowed time to have over-coloured Darnley's brutality. But the possibility that Mary could have been *enceinte* once more – it was now two months since the birth of Prince James – is an interesting one in view of Buchanan's accusations that Mary never again admitted Darnley to her bed after the child's birth. A ballad written in 1568 after Mary had fled to England, called *The Earl of Bothwell*, represented her as vowing after the murder of Riccio

> ... for a twelve month and a day
> The king and she would not come in one sheet

In view of Mary's conviction that Darnley had aimed at her death and that of her child, her refusal to grant him his conjugal rights would be easy to understand, but of course it could scarcely be expected to lead to happier relations between them. It is noticeable that his humiliation as a husband was one of Darnley's main points of complaint on the occasion when he voiced his grievances. Taking into account Mary's ill-health, the most likely state of affairs between them during July and August would seem to be an occasional reluctant acquiescence on the part of the queen to her husband's embraces, which did little to convince Darnley that she either loved or respected him. After Mary's illness, and especially once the matter of a divorce had been broached at Craigmillar, her abstinence from any physical relationship was certainly total: by then she clearly wished to have nothing more to do with him as a husband, and would therefore hardly have run the risk of another pregnancy.

On her return from Traquair to Edinburgh, the queen arranged for the transference of the little prince to Stirling Castle, the traditional nursery of royal princes. His cortège accordingly set off with four or five hundred harquebusiers round it for protection, and the prince was handed into the care of the Erskine family as his hereditary governors. In delegating the upbringing of her child in this manner, Mary Stuart was in no way deviating from normal practice, and certainly not showing herself a cold or unfeeling mother. Fosterage was on the contrary the standard custom of the Scottish noble families, who handed over their children in babyhood, and the custom of fosterage, being regarded as a mark of aristocracy, gradually came to be copied lower down the social scale. Mary, in her anxious watching over James's cradle, and her immense solicitude for the grandeur of his christening ceremony, which it was within her power to arrange, showed an almost pathetically strong maternal anxiety, borne out by her touching fondness for all other small children with whom she came in contact throughout her life. The preparations for his first nursery at Stirling were both detailed and sumptuous, done to the queen's personal command: there were to be buckets of gold and silver 'the finest that can be gottin', lengths of blue plaiding for the baby's cradle, fustian for his mattress, feathers for his bolster; his room was to be hung with tapestries, as well as adequately provided with blankets. The needs of Lady Reres in her capacity of wet-nurse were not overlooked: she too was to have plaiding to cover her bed and a canopy to go over it. The instructions were to be carried out without any delay, because it was all 'very needful to be had'.[26]

In September, Maitland, long out of favour with the queen, was reconciled to her, and returned to court; he was also reconciled with Bothwell. At the end of September there was a confrontation between Mary and Darnley in front of the French ambassador and many of the nobles, in which both stated their grievances. The emphasis was all on Darnley's status within the kingdom, and whether Mary was still allowing him his rights as king. Lennox first brought the matter up in a letter to Mary of 29th September when he told his daughter-in-law that Darnley was now so humiliated by his position that he intended to go abroad, having a boat all prepared for the journey.[27] As a result Mary faced Darnley the next day in front of the Council and du Croc, and made him a *'fort belle harangue'* in which she asked him in what respect she had offended him, and pleaded with him, with hands joined together, not to spare her anything, but to tell her the truth. The lords then joined in asking Darnley how they had offended him, and even du Croc chimed in with the view that if Darnley went abroad it would be an offence to the queen's honour. Darnley made little of this opportunity for airing his grievances against his wife, but merely said flatly that he had no particular cause for offence; his sting was in his deliberately melodramatic departure from the queen's side, without kissing her, and vowing in sybilline fashion that she would not see him again for a long time. Whereupon the lords and du Croc crowded round the queen and told her to continue in her present course of wise and virtuous behaviour, and the truth between her and Darnley would soon be generally known.*

* It is surely inconceivable that Darnley or Lennox would not have mentioned the subject of Bothwell's relations with the queen during the course of this long discussion on the troubles between Darnley and his wife, if indeed they had constituted a major source of dispute between the couple. Yet Bothwell's name

Two weeks later du Croc wrote to Catherine de Médicis of the newly excellent relations which existed between Queen Mary and her subjects, through her own efforts and good qualities – they were 'so well reconciled with the Queen as a result of her own prudent behaviour, that nowadays there was not a single division to be seen between them'. Darnley, on the other hand, was equally ill-regarded by both parties; having apparently learnt nothing from his recent experiences, he still wanted to rule everything; yet there was not a single noble who did not take his cue for his behaviour towards Darnley from the queen. Du Croc noted that preparations were already being made for the christening of the little prince, £12,000 being raised by direct taxation to pay for it, and he represented Catholics and Protestants as being equally enthusiastic about the coming celebrations. Indeed, he attributed much of Darnley's spoilt and sulky behaviour to the fuss which was going on about the christening: not only was Darnley jealous of Mary's reconciliation with the Protestant lords, but he was also fearful lest strangers should witness his obvious fall from favour at the ceremony – a prospect which was intolerable to his '*haute et superbe*' temperament.[28]

To the queen's attitude to the official religion of her country, as much as to the birth of an heir, must be attributed much of this Indian summer of warm relations with her nobility. The tender green shoots of a pro-Catholic policy which she had put out in the spring of 1566 had been rudely blighted by the sharp frost of Riccio's murder, which among other things demonstrated the strength of the Protestant lords who could even storm her apartments. For the rest of the fifteen months of her personal rule, Mary made no attempt to help the Scottish Catholic Church, but showed on the contrary a renewed warmth towards the organization of the reformed religion. On 3rd October an Act of Privy Council ordained that benefices worth less than 300 merks annually were to go to the Protestant ministers, and

was never introduced into the conversation. Describing the scene afterwards to the French court, du Croc did not mention it either.

there were now some instances of ministers being appointed to benefices. On 13th December a further law was enacted to help the Protestant administration; and on 20th December the Church received from the queen a direct gift of £10,000 as well as provisions.[29] Such an attitude to the religion which the majority of her subjects professed may seem to us today pragmatic in terms of government and admirable in terms of tolerance and good order. There could after all be no doubt of Mary's personal attachment to the Catholic faith, since quite apart from her early words to Throckmorton, she never wavered from the holding of her own personal Mass in Scotland, even at the times when it would have been most expedient to do so, and the Mass itself as we have seen was a most detestable symbol to the fervent Protestants. One may therefore applaud her far-sighted policy, all the more remarkable in one born after all in the year in which the Spanish Inquisition was founded. But of course Pius v, in distant Rome, could not be expected to view the situation in the same detached light: indeed, to him the flagging of his spiritual daughter's newly kindled zeal was a painful prospect, and one to be combated with the double weapon of a papal mission and a papal subsidy. A papal nuncio, the bishop of Mondovi, was dispatched, bearing 150,000 crowns in gold from the Pope, intended to help the queen combat the heretics; but now as before, Queen Mary showed an absolute disinclination to receive the nuncio on Scottish soil, on the grounds that his arrival would occasion 'great tumults'.[30] Mondovi was in fact lingering in France, awaiting permission to land, when the news came of Mary's serious illness in Jedburgh.

Jedburgh was one of the important towns in the Scottish border country, lying on the edge of the wild terrain which led across to the Anglo-Scottish border itself. Here Mary had arrived in early October to hold a justice eyre. She inhabited a 'bastel-house', or fortified dwelling, in the main street, still visible today in its original form. While she was in the midst of administering justice, news came that her lieutenant on the borders, Bothwell, had been seriously wounded in a foray there, and was now lying in danger of death at the castle of Hermitage. The queen did not immediately take any action, but five or six days later, when her business had been completed, she decided to pay Bothwell a visit, not so much to express her sympathy, as for the practical reason that he was her lieutenant and one of her chief advisers, especially on the perennially vexed border questions, and she needed to consult with him. Bedford, reporting the incident, and the earl's recovery, commented that the queen of Scots would certainly have been sorry to lose Bothwell, but made no remotely bawdy suggestion about the loss, which was by implication a strictly political or administrative one.

On 16th October, the queen, accompanied by her half-brother Moray and a large number of her court, as well as a quantity of soldiers, decided to ride over to the Hermitage, visit Bothwell, and since this border fortress was not prepared to receive the luxurious burden of a royal stay, return to Jedburgh that same day. Hermitage Castle was a thirteenth-century fortress, gaunt and forbidding in appearance, in the centre of Liddesdale. Lying on the left bank of the Hermitage water, twelve miles south of Hawick, it was a true military outpost, where up to 1000 men and 200 horsemen could be stationed in times of danger. Already it had acquired cruel and mournful memories from earlier violent scenes in Scottish history, and being close to the English border, it was understandable that the queen should not wish to linger there overnight. In any case the day's journey meant a ride of only a little over fifty miles. Although a good day's ride at the time was considered to be thirty to forty miles, it was always considered possible to ride more than fifty miles in emergencies: the ride was not an outstanding hardship to a queen accustomed to daily hunting and riding hard in the saddle all her life, who had ridden twenty-five miles pillion to Dunbar when six months pregnant. The decision to make the visit within the day was certainly a practical one under the circumstances.*

* On 16 October 1966, the 400th anniversary of Queen Mary's ride, an equivalent ride was mounted from Jedburgh to Hermitage and back, following the route which she was believed to have taken: Banchester Bridge (via the queen's well), Earlside, Stobs Castle, Barnes Farm, Priesthaugh, the rough country between Priesthaugh and Hermitage known as the queen's mire (where the enamelled watch

However, on her return from Hermitage Queen Mary fell violently and seriously ill. Undoubtedly the ride contributed to the final impetus of her collapse, but she had evidently been sickening in her habitual and, as it seemed, nervous fashion for some sort of breakdown for weeks, since the situation with Darnley seemed to admit no solution. In a confidential letter to Archbishop Beaton, Mary's ambassador in Paris, Maitland attributed her illness entirely to her disagreements with Darnley – 'he misuses himself so far towards her that it is an heartbreak for her to think that he should be her husband ...'[31] Physical and mental stress now apparently combined to produce an attack of illness so severe that many of those who observed Mary in the throes of it formed the opinion that she was unlikely to recover, even if she was not already dead. First the queen was seized by a prolonged fit of vomiting – 'more than sixty times' – so long and severe that she several times fell into unconsciousness; two days later, she could neither speak nor see, and had frequent convulsions. There was a temporary recovery, but by 25th October she had become so rapidly ill again – 'all her limbs were so contracted, her face was so distorted, her eyes closed, her mouth fast and her feet and arms stiff and cold' – that she was once more considered to be on the verge of death. Since she was generally believed to be sinking, Mary was publicly prayed for in the churches of Edinburgh as Knox's *History* testifies.[32] By her own account to Nau, Mary's servants thought she was dead, and started to open the windows of the little room where she lay; Moray was accused of trying to lay his hands on silver plate and rings; mourning dresses were ordered and funeral arrangements discussed. In Maitland's more laconic account to Cecil, it was admitted that

now in the museum in Queen Mary's House was later found) and finally Hermitage Castle which was reached at 12 noon, the expedition having left Jedburgh at 7 a.m. The return journey took from 1 p.m. to 7 p.m. The weather on this occasion was misty, and visibility was down to fifty yards over the queen's mire. But Miss Elizabeth Millar, twenty-six, who took the part of Queen Mary, not at the time accustomed to long hours in the saddle (unlike her prototype), told the author that she did not feel particularly tired at the end of the journey, and was able to attend a banquet in the evening without undue exhaustion.

her life had actually been despaired of for half an hour. The situation was saved by the queen's physician, Arnault, who seeing some signs of life in her arms, bandaged her very tightly, including her toes and legs from the ankle upwards, and then having her mouth opened by force, poured wine down it. He then administered a clyster, the queen vomited an amount of corrupt blood, and subsequently began to recover.[33]

Out of these facts, dramatic enough in themselves, Buchanan wove a lecherous fairy story in which the queen rode like a maniac to be by Bothwell's side the moment she received the news of his mishap (which as we have seen is quite contradicted by the facts), fell ill through having thus gratified her unlawful passions during her short stay at Hermitage (Moray's presence at the interview is ignored) and subsequently had Bothwell moved into the room below hers at Jedburgh, so that they could continue their love-making conveniently during their mutual convalescences[34] – once again almost ludicrously far from the truth. In fact, the queen was occupied at Jedburgh far away from Bothwell, once more in making provisions for her kingdom in the event of her death. When she felt herself to be *in extremis* she called the nobles into her room, including Moray, and attempted to dictate some sort of settlement which would ensure a calm inheritance for her son – for it is the son who is to succeed, not the father, and Mary specified that Darnley was not to seize the crown 'to which he laid claim by right'. Her first concern is for the young prince, who is to have no evil company around him during his 'youth head' – here perhaps Queen Mary was influenced by the example of Darnley, who often tried to excuse his failings on the ground that he had been corrupted by bad companions. Darnley is once more castigated for ingratitude: 'My lords, you know the goodness that I have used towards some whom I have advanced to a great degree of honour and pre-eminence above others; who, notwithstanding, has used ... ingratitude towards me, which has engendered the displeasure that presently most grieves me, and is also the cause of my sickness. I pray lord mend them.' Perhaps her most interesting words of all were on the subject of religion, where she pleaded for the tolerance which she had shown during her life to the Protestants to be shown after her death to the Catholics: 'I have pressed none of you that professes religion by your conscience ... I pray you, brother earl of Moray, that you trouble none.' When Father Edmund Hay, a Jesuit in Paris on his way to Scotland, reported the scene round the bedside of the apparently dying woman in a letter to St Francis Borgia of 6th November[35] he said that, although she affirmed her desire to die in the (Catholic) religion which her predecessors, the kings of Scotland, had practised for 1364 years, yet she frankly admitted that she had been neglectful not only in government of the realm, but also, and chiefly, in promoting the Catholic religion.

Throughout this period of illness, Darnley scarcely showed himself as the devoted husband. He was in the west of Scotland when Mary fell ill and did not, as Buchanan and Knox afterwards stated, come rushing to his wife's side. He paid the queen a brief visit eleven days after she first fell ill, and then returned to Glasgow. The queen's apologists have sometimes cited this in turn as an example of callousness; however, the Diurnal of Occurrents, an unbiased chronicle of events, suggests that as he was hunting and hawking, he did not even hear of the illness until 27th October, whereupon he rode to Edinburgh and the next day to Jedburgh.[36] At Jedburgh he received some fancied slight, of the sort Darnley was quick to perceive – so that he went back to Edinburgh and thence to Stirling. Possibly no special messenger had been sent to advise him of the illness: at any rate the picture of a breach in their relationship is a complete one.

The next episode in the mounting tragedy of Darnley took place at the end of November at the castle of Craigmillar, an enormous baronial edifice, founded by the Preston family, in the parish of Liberton, on the outskirts of Edinburgh. Mary was still in the hands of her physicians, since her illness, and was apparently in a state of deep depression. Du Croc, the French ambassador, wrote to Beaton in Paris that she often repeated the words 'I could wish to be dead'. Du Croc commented that no future understanding could be expected between the queen and her husband for the two reasons of his arrogance and her suspicion: 'The first is, the King will never humble himself as he ought; the other is, the Queen cannot perceive any nobleman speaking with the King, but that she presently suspects some contrivance between them.'[37] Ever since the murder of Riccio, Mary evidently regarded herself as permanently threatened by some possible conspiracy on the part of Darnley. But Mary's chief nobles, lodged with her at Craigmillar, were equally resolute in their hatred of Darnley, who had betrayed them over Riccio, and was yet still left nominally able to lord it over them as king of Scotland. Experience had not curbed Darnley's arrogance; nor were nobles of the temperament of Moray, Argyll, Bothwell and Maitland likely to forgive and forget.

According to the 'Protestantism' of Huntly and Argyll (written in January 1569 when Huntly and Argyll formed part of the Marian party), Moray and Maitland now broached the subject of a divorce to Argyll; Huntly was then brought in, finally Bothwell; then the queen was approached. Maitland opened up the argument by saying that means would be found for Mary to divorce Darnley, if she would only pardon Morton and the other Riccio assassins (who were still in exile). The queen promised her consent, but said that the divorce must be legally obtained without prejudice to her son. Maitland then suggested 'other means', and in a famous phrase told the queen that 'Moray would look through his fingers'. At this the queen quickly asked them to do nothing against her honour, and Maitland replied: 'Let us guide the matter among us, and your Grace shall see nothing but good, and approved by Parliament.'[38] This was in effect to be the case of Mary's supporters in later years, to prove her innocence over the death of Darnley. They maintained that the queen, although anxious to rid herself of Darnley, could not have known that the nobles actually intended to kill him, since Maitland had assured her that whatever happened would have parliamentary approval. But of course Mary was not, and was never intended to be, one of the executive conspirators; the details of the deed were not within the province of her concern. At Craigmillar she made it clear that she wished to be rid of Darnley, much as Henry II had once exclaimed 'Who will rid me of this turbulent priest?' of Thomas à Becket; she made two further points, of vital interest to her – firstly that her child must not run the risk of bastardy, and secondly that 'her honour' was not to be impugned. Maitland reassured her on both these points, but it was difficult to see what 'other means' he was contemplating except perhaps a treason trial of Darnley before Parliament, which would result in his execution. Mary, however, did not examine the situation so candidly in her own mind. She was a queen and a woman; as a woman she wished to be rid of an intolerable marital situation; as a queen she expected her nobles to help in a difficult governmental problem of order; there could be no benefit to her thinking too far or too early into how the nobles proposed to carry out her wishes. If Moray was quoted as intending to 'look through his fingers', Queen Mary, on the other hand, intended to keep her own hands tightly across her eyes.

It seems virtually certain that a bond was then drawn up and signed at Craigmillar by those nobles who intended to get rid of Darnley, including Maitland, Bothwell, Argyll, Huntly and James Balfour, with Morton signing later on his return to Scotland, much as a bond was signed before the murder of Riccio. Following the parallel with the Riccio bond, it is unlikely that the murder was specifically mentioned, for the death of Riccio had never been alluded to in the official document. The project could be put more vaguely, especially as Sir James Balfour, who had a legal training, probably played an important part in drawing it up. The hostile *Book of Articles* described the bond as follows: 'It was thought expedient and most profitable for the common wealth, by the whole nobility and lords underscribed, that such a young fool and proud tyrant should not reign or bear rule over them; and that for diverse causes, therefore, that these all had concluded that he should be put off by one way or another; and whosoever should take the deed in hand, or do it, they should defend and fortify as themselves.'[39]

But the actual bond does not survive for inspection, although its existence was mentioned in the confession of Bothwell's henchman, John Hepburn of Bolton, who said that Bothwell showed it to him, and later Ormiston, another henchman, executed in 1573, described it in his death-bed confession to a priest. The queen later told Nau that when she parted from Bothwell for the last time before the battle of Carberry Hill, he pressed into her hand a piece of paper and told her to guard it well, since it was the evidence of the complicity of the other lords in the murder – those very lords who were now drawn up in battle array against them, and accusing Bothwell alone of the crime. If this account is accepted, the incriminating paper must have been taken from her after her capture and destroyed. Moray's part in the whole affair remains obscure: he did not sign the Craigmillar bond although he certainly knew of its contents. He afterwards protested that he had taken part in, and approved of, nothing that was illegal. In view of Maitland's assurance to Mary that Moray would 'look through his fingers', it seems likely that it was Moray's intention to leave the actual execution of the deed to others, while approving the result and hoping to benefit from it. If he believed that it was intended to seize Darnley for trial for treason, and kill him in the act, he could perhaps stretch his conscience sufficiently to cover the statement that he had approved of nothing illegal.* Moray was therefore several degrees closer than Mary in his knowledge of what was planned, although in their general attitudes to the subject, the responses of brother and sister were not dissimilar.

In December the queen was able to turn her mind from her vexatious problems with her husband to the happier matter of her son's baptism. Shortly after the birth, messages had been sent to the king of France, the duke of Savoy and the queen of England to act as godparents. Darnley objected to the inclusion of Elizabeth, because of her animosity against him, but his

---

* This is the explanation for Moray's behaviour and his subsequent protests advanced by his biographer Maurice Lee. But Professor Donaldson points out that so long as Darnley remained king, it was still illegal for the nobles to arrest him for treason.[40]

objections were overruled by Mary who visualized a golden future for James if Elizabeth's goodwill could be secured. On 17th December the ceremony took place, according to the Catholic rite, in the chapel royal of Stirling Castle. The little prince, now just on six months old, was carried in the arms of the count of Brienne, proxy for the king of France, from the royal apartments to the chapel between two rows of courtiers, the whole scene lit by flaring torches. M. du Croc represented the duke of Savoy. The procession was followed by a list of Catholic nobles bearing the various official accompaniments of the Catholic christening – one the cierge, one the salt, one the basin and laver and one the rood. At the entrance of the chapel, the cortège was received by the archbishop of St Andrews and other Catholic prelates.

Queen Elizabeth had sent a magnificent gold font, weighing two stones according to the Diurnal of Occurrents,[41] as a present for her godson. But as Bedford, her emissary, was a leading English puritan, he could not stand proxy for her at the font. Jean, countess of Argyll, the child's aunt, acted as proxy godmother for Elizabeth, and held James in her arms. Prince James was duly christened according to the full Catholic rite, except that the queen refused to let the priest spit in his mouth as the custom then was, saying according to a later story that she was not going to have 'a pocky priest' spitting in her child's mouth. The Diurnal of Occurrents merely reported that the queen 'did inhibit' the use of the spittle. Throughout the ceremony, Bedford and the other Scottish Protestant lords stood outside the chapel.

The accomplishment of the ceremony was celebrated with all the magnificence which Queen Mary could command. She clothed the nobility at her own expense for the occasion, 'Some in cloth of silver, some in cloth of gold, some in cloth of tissue, every man rather above than under his degree'.[42] Moray was clothed in green, Argyll in red and Bothwell in blue (Buchanan afterwards chose to report that Mary had deliberately clothed Bothwell alone). There were fireworks and masques, with verses written by George Buchanan himself, evidently still at this date an admirer of the queen. The English party took offence at one masque in which some French-born satyrs deliberately turned in their direction and 'put their hands behind them to their tails which they wagged with their hands'.[43] This insult apart (and the English believed it sprang from uncontrollable Gallic jealousy of the honour which was being done to their national rivals) the merriment was general, and Bedford, puritan as he might be, graciously allowed the young gentlemen in his train to join in the dancing at night.

In all these rejoicings, there was only one mysteriously absent figure, that of the baby's father, 'King Henry' himself, although he was actually present within the castle of Stirling at the time. It has been suggested that his absence was due to his continued bad relations with Queen Elizabeth (who had never officially countenanced his marriage) and because Bedford had been instructed not to give him his due as king of Scotland. But no such instructions have been discovered. It seems more likely that Darnley, as du Croc suspected, hated the idea of the English, from whose ranks he sprang, whom he had once scorned, seeing how far he had fallen in prestige at the Scottish court; it would certainly be in his character to avoid any occasion of public humiliation, real or imaginary.[44] The change in his position was made all the more obvious to him, because on the day of the christening itself du Croc three times declined to give him an interview. The reason given was especially irritating. As Darnley was not now 'in good correspondence' with Mary, the French king had instructed du Croc to have nothing further to do with him. At the end of December, Darnley left Stirling abruptly and went to Glasgow, in the west of Scotland, the traditional centre of Lennox Stewart power, where he hoped to be more royally treated.

CHAPTER SIXTEEN

The Murder of Darnley

'I'll pity thee as much' he said
'And as much favour I'll show to thee
As thou had on the Queen's chamberlain
That day you deemedst him to die'
            Bothwell to Darnley, from the ballad Earl Bothwell

In October at Jedburgh Mary Queen of Scots had nearly died. At Glasgow in the New Year Darnley in his turn fell extremely ill. At the time it was given out that he had smallpox, but it seems more likely that he was actually suffering from syphilis. Bothwell, on his own narrative of events written during his captivity in Denmark, *Les Affaires du Conte de Boduel*, took the trouble to cross out the words *petite vérole* (smallpox) and insert *roniole* (syphilis) in his own handwriting. The Diurnal of Occurrents, a contemporary diary probably written by a minor official of the court, referred to the 'pox', a word often used at the time for syphilis, and Pitscottie stated that the king was stricken with 'a great fever of the pox'.[1] Darnley's skull, now in the Royal College of Surgeons at London, was analysed by Sir Daniel Wilson, at the request of Dr Karl Pearson, and discovered to be pitted with traces of 'a virulent syphilitic disease'.*[2] The queen did not immediately visit her husband, but

---

* W. Armstrong-Davison, in *The Casket Letters*, advances the further theory that Darnley was already suffering from syphilis when Queen Mary nursed him, apparently for measles, in April 1565. He states that it was by no means rare in the sixteenth century for a measles-like eruption to be succeeded by a smallpox-type eruption twenty-one months later, and for both to be symptoms of syphilis.[3]

she did show her habitual humanity: she sent him her doctor to Glasgow, and in early January, according to the accounts, gave orders for the royal linen to be cut into ruffs for the king's nightshirt.

Yet despite Mary's careless kindness – so typical of her nature – clearly she was still pondering in her mind legal ways and means of ridding herself of this degenerate creature as a husband. On Christmas Eve she duly pardoned Morton and his associates – a fact which lends conviction to the story of the Protestation that Mary believed herself to have struck a bargain with Maitland and other nobles: now that she had allowed Morton to return, it was up to these nobles to rid her of Darnley in such a way as would be 'approved by Parliament'. The return of Morton and his friends also of course substantially increased the numbers of Darnley's potential enemies within the boundaries of Scotland. A further step taken by the queen before Christmas shows that she was still considering the question of a divorce: the Catholic Archbishop Hamilton of St Andrews was temporarily restored to his consistorial jurisdiction from 23rd December until some date before 9th January, when the privilege was again removed. The intention was presumably to allow the archbishop to pronounce decrees of nullity between the queen and her husband. The brief restoration suggests that the queen was still casting around for ways to come about a decent divorce which would not compromise Prince James, and did not regard the subject as totally closed by Maitland's adverse advice; after all as a Protestant Scot he did not necessarily represent the views of Catholic Rome, which had not yet been officially sounded. In any case the marriages of royal persons were by Canon Law reserved for the consideration of the Pope himself, as *causae majores*. However, divorce for royal personages was by no means unthinkable in the sixteenth century, even within the structure of the Catholic Church. There had been some significant divorces in the French royal house. Mary and Darnley's mutual grandmother, Margaret Tudor, had been divorced from her second husband, the earl of Angus; and the marital problems of Henry VIII, which he had originally attempted so hard and so long to solve within the structure of the Church, were only a generation away.

For Darnley, with his teeth drawn, and threatened from so many quarters, was still in some respects a dangerous animal. He did not cease to intrigue as well as boast. He was clever enough to see that he had a possible line of attack against Mary in her determinedly *laissez-faire* policy towards the Scottish Catholic Church; he was unscrupulous enough to contemplate blackening her reputation in the eyes of the Catholic powers abroad with the aim of elevating himself, as the champion of the Catholic faith, in Scotland. In the summer of 1566 there had been some crazy story that he contemplated inhabiting the Scilly Isles and from there attacking England.[4] On 22nd October Robert Melville reported to Beaton in Paris that Darnley was trying to use his threat to leave the country to demand the dismissal of Maitland, Macgill and Bellenden, all strong Protestants, from the queen's counsels.[5] On 13th November, de Silva, the Spanish ambassador in London, reported to Philip II that Queen Mary had heard in Scotland that Darnley had written to Philip, the Pope, the king of France and the cardinal of Lorraine, that she was 'dubious in the faith'.[6] Nearly a year before Darnley had pictured himself in possession of the coveted crown matrimonial. Now his ambitions were strong enough still to picture himself set up as Catholic king of Scotland, at the will of a strong foreign Catholic power, ruling as guardian of his infant son – with his wife of course overthrown.

It will never be known exactly how much of this 'Catholic' plot existed in the imagination of Darnley, or indeed Darnley's enemies, and how much reality there was behind the rumours and the suspicions. But certainly at the turn of the year there were whispers that Darnley was once more intriguing against his wife which were loud enough to reach not only the queen's ears in Edinburgh, but also those of Beaton in Paris. In the words of the historian F. W. Maitland, it is very hard to remember that events now long in the past were once in the future. In January 1567 it was Darnley, out of the royal couple, who had been shown to be the plotter, who had aimed at the crown matrimonial and perhaps more, by a conspiracy. So far Queen Mary had only been plotted against during her reign, and ever since the Riccio affair had kept, as du Croc pointed out, an extremely wary eye on Darnley for 'further contrivances'. Now she believed she had stumbled on news of such contrivances: she wrote to Paris in January to tell Beaton that there was a rumour of a plot by Darnley to seize the person of Prince James, and thus control the reins of government.[7] The story had been brought to her at Stirling by a servant, William Walker: 'How it was not only openly bruited, but also he had heard by report of persons whom he esteemed lovers of us [the Queen] that the King, by assistance of some of the nobility, should take the prince our son and crown him, and being crowned, as his father, should take upon him the government ...' Walker gave as his reference another servant, William Hiegate. But Hiegate, when questioned, denied the whole thing, and merely repeated a rumour to the opposite effect, that he had heard how the king was about to be put in ward by the nobles.

The queen duly conveyed this atmosphere of plot and counter-plot to Beaton in Paris. But at the end of her letter she merely concluded rather dourly that God knew how her husband had behaved towards her, and the outside world knew as well as God; as for her subjects, she did not doubt that they too, in their hearts, condemned him for the way he had treated her. Darnley was always inquiring for news about her doings, and in Mary's view, both he and his father Lennox, with their adherents, would be delighted to do her some mischief, if their strength were equivalent to their wishes. Luckily, wrote Mary, God had seen to it that their power was moderated, so that they had little means to execute their evil intentions. In any case Mary declared herself sceptical as to whether any in Scotland – beyond the immediate Lennox party – would truly approve of an action against their queen. Despite Mary's boasted self-confidence, she did take one precaution against the possible malevolence of Darnley: she had the little Prince James brought out of Stirling Castle, where he was considered to lie too close to the dangerous Glasgow area. On 14th January he was installed with his mother in the palace of Holyrood. Other rumours of danger to the queen had already reached Beaton in Paris, before the arrival of her letter; these came in the form of a hint from the Spanish ambassador that 'there be some surprise to be trafficked to the Queen's contrary'. The Spanish ambassador in London heard from the same source that there was a plot forming in Scotland against the queen.[8] Beaton's reaction to these innuendoes was to send Mary a warning letter, in which he begged her to re-establish good relations with her husband, lest some peril ensue from him in the future to destroy her. Unfortunately this letter, full of good sense, reached Mary too late, when Darnley was already dead.

On 20th January Queen Mary set off for Glasgow to bring back her sick husband on a litter to Edinburgh, to finish off his convalescence in her own company. In view of the dispassionate contempt which she quite openly expressed for him in her letter to Beaton, written on the very day of her departure, it is necessary to consider exactly what prompted her to make the journey. It is true that Mary had always displayed courteous kindness towards Darnley's sufferings; but some more compelling argument than sheer humanity must be advanced to explain her actions – and also to explain what is every bit as mysterious, why Darnley so readily agreed to follow her back. One must therefore examine the actions of the conspirator nobles during the period in January leading up to the queen's expedition. It was on 6th January – the last Twelfth Night that the queen of Scots who loved these celebrations so much was ever to spend outside prison walls – that Maitland at last achieved his wish and married the voluptuous Mary Fleming in the chapel royal at Stirling. By this marriage to the chief of the Maries, the queen's own kin, Maitland was further entwined in Mary's inner court circle, to which he had been re-admitted in the previous September. In January also some sort of conference took place at Whittingham, one of the Douglas castles, between Bothwell, Morton, newly returned to Scotland, his cousin Archibald Douglas, and Mary. The exact truth of what happened at this conference is impossible to establish, since afterwards, once the nobles concerned were on different political sides, each accused the other of having raised the subject of Darnley's murder.

Morton, in his confession, some fifteen years later, said that Bothwell suggested the killing of Darnley to him, at which Morton begged himself off on the grounds that he had only just recovered from his disgrace over Riccio – 'I am but newly come out of a great trouble ...' According to Morton, Archibald Douglas was then dispatched to Edinburgh to see if the queen would give some written authority for the dispatch of her husband, but Douglas returned with the quite definite answer: 'Show to the Earl of Morton that the Queen will have no speech of the matter.'[9] Bothwell, on the other hand, represented himself as being anxious 'for rest and a peaceful life after the imprisonment and exile I had suffered', whereas it was Morton who was determined to spur him forward to annihilate Darnley, as a revenge on him for his treachery.[10] There is little to choose between these two versions of the same story, and it is hardly necessary to decide which of these two ambitious and daring men should be given the honour of first broaching the subject. But it is important to notice that neither party suggested that the queen had any foreknowledge of their plans; according to Douglas, she had even gone further and specified that she wanted to hear nothing more about such a blood-thirsty enterprise. The queen's dissent, combined with her known merciful character and clemency, which made her ever ready to pardon those who were sometimes best left unpardoned, gave the conspirators a strong motive for the future in not involving her in their plans. She had a horror of violence: as she said herself years later, she would rather pray with Esther than take the sword with Judith. Yet the nobles had every reason to believe, after the conference at Craigmillar, that she would approve the end result. The argument for proceeding with their plans without informing the queen further was overwhelming.

There was, however, one detail in which the queen could help them: their plan did demand that Darnley should be in Edinburgh or thereabouts, rather than Glasgow; there he was surrounded by his own Lennox Stewart adherents, in feudal fashion, but Morton's Douglases and Bothwell's Hepburns were at a distance. It is possible that Maitland indicated to Mary that in practical terms it was unwise to allow Darnley to remain in Glasgow where he might manage to work up an effective conspiracy against her. During the period leading up to the murder, according to Nau, a man called John Shaw came to the queen and told her that Ker of Fawdonside, whom she particularly loathed for his part in the Riccio murder – it was he who had held the pistol to her stomach – was back in Scotland: 'He having boasted to certain persons … within fifteen days he assured them, there would be a change at court, and he would be more than ever in credit; and then he inquired boldly how their queen was.'[11] Or it may have been Bothwell who dropped the hint – Bothwell, whose record of loyalty was impeccable in the last two years. Equally the queen herself may have needed no particular prompting to see that it was safer to have Darnley under her own eyes where experience had taught her that it was easier to control him, than loose in the countryside, either plotting or breeding dissension with his wild schemes. At all times during the past year, she had shown herself to be extremely upset when Darnley broke loose from the court and wandered off by himself, presumably because she trusted him even less once he was outside the sphere of her influence. Her journey to recall the errant Darnley made sense in terms of her own personal security, whether prompted or not by one of her nobles. But being both frank and feminine, or in her own phrase 'undissembling', Mary, in her letter to Beaton, made no attempt to pretend a passionate love for Darnley which she was by now far from feeling.*

* The only documents ever produced which were supposed to date from the period before the murder, to prove that the queen enjoyed an adulterous liaison with Bothwell, were the highly dubious Casket Letters. These will be considered in Chapter 20. In order to explain the many inconsistencies in these letters (whose originals have vanished) some sort of theory of interpolation has often been adopted, i.e. genuine letters from Mary interposed with passionate love letters to Bothwell from another woman. If this theory is correct, then the so-called Long Casket Letter, supposed to be written while at Glasgow by the queen to Bothwell

If her motives are plentiful enough, the question still arises exactly how Mary induced her husband to accompany her back to Edinburgh: for it is clear that once Mary arrived in Glasgow, she experienced no difficulty in persuading him to make the move. Darnley freely consented to the plan, and this despite the fact that he had heard some rumour of what had transpired at Craigmillar, as his servant Crawford later deposed. Darnley had learned apparently that something had been plotted against him in the autumn, but that Mary had refused to be a party to it: in Crawford's words,[12] he knew that 'a letter was presented to her in Craigmillar, made by her own device, and subscribed by certain others, who desired her to subscribe the same, which she refused to do. And he [Darnley] said that he would never think that she [the queen] who was his own proper flesh, would do him any hurt ...' Darnley's confidence in the gentle nature of his wife on eighteen months of marriage is significant. However, this confidence in itself would not have been enough to persuade him to return from Lennox-dominated Glasgow to Edinburgh, inhabited not only by the queen but by many nobles with far from gentle natures. The promise which Mary seems most likely to have held out to Darnley was the resumption of full marital relations on his return to Edinburgh. Mary's coldness as a wife had been one of Darnley's complaints against her: it wounded his vanity as a man, and also, he felt, threatened his status as a king, there being more to the embraces of a queen than the mere feel of her arms around him. This promise would have been enough to rouse Darnley's ambitions all over again, to rekindle his hopes of future grandeur as king: in this way he went willingly out of his own feudal domain of influence into hers. The attitude of Mary to the journey was totally different: convinced that Darnley was once more plotting against her, convinced also that Darnley had once attempted her own death and might do so again, she felt little love or any emotion of any

(although containing the unnecessary reminder 'remember you ... of the Earl of Bothwell') might be the draft of another similarly frank letter from Mary describing her feelings for Darnley, interpolated with a genuine love letter to Bothwell from another woman.

sort for her husband, as her letter to Beaton shows. Nevertheless it still seemed safer for herself and her child to have him lodged in Edinburgh under her own eyes, than let him loose in the west of Scotland, free to plot. Mary led Darnley to Edinburgh with kind words and hints of happiness as once before she had won him over on the dramatic day after Riccio's murder, for the same cogent reasons of self-preservation.

The only subject on which the queen and king now disagreed was the place where Darnley should spend the rest of his convalescence: he needed constant baths to improve his condition, and his face was still shrouded with a piece of taffeta. Mary had intended to bring him to the castle of Craigmillar a little way outside Edinburgh, that same castle where the bond had been signed. Darnley, however, declined to enter the stronghold, as his own servants testified. Perhaps he was afraid to do so. He chose instead – and once again there is general agreement that the choice was his, not the queen's – a house of moderate size on the outskirts of Edinburgh town proper, but still lying just inside the town wall. It was situated within the quadrangle attached to the old collegiate church of St Mary-in-the-Field, as it had once been called, which was now known as the Kirk o'Field, and it was about three-quarters of a mile distant from Holyrood palace, along hilly streets. This house, known as the old provost's lodging, because it had once been the house of the provost of the collegiate church, now actually belonged to Robert Balfour, brother of Sir James Balfour, but was often said to belong to Sir James himself. Within the same quadrangle lay the considerably larger Hamilton House, belonging to the duke of Châtelherault. Darnley's servant Nelson, while agreeing that Darnley himself made the choice of Kirk o'Field, stated in his deposition that Darnley had then expected to be lodged in Hamilton House and was surprised to find himself in the old provost's lodging.[13] But no other mention is made of Darnley's surprise, whereas there is general agreement that Darnley made the choice after the royal cortège left Glasgow. In addition one may doubt whether Darnley would actually have wished or expected to be lodged in the house of his hereditary family enemies, the Hamiltons. The main point to be grasped about the old provost's lodging, apart from the Balfour connection of the house, is that the venue of Darnley's lodging had been changed suddenly and unexpectedly at his own request: therefore any plans centred on his dwelling would necessarily have an improvised and makeshift quality, since they could not have taken longer than a few days to both plot and put into action. This need for speed at the cost of efficiency may explain some of the confusion of the tangled events which followed.

But of course the many seemingly irreconcilable contradictions of what followed at Kirk o'Field – the most debatable, as well as surely the most worked over murder in history – have a deeper cause than the essentially makeshift nature of the crime. They arise principally from the extraordinarily untrustworthy nature of the evidence. The basic difficulty in the way of reconstructing the truth about Kirk o'Field is the fact that the lesser executive criminals were subsequently executed for the crime at the instance of the great nobles who had approved or inspired it. There is thus a veil of unreality over the depositions of these minor figures, as in the trial of criminals in some twentieth-century totalitarian state, since their words had to be carefully tailored not to incriminate the men then in power in Scotland. Equally it was desirable to throw all the blame possible on one noble who had vanished from the scene, after quarrelling with his former associates – Lord Bothwell. The evidence is affected further by the circumstances of Mary Stuart's own trial in England in late 1568: as with her alleged adultery with Bothwell, it will be found that once again the *Book of Articles* related a series of demonstrable untruths, the intention of which was to keep her in captivity in England while Moray remained regent safely in Scotland. In short, the unreliability of the depositions, many of them made under torture, and the political 're-writing' of history which went on at the time of Mary's trial means that the detailed story of Kirk o'Field can only be guessed at, or pieced together, rather than established with total certainty.

The house in which Darnley now settled for the last days of his recovery was in many ways ideally suited for the state of convalescence. According to Nau, a raven had hovered over the royal caravan on its way from Glasgow, and now settled on the roof of the lodging. But there were certainly no other evil omens to be discerned in the actual structure of the building. The house lay on a slight eminence, overlooking the Cowgate, and the site was open and healthy compared to low-lying Holyrood; as Leslie said, the air was thought by the doctors to be the most salubrious in the whole town.[14] The quadrangle in which it lay and its recent connection with the church must have given the lodging something of the atmosphere of a house in a cathedral close in an English provincial town. It was far enough from Holyrood for the king's illness not to be an embarrassment to him, yet it had the security of lying just within the town wall, which had been begun to be built round Edinburgh at the time of Flodden. Edinburgh during this period had a nightly town watch, numbering a total of thirty-two men, of whom twelve were stationed at the various gates, or the Leith Wynd gap in the wall, and ten perpetually perambulated the streets – providing a considerable sense of security to its citizens, and a continual threat to anyone who might stray in its streets by night without a lawful excuse to do so. This town wall, six feet wide at its base, and tapering to a flat top, skirted the back of the house; and the characteristic gallery which extended off the first floor chamber of the lodging rested on it.* The house had its own east garden, with a door into it, and on the other side of the town wall lay further gardens and orchards, once part of the fields, but divided off by the building of the wall. All these details can be clearly distinguished in the sketch of the scene after the murder sent to Cecil in London, which is also vital to our understanding of the geography of Kirk o'Field. From it, it can be seen that the old provost's lodging lay on the south side of the quadrangle; two of the other sides were occupied by

---

* There is no trace of St Mary, Kirk o'Field, its quadrangle and the little houses round it in modern Edinburgh. The site of Darnley's last lodging lies somewhere beneath the Adam-designed quadrangle, which is the central establishment of the university of Edinburgh, off South Bridge Street.

smaller houses, still standing in the sketch, and the third contained slightly larger houses such as Hamilton House. The quadrangle has been estimated to be eighty-six feet by seventy-three feet.*

Although Buchanan tried to make out that the lodging itself was ruinous and uncomfortable – in order to blacken the character of Queen Mary who was erroneously stated to have chosen it – it was in fact a pleasant house of moderate size, by the standards of the day. Mahon calculated the house to have been about sixty-one feet long and twenty-five feet deep compared to King James's Tower at Holyrood, containing all the state apartments, which is seventy-four feet by thirty-seven feet. Besides the door into the east garden already mentioned, the house had two other doors, into the quadrangle, and through the postern gate in the town wall (visible in the sketch) into the alleyway beyond. No trace has ever been found of a secret tunnel connecting the lodging with Holyrood; when Lennox furiously and crazily accused the queen of coming disguised in men's clothing to witness his son's murder by 'secret ways', in his *Narrative*,[15] he was presumably thinking not of a tunnel, but of the back streets of Edinburgh. The obvious route from Holyrood to the provost's lodging lay down the Canongate, through the town wall at the Netherbow Port, down the Blackfriars Wynd, crossing the Cowgate, and so to the purlieus of St Mary's. But sixteenth-century Edinburgh was a network of smaller streets, off the main thoroughfares, and it would have been possible to take an altogether more circuitous route along the back wall of the south Canongate gardens to St Mary's Port, and thence, where the town wall was as yet unbuilt, through the gardens and fields of the old Blackfriars Priory to the east garden of the Kirk o'Field house. This would avoid the town wall, and the challenge of the watch; the only remaining problem

---

* By Major-General Mahon, whose *Tragedy of Kirk o'Field*, 1923, contains by far the most detailed investigation into the geography and circumstances of the events now to be related. Later writers, whether they agree with his conclusions or not, must acknowledge a debt of gratitude for his painstaking consideration of even the minutest aspect of the crime.

would be the curious eyes of the ten watchmen nightly patrolling the streets of the city.

The lodging contained two bedrooms for Darnley and the queen, Darnley's lying directly above that of his wife, a presence chamber (or *salle*), two *garde robes*, a kitchen and vaulted cellars beneath. The drop from the gallery, which extended out of Darnley's bedroom on to the town wall, to the ground, was only about fourteen feet, since the level of the ground beyond the wall was higher than within the quadrangle. The house was not only pleasantly situated and healthy, with gardens, but it was also well if hastily furnished for Darnley's benefit, once he had selected it, from the store of royal furniture at Holyrood. The inventories testify not only the suddenness of the decision to use the provost's lodging, but also the amount of furniture and ornaments now brought down from Holyrood.[16] A series of seven pieces of tapestry representing the 'Hunting of the Conies' were brought for the *garde robe*, as well as a canopy of yellow taffeta to enclose the *chaise percée*. Five pieces of tapestry were brought for the *salle*. For Darnley's bedroom, six pieces of tapestry, originally taken from Strathbogie after the defeat of Huntly, were ordered, a little Turkish carpet, two or three cushions of red velvet, a high chair covered in purple velvet, and a little table covered with green velvet which had also once belonged to Huntly, as well as a bed which had once belonged to Mary of Guise, which Mary had given her husband in the previous August – hung with violet-brown velvet, embroidered with ciphers and flowers, trimmed with cloth of gold and silver, and having three coverlets, one of them blue quilted taffeta.* A bath stood

---

* It is characteristic of the confused nature of the evidence about Darnley's death that Buchanan later in his *History* accused Mary of deliberately having her own bed changed in order to save it from the blast: this contradicted not only his own story in the *Book of Articles*, but also the deposition of Darnley's servant Nelson (who said that it was Darnley's bed the queen had changed). Nelson reported that a new black velvet bed was sent away in favour of an old purple-brown one; in fact the black bed was probably lying at the lodging when Darnley arrived at short notice, and was later changed for Darnley's favourite royally-ornamented purple-brown bed. The inventories record that this was specially brought down from Holyrood; they record no other exchanges made on a later date.[17]

beside the bed – baths being a necessary part of the con-valescence – and one of the makeshift aspects of the visit was the fact that one of the doors of the house was taken off its hinges to serve as a lid when it was not in use. The chamber beneath that of Darnley, which had a window looking north over the quadrangle, contained a small bed of yellow and green damask with a furred coverlet, in which the queen could sleep if she so wished.

Darnley took up residence in his new dwelling on Saturday 1st February. The last week of his life was pleasant and almost domesticated. Queen Mary felt confident that her husband had for the time being no opportunity to weave any plot against her, especially as his father Lennox, so often his evil genius in feeding his childish vanity with praise, was still in Glasgow. The mass of courtiers, Privy Councillors and attendants who inevitably moved with the queen as she progressed through Edinburgh, settled into a routine of visiting Darnley at Kirk o'Field and then returning to the royal palace at Holyrood for the other formal ceremonies of court life. Relations at this point between Darnley and his wife were perfectly amicable. On the Wednesday the queen spent the night at Kirk o'Field in the chamber beneath Darnley's. According to her own account, propinquity now led to newly friendly relations between them. They had certainly seen little enough of each other lately: when Mary fetched Darnley from Glasgow at the end of January she had not seen him since his abrupt departure from Stirling at the end of December; in October and November she had been ill, and separated from her husband. On the Friday, 7 February, Darnley was actually inspired by this novel amity to discuss with his wife some information he had of plots against her. He begged her in touching language to beware of the people who tried to make mischief between them, adding with self-righteous horror that it had even been suggested to him that he should take his wife's life.* This sort of volte-face was typical of

---

* Buchanan's *Book of Articles* and his *Detection*, both luridly accusatory, later tried to turn the whole incident round to the queen's disadvantage, accusing Mary of trying to work up a quarrel between Darnley and Lord Robert Stewart on this Friday, a fracas to which Moray also was supposed to have been a witness.[18]

Darnley: Mary, being the stronger character of the two, was always able to win his loyalty for the time being by force of personality, provided they were face to face, as the denouement of the Riccio affair had demonstrated. It was on this very Friday also, according to Lennox, that Darnley wrote to his father concerning the improvement of his health, which had occurred so much sooner than he had expected, through the kind treatment of 'such as hath this good while concealed their good will, I mean my love the queen, which I assure you hath all this while and yet doth use herself like a natural and loving wife'.[19] It would seem therefore that Friday, from the point of view of the husband and wife, was outwardly another day of uneventful convalescence. The Friday night was once more passed by the queen at the old provost's lodging, under the same roof as her husband.

Is it possible to construct out of Darnley's outburst of penitence to his wife, Mary's suspicions and the warnings received from abroad, evidence of an actual plot by Darnley against Mary, based on his residence at Kirk o'Field? It has been suggested that Kirk o'Field was in fact a monstrous conspiracy against Mary, which reacted in the end against its own perpetrator, Darnley.* Darnley was certainly by nature an intriguer and an ambitious one. But the fact that he was plotting in general is not evidence that he was plotting in particular at Kirk o'Field. He was here, impaired in health, virtually confined to his bed, with few of his supporters about him, surrounded by those of the queen, in the house of the brother of one of the nobles who hated him. Mary, far from being the immobile pregnant woman of a year back, was now active and energetic, flitting between Holyrood and Kirk o'Field, whereas Darnley

Although the *Book of Articles* made out that Mary's intention was to get her husband killed accidentally, it is notable that Moray made no mention of this remarkable scene, at which he was alleged to have been present, either at the time, or in any later indictment against Mary.

* Principally by Major-General Mahon, *op. cit.* R. Gore-Brown, in *Lord Bothwell*, follows Mahon in believing that Darnley planned the explosion against Mary, while admitting that Bothwell actually ignited it, having discovered Darnley's treachery in the nick of time, and determined to pay Darnley out with his own coin.

was stationary. This was not a roundabout age in the manner of its killings. Kings and nobles died violently, but they died openly. The regent Moray died at the hand of an assassin, who shot out of the window into the street; the Riccio plot had aimed at the queen's life in the crudest possible manner. Queen Mary, who rode freely and frequently among her people, would at all times present an excellent target for an assassin: if gunpowder had been in Darnley's mind, it would have been aimed at a dwelling where there was not the faintest doubt that the queen would be present, at a time when he was in perfect command of himself. Kirk o'Field was so very far from being the ideal situation for Darnley to plan to kill Mary that, in the absence of concrete proof that he did so, it is surely more logical to regard the crime as aimed straightforwardly at the man it did in fact kill – Darnley. It is in the participants and the accessories to the crime, rather than the intended victim, that the complexities of the plot lie.

For while Darnley and Mary jogged through their last week of marriage in comparative peace, the conspirators had been hard at work to compass the death of one and the deliverance of the other. Friday seems to have been the critical day. Darnley could not be expected to stay in the lodging forever and Holyrood with its guards obviously presented more of a problem from the point of view of assassination than Kirk o'Field. Sir James Balfour told the lords in the summer, when he made his peace with them, that he first knew of the plot on Friday. Morton admitted in his own confession years later that he first knew of the plot from Archibald Douglas a little before, possibly on the Friday. The *Book of Articles* went further and said that this was the day originally intended to perform the murder, but the preparations were not ready. John Hay of Tallo in his deposition stated that it was on Friday that Bothwell said to him: 'John, this is the matter. The King's death is devised. I will reveal it unto you for if I put him not down, I cannot have a life in Scotland. He will be my destruction!'[20] John Hepburn, Bothwell's kinsman and henchman, deposed that the original purpose had been for certain of the nobles to kill the king by each sending two of their servants 'to the doing thereof in the fields'[21] – this corporate fate, so characteristic of gang vengeance, whether in Scotland or Sicily, would not only have wiped out Darnley's treachery but would also of course ritually involve all the nobles in the act, much as Riccio himself had received over fifty dagger-wounds in his body including Darnley's own dagger planted by George Douglas. It would thus not have been possible later for some of the nobles to have denied their involvement.

The dagger being the natural murder weapon of the time, it is interesting to speculate what made Bothwell change his plans and turn to the much less malleable weapon of gunpowder. The reason he gave John Hepburn was probably the true one – because it was the obvious one. With servants openly at work, the death of Darnley in the fields would inevitably have been pinned upon the nobles who had concocted it. Bothwell was already in his agile opportunist's mind aiming at the position of king. He knew Mary had formally indicated that she wanted no violence done to Darnley. It was no part of his plan to be blamed for the crime: he certainly did not wish to suffer for it, merely to enjoy the result. Ironically enough, the use of gunpowder, and the blowing-up of the house which gave its incredibly flagrant character to the crime – and made Mary's cheerful tolerance of the perpetrators give such appalling scandal throughout Europe – seems to have been planned in simple good faith that a hearty explosion would cover the tracks of the killers, and make it impossible afterwards to prove who had done it, even if it was only too easy to guess. Such bold but straightforward reasoning was typical not only of Bothwell but of the age in which he lived.

The testimony of the page 'French' Paris (although extremely suspect, because it was wrung from him by torture) does at least confirm that Kirk o'Field was not a subtly planned crime.[22] Paris, once Bothwell's servant, was now in the queen's service, and attended her at the old provost's lodging. It was on the Wednesday or Thursday that Bothwell came into the queen's chamber, below that of Darnley, and told Paris that he found himself ill of his 'usual illness' which was a flux of the blood. He asked Paris whereabouts in the house he could '*faire mes affaires*', and Paris, in view of the urgency of the situation, found Bothwell a corner; it was here, as Bothwell availed himself of the slight privacy to relieve himself, that Bothwell outlined to Paris that he had in mind to kill the king. Paris hesitated. Bothwell told him angrily that he was an utter fool if he thought that he, Bothwell, would enter such an enterprise all on his own – Bothwell then named Maitland, Argyll, Huntly, Morton, Ruthven and Lindsay as his accomplices. Paris inquired about Moray. Bothwell replied that he was neutral.* When Paris resisted Bothwell's demands, Bothwell only exclaimed impatiently, 'Why did I put you in the Queen's service if not to help me?' and it was at this juncture that Paris pointed out that Bothwell had bullied him for more than six years, kicking him in the stomach to make him do what he wanted. Paris was, however, insistent that Bothwell wanted the keys of the house of lodging from him – a point which incidentally points to the innocence of the queen, since she could presumably have provided them easily herself, had she been aware of the details of the plot. On Saturday, 8th February, Paris had apparently obtained these keys while no one else was in the room and taken them to Bothwell at Holyrood.

Sunday, 9th February, was to be the last day of Darnley's convalescence. It was announced that he would return to Holyrood early on the Monday. It was also the last Sunday before the beginning of Lent, and, as such, a day of carnival and rejoicing; two events typical of the life of Queen Mary's court were planned to take place. In the morning Mary's favourite valet Bastian Pages married Christiana Hogg; being a Catholic it was his last opportunity to do so before the beginning of Lent. The wedding dinner took place at noon, and the queen was present: Bastian was an amusing high-spirited Frenchman,

---

* By the date this deposition was made, later in 1568, it must be remembered that Moray was regent of Scotland: Paris's interrogators would have a strong motive for not wishing to incriminate their ruler.

who shared the queen's own love of masques. It was he who had devised that masque at the baptism of Prince James, with the satyrs wagging their tails which had so much enraged the English visitors that Hatton exclaimed that if it had not been for the presence of the queen, he would have put his dagger in the heart of 'that French knave Bastian'. The second court event was a formal dinner given at four o'clock by the bishop of the Isles in the house in the Canongate for the returning ambassador of Savoy. The queen attended this dinner, accompanied by her chief nobles, Argyll, Huntly, Bothwell and Cassillis – but not Moray. He had that very morning slipped out of Edinburgh, on the excuse that his wife was sick with a miscarriage. Maitland was also absent, and Morton was not yet sufficiently in the queen's personal favour to be admitted to court events. This duly accomplished, the queen and her court rode down to the provost's lodging again, in order to spend the evening with Darnley. The queen planned to sleep Sunday night at Kirk o'Field once more, at the end of her day of revelry, as she had done on the Wednesday and the Friday.

There was a crowded scene at Kirk o'Field, as there had been on many previous evenings there during the previous week. The royal entourage – 'the most part of nobles then in this town', said the queen[23] – crowded into the king's chamber. The nobles, including Huntly, who had been at the bishop's dinner, played at dice on that little table with a green velvet cloth which had once belonged to Huntly's father, still in their carnival costumes. Bothwell was an especially striking figure in black velvet and satin, trimmed with silver. The queen chatted pleasantly to the king. There was probably some music, a song in the background to the sound of the lute or the guitar. It was the sort of evening the queen much enjoyed whether at Holyrood or any of her other Scottish palaces: she may even have appreciated the comparative adventure of sleeping at the Kirk o'Field. But at ten or eleven o'clock her intention to do so once more was forestalled. Something – or someone – reminded Queen Mary that it was the hour of Bastian's wedding masque which she had promised to attend. Queen Mary was unable by nature to resist this sort of obligation and Bastian's masque was of special importance in view of the fact that he had designed one of hers only six weeks previously. It now seemed unnecessarily inconvenient to return once more to the provost's lodging after the masque, to sleep there, since Darnley was coming back to Holyrood early the next morning, and the queen herself had also planned an early ride to Seton – according to Lennox's *Narrative*, it was 'Bothwell and others, who seemed to bear a good countenance' who reminded her of this last point. Darnley was sulky at the idea of the change of plan, making the petulant demur of a sick man, from whom the centre of amusement was being suddenly swept away. According to Moretta, the Savoyard ambassador, the queen lightly gave him a ring as a pledge of her goodwill.[24] She then bid him goodbye. Down the staircase went the queen, out to the door where the horses of the court were ready to bring her back to her palace. As she stood to mount her horse, she paused for a moment, puzzled. She saw in front of her her own page, Bothwell's former servant, French Paris. 'Jesu, Paris,' said the queen. 'How begrimed you are!'[25]

Little did the queen know that her innocent observation touched at the core of the secret happenings within the provost's lodging. For at some point during the day which the queen had spent in the formal court ritual of a servant's wedding and an ambassador's dinner, with the prospect of another court masque ahead of her, enough gunpowder had been placed in the vaults of the cellar of the house to blow it sky-high, and reduce it to the heap of rubble to be seen in the Cecil sketch. It is impossible to be sure with any accuracy exactly when the gunpowder was introduced and by whom. The henchmen employed in carrying out the practical details of the plot were apparently nine in number: John Hepburn, John Hay of Tallo and John Spens, kinsmen of Bothwell, William Powrie, his porter, George Dalgleish, his tailor, French Paris, his former servant, James (Black) Ormiston and Hob Ormiston, two further kinsmen, and Pat Wilson. At no point do their subsequent depositions seem more improbable than on the subject of the gunpowder.

According to the official story given by the arrested criminals later, the gunpowder was brought openly through the streets of Edinburgh by William Powrie, during the evening of Sunday, since it had been for some unaccountable reason stored in Bothwell's apartments at Holyrood in a barrel. The gunpowder was supposed to have travelled in two trunks. But William Powrie subsequently changed his story from one journey with two horses, to two journeys with one horse.[26] There was incidentally no explanation given as to why Bothwell should have already brought gunpowder from Dunbar, well before the Friday when he was first supposed to have broached the idea of an explosion. Powrie took the gunpowder to the gate of the Blackfriars Monastery and helped to carry the gunpowder in 'polks' or bags over the wall. According to Paris's story, the gunpowder was now placed openly in a heap on the floor of the queen's chamber (with the entire court, in Buchanan's words 'a great attendance', revelling in the room above). Bothwell himself was even supposed to have come down in the course of the evening to see how matters were progressing. Powrie now made his way back up the Canongate accompanied by Wilson; together they conveyed the empty trunks; as Powrie went, he saw the torches of the queen's party flaring ahead of them, and heard the hooves of the royal horses clattering on the cobbles.

This whole story is so improbable that too much time need not be wasted in demolishing it: in any case it has been constructed out of depositions which are in many respects mutually contradictory. But certain salient points should be noticed: firstly, the amount of gunpowder which could have been conveyed on horseback in two trunks was certainly not adequate to demolish the house at Kirk o'Field. At most, this amount could not have been more than two hundredweight.[27] The strength of gunpowder in the sixteenth century was also considerably weaker than today. Yet it was suggested that this amount of gunpowder, loosely placed in a heap on the floor of the queen's bedroom (the ground floor of the house), was sufficient to produce an explosion which by every contemporary account reduced the whole house to rubble. If the gunpowder

was to produce any sort of blast, it would have had to have
been tamped in rather than left in a heap; it would also have
needed to be placed in the vaults of the house rather than on
the ground floor. Left in a loose heap on the bedroom floor,
there was no certainty it would have produced any sort of
explosion at all: it might merely have flared and burnt itself out.
It therefore becomes clear that the detail concerning the heap of
gunpowder on the floor of the queen's bedroom was particularly
inserted in Paris's deposition in order to incriminate her: for
quite apart from the impossibility of producing an explosion
from there, the heap of gunpowder would only too easily have
attracted the attention of Darnley's servants as they passed to
and fro on their way to the kitchen. Not only Darnley's
attendants but the entire court were thronged into the room
above, and there was no guarantee that they would all stay
peacefully within the confines of the upper room. Like Bothwell,
on a previous occasion, they might have searched out the
garderobe.

The second point to notice in the depositions is that Holyrood
Palace would have been an extraordinary place to choose to
store gunpowder: not only was it patrolled by the royal guards,
but the conspirators inevitably risked detection once more when
they had to convey the gunpowder through the streets of
Edinburgh, patrolled in turn by night watchmen, to the distant
Kirk o'Field. Thirdly, the movements attributed to Bothwell
present him with an impossible schedule to fulfil, since he had
already a full list of engagements to carry out in the course of
the day, in official attendance on the queen. The figure who was
far more involved in the practical details of the crime than the
depositions revealed was Bothwell's then close associate Sir
James Balfour. The reason for the obscurity which was cast
over his actions is not difficult to find: by June 1567 he had
abandoned Bothwell's side for that of the lords in power, and
they therefore had an excellent motive for keeping his name out
of trouble and at the same time blackening that of Bothwell still
further. This remarkable but unlikeable man was later described
by Queen Mary as 'a traitor who offered himself first to one

part and then to the other"[28] and his career seemed certainly to justify her condemnation. Balfour had every reason to know the geography of the old provost's lodgings, since both it and the house next door (the new provost's lodging) belonged to his brother.* A few days after the explosion Drury reported to Cecil that James Balfour was known to have brought powder to the tune of £60 Scots.[30] If any explosion was planned, it would certainly have been infinitely more practical to bring the gunpowder, in sufficient quantities, from some comparatively obscure house much nearer the provost's lodging than from Holyrood Palace. The inconsistencies of the depositions make it clear that others involved were being shielded, and although it cannot be proved, Balfour seems the most likely candidate for the chief accomplice whose name was afterwards shielded. It would have been easy for Balfour to store the large quantity of gunpowder needed in the vaults of his brother's house, and from there transfer it silently to the vaults of the house next door. With his knowledge of Darnley's house and of the district, he could have chosen the time and place at his leisure, when he and his assistants were not likely to be detected.

Queen Mary, in happy ignorance that the house in which she had just spent a relaxed evening was in fact heavily mined with gunpowder – if she had known, one can hardly believe that she would have rested in it so contentedly – now proceeded down the Canongate to Holyrood. Here she attended the masque in honour of Bastian's marriage. She did not stay particularly long there, having made her *acte de présence*, and in any case the party seems to have been almost over when she arrived: it was time to put the bride formally to bed, according to the custom of the period. Mary now went to her apartments, where she took part in a long and earnest conversation until about midnight with Bothwell and John Stewart of Traquair, the captain of her guard. What was the subject of this conversation? No record

---

* The Continuator of Knox's *History*, writing at a later date, had come to believe that Balfour himself owned the house where Darnley died, having 'lately bought it'.[29]

was ever kept, and no contemporary suggestion ever made. But of one thing we can be certain – Bothwell did not take this opportunity to impart his plans for the destruction of Darnley to the queen. There could be no conceivable point in doing so at this juncture. The conspirators had no need to drop the slightest hint to the queen, so long as she fell in unconsciously with their plans. What could be their motive in informing her of the conspiracy at this late hour? If Mary showed signs of lingering at Kirk o'Field, it took only a gentle reminder from a courtier to recall Bastian's masque to her attention, a ceremony which she would be loath to miss. On the Friday the conspirators may have supposed that the masque would keep her away from the lodging altogether on the Sunday evening. Now that the lodging was heavily mined and Mary safely stowed at Holyrood, there could be no hitch in their plans – unless of course they chose to make a last-minute revelation to the queen. Mary, with that soft heart, that horror of bloodshed, that inclination towards mercy, to say nothing of love once felt towards Darnley, extinguished perhaps from the senses but not from the memory, might suddenly experience a last-minute feminine revulsion for what was proposed. She still had it in her power to wreck everything, with a lightning message of warning to Kirk o'Field. The arguments for not implicating her were now, as they had been previously at the conference at Whittingham, over-whelming. Queen Mary retired peacefully to sleep in her apartments in Holyrood. It was a cold evening; there had been a new moon at six o'clock that morning; outside a little snow powdered the streets and fields between Holyrood and the old provost's lodging.

It was now time for Bothwell, released from the royal presence, to join his underlings at the scene of the crime to supervise the lighting of the fuses. Going to his room, he changed out of his splendid silver and black carnival costume; his black velvet hose 'trussed with silver' were exchanged for a sober plain black pair, and a canvas doublet. He wrapped his riding cloak around him: George Dalgleish, with his tailor's eye, added in his deposition that it was of that 'sad English cloth, called the new colour'.[31] He collected the unwilling Paris, who by his own account showed no enthusiasm for the dangerous project. He now had the problem of reaching Kirk o'Field undetected, or at any rate comparatively so. We may dismiss the stories given in the depositions, which related that Bothwell now marched boldly down the Canongate and through the town wall at the Netherbow port. Here he was supposed to have answered the challenge of 'Who goes there?' from the watch with the piece of blatant self-advertisement: 'My lord Bothwell's men.' Bothwell, who had abandoned the dagger and turned to gunpowder, had obviously no desire to have the crime pinned on him. It is more likely that Bothwell went to Kirk o'Field by back streets, perhaps availing himself of the unbuilt section of the town wall, and thus approaching the lodging through the east garden, into which, as we have seen, the house had its own door; of this door, Bothwell had either been given the keys by Paris as the servant deposed, or else had had false keys made by an Edinburgh blacksmith, as one of the anonymous placards after the murder suggested. Bothwell was now ready to supervise the lighting of the fuses. He was not the only nobleman present among the gang of conspirators. The movements of Sir James Balfour are obscure, but from the nearby Douglas house came Archibald Douglas and some of his men; although the Douglases were kinsmen to Darnley (through his mother Margaret, born a Douglas) they were under the leadership of Morton, and were sworn to the destruction of the man who had betrayed them over Riccio. It was said that Archibald Douglas left one of his velvet slippers – 'his mule' – at the scene of the crime, but at Douglas's trial in 1586, his servant John Binning said that after supper, Douglas, wearing secret armour and a steel helmet, took Binning and another servant by the back door of his house to the scene of the crime and Douglas was rightly able to pour scorn on the idea of wearing velvet slippers with armour.[32] It is far more probable that the gang of Douglases were heavily armed as they thronged round the house, either in the east garden, or the alleyway beyond the town wall.

Meanwhile within the doomed house, Darnley sulkily made

preparations for his early departure the next morning to Holy-rood. He ordered the 'great horses' for 5 a.m. For an account of how he spent his last hours we are dependent on the narrative of his father Lennox.[33] Lennox paints an affecting picture of the lonely young boy (his 'innocent lamb') reciting the Fifth Psalm with his servant, 'My voice shalt thou hear in the morning, O Lord; in the morning will I direct my prayer unto thee, and will look up.' It is, however, a picture which ill accords with Darnley's known tastes during the rest of his life. More in keeping with his character was the fact that he called for wine from the kitchen downstairs, presided over by the cook Bonkil. Did he repeat to his servant, as Lennox suggested, some ominous words of the queen's that evening – 'It was about this time of year that David Riccio was killed ...'? It seems likely that, as with the psalm, this dramatic detail sprang from Lennox's imagination. They were not at Holyrood, after all, where Riccio was killed, and it was a full month off the Riccio anniversary. There would have been little point in the queen taunting her husband on the subject, and in any case there is general agreement that their last interview was polite and friendly. One of his servants suggested that he should play the lute, but Darnley said that his hand was not given to the lute that night. They compromised on 'a merry song'. Darnley then retired for the night, with Taylor his valet sleeping in the same room, and Nelson, Symonds and Taylor's boy sleeping in the adjoining gallery, which overhung the town wall. Two grooms, Glen and MacCaig, were in attendance. There was a light burning in the window of Hamilton House, within the quadrangle, otherwise outward calm and silence over the Kirk o'Field.

At two o'clock in the morning, or thereabouts, the silent air was rent by an explosion of remarkable proportions. The Keeper of the Ordnance afterwards likened it to thunder. Paris said that the air was rent by the 'crack', and that every hair of his head stood on end. The *Memoirs* of Herries described it thus: 'The blast was fearfull to all about, and many rose from their beds at the noise.'[34] At distant Holyrood, the queen in her bed was wakened as by a sound likened at the time to that of a cannon fire and sent messengers to find out what had happened. Her guards heard it, and said: 'What crack was that?' People in the nearby Blackfriars Wynd came rushing out into the streets in fear to see what had transpired. We know from the Cecil sketch the sight which met their eyes – the house in which their king was lodged, totally reduced to a pile of rubble. Obviously the first immediate reaction was to imagine that the king had been killed. The first man to rush out into the street – a Captain William Blackadder, a henchman of Bothwell – was promptly arrested, although he swore he had merely been drinking in the nearby house of a friend. But now it was seen that on the top of the town wall, which was still standing, stood Nelson, one of Darnley's servants, who had survived the blast, calling to the people for help. If Nelson had survived, why, so might the king. The next discoveries put an end to this hope. In the garden outside the town wall lay the dead bodies of the king and his servant Taylor. The king was still in his nightgown, and naked beneath it. Beside him was a furred cloak, a chair, a dagger and some rope. There was no mark or mutilation on either body, 'no fracture, wound or bruise' as Buchanan put it[35] – and no sign of the work of the blast. The king and his servant had been strangled.

The famous gunpowder plot of Bothwell had proved in the end all in vain – although Bothwell himself may not have known it as he returned to Holyrood once more. Indeed, he himself looked like perishing in the ruins of Kirk o'Field at one point, alongside Darnley. Having lit the fuses, he retired to watch the explosion; but, according to John Hepburn, as the train of gunpowder did not 'take fire so quickly as the Earl had expected', Bothwell impatiently began to approach the house once more. 'Thereupon the train suddenly emitted fire', and Hepburn, noticing it, was able to drag back his master in the nick of time, before the whole house collapsed upon him.* With the explosion

---

* Related by John Hepburn in prison 'in the very agony of death' to a fellow-prisoner, Cuthbert Ramsay. Ramsay told this story nine years later, when he was giving evidence in Paris for the nullification of Bothwell's marriage to Mary.[36]

completed, it was time for Bothwell to return to Holyrood once more; if the depositions are to be believed, Bothwell answered the challenges of the watch with the same self-advertisement, as he made his way through the town back to the royal palace. According to Paris, the keys of the house were dropped down a deep well the day after the murder. But Bothwell scarcely needed to perform this symbolical action to expunge any guilty feelings concerning the death of Darnley. From the point of view of a border adventurer and bold warrior, it had been a satisfactory night's work, in which an eye – Darnley's – had been given for an eye – Riccio's. Bothwell's own personal fortunes also stood to gain from the enterprise. The paradoxical almost ludicrous element in the whole situation – that Bothwell had not actually killed Darnley by his mighty explosion – was probably unknown to him at the time when he sank thankfully into his bed at Holyrood.

For Darnley in fact died at other hands than those of the earl of Bothwell. Something frightened Darnley, as he lay within the mined house, and frightened him so badly that he escaped out of the provost's lodgings in only a nightgown, and attempted to make his way across the gardens beyond the town wall to safety. He had had no time to dress himself, and although his servant clearly picked up a cloak, Darnley was not wearing it when he died. They had one dagger between them. The chair and rope indicate the improvised method of their escape – a chair let down by a rope out of the gallery window into the alleyway, a drop of only fourteen feet as we have seen, and so through the next gate into the garden. There had been no time to alert the grooms (who died in the explosion) or the other servants. Darnley acted with the speed of panic.

The most likely explanation of Darnley's precipitate departure would be that he was originally wakened by some noise (possibly the laying of the gunpowder trail within the bowels of the house); he then looked out of his window, and saw the gathering of Bothwell's men and the Douglas faction in the east garden, on to which the window looked directly. Gunpowder would not have immediately sprung to mind (unless some hint of it had already been dropped, which now fell into place in his conjectures) but fire would. Burning the enemy's house over his head was a comparatively common sixteenth-century Scottish practice. The sight of Bothwell and his Hepburns and the hostile Douglases milling outside his house would certainly have suggested some imminent danger of fire, if not assassination to Darnley. Put at its mildest, there were no arguments to linger. But for Darnley, even once outside the house, there was no escape. The fleeing figures in their white nightgowns were discerned by some of the Douglas men who pursued them into the gardens. Here they were quietly and efficiently strangled, even as the house itself exploded in a roar of flames and dust. Some women living in the nearby houses said afterwards that they overheard the wretched last plea of Darnley for mercy to the Douglas men who were after all his relations: 'Pity me, kinsmen, for the sake of Jesus Christ, who pitied all the world ...'[37] The plea went unanswered. Darnley died, a boy of not yet twenty-one, as pathetically and unheroically as he had lived.

CHAPTER SEVENTEEN

The Mermaid and the Hare

'Certain stars shot madly from their spheres
To hear the sea-maid's music'

Shakespeare in A Midsummer Night's Dream
(said to be a reference to Bothwell and Mary)

At the palace of Holyrood Queen Mary was woken from her sleep by a noise like twenty or thirty cannon. Shortly afterwards messengers brought her the news that the house at Kirk o'Field had been totally destroyed, and her husband's dead body found lying at a distance of sixty to eighty paces. Her first reactions were horror and shock – horror at what had happened and shock at the feeling that she herself had had such a narrow escape. Bothwell described her in his narrative as '*fort épleurée et contristée*'.[1] She wrote the same day – Monday, 10th February – to her ambassador Beaton in Paris, pouring forth her amazement and distress, although it is noticeable that her conventional grief for Darnley is outweighed by her conviction that the conspiracy had been aimed at her personally; shortly after the event, the Venetian ambassador in Paris also reported that the crime was the work of heretics (Protestants) who had intended to kill Mary too.[2] 'The matter is so horrible and strange,' wrote the queen, 'as we believe the like was never heard of in any country.'[3] She retailed Darnley's fate (still apparently unaware that he had been strangled, and not killed by the blast) and reported the utter demolition of the building 'with such a vehemency, that of the whole lodging, walls and other, there is nothing remaining, no, not a stone above another, but all carried far away, or dung in dross to the very groundstone. It must have been done with the force of powder, and appears to be a mine.' The queen did not yet know who was responsible, but is certain that with 'the diligence our Council has begun already to use ... the same being discovered ... we hope to punish the same with such rigour as shall serve for example of this cruelty to all ages to come'. She continued: 'Always who ever have taken this wicked enterprise in hand, we assure our self it was dressed always for us as for the King; for we lay the most part of all the last week in that same lodging, and was there accompanied with the most part of the lords that are in this town that same night at midnight, and of very chance tarried not all night, by reason of some mask in the abbey; but,' the queen concluded piously, 'we believe it was not chance but God that put it in our head.'

It is evident that at the moment when she wrote this letter, a few hours after the crime, it had not yet struck the queen that any of her chief nobles were involved in its execution. The sheer outrageousness of the explosion had distracted her from considering the known enmities between Darnley and many of the nobility – as Bothwell must have planned that it should; nervously convinced that she herself had only escaped death by a miracle, the queen was at first more inclined to ponder on her own enemies than on Darnley's. The official letter sent to France by the lords of the Council on the same day also emphasized the danger to the queen. So far, then, Bothwell's strategy had succeeded. He himself was officially notified of what had happened when George Hackett came and woke him from his bed at Holyrood, with the news that the king was dead. 'Fie, treason!' exclaimed Bothwell, jumping out of bed, and pulling on his clothes, which he had discarded only an hour before.* As sheriff of Edinburgh, it was now Bothwell's duty to lead a party of soldiers from Holyrood to the scene of the crime;

---

* In his own narrative, *Les Affaires du Conte de Boduel*, Bothwell announced that he had spent the whole night in bed with his wife – the classic alibi of the criminal.[4]

whereupon the king's body, bearing as Knox said 'no mark of fire', was carried into the next-door new provost's lodging. Here it was inspected by surgeons, then members of the Privy Council, and also by the general public, who were allowed to exercise their natural curiosity. It was at this point that the news that Darnley had in fact been strangled began to spread abroad – the variety of rumours on the nature of the weapon included his own belt, the sleeves of his shirt, his garters, a serviette, a napkin steeped in vinegar (Lennox's lurid contribution), and waxed cord. The old women in the Blackfriars Wynd – who were later examined by the council and dismissed for involving too indiscreetly the names of the great – began to chatter of the men they had seen round the house and that last poignant cry of Darnley. His body was now carried on a board to Holyrood, embalmed by an apothecary and a surgeon, and laid formally in state for several days, before being buried in the vaults of the chapel royal, as was his due as a king of Scotland.

So far the royal widow had behaved with perfect correctness. She ordered the court into mourning, for which £150-worth of black was ordered. Although, according to Knox's *History*, Mary showed no outward sign of joy or sorrow when shown the corpse of Darnley, her strange composure – so unlike her usual ready tears – may well have been due to simple shock.⁵ She herself embarked heavily on the traditional forty days' mourning for her husband, permitting herself, however, to attend the wedding of Margaret Carwood, her favourite bed-chamber woman, on the Tuesday after the murder; she had paid for the wedding-dress – £125⁶ – and either considered a promise to a beloved servant too important to break, or else was too dazed to realize the significance of what had just happened. Her spirits had never recovered properly from her Jedburgh illness; at the time of James's baptism at the end of December du Croc had prophesied gloomily that her nerves would give them some trouble yet – 'nor can I be brought to think otherwise so long as she continues to be so pensive and melancholy ... She sent for me yesterday and I found her laid on the bed, weeping sore. She complained of a grievous pain in her side.'⁷ Now her nervous health became so critically weakened by the shock of the crime that, according to Leslie, the Privy Council were earnestly exhorted by her doctors to let her get away from the tragic and gloom-laden atmosphere of Edinburgh for a while, lest incarceration in the closed chamber of the widow should cause a total breakdown – the doctors emphasized 'the great and imminent dangers of her health and life, if she did not in all speed break up and leave that kind of close, solitary life and repair to some good wholesome air'.[8] Accordingly, the queen went to Seton, one of her favourite haunts close to Edinburgh, a week after the murder, and spent three recuperative days there. Although Mary's enemies subsequently accused her of dallying at Seton with Bothwell, it was the task of Bothwell and Huntly, as chief nobles of the kingdom, to remain at Holyrood to guard the person of Prince James.

In the course of her further reflections, once the first distressing impact of the murder wore off, it could not fail to occur to Mary that this was no hideous outrage by unknown assassins, but a deliberately planned coup on the part of those nobles who had hated Darnley, and who had openly discussed his removal with her at Craigmillar. It must now have become apparent to her that she herself had been in no personal danger, but that Darnley had paid the penalty for his treachery in the violent and bloodthirsty manner which she had by now come to associate with Scottish vengeance. Possibly she taxed Bothwell with complicity or possibly she was informed of it from another source; but in any case by the mere process of reasoning she could hardly have been ignorant as to who were the authors of the crime, when the first shock had subsided. In the meantime rumours as to the truth of the matter, and the fact that Mary's chief nobles had been involved, began to reach both England and France. By March the Venetian ambassador in Paris had heard a comparatively accurate account of events from Moretta, the returning ambassador of Savoy, and commented further: 'It is widely believed that the principal persons of the kingdom were implicated in this act, because they were dissatisfied with the King', amongst whom he singled out Moray for having had a quarrel with Darnley.[9] Both Catherine de Médicis and Elizabeth reacted predictably to these rumours: a king had been killed; Mary's leading subjects were said to be involved in the crime; it was now up to Mary herself to dispense public justice with a heavy hand, whether it was directed towards the true criminals or not being less important than the fact that justice should be seen to be done. The two queens, French and English, wrote long admonitory letters to the third Scottish queen to this effect.

Rumours were not only rife on the Continent and in England, they were also percolating rapidly round Edinburgh itself. A quantity of people, many of them servants, had been involved in the murder; it was hardly likely that an outrage of this magnitude would remain a total mystery for very long. Tongues wagged. There were dark hints, and others a good deal plainer. One story said that Sir James Balfour had had one of his underlings killed, because he threatened to reveal the truth out of a crisis of conscience.[10] Placards began to appear in the streets – the art of the anonymous placard having been recently imported from France. The first placard was nailed up on 16th February, a week after the murder, naming Bothwell and Balfour, and asserting that the queen had consented to the murder, as a result of the witchcraft of Janet Beaton, the lady of Buccleuch. The second placard on 18th February took a more xenophobic line, naming three foreigners in Mary's household – Bastian, Francisco, and Joseph Riccio. In a letter of 28th February to Cecil, Drury spoke of other bills bestowed upon the church doors, even of one posted upon a tree which mentioned a smith who would step forward if necessary and say he was the maker of the false keys for the house (if the man existed, it casts further doubt on Paris's deposition in which he said he was instructed to steal the keys of Kirk o'Field).[11] The sound of voices crying that Bothwell was the murderer of the king was heard through the night in the streets of Edinburgh. On 1st March the most famous and most virulent of all the placards appeared: it showed Queen Mary as a mermaid, naked to the waist, with a crown on her head, and Bothwell as a hare – the crest of the Hepburns – crouching in a circle of swords.

The implication behind the use of the mermaid was not romantic, as might appear to modern eyes, but deliberately insulting, since the word was commonly used in the sixteenth and seventeenth centuries to denote a siren, and thus by analogy a prostitute.*

This was the supreme moment for Mary to show herself the prudent and ruthless sovereign, and benefit from the actions of others to make her own position thoroughly secure. Her Achilles' heel in Scotland – her husband Darnley – had been eliminated from her path by her own nobility. She had not known of the crime beforehand, and was not implicated in its details. Now her best course was to pursue the so-called murderers with public vengeance, in order to establish once and for all her own innocence of any possible complicity. After all, once the nobles came to power they took great care to produce some criminals publicly, as we shall see, in order to exculpate themselves; Mary herself should have been at least as practical while she still had the opportunity. Even if she could not go so far as arraigning Bothwell himself, there were underlings to be sacrificed. As it was, her conduct bordered on madness. The Privy Council had announced a reward of £2000 for the capture of the criminals, immediately after the deed; there had been vague questionings of Nelson and the old women; but beyond that no further steps were taken to secure any arrests. Neither the placards, the rumours, the letters from abroad, nor Lennox's furious denunciations of his son's murderers – about whose identity he was personally in no doubt – seemed to have the power of penetrating Mary's passive state of despair and melancholy. Since health and shock had clearly robbed her of any shred of political judgement, she was exceptionally dependent upon her advisers. But the advisers who surrounded her were all for one reason and another

---

* The description of a mermaid was one which was thought especially applicable to Mary: Shakespeare used it in *A Midsummer Night's Dream* when he wrote of

> A Mermaid on a dolphin's back
> Uttering such dulcet and harmonious breath...
> that Certain stars shot madly from their spheres
> To hear the sea-maid's music.

The stars were intended to represent Bothwell.

incapable of pointing out the true facts of the situation; never was Mary Stuart's pathetic lack of loyal disinterested consultants more disastrous to her than in the period immediately after Kirk o'Field.

Moray's first concern was to clear himself of any possible guilt in the eyes of his English friends: Moretta, after all, had believed Moray implicated above all others because of his notorious hatred for Darnley. In a letter to Cecil of 13th March, Moray anxiously excused himself and also asked for a passport so that he could come to London.[12] In this crisis of his sister's affairs, Moray was eager to put as much distance as possible between himself and the Scottish court, partly so that he should not be involved in the contentious struggle for power which he saw coming, in which the strength of the hated Bothwell seemed to be growing hourly, partly so that he could ingratiate himself in England. He departed for London at the beginning of April – incidentally making his sister guardian of his daughter, in his will. Queen Mary wept at his departure, and wished 'he were not so precise in religion'.[13] Of the queen's other possible advisers, Maitland had been involved in the plot, and could therefore scarcely advise her to pursue its punishment vindictively. Bothwell was hardly likely to counsel a course so alien to his own interests. There was thus no force to conjure the queen out of her mood of lassitude and melancholia. Her foreign correspondence ceased – that immense flood of letters to her Guise relations, in whom she had taken such a touching, detailed domestic interest ever since she left France, dried up; there is no more poignant evidence that Mary Stuart had fallen into a state of despair. The Scotland of her dreams and early happiness now seemed to her a cruel and barbarous country where deeds of violence succeeded each other in remorseless succession; her secretary and now her husband had been done to death within a year, not by low assassins but by the chief men of the kingdom. The renewed bloodshed less than twelve months after the death of Riccio horrified her. In her sad passivity, she allowed herself to lean increasingly on the one man close to her who still showed strength of purpose, energy and determination – and was also only too anxious to direct the affairs of the state. Unfortunately for Mary, that man was Bothwell, who, whatever his dominating qualities, was also the chief suspect of her husband's murder.

On 8th March, the queen received a formal visit of condolence from Killigrew, Elizabeth's envoy. He found her, by his own account, 'in a dark chamber, so as I could not see her face, but by her very words, she seemed very doleful, and did accept my sovereign's letters and messages in a very thankful manner ...'[14] On 14th March, an effort was made to punish the author of the defamatory placards, and James Murray of Tullibardine was accused of having 'devised, invented and caused to be set up certain painted papers upon the Tolbooth door of Edinburgh, bending to her Majesty's slander and defamation'.[15] On 19th March, Bothwell began to show his mettle as director of Mary's policies: it was time for Prince James to be returned to the royal nursery at Stirling, from which his mother had plucked him a month before, when there were rumours that Darnley was threatening his safety. While Argyll and Huntly conveyed him there, his governor, Lord Mar, was presented with the governorship of Stirling Castle. This meant, in turn, that Mar could be deprived of the vital governorship of Edinburgh Castle – which he had held loyally for the queen in August 1565. This fortress Bothwell now bestowed on his own ally Sir James Cockburn, but later, even more fatally, gave to his associate Sir James Balfour – presumably as a reward for his part in the murder.

Bothwell's ambitions to become effective ruler of Scotland, which one may conjecture he had nourished since the summer of 1566, had been given a further fillip at the end of February by the serious illness of his wife Jean Gordon: she hovered on the brink of death, and one ambassador went so far as to announce that she had actually died. There is no need to attribute poison to Bothwell to explain the illness, since divorcing Jean later proved extremely easy – but it must surely have had the effect of sending his thoughts racing forward to his future plans. His finances were also no better than before and in February he had to sell more land to Alexander Home, which gave him another powerful motive to press forward towards a position in which his finances would be at least unassailable. By the end of March, a story had reached the English ambassador in Paris that a marriage might be forthcoming between Mary and Bothwell and, at roughly the same date, Drury reported to Cecil in London that 'the judgment of the people' was that Mary would marry Bothwell.[16] For once more in her history, as at her birth, and after the death of Francis, the queen's new marriageability made her a target for any ambitious man who wanted to make himself a king. And Bothwell was certainly such a man inspired either by family tradition of advancement through queens, or plain personal ambition, unmarked by any trace of sentiment or sensitivity.

On 23rd March, the fortieth day after Darnley's death, the queen's period of mourning officially came to an end with a solemn Mass of Requiem and a dirge for Darnley's soul. In fact her sorrows were only just beginning. The vociferous demands of Lennox for vengeance had reached a pitch when even Mary, advised by Bothwell, felt herself unable to ignore them. In a letter of 24th March she agreed to allow him to bring a private process in front of Parliament against Bothwell as the slayer of his son, and the process was set up by an Act of the Privy Council on 28th March to take place on 12th April. It was hardly surprising that in two letters of 29th and 30th March, Drury reported the queen to be in continuous ill-health – 'She has been for the most part either melancholy or sickly ever since, and especially this week upon Tuesday or Wednesday often swooned ... the Queen breaketh very much.'[17] The trial of Bothwell was not even instituted officially by the queen, but allowed to stand at the private petition of Lennox. But Lennox understandably shrank from appearing in Edinburgh with the six followers permitted to him by law, in view of the fact that the city was swarming with 4000 of Bothwell's adherents.

On the appointed day, Bothwell rode magnificently down the Canongate, with Morton and Maitland flanking him, and his

Hepburns trotting behind. The queen, with Mary Fleming, now Maitland's wife, watched them go from the window at Holyrood. Although the due processes of justice were observed at the trial – which lasted from noon till seven in the evening – the absence of the accuser Lennox meant that Bothwell was inevitably acquitted; the wily Morton excused himself from the jury, on the grounds that he was kin to the victim, and thus cunningly, with an eye to the future, did not partake in Bothwell's acquittal. The Diurnal of Occurrents, written by a comparatively impartial court observer, commented sourly that Bothwell was 'made clean of the said slaughter, albeit that it was heavily murmured that he was guilty thereof'.[18] Another omen for the future was the fact that a last-minute messenger from Elizabeth arrived at Holyrood at 6 a.m., and attempted to get the trial postponed, presumably until Lennox could be present. The messenger was, however, not admitted to the Scottish queen's presence, and treated with little courtesy.

Bothwell reacted characteristically and braggartly to his acquittal: he sent a crier round the town, and had bills stuck on the town gates and the Tolbooth, emblazoned with his arms, offering to defend his innocence with personal combat. However, that night, an anonymous acceptor of his challenge on a placard offered to prove that Bothwell was the 'chief author of the foul and horrible murder by law of arms', showing that the Scots spirit was not to be bullied. The next Wednesday, the queen rode to Parliament, with Bothwell carrying the sceptre, Argyll the crown and Crawford the sword once more as a year ago, but on this occasion, her nerve had evidently gone sufficiently to surround herself with hagbutters, no longer trusting the bailies of Edinburgh. At this Parliament, the proceedings of Bothwell's trial were officially declared to be just according to the law of the land; all subjects were ordered to live in unity, despite their religious differences, and even more significantly, grants of land towards certain nobles were confirmed – the lands that went with Dunbar Castle were confirmed to Bothwell, and Huntly and four other Gordons were confirmed in their estates, although unofficial restitution had been made two years before. These were the practical aspects of the fall of Darnley.

Bothwell's next move was absolutely in keeping with his character and the conditions of the time: if he was to make his power even more effective by occupying the position of king, he needed the support of at least some of his fellow-nobles. The contemporary expedient of a bond was once more called into play, as twice before over the murder of Riccio and the murder of Darnley. In order to secure adherents for this new bond, on Saturday 19th April, at the end of the sitting of Parliament, Bothwell duly entertained twenty-eight of the nobles and prelates then in the capital to a lavish feast – contemporary reports differing as to whether this banquet took place in his own apartments at Holyrood, or in Ainslie's Tavern in the town itself. What was sure was that at the end of this momentous supper party, Bothwell produced a long document, the main point of which, apart from his own innocence of the murder of Darnley, was that the queen was now 'destitute of a husband, in which solitary state, the commonwealth may not permit her to remain'.[19] It continued ingenuously: if the 'affectionate and hearty service of the said Earl, and his other good qualities' might move the queen to select him as a new husband – and the document suggested that another reason for such a choice, quite apart from Bothwell's noble nature, might be the fact that Mary would prefer 'one of her native-born subjects unto all foreign subjects' – then the signatories were to promise themselves to promote the marriage by counsel, vote and assistance. To this remarkable manifesto, known by the name of the tavern as the Ainslie bond, eight bishops, nine earls and seven barons now put their signatures including Morton, Maitland, Argyll, Huntly, Cassillis, Sutherland, Glencairn, Rothes, Seton, Sinclair, Boyd and Herries.* Although the motives and loyalties of some of the signatories must be considered to be highly suspect – for surely to Morton and Maitland King James Hepburn would be no more acceptable than King Henry Stuart had been – nevertheless

---

* Although one contemporary report said that Moray also put his signature to the bond, this seems unlikely as he was by now in London.

Bothwell now had in his pocket the document he considered he needed for his next bold move forward.

The queen having gone to her favourite Seton, Bothwell now followed her there with Maitland and Bellenden. According to Queen Mary's own story, it was here that he first paid suit to her, suggesting both that she needed a husband, and that he was the best man to fill the role, since he had been selected to do so by her nobles. This direct request threw the queen into a state of confusion: 'This poor young princess, inexperienced in such devices,' wrote Nau,[20] 'was circumvented on all sides by persuasions, requests, and importunities; both by general memorials signed by their hands, and presented to her in full council, and by private letters.' We can certainly believe Mary's account that she did not know what to do, especially when Maitland assured her what she knew only too well, that it had become absolutely necessary that some remedy should be provided for the disorder into which the public affairs had fallen for want of a head. Now her chief nobles were apparently pleading with her to accept Bothwell – 'a man of resolution well adapted to rule, the very character needed to give weight to the decisions and actions of the council'. However, Queen Mary always asserted afterwards that she refused Bothwell's proposals at this point, on the grounds that there were too many scandals about her husband's death, despite the fact that Bothwell had been legally acquitted of complicity by Parliament.

With this refusal still uppermost in her thoughts, the queen proceeded to Stirling to pay a visit to her baby. She arrived on Monday 21st April, and spent the whole Tuesday enjoying the company of her child. James was ten months old. The queen played with him in peace, happily unaware that this was the last meeting she was ever to have with her son. While she was at Stirling, she also wrote to the former papal nuncio, the bishop of Mondovi, now back in Turin, protesting her devotion to Scotland, to the Pope, and the Holy Catholic Church – in which she intended to die.[21] It is difficult to know for certain what thoughts of the future inspired this strange guilty little letter, but Mondovi's reaction, written before he had heard news of her abduction and marriage to Bothwell, is significant: he prophesied that unless the queen of Scots was given strong support by the papacy, she might give way to the natural impulse of a young woman and seek support elsewhere from a husband instead; as a candidate for this post, Mondovi put forward the name of Bothwell 'who has ever been the Queen's most trusty and obedient adherent'.[22]

On the Wednesday Mary started back to Edinburgh. The visit to Stirling had ostensibly been a secret one, and she had with her only Maitland, Huntly, James Melville and about thirty horsemen. Mary's health was still poor. On the road back she was seized with a violent pain and had to take rest in a roadside cottage. That night she slept at the palace of Linlithgow, the peaceful palace overlooking its lake, where she had been born. The next morning, Thursday 24th April, the ninth anniversary of her marriage to Francis, the queen and her little troupe started back on the road for Edinburgh. But as they reached the Bridges of Almond, about six miles from Edinburgh, close to the point where the Gogar Burn joined the Almond River, and travellers were ferried across, Bothwell suddenly appeared with a force of 800 men. He had spent the night at the nearby castle of Calder, apparently on his way into Liddesdale. Bothwell rode forward, put his hand on the queen's bridle, and told her that since danger was threatening her in Edinburgh, he proposed to take her to the castle of Dunbar, out of harm's way. Some of Mary's followers reacted disagreeably to the sudden appearance of Bothwell, but the queen said gently that she would go with the Earl Bothwell rather than be the cause of bloodshed. Docilely, without more ado, she allowed herself to be conducted about forty miles across the heart of Scotland, skirting the capital itself; she seemed to accept Bothwell's story so totally that she made no attempt to seek rescue from the country people as she passed. Her only positive action was to send one James Borthwick to Edinburgh to issue a warning of possible danger. When Borthwick told the provost what had happened, a very different view was taken of the disappearance of their sovereign. The alarm bell was rung and the citizens were begged to attempt a rescue. But by this time there was little that they, or anyone, could do. At midnight, the queen was within Dunbar Castle, surrounded by a force of Bothwell's men. The gates of the castle were firmly shut behind her.

This abduction – if the word can truly be applied to anything so calm and placid as these proceedings at the Bridges – represented a typical example of Bothwell's thinking. Even if earlier hints of Bothwell's predilection for abduction, in Arran's story, are disregarded, Bothwell clearly had the mentality which considered that a sufficiently public outrage covered in some curious way a multitude of sins. This had been his reasoning over Kirk o'Field. Now he confidently believed that an abduction would not only put an end to further consultation and discussion about the marriage – in which his reasoning was perfectly correct – but also distract public attention from his connection with Darnley's death by the very flagrancy of the act; here of course his reasoning was disastrously wrong. Was Queen Mary enlightened in advance as to her prospective fate? Although we cannot have the certainty of definite proof, the contemporary evidence points strongly to the fact that Mary knew of the plan beforehand, and agreed to it weakly, as a possible way out of the morass in which despair brought on by ill-health seemed to have landed her. The intended abduction was certainly widely known about beforehand among her nobles. Lennox knew about it on the Tuesday, and Kirkcaldy of Grange, Bothwell's bitter enemy, mentioned it on Thursday, the day it actually happened.[23] In a fury at Bothwell's rising eminence, Kirkcaldy wrote to Bedford in the same letter that the queen had been overheard saying that she would go to the end of the world in a white petticoat with Bothwell – but as Kirkcaldy did not reveal by whom or under what circumstances this extraordinary declaration had been overheard, and as he subsequently became one of Mary's loyalest followers, it seems likely that he was allowing his dislike and jealousy of Bothwell to taint his imagination. Maitland must surely have known of the plan. Paris, in his deposition, said Bothwell's man, Black Ormiston, came to Linlithgow Palace secretly the night before the abduction and had a long earnest conversation.[24] It seems inconceivable that the scheme should not have been outlined also to the queen, if only to secure her co-operation. Mary, still envisaging Bothwell as her help and support among the nobles, and not as the reprobate adventurer whom his enemies later built up in their writings, felt in no position to withstand his latest proposition; it was presented to her by Bothwell, using the same arguments which he had used to himself, as a convenient solution to her difficulties.

Once within the castle of Dunbar, Bothwell made his second planned move – an equally characteristic one, although in this case the queen was not consulted beforehand. He decided to complete his formal abduction of her person by the physical possession of her body. His intentions in this aggressive act were as before perfectly straightforward: he intended to place the queen in a situation from which she could not possibly escape marrying him. Bothwell was certainly not in love with Mary, although he may have accompanied his actions with some sort of protestations, such as he thought suitable to the occasion. But in the course of the gratification of his ambitions, rape was not the sort of duty from which Bothwell was likely to shrink. Melville, who was present in the castle at the time, and only allowed to go free the next morning, was quite certain that the ravishment had taken place: 'The Queen could not but marry him, seeing he had ravished her and laid with her against her will.'[25] It was Melville who tells us that Bothwell had already boasted that he would marry the queen – 'who would or would not; yea, whether she would herself or not'. A fortnight later Mary gave a very vivid description of her experiences to the bishop of Dunblane, who was instructed to explain her hasty marriage to Bothwell to the French court: first of all Bothwell 'awaited us by the way, accompanied with a great force, and led us with all diligence to Dunbar' and there, in words which seem positively touching: 'Albeit we found his doings rude, yet were his words and answers gentle.' Now Bothwell, not accepting her promise to marry him, refused to have the consummation of the marriage delayed, but kept up a continuous barrage of importunity, 'accompanied none the less by force' until 'he has finally driven us to end the work begun at such time and such form as he thought might best serve his turn'.[26] It is interesting to note that Bothwell's and Mary's contemporaries believed instantaneously and strongly that the abduction scheme had been a rigged one and intended to save the queen's face. Within three days Drury wrote that although the manner seemed to be forcible, it was known to be otherwise.[27] But it was also widely believed that Bothwell had completed his scheme by making love to the queen, and that this was probably against her will. These were the conclusions drawn by those able to observe at first hand the bold and scheming character of Bothwell, and the markedly straitlaced attitude of Queen Mary to matters of sexual morality.

It is sometimes suggested that Mary found a sexual satisfaction with Bothwell which she had not experienced with either of her previous husbands. This may or may not be true: it can certainly never be proved, since the queen herself certainly never ventured any opinion upon the subject, and to the end of her life always firmly attributed her marriage to Bothwell to reasons of state rather than the dictates of the heart. In fact, the events leading up to her marriage to Darnley point far more clearly to the workings of physical infatuation, than those leading up to the Bothwell marriage. In spring 1565 Mary Stuart was a young and beautiful woman, healthy and energetic, long widowed, eager to be married; in spring 1567 she was broken in health, distraught, nervously concerned about the future of her government in Scotland. Quite apart from the evidence of events, it seems extremely doubtful whether they were the sort of couple who would have been drawn to each other if political considerations had not been involved. Practical ambition had driven Bothwell to woo the queen: this elegant, coquettish, literary-minded, slightly cold woman, with her graceful, leaning figure, her red-gold hair, her laughing flirtatious ways, her demand for obeisance to which she had been accustomed from her earliest years, was not the type to appeal to Bothwell, the lover of the lusty

Bessie Crawford, the dominating courtesan Janet Beaton or the plaintive, submissive Anna Throndsen. Of all Mary Stuart's qualities, her courage and gaiety, her ability to make quick decisions and pull herself rapidly out of an untenable situation were those most likely to appeal to Bothwell but these had been strangely in abeyance since her virtual nervous breakdown at Jedburgh. The important fact about Mary Stuart in Bothwell's eyes was that she was queen regnant of Scotland, with the power to make her husband king consort and effective ruler of the country.

Of course it would not be essential for Bothwell to love Mary for her to respond to him: she might even have experienced some perverse satisfaction in domination by this straightforward and brutal man, so different from her other husbands, and her potential courtly lovers. Bothwell's intellectual curiosity certainly extended into matters of sex. Apart from the common contemporary rumours of his vicious life, there was a *canard* that he practised homosexuality.* The feelings which Queen Mary felt for Bothwell can only be estimated in terms of the importance which as a woman she gave to the whole subject of sex. In early youth she naturally paid little attention to such questions, and during the period of her first widowhood also was remarkable for the discretion with which she conducted herself. Her disastrous marriage to Darnley, springing from physical attraction, gave her every reason to adopt an extremely suspicious attitude towards passion and its consequences. If, despite all these considerations, she experienced some genuine fulfilment in Bothwell's embraces, it is remarkable how little effort she made to keep in touch with her husband, once she was in captivity: from the moment of her abdication onwards, she seems to have lost all interest in Bothwell, as though he belonged to some previous, unsuccessful, political phase in her life. Another interesting aspect of her captivity is that she made

---

* A broadside ballad published in Edinburgh after Mary's abdication, *An Declaration of the Lord Just Quarrel*, written by Robert Sempill, an extremist Protestant, exclaimed:
      Such beastly buggery Sodom has not seen
      As ruled in him who ruled Realm and Queen.[28]

absolutely no attempt to quench any desires of the flesh, if indeed she felt them, during the whole nineteen years: there is no rumour, which bears investigation, of the sort of liaison which would surely have occurred had she become, under Bothwell's tuition, the *grande amoureuse* of so many imaginings. On the contrary, from the age of twenty-five onwards, the queen led a life of total chastity.

Whatever Mary's inner feelings for Bothwell during the short period of their concubinage – three weeks from Dunbar to the marriage, and four weeks thereafter – their union was certainly not founded originally on the flimsy basis of passion. Mary's confessor Mameret later solemnly swore to the Spanish ambassador in London that, until the question of her marriage to Bothwell was raised, he had never seen a woman of greater virtue, courage and uprightness – and he therefore, with all the intimate knowledge of her character gained in the confessional, utterly believed that Mary had only taken up with Bothwell in order to settle the religious situation in Scotland.[29] In fact the queen had not one but three pressing and – as it seemed to her – good reasons for giving her consent to the marriage with Bothwell. In the first place he had succeeded in convincing her that he would at last provide her with the able and masterful consort whom she had so long sought to share with her the strains of the government of Scotland. He had subjugated her by the undoubted strength of his personality at a time when broken health had induced in her a fatally indecisive, even lethargic state of mind, so that faced with the reality of Bothwell and his positive aims, she was unable to see clearly where her own best interests lay. Secondly, Bothwell was able to show to Mary the Ainslie bond which proved to her satisfaction that the majority of her nobility – not only Seton and Huntly but also the more contumacious Morton and Argyll – were prepared to accept him as their overlord. Mary had married Darnley defiantly against the advice of most of her nobles: she did not intend to make the same mistake twice. The Ainslie bond and the apparent approval of the nobility were worth more to Bothwell in furthering his suit than all the magic arts and enticements with which he was afterwards credited by Mary's partisans in order to explain his seduction of her.* Thirdly, Bothwell had effectively ensured that the queen would not be able to go back on her word once she was back in her capital, by the act of physical rape which he had performed at Dunbar. The union had already been consummated: it remained to transform it into a legal marriage.

Having secured the queen's acquiescence, Bothwell now faced the problem of ridding himself of his existing wife, to whom he had been married just over two years before. This did not prove difficult, since Jean Bothwell seems to have raised no objections: her marriage had been brought about by political considerations, and she was now content to have it dissolved for the same good reasons. There were already rumours by the end of March that her brother Huntly had agreed in principle to the deal. On 3rd May Lady Bothwell was given judgment against her husband in the Protestant commissary court, which had replaced the old church courts in matrimonial cases: the grounds given were his adultery with Bessie Crawford. In order to make assurance doubly sure, their marriage was then formally annulled on 7th May by the Catholic Archbishop Hamilton, on the grounds that they had not received a dispensation for their marriage, although they were within the fourth degree of consanguinity, Bothwell's great-great-grandfather having married a Gordon. The cynicism of this gesture may be judged by the fact that not only had a dispensation actually been given, but it had been given by Archbishop Hamilton himself.[31] Despite the ease of the divorce, Bothwell's servants took the opportunity in the course of it to threaten violence to Master John Manderstoun, canon of Dunbar collegiate church, who was told that if matters did not move fast enough 'there shall not fail to be noses and lugges (ears) cut, and far greater displeasures ...'[32] On 6th May Bothwell brought the queen back into Edinburgh; at the end of

* Both Leslie and Lennox, from different sides, accused Bothwell of using black magic to seduce the queen. Today he would probably have been accused of drugging her. In his *Confession*, a suspect document, Bothwell admits to using magic to secure the queen's affections.[30]

April she had received an offer of rescue from Aberdeen, which she had rejected. She was now regarded as firmly committed to Bothwell's rule. The couple entered Edinburgh by the West Port and then rode up the Bow towards the castle. Both Huntly and Maitland were in their train. Although the artillery of the castle shot off magnificently for the queen's arrival, it was generally remarked that Bothwell's power was not absolute. The Diurnal of Occurrents recorded that the Earl Bothwell led the queen's majesty by the bridle of her horse, as though she were a captive.[33]

As Queen Mary moved in a trance towards her public union with Bothwell, already the forces of aristocratic reaction were coalescing against his meteoric rise. Furious at the realization that Bothwell – one of their own number – had made himself a virtual dictator, on 1st May a party of dissidents gathered at Stirling. They vowed in yet another communal bond to strive by all means in their power to set their queen at liberty, and defend her son Prince James. In this meeting at Stirling, it is significant that the key figures were Morton, Argyll and Atholl – all three of whom only a week before, out of either cunning or weakness, had signed the Ainslie bond promising to forward Bothwell's suit of the queen. Bedford was now asked by Kirkcaldy to write to Moray and ask him to return, and Robert Melville wrote for English support against Bothwell, threatening French support if it was not forthcoming. The pattern of Scottish politics was forming once more into the same shapes of family alliances and feuds, in which the power of one noble could not be allowed to grow unchecked, and in which English help was like the joker in the pack of cards. The Stirling conspirators diverted themselves with a drama called *The Murder of Darnley and the Fate of Bothwell* – in which the boy actor who played the part of Bothwell was hanged so realistically that it took some time to restore him to life. These same nobles sent a message to Mary offering her their support against the Lord Bothwell. But since Bothwell was firmly governing all matters around her, the queen could scarcely credit that he had already lost the support of the fickle Scottish lords: it was after all only a few weeks since the signing of the Ainslie bond, which had convinced her that the majority of her nobility especially desired this Bothwell marriage.

The days passed with horrible speed towards her wedding-day. When John Craig, Knox's colleague in the parish church of Edinburgh, refused to proclaim the banns of the marriage without a writ from the queen, he was brought a command signed by her personally saying that she had been neither ravished nor yet retained in captivity. But when Craig did make his proclamation, he was still brave enough, on 9th May, to express contemporary disgust at the speed of events, by a denunciation in front of the Privy Council of Bothwell's behaviour: 'I laid to his charge, the law of adultery, the ordinance of the Kirk, the law of ravishing, the suspicion of collusion between him and his wife, the sudden divorcement, and proclaiming within the space of four days, and last the suspicion of the King's death which her marriage would confirm.'[34] Angrily Bothwell threatened to hang Craig; but Craig spoke no more than what the common people of Edinburgh, once so devoted to Mary, their dream figure, their beautiful young queen, felt themselves at seeing her thus recklessly and carelessly allow herself to be trampled in the mire of Bothwell's ambition. On 12th May Mary created Bothwell duke of Orkney and lord of Shetland (titles once borne by his ancestor, the 1st earl) and placed the ducal coronet on his head with her own hands. Four of his followers were knighted, including Black Ormiston of Kirk o'Field fame. To many the queen seemed like a mindless zombie under the power of Bothwell's authority: Beaton in Paris was naturally growing distracted at the madness or folly of his young mistress, but Clernault reported to him on 14th May that Mary neither listened to nor inspected any communication he brought her from Beaton or others of her advisers abroad.[35] On the same day the queen officially pardoned those nobles who had signed the Ainslie bond.

On Thursday, 15th May, twelve days after his own divorce, just over three months after the death of her own husband, Mary and Bothwell were married in the great hall at Holyrood. Lines from Ovid were posted upon the gates of the Palace –

'*Mense malas maio nubere vulgus ait*', or as the people murmured significantly: 'Wantons marry in the month of May'.* A greater contrast to the two previous weddings of the queen could hardly be imagined. The very fact that the ceremony took place according to the Protestant rite showed how much the queen had lost control of her destinies, although it is possible that she herself heard a Mass earlier in the day, out of which her adherents later tried to construct a story that they had been married under both forms. At the service, Adam, bishop of Orkney, preached a sermon in the course of which he chose to announce Bothwell's penitence for his former evil and wicked life. After the wedding, there were no masques as there had been at the Darnley wedding, or 'pleasures and pastimes' as there had always been before when princes married.[36] There was merely a wedding dinner, at which the people were allowed to watch Mary eating her meal at the head of the table, with Bothwell at the foot.

Equally significant of the queen's state of mind is the fact that there were no rich presents for Bothwell as groom as there had been for Darnley, and certainly no lavish replenishment of her own wardrobe. Whereas Darnley had received violet velvet, furs, a cupboard for perfumes, cloth of gold for his horse's caparison, blue bonnets with feathers for his fools, and other tokens of Mary's love, Bothwell merely received some genet fur from one of Mary of Guise's black cloaks for his dressing-gown – his solitary present. Furthermore, the queen seems to have paid no attention to the subject of her own clothes, once so important to her. There are only two entries in the inventories of her wardrobe in May 1567 – one being for Bothwell's fur – compared to thirty in July 1565, the month in which she married Darnley.[37] Her sartorial preparations were confined to having an

---

* There was a rooted prejudice in Scotland against May marriages – or, as a similar Scottish saying had it: 'Marry in May and regret it for ay'; and the records show a remarkable decline in the number of marriages practised during that month. Ovid's line (from the fifth book of the *Fasti*) described the similar prejudice of the ancient Romans, said to have been due to the fact that the Lemuralia, or three-day feasts to appease the spirits of the dead, began on 9th May.

old yellow dress relined with white taffeta, an old black gown done up with gold braid and a black taffeta petticoat relined. Of all the sad events in the life of Mary Stuart in Scotland, this squalid, hurried wedding, of a rite she did not profess, without any of the preparations she so loved, is surely the most pathetic.

Judged from the comments of observers, Mary's brief married life with Bothwell brought her absolutely no personal happiness. Already on their wedding-day, du Croc reported that a strange formality was noticed between the queen and her new husband. Mary tried to excuse it, by saying that she did not wish to be merry. To Leslie, she was more explicit: she sent for him, and in floods of tears told him how much she already repented of what she had done, especially her Protestant marriage ceremony.[38] She promised him desperately she would never do anything again opposed to the Catholic Church. In front of others, Mary's sadness was even more fearful and more desperate. Melville heard her actually ask for a knife, to kill herself in front of Arthur Erskine, her equerry, the day after the wedding, and when he remonstrated with her, the queen threatened to drown herself.[39] It has been suggested that Mary's unhappiness was due to the fact that Bothwell now made some revelation to her about his past – his guilt at Kirk o'Field, for example, or even his father's supposed liaison with her mother Mary of Guise. But Mary Stuart's state of mind was now too immediately disturbed for such past scandals to be able to affect her, and Bothwell's involvement in her husband's death was certainly no surprise to her at this point. The hysterical nature of Mary's reaction shows not only how far she was from feeling any kind of personal love for Bothwell, but also how desperately close her nerves were to the surface and how far her self-control had vanished. As it began to dawn on her that she might have betrayed her whole reputation in order to marry a man who was no more suited than Darnley to advise her, control the nobles, or govern Scotland, her future began to look very black indeed.

Melville reported that Bothwell's beastly and suspicious nature was such that 'not one day passed' during their time together without the queen shedding abundant tears. Maitland told du

Croc a little later that since the day of the queen's marriage there had been no end of tears and lamentations, since Bothwell was furious and jealous if she looked at anyone except him – he accused her of having a pleasure-loving nature, and liking to spend her time in frivolous worldly pursuits, like any other woman.[40] In short there was now no lute-playing, hunting and hawking, as in the early days with Darnley. Even before their marriage, Bothwell's unkindness had led to half a day's quarrel between them. Bothwell's language was said to be so filthy that even Melville was constrained to leave his presence. Gossips in London suggested that Mary suffered tortures of jealousy because Bothwell's former wife Lady Jean still remained installed in his own castle of Crichton. Maitland helped to stir up trouble by telling Mary that Bothwell had written to Jean several letters assuring her that he only regarded Mary as his concubine – Jean was still his only lawful wife. Du Croc took care to pass the story on to the French court, adding spitefully: 'No one in this kingdom is in any doubt but that the Duke (Bothwell) loves his former wife a great deal more than he loves the queen.'[41] In fact property was probably at the bottom of Bothwell's relations with Jean: it is unlikely that he could have turned her out of Crichton, even if he had so wished, since her dowry had redeemed the mortgage, and Jean Bothwell, as we have seen, had a commendable sense of property values.

But Bothwell in his treatment of Mary was less concerned with the niceties of their legal relationship than with the power that it brought him. In their bond of 16th June, the lords announced that Bothwell had kept Mary as the virtual prisoner of his ambition. None of their number had been able to speak to her, even on lawful business, without Bothwell being present; so suspicious had Bothwell become, that he kept the queen's chamber door perpetually guarded by his own men of war. Drury reported on 20th May that the queen's distress was the talk of the court: never, it seemed, had a woman changed so much in appearance in so short a space of time. It was even rumoured that she was suffering from the falling sickness (epilepsy) to explain her deranged behaviour.* The mermaid and the hare were evidently as ill-suited to live together as might be expected of a half-fairy sea creature and a wild animal of the earth.

One of the first tasks the queen and Bothwell had to face after their hasty marriage was that of explaining it away to both the French and English courts. Mary's instructions to the bishop of Dunblane,[43] who was entrusted with the mission to France, and the letter she sent along the same lines to Beaton, have a strongly apologetic note, as though she was all too aware of that unpleasant French proverb, *qui s'excuse, s'accuse.* Apart from her accounts of events leading up to the marriage, already quoted, she stressed her continued loyalty to the Catholic Church – she would not 'leave her religion for him, nor for any man at all' – aware that her actions had once more cast this seriously in doubt. Her instructions emphasized Bothwell's loyal service to the Scottish crown, and glossed over their previous disagreements which she attributed to the jealousy of other nobles. 'As envy follows virtues, and this country is of itself somewhat subject to factions; others began to mislike his proceeding, and so far by reports and misconstructing his doings, went about to put him out of our good grace ...' Then Mary stressed the fact that Bothwell had won over the other nobles to the marriage project – 'He obtained an writing subscribed with all their hands, wherein they not only granted their consent to our marriage with him, but also obliged them to set him forward with their lives and goods.' Finally she described her own helpless and broken spirit, how she felt herself inadequate to deal with the Scottish situation singlehanded – 'this realm being divided in factions as it is, cannot be contained in order, unless our authority be assisted and forthset by the fortification of a man who must take upon his person in the execution of

---

* From this comment Mahon argues that the queen suffered from mild epileptic seizures all her life, citing her dementia, stupor and apathy after Kirk o'Field as signs of temporary post-epileptic insanity. But the evidence of her captivity – when her health was closely observed and recorded – does not confirm the epileptic diagnosis.[42]

justice ... the travail thereof we may no longer sustain in our own person, being already wearied, and almost broken with the frequent uproars and rebellions raised against us since we came in Scotland'. Despite this plea for sympathy in her situation, which has the ring of truth, Mary felt it necessary to outline answers to two possible objections – the lawfulness of the marriage she defends by saying that Bothwell's previous marriage was dissolved, and her failure to bring the nuncio to Scotland she defends by saying rather ingenuously that she had done all she could in this respect, and that if the nuncio had arrived such terrible events might not have happened.

Robert Melville's instructions for breaking the news to Queen Elizabeth ran along very similar lines.[44] The difficult quarrelsome nature of the Scottish people is once more emphasized, as is Mary's personal exhaustion and despair for lack of a husband to support her in this impossible situation. Mary met the principal objection of Elizabeth – that she had married the man suspected of her husband's death – with the point that he had been formally acquitted of the crime by the Scottish Parliament. Despite the fact that Mary accompanied her instructions with a personal and charming letter to Cecil, begging him to help her cause with Elizabeth, neither the English queen nor the French queen allowed themselves to be distracted by Mary's excuses from the patent facts of the case. From the point of view of either France or England, the Scottish queen had totally lost her head in thus allowing herself to be wedded to the disreputable Bothwell. The only real line of defence was after all that which Mary took in her letter to Beaton: 'The event is indeed strange and otherwise nor (we know) you would have looked for. But as it is succeeded, we must take the best of it.'

Ironically enough, if the Scottish situation had not been so factious, if Bothwell had not by the flagrant manner of Darnley's death provided such a convenient handle against himself, if he had understood in any way how to persuade his fellow-nobles into accepting him as consort – as he attempted unsuccessfully to do through the Ainslie bond – he might not have made a bad ruler of the country. The union of Mary and Bothwell might have turned out a marriage of convenience, if not a love match. Bothwell had strength and he had intelligence; as for his tendency to search for violent solutions to problems, he was certainly not alone in possessing this failing in this epoch. He showed reverence for the queen's position if not her person, refusing to cover himself in her presence until she took his cap and put it on. When they rode abroad together, they put up a good public front of content. Bothwell's actions during his five weeks as consort were positively encouraging for the future of the country, were it not for the fact that his fellow-nobles were by now seething in almost open revolt. The machinery of the Privy Council, for example, was overhauled to provide for more regular attendance; a law was passed against bringing false money into Scotland; more important still, on 23rd May the proclamation concerning the religion of the country which Mary had enacted on her first arrival in Scotland in 1561 was re-enacted formally to reassure the troubled minds who had heard false rumours about its validity. It was pointed out that by allowing certain persons to practise their own (Catholic) religion, the queen had intended no violation of the Act. Scotland was still very much officially Protestant. All this was done with the advice of Mary's 'dearest husband, James Duke of Orkney, Earl Bothwell, etc.' Bothwell's own letters to France and England, backing up Mary's explanations of their marriage, revealed a certain native diplomatic ability. To Queen Elizabeth, Bothwell wrote: 'I will thus boldly affirm that, albeit men of greater and birth and estimation might well have been preferred to this room, yet none more careful to see your two Majesties' amity and intelligence continued by all good offices ...' He wrote in the same vein to Charles IX of France; Archbishop Beaton he tactfully requested to excuse him in so far as some of his behaviour might seem rather unceremonious and lacking respect.[45] Such intelligence might have stood Mary in good stead, if she had ever been allowed the time to enjoy it. It was in exchange for his strength and support in the future that Mary had endured the humiliation of her wedding-day to Bothwell.

But the cruelty of fate ensured that she was never allowed the time to enjoy her part of the bargain.

Fast as events had moved before Mary's wedding, the speed only increased after the ceremony. By the end of May the clouds of war were gathering round Bothwell's head with such menace that on 30th May the queen and duke were constrained to summon their people to meet them at Melrose on 15th June, with a view to taking arms. The granting of Tantallon to Morton and Edinburgh Castle to Balfour made neither of them more agreeable to see Bothwell elevated above them. Mary described the genesis of a new conspiracy in Scotland to Nau as follows:[46] 'It may have originated in some secret feuds among the lords of recent date, or possibly from grievances of remoter origin which though long hidden, at last came to scatter their poison on the surface.' What distinguished this new fracas from the Huntly affair, the Chaseabout Raid, the Riccio killing and even the murder of Darnley, was that it now proved convenient to bring in a new dimension of morality, in order to blacken the case against Bothwell, and gloss over the previous commitments of Morton and Maitland. Undoubtedly the hatred of Bothwell and Maitland for each other proved a telling point in the rallying of the nobles against the queen. This animosity was so well known that Maitland was actually rumoured to have been killed by Bothwell at Dunbar. In the end Maitland placed his feelings for Bothwell above his loyalty to Mary, and on 6th June finally left the royal court for the west. He told Cecil that he had been in fear of his life, since Bothwell had tried to kill him in a fit of ungovernable rage in the queen's own presence, and would have succeeded in doing so if Mary had not rushed to Maitland's assistance. Maitland refused to admit that his disappearance at this critical juncture involved any disloyalty. To Cecil he explained smoothly that he had only remained at Mary's side for so long, with so many hazards to his life and honour, because of his ancient affection for the queen. Now he could endure no more.[47]

Many of the conspirators, such as Kirkcaldy, belonged to the old Protestant party of Moray, who had hated Bothwell since Chaseabout days and before. Bothwell had many virulent enemies. After Home and Murray of Tullibardine joined, Tullibardine brought in his brother-in-law Mar, the more inclined to come over because Bothwell had deprived him of Edinburgh Castle. The allegiance of Atholl was the easier to procure because his wife was sister to Maitland's wife Mary Fleming; Morton also dangled the prospect of the marriage of his rich young ward the countess of Angus with Atholl's son before the earl's eyes, although in the end the young lady was married off to Mar's son instead. In this network of allegiances and betrayals the treachery of Sir James Balfour surpassed that of anyone else: for he, the closest involved in the murder of Darnley, who had probably drawn up the Craigmillar bond, and who had been granted the custody of Edinburgh Castle as a reward for his complicity, now secretly treated with the conspirators and agreed to support their cause, on condition that his custody of the castle was confirmed. Yet another bond was made in which Sir James Balfour promised to put Edinburgh Castle at the disposal of the nobles, on the grounds that Bothwell was wickedly keeping their sovereign's person in thrall. A further condition of Balfour's adhesion was a total indemnity for any past crimes he might have committed up to the present moment – which included of course his participation in the murder at Kirk o'Field.

On 6th June, Bothwell took Mary from Holyrood to the castle of Borthwick, a stark twin-towered fifteenth-century fortress set down beneath a low hill in a valley watered by a tributary of the Esk, about twelve miles to the south of Edinburgh. The lord of Borthwick was Bothwell's neighbour and ally: from the battlements of Borthwick, the tip of Bothwell's own castle of Crichton, only two miles away, could be discerned. Mary evidently considered her stay would be tranquil enough, for the Demoiselle de Courcelles specially brought down the royal silver hand-basin for the queen to use while she was there.[48] Her hopes were disappointed. Borthwick was surrounded by the insurgents. Bothwell, with his military knowledge, realized that it was ill-situated to withstand a siege, and therefore slipped away through a postern gate, with only one companion, the son of the laird of Crookston. The boy was captured, but Bothwell galloped clean away, leaving Mary to hold the castle. The besiegers called up to the queen to abandon her husband and accompany them back to Edinburgh. When she proudly refused, they shouted insults up to the steep and forbidding walls, of a nature 'too evil and unseemly to be told', wrote Drury in a letter to London, as he described the new plight of 'this poor princess'.[49] The poor princess had not, however, lost all her old spirit. She sent two messengers to Huntly for help, both of whom fell into Morton's hands. The besiegers felt unable to attack without the arrival of Mar and Lindsay, and decided to return to Edinburgh. In the meantime Mary disguised herself as a man, and escaped out of the castle by night to the nearby Black Castle at Cakemuir, which belonged to the Wauchopes, also neighbours and adherents of Bothwell. Here she met Bothwell, and together they made their way to Dunbar, by Fala, skirting the Lammermuir hills to the north to avoid detection.

It was at Dunbar that the ultimate treachery of Balfour revealed itself: for it was his message to the queen that she would do better to return to Edinburgh, where the guns of the castle, under his command, would support her, which brought her out of this comparatively safe place, before the royal forces had mustered to anything like a secure strength. In answer to this reassuring summons, Mary and Bothwell now issued forth from Dunbar, with 200 hagbutters (musketeers), sixty cavalrymen, and only three field guns taken from the castle itself. All the queen's belongings and wardrobe had been left behind in Edinburgh or at Borthwick from which she had escaped in her male disguise; she was now dressed in clothes hastily borrowed at Dunbar: a short red petticoat, a muffler, velvet hat and sleeves tied with bows, such as the women of Edinburgh wore. Her charm and dignity were undiminished by her costume: it was her reputation which no longer had its pristine purity in the minds of her ordinary subjects and, in a tragic phrase, as the royal cortège passed, 'the people did not join as was expected'. By the time the queen reached Haddington she had about 600 horses – the faithful Seton had joined her, but Lord John Hamilton and Fleming did not appear; as they debated the best route to take, Huntly and the rest of the Hamiltons stayed, either dispiritedly or indecisively, within Edinburgh Castle. Bothwell found himself relying on the inferior contingents of border lairds such as Ormiston, Langton, Waughton, Wedderburn and Bass. At Gladsmuir, those royal supporters to be seen were treated to a proclamation saying that the conspirators, under the pretext of saving the life of Prince James, were trying to dethrone the queen, in order that they might rule in their own fashion. Queen Mary was therefore compelled to take up arms, and those faithful subjects who had come to her assistance would be rewarded with the lands and the possessions of the rebels. The army then marched on to Leith, and reached Prestonpans, where they spent the night. Mary and Bothwell passed the night – their last together – at the palace of Seton, the house which Mary had loved so long and happily in her six years in Scotland.

At 2 a.m. on the Sunday morning, 15th June, 1567, the confederate lords marched out of Edinburgh towards Musselburgh. In the van of their procession was borne a white banner showing a green tree, with the corpse of Darnley lying underneath it, and his infant son kneeling before him, with the legend: 'Judge and avenge my cause, O Lord'. Otherwise the rebel lords were each marked by the banner of their family. A few hours later, the royal army under Bothwell also moved out, and took up a commanding position on Carberry Hill. About eight miles east of Edinburgh, above their heads flew not family banners, but a series of banners bearing in each case the cross of St Andrew; and the position of the queen herself was marked by the solitary rampant red lion of Scotland. These nobles now took up their position on a hill opposite – Morton and Home with the cavalry, and behind them, Atholl, Mar, Glencairn, Lindsay and Ruthven with the main body of troops. It was a blazing hot day. Both parties suffered from thirst although by one account the lords had the advantage of some wine to sustain them. In between these two armies, neither of them exactly certain as to how they should proceed, the queen lacking troops, and the nobles lacking authority, there appeared the figure of du Croc, the French ambassador, who had panted out from Edinburgh after the insurgents.[50]

Du Croc was now deputed by the rebels to beg Mary to abandon Bothwell, at which they were to restore her to her former position, while they themselves would continue to be her loyal subjects. This Mary absolutely and furiously declined to do. She pointed out in a passion of indignation to du Croc that these same lords had signed a bond recommending marriage with the very man they were now opposing vehemently – 'It was by them that Bothwell had been promoted' she kept repeating. By her account, Mary had no inkling at this point that the lords intended to charge Bothwell with the murder of Darnley, but certainly she felt absolutely no temptation to desert Bothwell. In the first place, Bothwell, with all his faults, had shown himself loyal to her throughout her adversities and his own, and was pledged to her support; she felt no such confidence about the behaviour of men of the calibre of Morton, Lindsay and Ruthven. Secondly, the queen, who miscarried a child at Lochleven in the middle of July, must by now have realized herself to be pregnant by Bothwell. The fact could not fail to seal their union in the mind of such a philoprogenitive woman. A single child was scarcely enough to ensure the royal succession of Scotland – or England – as history had all too often proved: it was no coincidence that Mary's marriage contract to Bothwell had specifically stated one of the objects of the match to be 'that of her royal person succession might be produced'.[51]

As Mary refused to relinquish Bothwell, both sides now gave themselves up to a series of chivalric parleys, reminiscent of medieval warfare, in which challenges to personal combat were given and taken with great enthusiasm, but no actual battles took place. The first challenge came from the lords, who probably thus hoped to delay matters, until their reinforcements reached them. Bothwell, whom du Croc described as being in high spirits – 'a great Captain, speaking with undaunted confidence, and leading his army gaily and skilfully ... he could not count on half his men, and yet was not dismayed' – accepted the challenge and rode out in front of the troops, sending a herald forward. James Murray of Purdovis was the first to step forward, but the queen refused to tolerate the encounter, on the grounds that his rank was so much inferior to that of the duke. Bothwell then indicated the sly Morton as a suitable recipient of his challenge. Morton characteristically delegated the job to the spirited Lindsay, who took off his armour and rested his limbs in preparation for the combat. Morton then clasped round his waist the great sword which had once belonged to his ancestor Archibald Bell-the-Cat. But even as these parleyings and preparations were proceeding, the royal troops were melting away, as can be seen in the contemporary sketch of the battlefield. This was probably the intention of the rebels, for in the end, despite these splendid preparations, no one ever did come forward to meet Bothwell's challenge. Like an ancient hero he stood alone while his troops vanished. It was too late now to attack his enemies up hill, and his men were insufficient. There was no sign of the Hamiltons, who it was hoped might reinforce them.

At evening the rebels decided to press their advantage with a new parley. Atholl and Maitland both lacked the courage to confront the queen they had betrayed, but Kirkcaldy rode forward. Bothwell's spirits were very far from being either broken or cowed, but as a good general he was aware that the royal party suffered from a striking lack of troops. It would be highly unwise to choose this moment to challenge the lords, when there was a possibility of rallying much more support to Mary's side in other parts of the country. He therefore suggested to Mary that they should retreat to Dunbar: first of all the castle had a strong, virtually impregnable position on the sea; secondly it would serve as a rallying-point for new supplies of royalists. But Mary could not believe that the situation was so desperate. She still believed in Kirkcaldy's honour. She considered that the wisest course for her to pursue in the interests of peace and the avoidance of bloodshed was to accept a safe-conduct for

Bothwell, and trust herself to the confederate lords, whom she now apparently thought would investigate everything anew by Parliament. Kirkcaldy assured her that the crown as such was not being attacked; afterwards Mary told Nau that both Maitland and Atholl had assured her privately that they were not with the rebels at heart.[52] Bothwell, it was agreed, would gallop off to Dunbar, either to raise further troops, or to await parliamentary developments in the capital. With renewed trust in her nobles, Mary bade farewell to the man for whom she had sacrificed so much in terms of honour and reputation. They embraced in full view of both armies. It was at this point that Bothwell entrusted to Mary the bond signed at Craigmillar, which gave her the proof of Morton's and Maitland's complicity in the murder; perhaps because he had been raised among them he had less optimism than his wife about her future at the hands of the rebels. At sunset Bothwell mounted his charger, and after five weeks of power galloped away down the road of Dunbar. It was the last sight Mary was ever to have of him.

The queen of Scots was now thoroughly alone. And her entry into the camp of the rebels immediately and rudely jolted her confidence in the love which she still believed her subjects bore for her. Here was no enthusiastic reception, no cheers, no protestations of devotion. On the contrary, the soldiers shouted crude insults at her. The queen's spirit still held. She said loudly and openly to Morton: 'How is this, my lord Morton? I am told that all this is done in order to get justice against the king's murderers. I am told also that you are one of the chief of them.'[53] Morton slunk away. But Mary Stuart needed all her courage to endure the ordeal before her, for which she seems to have been ill-prepared. She, who all her life had been greeted publicly with adulation and enthusiasm, now heard the soldiers shout, 'Burn her, burn the whore, she is not worthy to live,' as they conveyed her along the road into Edinburgh. 'Kill her, drown her!' they cried. Close to Mary's side rode Drumlanrig and Cessford, two notorious young thugs, who joined their insults to the soldiers' as they rode. Amazed, almost stunned, the queen allowed tears of shock and humiliation to pour down her cheeks, as she rode forward in the clothes she had acquired at Dunbar – now 'all spoiled with clay and dirt'. For the first time she began to realize what the effect had been on the ordinary people of Scotland – the people who had once loved her – of her reckless action in marrying her husband's assassin, and of those weeks of propaganda by the enemies of Bothwell. To them she was now no longer their young and beautiful queen, but an adulteress – and an adulteress who had subsequently become the willing bride of a murderer.

In Edinburgh, the queen was not taken to either of her own residences, Holyrood or Edinburgh Castle, but to the house of the laird of Craigmillar, the provost of Edinburgh, who was Maitland's brother-in-law. The nobles sat down to a hearty supper, but the queen retreated in a daze of horror at her experiences into her bedroom – even here, however, she could not find peace, since the guards insisted on remaining with her inside the room, so that she could not even undress. Mary now lay down on the bed, deprived of any furniture or bedding proper to her station as a queen, still in the red petticoat in which she had come from Dunbar, and gave herself up to the wastes of despair. There seemed no hope, and certainly no honour in Scotland, since the nobles, to whom she had freely surrendered, now held her a humiliated and unconsidered captive. Looking out of her window, she caught sight of Maitland – Maitland of Lethington who had risen so high in her favours, Maitland, her earliest counsellor, Maitland, her secretary, 'her Lethington' who owed so much to her for kindnesses in the past. In a piteous voice, and through her tears, she cried out the name; she called him: 'Lethington, Lethington.'[14] But Maitland pulled his hat over his ears and pretended not to hear her. In the meantime that cruel white banner was stationed in front of her window, with its corpse and its legend, which had accompanied her all the way to Edinburgh, the first thing to meet her impassioned gaze.

By the next day Mary's self-control had utterly collapsed. She came to the window and cried out to the people that she was being kept in prison by her subjects who had betrayed her. The sight of her brought about rioting outside and more mockery and more insults. The lords pulled her back, saying that shots might be fired, and that they could not guarantee her safety. But before they did so, many of her subjects had seen the distraught woman, as she showed herself at the open window – her hair hanging down about her face, her clothes torn open so that the upper half of her body was almost bare, her beauty ravaged, her courage gone." Where now was the exquisite princess who had fascinated the French court and half Europe, the '*belle et plus que belle*' of Ronsard's poetry, in this wretched, near demented creature hanging out of the window of an Edinburgh prison, half naked, her bosom exposed, shrieking out that she had been betrayed? The people of Edinburgh, their innate decency overcoming their moral disapproval, were shocked into pity and compassion at the sight. It was four weeks since Mary's marriage to Bothwell, and not quite two years since her boldly triumphant marriage to Darnley, attended by all the panoply of the Scottish court. This was the nadir of Mary Stuart.

CHAPTER EIGHTEEN
Lochleven

⁓

'How the Mouse for a pleasure done to her by the
Lion, after that, the Lion being bound with a cord, the
Mouse chewed the cord, and let the Lion loose....'
Aesop's fable of the mouse and the lion, quoted in the deposition
of a servant after Queen Mary's escape from Lochleven

The confederate lords were aware that they were on
extremely delicate ground with regard to the queen's
imprisonment, since this imprisonment had followed ruth-
lessly on her own voluntary surrender in the interest of civil
peace. Mary herself had genuinely, if naïvely, expected a parliamentary investigation into the murder of Darnley to follow
her surrender. Under these circumstances, the lords decided that
it would be too dangerous to keep the queen in ward in
Edinburgh itself. The people of the city regarded the queen's
wretched state with sad astonishment: it would certainly be
easier to keep their moral disapproval of her behaviour at fever-
point during her absence, when rumours of her depravity could
be spread without fear of contradiction. But even *in extremis*
Mary retained enough of her former decisiveness to send a
message to the captain of Edinburgh Castle, begging him to
keep 'a good heart' towards her, and to preserve the fortress
from the rebel lords. There is no proof that Mary wrote to
Bothwell on the night of her arrival swearing to be true to him:
Melville believed the story was invented by the lords themselves
to lend colour to the theory of the queen's infatuation;¹ in any
case no such letter has ever been found. The queen did succeed

in having an interview with Maitland on Monday evening (she told Nau that, in the course of it, he was never able to meet her eyes) in which she continued to demand a full inquiry into the circumstances of the late king's death.² It was just this inquiry which Morton, Maitland and Balfour in particular had good reason to fear, and against the possibility of which they were so determinedly blackening the name of their former colleague Bothwell. All things considered, it was clearly in their interests to remove the queen as fast as possible to some secure prison, where she could no longer make these inconvenient demands, or if she did so, her utterances need not necessarily be reported accurately beyond the bounds of the four walls which would confine her.

On the Monday evening, therefore, the queen found herself being taken down to her own palace of Holyrood, where she was reunited with her own women including Mary Seton and Mary Livingston (Sempill). Some supper was prepared for her. This was the first meal she had eaten since before her surrender at Carberry Hill, for she had been at first too upset, and later too frightened by the idea of poison, to eat anything while she was in the provost's house. Morton stood behind her chair while she ate. In the middle of the supper he sent a message to find out if the horses were ready and, on hearing that they were, told the queen to leave her meal and get ready to ride on horseback. At this point, Mary had some vague idea that she was being taken to Stirling Castle, to join her son. She was not allowed to take any of her ladies-in-waiting with her, but only two *femmes-de-chambre*; nor was she allowed to take any clothes, not even a nightdress or linen. At this news, the women around her set up a great wailing. Against the background of this melancholy sound and under cover of darkness, the queen was once more conducted out of her palace.

Mary found herself being taken at great speed not to Stirling, but fifty miles north, to Kinross-shire. The two lords whom she had most reason to fear for their previous boorish conduct to her – Ruthven and Lindsay – were put in charge over her. Still scarcely able to credit what was happening to her, Mary had got as far as Leith, which was posted full of soldiers, when a rumour reached her that the Hamiltons were going to mount a rescue attempt. The queen tried to slow down the pace of her horse, but the gesture was in vain, since her escorts whipped it on. Late at night Mary reached the vast waters of Lochleven. Here, on one of the four islands in the middle of the loch, lay the dour castle of Sir William Douglas. Douglas was a most trustworthy jailer from the point of view of the lords: he was the half-brother of Moray, being the son of Moray's mother Margaret Erskine by her legal husband Robert Douglas; he was the nephew of the earl of Mar, Margaret Erskine's brother; he was cousin and heir presumptive to Morton. The lords could certainly rely on his interests being bonded to theirs. The queen was now rowed across the bleak waters of the lake. On arrival she was conducted quickly and unceremoniously to the laird's room; it had in no way been prepared for her visit, and lacked any sort of furniture, equipment or even bed suitable to her rank and condition. Mary sank once more into a stupor in which sickness, aggravated by pregnancy, despair and exhaustion, all played a part. She remained in this semi-coma for a fortnight, neither speaking to anyone nor, as she remembered afterwards, eating or drinking, until many of those within the house actually thought she would die.

Beyond the laird himself, the inmates of Lochleven consisted of his mother Lady Margaret – 'the old lady' as she was known – who as the mother of the bastard Moray by Mary's own father, James v, was said to bear a natural, if illogical, grudge against the queen for occupying the throne from which fate had debarred her own son. Also within the castle was one of the old lady's younger sons, George Douglas who was nicknamed 'pretty Geordie', a handsome and dashing young man, very unlike his half-brother Moray both in appearance and in the romanticism of his character. Mary had visited the castle itself previously under happier auspices, using it as a centre from which to hunt in Kinross-shire: it was here in its great hall that she had debated with Knox in the spring of 1563. But by nature, Lochleven was indeed more suited to be a prison than a pleasure haunt.* In the sixteenth century, the island on which it stood was so small that it hardly extended beyond the walls and garden of the fortress – the present-day slightly larger island being the result of a considerable fall in the water level of the lake in the last century. Its dominating, square main tower, from which an excellent view of the shore was to be obtained, stuck up out of the lake like a signpost pointing to its inviolability. This tower had been built in the late fourteenth century, and contained five storeys, with the entrance only on the second floor; in this tower the laird and his family lived. The castle also contained another round tower, built in the corner of the courtyard, and here the queen was eventually incarcerated, on the grounds that this would make it more difficult for her to signal to the shore. The lake itself, then twelve miles across, was a bleak place even in August, with the Lomond hills lowering over it, and the flat grey waters punctuated only by the occasional dark trees of the islands; during the winter, the winds and rain would sweep across the lake and make it a desolate place indeed. It was certainly a prison from which escape would prove a virtual impossibility without connivance from the inside.

On 16th June the warrant for the queen's imprisonment was signed by nine lords including Morton, Glencairn and Home, who only eight weeks before had put their signatures to the Ainslie bond supporting the Bothwell marriage. The lords left in power in Edinburgh – for Lindsay and Ruthven remained at Lochleven to guard the queen – like robber barons, did not fail to take possession of the queen's silver plate, jewels and other goods which she had involuntarily left behind her. Calderwood wrote that the lords went through her belongings, as well as overthrowing the religious furnishings of her private chapel, as soon as she was gone to her prison. Mary herself told Nau that the silver and furniture and her multitudinous wardrobe were handed over to the lords by the treachery of one of her Italian servants – who probably felt himself unable to resist the new

---

* Later the earl of Northumberland was also imprisoned there by Morton when he fled to Scotland in 1570 after the failure of the northern rebellion.

powers in the land. Certainly by 10th July arrangements were made for twenty-seven pieces of the queen's plate to be delivered over by her chamberlain, Servais de Condé, to be melted down into silver coin.[3] In view of the fact that the previous bond of the rebel lords had expressly referred to their intention of releasing Mary from the thraldom of Bothwell, and restoring her to liberty to rule as before, it was small wonder that the queen now felt herself totally betrayed – being in closer thraldom than ever, with her belongings sequestrated and her liberty far more grievously curtailed than it had ever been in the days of her marriage to Bothwell.

In the meantime Bothwell himself was still at liberty. From Carberry Hill he had gone to Dunbar, but on hearing of the queen's imprisonment, he sallied forth from the castle, and during his remaining two months within the bounds of Scotland attempted with great energy and singlemindedness to raise some sort of support for her. At first he enjoyed a certain success, with the Hamiltons at Linlithgow, and then at Dumbarton which Lord Fleming still held for the queen; Argyll and Boyd actually rejoined the royal cause, showing once more the chameleon-like character of Scottish family allegiances. The speed of Bothwell's movements defied capture by the lords, even after 1000 crowns was offered for his apprehension as a result of the protests of the Assembly of the General Kirk; he was able to make a quick visit to the borders, where he hoped to be able to galvanize his family adherents.

He was now called to the Tolbooth officially to answer for murdering Darnley, kidnapping the queen, and making her promise to marry him: having ignored the statutory three weeks' notice to appear, Bothwell was formally declared an outlaw and a rebel, with his titles, offices and dignities forfeit. The outlawry cracked the somewhat weak nerves of the royalist party, who feared for their own possessions: Seton and Fleming withdrew from the connection; Huntly, whom Bothwell visited at Strathbogie, discerned how little backing Bothwell now had in the Lowlands and lost heart at the idea of raising the Highlands; his sister Jean Bothwell shortly afterwards abandoned the castle of Crichton and returned to her mother at Strathbogie, pausing on the way to inform the countess of Moray that she wished to have nothing more to do with her outlawed ex-husband. With the queen immured silently at Lochleven, the royalist party crumbled away, despite all Bothwell's energetic foraging for support from one end of Scotland to the other. Bothwell was eventually compelled to withdraw to the palace of his kinsman, the bishop of Moray, at Spynie in the far north. Here he was betrayed to his enemies by the bishop's illegitimate sons, but even so, managed to make his way to the Orkneys, where as their duke, and also as lord high admiral of Scotland, he hoped either to rally support once more by sea, or at least to continue to elude capture.

Unlike Mary herself, the lords now took care to pursue with relentless ferocity those of Bothwell's underlings who had been involved in the murder of Darnley. This process, which continued throughout the rest of the year, was intended to distract public attention from the complicity of the new governors of Scotland, Morton, Balfour and Maitland, in the crime. William Blackadder – he who maintained he had merely run out of a nearby tavern when he heard the explosion at Kirk o'Field – was the first to be captured; he was hanged, drawn and quartered, and his limbs posted up on the gates of the leading burghs of Scotland. William Powrie, who had been in charge of transporting that suspiciously small amount of gunpowder through the streets of Edinburgh, was caught; under threat of torture he provided two separate depositions, contradicting each other in many respects, and he was finally hanged. Bastian and Francisco Busso were imprisoned in the Tolbooth. Another of Bothwell's men, John Spens, was given his life, in return for handing over the coffers full of his master's money. John Hepburn and John Hay of Tallo were caught and executed before the turn of the year; in each case they made self-incriminatory depositions before the end. It was another year before the lords managed to lay their hands on 'French' Paris – he who described how he had been kicked and bullied by Bothwell into participation in the murder; by this time Mary was in an English prison and

Moray securely installed as regent; Paris's deposition therefore proved the most fruitfully damning of them all. But when Cecil sent a request from London that Paris should be sent down for cross-examination, the page was promptly hanged in Scotland. Black Ormiston was hanged in 1573, after making a highly dubious death-bed confession to a priest. Pat Wilson and Hob Ormiston were never caught.

The most dramatic capture, from the point of view of the future, was that of the tailor, George Dalgleish, he who had watched Bothwell while he changed his carnival clothes to a cloak of 'sad English cloth'; his seizure was afterwards said to have marked the first appearance of those most debatable of all controversial documents – the Casket Letters. The alleged circumstances of their discovery were not made public until eighteen months later, at the Conference of Westminster in December 1568, in a declaration given by Morton. But it is worth giving the declaration's story in detail here, at the moment in history at which these events were afterwards said to have taken place, in order to see how far this later declaration fits in with the happenings of the time. The story of Dalgleish's apprehension was given by Morton as follows.[4] On 17th June Morton was dining with Maitland in Edinburgh Castle when a spy reported to them secretly that Dalgleish was known to have come into the castle from Dunbar, with the parson of Oldamstocks. Archibald Douglas was sent to catch the clergyman, but Dalgleish himself had almost escaped when his whereabouts were betrayed. Dalgleish protested that he had only arrived on a simple errand to fetch his master's clothing, but after being threatened by torture he changed his story, and according to Morton's statement, led his interrogators to a house in the Potterow where he produced from under his bed a silver casket. This was the first appearance of the famous silver casket in which the Casket Letters were said to have been discovered, and it will be seen how dubious the circumstances of its discovery were from the first, with the threat of torture playing a sinister role. Morton's declaration went on to state how on 20th June he had the casket formally opened; the papers within it were presumably read, but no note was taken of their contents, beyond the fact that the documents pertained to Bothwell. There was absolutely no mention of the queen, or of letters in her handwriting. Morton sealed up the casket again and took it into his own possession, where it remained.

The strange fact about this declaration, and the whole affair of George Dalgleish's capture, was that absolutely no mention was made of these remarkable facts at the time. According to Morton's December 1568 statement, the lords were from 20th June, 1567 onwards in full possession of the vital evidence of the Casket Letters; but although these letters thoroughly incriminated Mary in Darnley's murder, it was remarkable that the lords still made no mention of her guilt three weeks later when they made a series of accusations against Bothwell at the Tolbooth. As has been seen, throughout the summer of 1567, the blame for Mary's downfall was heaped by the lords on Bothwell; the queen's crime was considered to be her refusal to abandon him; there was no suggestion that she had participated personally in Darnley's death. Yet the lords were nothing if not anxious to retain the queen in her prison at Lochleven; it seems inconceivable that they should not have used this damning evidence against her at this point, if indeed they possessed it. More extraordinary still, if Morton's declaration was to be believed, was the matter of George Dalgleish's deposition.[5] The unfortunate tailor, although later described as so instrumental in its discovery, was asked no questions at the time about the silver casket, nor cross-questioned in any way about its contents. His interrogators concentrated entirely on the subject of Darnley's murder. By the time the subject of the Casket Letters was raised in England, eighteen months later, George Dalgleish had long since been executed.

It was hardly likely that such untoward events in Scotland would pass unnoticed or undigested in England and France. Queen Elizabeth's first reaction was strong distaste for such unmannerly treatment of queens, and her second characteristic reaction was to see what advantage could be obtained from the situation for England. She sent Throckmorton north to parley with the lords, and also to see if there would be a possibility of obtaining the wardship of the little Prince James whom she now suggested could be brought up conveniently in England by his grandmother the countess of Lennox, conveniently forgetting that day when Elizabeth had flung her into the Tower out of rage at the marriage of James's parents. The French were animated with the same happy idea of bringing up the young prince; the discussions over his welfare were strongly reminiscent of the arguments over Mary's own custody during her infancy. Throckmorton reached Edinburgh before the middle of July; his letters back to London provide a valuable insight into the state of affairs in the Scottish capital, since he brought the fresh mind of an outsider to his commentary. It is more difficult to assess Mary's own state of mind during the crucial early weeks of her captivity: none of her own letters from this period has survived, with the exception of two or three smuggled out of the island towards the end of her stay there; it is more than probable that the strict conditions of her confinement simply did not permit her to write them. The narrative of her secretary, Nau, dictated by the queen while in captivity in England, is the only guide extant to her personal feelings, and it suffers from the obvious disadvantage of having been written many years after the events in question took place, by one who had not himself been present on the island.

The first fortnight of Mary's incarceration was an agonizing experience, not only on account of her wretched health. Throckmorton heard that the queen was kept 'very straightly'; the lords did not intend that there should be any dramatic moonlight flittings from Lochleven. After a fortnight her total nervous collapse seems to have drawn to an end; Drury heard from Berwick that she was 'better digesting' her captivity, and could even take a little exercise. Bedford heard about three weeks later that her health was improving.[6] With the return of her strength, some of her personal magnetism seemed also to be exerting itself, since Lord Ruthven, son of that Lord Ruthven who had appeared like a vengeful ghost at the murder of Riccio, was considered by his colleagues to be falling under her spell, and was removed from his post. According to the queen's own account,[7] he made advances to her, throwing himself on his knees near her bed, promising that he would free her if only she would love him. From the amorous behaviour of this former enemy of Mary's can be deduced either the glamorous effect of her personal presence or, more cynically, the quickness of Ruthven's wits. He may have realized already that the departure of Bothwell made the queen once more potentially marriageable, with all the advantages likely to ensue from such a match.

The queen still absolutely refused to hear of divorcing Bothwell: her reasons for this, as before Carberry Hill, were twofold. Her pregnancy by Bothwell was now thoroughly established in her own mind, and she feared more than ever to compromise the legitimacy of her unborn child; secondly, her extreme suspicion of the intention of the lords towards her own person had only been deepened by their behaviour since Carberry Hill. Although Maitland told her that if she agreed to divorce Bothwell she would be restored to liberty and freedom, Queen Mary must have doubted whether the lords would have carried out their part of the bargain. Why should the same men who had planned to ward her in Stirling Castle eighteen months before have agreed to release her now, even if she put away Bothwell as they suggested? Her return could not fail to threaten their newly acquired power, as well as bringing out into the open once more the events leading up to the death of Darnley. Had the lords really wished to re-establish her, they had an excellent opportunity after Carberry Hill, instead of which they locked her up on Lochleven. The existence of the infant Prince James, held at Stirling Castle under the governorship of the earl of Mar, one of the principal confederate lords, which had once seemed to promise so much for Mary's future, now told as strongly against her. A long royal minority, with a series of noble regents, was traditionally regarded by the Scottish aristocracy as a time for aggrandizement. It should be borne in mind that on 8th December, 1567 Mary herself was approaching her twenty-fifth birthday, on which date it was possible by custom for a sovereign to call back wardships and properties given out during his or her own minority. To the Scottish nobility, the rule of the thirteen-month-old James was an infinitely preferable prospect to that of his twenty-five-year-old mother, whether she divorced Bothwell or not.

It is noticeable that Throckmorton was deeply shocked by the brutal attitude of the Scots towards their sovereign on his arrival from England. He was genuinely convinced that her life was in danger, and believed that it was his appearance and intervention which actually saved her; otherwise she too might have died as violently as Riccio and her husband. The common people too he found to be highly hostile to their queen, especially the women: Tullibardine took the opportunity of explaining to him that Mary would be in danger of death if they released her. But of course this attitude was only increased by the propaganda of the nobles in her enforced absence: what especially shocked Throckmorton was to find that noble families like the Hamiltons, who had a vested interest in the succession, were ready to join the lords if Mary died, and on 18th July he wrote to England that the Hamiltons would concur with the confederate lords in all things, 'yea, in any extremity against the Queen', as long as they were assured that Darnley's younger brother, Charles, would not be preferred in the Scottish succession over them, if Prince James died.[8] On 7th August Murray of Tullibardine went as far as to tell Throckmorton that the Hamiltons, Argyll, Huntly and others in their groups only refrained from joining the confederates because they had so inconveniently allowed the queen to live. The Hamiltons were ambitious enough to see how their chances of succession were greatly improved with the disappearance of Mary; there was now only the little king to be eliminated 'and then we are home'.[9] The behaviour of Maitland was as before highly ambivalent: Throckmorton accused him also of threatening the queen's life, and pointed out to him that her death, apart from being an outrage, would only clear the way for the Hamiltons; Maitland in turn accused Throckmorton of having liberty in his mouth but not in his heart. At all events, by 9th August Throckmorton was convinced that his intervention had saved the Scottish queen's life and that 'this woefull Queen' would not now die except by an accident, although he could not forbear from commenting, when he heard of the new agreement between the lords and the Hamiltons, that he hoped their accord would not be like that of Herod and Pilate who agreed to put Christ to death.[10]

On one point the lords were adamant: Throckmorton should not visit the queen personally, despite his many requests to do so. He was thus compelled to depend on their own bulletin as to her state of mind. They assured him that Mary was still madly infatuated with Bothwell, and said in addition that she would be willing to abandon her kingdom for him and live like a simple damsel (a statement for which there was no other confirmation and on which Mary's subsequent career casts considerable doubt). On 16th July Throckmorton heard that the queen was in great fear of her life, and had said to some of the lords about her that she would be well contented to live in a close nunnery in France or with her grandmother, Antoinette of Guise.[11] These sentiments, if indeed Mary expressed them, must be regarded as coming out of the depths of her despair and physical weakness. More importance can be attached to her first communication to Throckmorton, which he reported on 18th July, when she sent word that she would in no way consent to a divorce from Bothwell 'giving this reason, that taking herself to be seven weeks gone with child, by renouncing him she should acknowledge herself to be with child of a bastard and forfeit her honour'.[12] It was now some eight weeks since the queen's marriage to Bothwell: in her letter she therefore suggests that the baby had been conceived subsequent to the marriage. But at some date before 24th July, no doubt as a result of privations and stress, she miscarried the child, and according to Nau, who inserted the phrase very carefully as an afterthought on the page, found herself to have been bearing '*deux enfants*'.[13] If the twins had been conceived at Dunbar, on or about 24th April, they were about three months old at the moment of miscarriage, and the double gestation would have been easily recognizable. Even at eight weeks, the foetus is just over one inch in length; but at twelve to thirteen weeks, the foetus is three and a half inches long, which would have made the recognition of '*deux enfants*' perfectly possible. On balance of probabilities, it seems likely therefore that the queen conceived the twins at Dunbar at the end of April, and that by Carberry Hill, at least, if not earlier, knew for certain that she was pregnant by Bothwell; uncertainty on the subject could have been a factor in hastening on her actual wedding date in May.

What is virtually impossible is the suggestion, sometimes made since by historians, that the queen could have conceived twins by Bothwell in January before Darnley's death, and carried them in complete secrecy, without the faintest contemporary report of her pregnancy, throughout the vital months following the Kirk o'Field tragedy. It was mid-June before Bedford heard that the queen was pregnant; although Guzman, the Spanish ambassador in London, wrote to Philip II on 21st June, saying that the Scottish queen was five *months* pregnant,[14] he probably mistook five months for five weeks, since there is no reference of any sort through March, April and May to the royal pregnancy, which would have been becoming rapidly more apparent as the queen's figure changed. This was an age in which such facts were speedily known by the accurate news service of servants' gossip: as a girl queen in France, Mary's prospects of becoming a mother had been intimately assessed by the ambassadors at the court. Randolph's extraordinarily early reports of Mary's pregnancy with James in the autumn of 1565 will be recalled – he heard the first rumours of her condition about five weeks after conception, giving as his reference such 'tokens … annexed to the kind of them that are in that case'.[15] The spring months following the Kirk o'Field tragedy were among the most critical of Mary's existence, in which her every word and action were watched, checked and reported: how inconceivable is it then that an event of such moment as her growing pregnancy outside the bonds of marriage should have passed quite unnoticed until the sixth month, by observers who would certainly have grasped joyfully at such a convenient weapon to destroy, if not Mary, at least Bothwell, the child's father.*

The queen's miscarriage proved a turning-point in her attitude to Bothwell, for it removed one important obstacle in the way of divorce. By 5th August Throckmorton no longer despaired of securing her consent to the divorce, as he had done pre-viously.[17] It has occasionally been supposed that Mary did not in reality miscarry the child, but merely concealed her pregnancy; according to this legend, she gave birth to the baby – a daughter – in the following February; the little girl was smuggled away to France and there grew up as a nun in the convent of Notre Dame de Soissons. Alas, nothing would have been more impracticable than for the Scottish queen to have concealed her condition in the confined space of Lochleven, quite apart from the fact that there is no contemporary evidence to back up the story.† It is also highly unlikely that Mary would have ignored the continued existence of such a daughter – next heiress after James to the Scottish and English thrones – in the later years of her captivity when she quarrelled with her son. Such a daughter could have been introduced with effect into her last testaments.

* Dan McKenzie in his short article on the subject, 'The Obstetric History of Mary Queen of Scots at Lochleven', *Caledonian Medical Journal*, suggests that the time of conception might be 'about the time of Darnley's murder' (9th February) on the evidence of Guzman, although he does not make any suggestion as to how the queen concealed all signs of her condition until mid-June. Professor Donaldson, although giving McKenzie as a reference, goes further and suggests that Mary 'knew or feared' she was pregnant on 20th January, when she went from Edinburgh to Glasgow to fetch back Darnley, and this provided her with the motive for the reconciliation.[16] This of course suggests a conception date of early January, which makes her concealment of her condition until six months later still more remarkable.
† The story was first given credence in the edition of the memoirs of Castelnau, with notes by Le Laboureur, written in 1659, and published in 1731; Le Laboureur added the information in a footnote.[18] On the grounds that Le Laboureur occupied a post of confidence at the court of France as counsellor and almoner of the king, and therefore might have special access to this sort of information, Lingard accepted his story, as did Prince Labanoff, in his edition of the letters of Mary Queen of Scots. The whole story has been the subject of a historical novel – *Unknown to History* by Charlotte M. Yonge – in which sphere it rightly belongs.

It was while the queen was lying in bed after her miscarriage, by her own account 'in a state of great weakness' having lost a great deal of blood, and scarcely able to move, that Lindsay came to her and told her that he had been instructed to make her sign certain letters for the resignation of her crown. Mary now believed herself once more to be in great personal danger, on this tiny island, in the midst of an enormous lake, whose waters could claim any victim silently without the circumstances of their death being ever properly known. Despite her fears the queen was outraged at the monstrousness of the request, and continued to demand that she should be taken in front of her Estates for the parliamentary inquiry which had been promised to her; but Lindsay's rough words on the subject, that she had better sign, for if she did not she would simply compel them to cut her throat, however unwilling they might be to do so, only convinced her further of her own personal danger. She had no allies to assist her, except the two *femmes-de-chambre* she had been allowed to bring from Holyrood. In a state of terror and despair, she declared that she refused to leave the house. When Lindsay threatened her with forcible removal she replied that she would have to be dragged out by the hairs of her head.

It was at this point that Robert Melville hinted to Mary that by no means every member of the Douglas family was as hostile to her as the laird of Lochleven himself: his brother, for example, the young debonair George Douglas, was already showing himself susceptible to the charms of the beautiful if unfortunate prisoner: he showed his sympathies by persuading the servants of the house to rise up in rebellion at the project of her removal. But from the actual signing of the letters of resignation there was no escape. Mary told Nau later that Throckmorton had managed to smuggle her a note in the scabbard of a sword, telling her to sign to save her own life, as something so clearly signed under duress could never afterwards be held against her.[19] Certainly if duress was ever held to affect questions of legality there could be no possible legality about such a document, by which Mary signed away the crown she had inherited twenty-four and a half years ago, in favour of her own son, and a regency of her half-brother, on a lonely island, without any advisers and surrounded by soldiers, under the command of the new regent's own brother. Shortly afterwards, Mary fell seriously ill again: her body began to swell up, chiefly in one arm and leg; her skin turned yellow, and she broke out in pustules, so that she began to believe she might have been poisoned. This disease, which seems to have had something to do with the liver, was relieved by bleeding, and a potion which was said to strengthen the heart.

As a result of the instruments which his mother had been compelled to sign in this manner, on 29th July James was crowned king of Scotland at the Protestant church, just outside the gates of Stirling Castle, at the tender age of thirteen months. The oath was taken on his behalf by Morton and Home. The circumstances strongly recalled those of Queen Mary's own coronation twenty-four years before: once more the Scottish crown was in the grasp of a puny child, hedged round by a grasping nobility, whose powers seemed to have been curtailed very little in the intervening years. Letters of commission signed by the ex-queen were read out – one established a regency in the name of Moray, and after him Morton, during the king's minority; one resigned the crown and kingdom on Mary's behalf; a third appointed a Council to act with Moray. On the day of the coronation, the gloomy peace of Lochleven was disturbed by all the artillery of the house being discharged; the queen, sending to find out what the matter was, discovered that bonfires had been lit in the garden, and that the laird was celebrating riotously at the news. He asked her mockingly why she too was not making merry at the coronation of her own son, at which Mary started to weep and went indoors.[20]

No further excitements disturbed the queen's close imprisonment, until her half-brother returned to Scotland to assume the position of regent. Some of Mary's supporters had hoped that Moray's arrival would result in some amelioration of her condition, remembering the many benefits which she had bestowed upon him in the past. George Douglas, falling further under the spell of Mary's charm, chose to remind Moray of how he had been used to call himself the queen's 'creature'. But Moray had now no call to term himself anyone's creature, with the prospect ahead of him of at least twelve or fourteen years' rule of Scotland, during his own nephew's childhood. When he arrived at Lochleven, it was in a cold and punitive mood. To Mary's surprise, her brother was now addressed as 'Grace', a title usually reserved for kings or their children. In their first interview, he chose to harangue her in a tone of angry condemnation, which justified Throckmorton's description of him as leading his people like the ancient prophets of Israel. It was true that Moray's lofty sermon on Mary's past imprudences, unattractive as it might be, contained many observations which were most applicable to her case: he told her that the Scottish people were dissatisfied with her conduct, and even though innocent before God, she should have had regard to her reputation in the eyes of the world, 'Which judges by the outward appearance and not upon the inward sentiment'. On the subject of her marriage to Bothwell, and the rumours it had aroused concerning the death of Darnley, he observed perfectly correctly that it was not enough to avoid a fault, but also the occasions of being suspected of it. Such admirable pieces of advice would have been the more effective if the lords associated with Moray in the government of the realm had not been far more practically implicated in the death of Darnley than the unfortunate queen.

Moray gave a full account of his interview to Throckmorton on his return to Edinburgh.[21] Sometimes, he said, Mary had wept bitterly, sometimes she acknowledged her imprudence and misgovernment, some things she did confess plainly, some things she did extenuate. Almost certainly Moray went so far as to threaten Mary with execution, for their interview took place on two consecutive days, and the first night, as he told Throckmorton, he left her with the hope of nothing but God's mercy. Throckmorton was impressed with Moray's grave and pious character – as the English almost universally were – and praised his sincere qualities to Queen Elizabeth. But in fact there was little to admire in such cruel hectoring of his sister, who on Lochleven was totally at his mercy. Nevertheless the ruse worked. Mary once more passed a night of horror and fear; now even her own brother seemed to have turned against her; the next day she begged Moray to accept the regency. Moray told Throckmorton that Mary kissed him and asked him not to refuse it. She had of course extorted no concessions of any sort from him in return for the offer – neither the promise of liberty nor any other hint that she might enjoy freedom in the near future. In the meantime Moray was able to assure Cecil on 30th August that his new public state was neither welcome nor pleasing,[22] and even repeatedly assured Mary herself that he had no personal wish to assume the regency for his own private tastes led him to shun such grandeur and ambition, as she well knew. He might, however, be able to be of service to her as regent, where another in the same position would ruin her. Mary's own account of the interview to Nau put herself in a less desperate, more spirited light than Moray's account to Throckmorton. Although more reliance should be placed on Moray's account since it was delivered immediately, Mary did deliver herself of one significant aphorism on the subject of ruling Scotland. She warned Moray that if she, a born queen, was rebelled against by her people, how much more would the people rebel against him, a bastard by birth and origin. She quoted the maxim: 'He who does not keep faith where it is due, will hardly keep it where it is not due.'[23]

On 22nd August James Stewart, earl of Moray, was proclaimed regent of Scotland. One side-effect of his new status was the opportunity which it gave him to take possession of Mary's rich hoard of jewellery. It was a subject on which the queen felt strongly, and continued to do so for the rest of her life: the rape of her jewels by Moray caused her as much indignation as any other single injury he did to her. Moray was cunning enough to tell Throckmorton that Mary had actually begged him to take charge of her jewels on Lochleven in order to preserve them for herself and her son, but Mary afterwards accused Moray of simply stealing them. According to Nau, Mary pointed out to her brother not only that she wanted many of the jewels to be permanently united with the crown of Scotland (as she had specified in her will of 1566) but also that a preponderance of the jewels had been given to her by King Henry of France, or her husband Francis, and were therefore her own private property. Strong feelings on all sides were roused by the thought of this glowing prize. On 10th September Melville reported that Moray's acquisition of the jewels had 'colded many stomaches among the Hamiltons'.[24] The one thing which Moray did not do with the jewels was to unite them permanently to the honour of the Scottish crown, as Mary intended. He gave some to his wife. Others he sold to Queen Elizabeth the following April in order to remedy his forlorn finances. The latter action may perhaps be justified, if not excused, as an act of state – but the former cannot. The pearls, which were shown to Elizabeth on 1st May, 1568, in front of Pembroke and Leicester, consisted of six rows, strung like rosaries, and separate pearls as large as black grapes. They were thought to be of 'nonpareiled' beauty; there were also rings of lesser value, and a piece of heavily bejewelled narwhal tooth; the pearls seem to have been those intended in Mary's will to be divided between the crown of Scotland and the house of Guise, and the narwhal tooth for her favourite nephew Francis Stewart. From France Catherine de Médicis scented out the secret disposal of the pearls she had once admired and envied round her daughter-in-law's white throat at Fontainebleau, and tried in vain to obtain them for herself.

The proclamation of Moray as regent, coupled with the disappearance of Bothwell from the Scottish scene, led to a period of comparative calm on the little island of Lochleven. The queen's health gradually returned, after her privations and her miscarriage, since the enforced seclusion, however odious, did at least ensure her the rest which she so grievously needed. With health and the sinking away of hysteria returned also resolution and calm positive thinking. By the beginning of September, she was able to write to Robert Melville far more in her old vein of practical decisiveness, as though the year from the birth of James onwards had been lived under some black and disastrous shadow, now fortunately rolled away. She asked for materials, silks to embroider, and clothes for her ladies including her favourite Mary Seton who had recently been allowed to join her – 'for they are naked'.[25] On 23rd September Moray was able to tell Bedford that her health was good, and she herself was 'merrily disposed'.[26] The question of her clothes was now better resolved: much of her gilded wardrobe was gone forever, seized by the confederates, and not a great deal of attention seems to have been paid to her luggage-less state until after the arrival of Moray, when Mary accused him of bringing her some old and mean garments, very roughly made up, in place of her own clothes.

But the private aide-mémoires of her chamberlain, Servais de Condé,[27] show that even in June some clothes were of necessity brought, to supplement the clothes in which she had travelled: such as a red satin petticoat furred with marten, some satin sleeves, a cloak of Holland, a pair of black silk tights, or *chausses*, and more practically, some pins and a box of sweetmeats. In July she received another box of sweets, various stockings and garments of a utilitarian nature, such as leather shoes and wool chemises as well as a little red velvet box with crossed Fs on it in silver. From August onwards she began to receive supplementary provisions, the lists of which sound like any parcels sent to prisoners of war or state in any century: boxes of sweets, more pins, lengths of Holland material to make clothes, soap, Spanish silk and gold and silver thread for embroidery to while away the hours, handkerchiefs, an embroidered peignoir and a little blue box of taffeta full of '*poudre de santeur*'. In October she received what must have been a welcome parcel – her perukes of false hair, and other accessories to arrange her coiffure. In November she received a striking clock with an alarm or '*réveille matin*', more pins and linen. To a queen accustomed to the lavish grandeur of royal state since childhood, this was the diet of captivity. There was certainly no mention of the gorgeous dresses of the earlier inventories of the royal wardrobe in these lengths of Holland for her ladies to make up clothes. But, as captivities go, it was not particularly stringent, and on Lochleven, once her health was recovered, the queen began to develop those harmless, agreeable but petty activities with which royal prisoners while away their time – an unwitting dress rehearsal for the long years of imprisonment which lay ahead. She began to dance once more, and played at cards. She embroidered. She walked in the garden. She also looked out of the window towards the dark sedge of reeds along the distant edge of the lake and fed by the prisoners' fare of hope pictured the moment when she too would be standing on that wind-blown shore, once more at liberty.

If the queen dreamt of freedom, in the manner of all prisoners, it is unlikely that she also dreamt of Bothwell. Melville's hint to her concerning George Douglas had borne fruit. The young man was personable, gallant, and only too happy to see in his sovereign a frail and helpless woman, the victim of a cruel fate. Her fragile beauty drawn with suffering, coupled with her romantic history, could not fail to move him further; Cecil said afterwards that he fell into 'a fantasy of love' with the queen. By August, the queen was attempting to draw over the inhabitants of Lochleven to sympathize with her by the exertion of her famous personal charm and gentleness; even Lady Margaret was thought to be succumbing. By the end of October, even Drury from Berwick was able to report to Cecil in London that there was a nasty suspicion of over-great familiarity existing between the queen and Mr Douglas.*[28] Although George Douglas's heart was genuinely stirred by the presence of this romantic heroine, Mary's aim in this relationship, however much she appreciated the admiration, was quite clearly to escape from Lochleven; she now hoped to have found in George Douglas the weak link in the Douglas chain. But she was also able to extend her allure and her promise beyond even that of her own affections: for as

---

* Out of this statement, an absurd story had been built, quoted by Bishop Burnet in his *History*, that Mary Stuart conceived and bore a son by George Douglas while on the island of Lochleven. This son was said to have been the father of Robert Douglas, the covenanting divine who preached at the coronation of Charles II at Scone in 1651. There is no contemporary evidence whatsoever to support this story which is, in terms of time alone, scarcely possible.

Bothwell had now disappeared, there was in theory no reason why George Douglas should not aspire to her hand. This in turn did not necessarily displease his ambitious mother Margaret, who could imagine a worse future for her younger son than seeing him the husband of the queen of Scotland, with her other son the regent, able to restore his sister to power at any moment. As these projects buzzed in the minds of its inhabitants, during the autumn the island of Lochleven ceased to be an absolute slough of despair for the imprisoned queen of Scots.

The disappearance of Bothwell was the key to this new hope, as it was also to the temporary stability of Scotland. Beyond the confines of the island, Bothwell had been pursued to the Orkneys by his inveterate enemy Kirkcaldy of Grange, who promised to bring him dead to Edinburgh or die himself. In the event, neither death took place, for although Bothwell's capture was scheduled to take place before the end of August, at the beginning of September Moray was still obliged to observe warily on the subject: 'We cannot merchandise for the bear's skin before we have him.'[29] Kirkcaldy lived on, to become later one of the queen's most loyal adherents; Bothwell escaped to the Karmoi sound on the coast of Norway, but here had the misfortune to encounter some kinsmen of his former mistress Anna Throndsen, as well as some creditors from his previous Scandinavian travels. The combination resulted in him being officially captured and taken to Bergen on 2nd September, with two ships and 140 men. By the end of September he was being held in Copenhagen Castle, since King Frederick, joint sovereign of Denmark and Norway, quickly perceived in his uninvited guest a useful pawn in international politics, who as the husband of the queen of Scots, heiress-presumptive to the English throne, could certainly be used against the English queen. Although Moray pressed for his extradition, and Bothwell himself wrote anxiously to the king of France, asking for help, he was destined to remain in a series of Danish prisons, of increasing squalor, for the rest of his life.*

---

* It was while in the Castle of Copenhagen that Bothwell wrote his own narrative,

Throckmorton returned to England at the beginning of September, having never succeeded in achieving that audience with Queen Mary on Lochleven which he had so earnestly desired. On instructions from the English queen, he refused the silver plate given to him on his departure in the name of King James, on the grounds that Queen Elizabeth did not acknowledge Queen Mary's abdication from the throne of Scotland; nor did she acknowledge the regency of Moray, despite his many friendly overtures to England. Despite this disapproval from across the border, the Marian party in Scotland seemed temporarily in abeyance: Huntly and Herries had recrossed to Moray's side; Dunbar surrendered to the regent; Dumbarton, in the west of Scotland, was the only fortress left, and its effectiveness was considerably annulled by the fact that it lay in the centre of Lennox country. By the middle of October, Moray was able to write to Cecil that Scotland was quiet.[30]

Scotland might be quiet, and no part of it quieter than the tiny island in the middle of Lochleven which held the imprisoned queen. Nevertheless the course of Mary's fortunes did not stand still. The winter of 1567 was remarkable for an unpleasant new development in her affairs. The governing lords found that circumstances dictated they should change their attitude both towards her and towards the official reasons for her imprisonment. It was not enough to keep Mary incarcerated, having procured her abdication; the lords needed to provide some further public justification for their behaviour towards her. Originally they had claimed to be freeing Mary from Bothwell's tutelage at Carberry Hill – there was no question of implicating Mary personally in Darnley's murder. But now that Bothwell had disappeared from the Scottish scene and Mary was in prison

---

Les Affaires du Conte de Boduel, referred to earlier over the events of Kirk o'Field. Completed by 5th January, 1568, it was intended to procure his release. It is to be distinguished from his so-called death-bed *Confession*, a dubious document which was probably written much later on Mary's behalf to secure her release. Bothwell would in any case have been unable to write a death-bed confession, since he died insane.

at Lochleven, they could hardly continue to criticize her on the score that she was unduly influenced by Bothwell. Some other reason had to be put forward to justify her continued confinement. It was time for the lords to gloss over the deep implication of some of their number in the murder at Kirk o'Field. The Craigmillar bond of November 1566, to get rid of the king, had been signed by Maitland, Morton and James Balfour amongst others; now this was conveniently forgotten. In December 1567, nearly a year after the event, Mary was herself publicly blamed for the death of Darnley.

The existence of certain documents which implicated Mary in the crime was mentioned for the first time in front of the Privy Council on 4th December.[31] The text of these writings was not quoted, nor were the actual documents produced; but their existence was used to justify a new Act of Council which stated that the official cause of Mary's detention was her involvement in her husband's death. Mary was said to have encouraged the outrage 'in so far as by divers her privy letters written and subscribed with her own hand and sent by her to James Earl Bothwell, chief executioner of the horrible murder'. At the Parliament convened by Moray on 15th December, Mary's abdication of the government was said to be 'lawful and perfect'; James's investiture and coronation was described as being as valid as those of his ancestors, since it was to be considered as though his mother were actually dead. Moray's appointment as regent was confirmed, and the lords who had taken up arms at Carberry Hill were formally vindicated in that Queen Mary had been 'privy, art and part of the actual devise and deed of the forenamed murder of the King her lawful husband'.[32] This was quite a new departure from the line which the lords had actually taken on the eve of the battle. Then all the talk had been of Bothwell's guilt; now for the first time the subject of Mary's guilt was introduced. It was a change of emphasis which boded no good for Mary's future.

Although Mary herself on her island was unaware of the turn which matters were taking, the news that Moray was summoning a Parliament was enough to cast her into a state of fervour agitated by frustration. She addressed a long letter to her brother, asking that she should be allowed to vindicate herself before it, as previously arranged; she touched on her relationship to Moray, the favours she had shown him, his promises to the French court to support her, and earnestly suggested that she would submit to any law, even laying aside her queenly rank, if only she could be allowed a hearing; Queen Mary also pointed out pathetically her past virtues as a ruler – how she had never been extravagant or embezzled her subjects' money, like so many sovereigns.[33] To this *cri de coeur*, in which can be heard the desperation of the captive who will promise anything, if only he or she can be allowed a hearing from the outside world, Moray sent only a few lines of acknowledgement. On his next visit to Lochleven, when he brought James Balfour and Morton, relations between the brother and sister were cold and quarrelsome. Yet by mid-winter the graph of Scottish loyalties was rising once more in Mary's favour. For one thing, the Hamiltons were annoyed that Moray had assumed the regency, which they thought belonged rightfully to their family, as in the past, and did not attend the December Parliament. Kirkcaldy and Maitland were both privately concerned lest Mary's abdication under duress might be considered illegal in the future. It was not long before Maitland began to display his usual political ambiguity: in her prison the queen received secretly an engraved ring representing Aesop's fable of the lion and the mouse.[34] The gift was said to come from Mary Fleming, but at the time it was generally believed that its true significance was the promise of future support from her husband Maitland – the grateful mouse who would gnaw through the bonds of the lion, Mary.

The Scots people, who had been told that their queen had been removed for complicity in Darnley's murder, could see for themselves that many nobles, far more intimately involved than she, were not only at liberty, but forming part of the government of the country. Moray's persistent hunting down of the lesser criminals was intended to distract attention from this patent fact, but when John Hay of Tallo was publicly executed at the beginning of January 1568, he stood up on the scaffold and declared boldly to the large crowd assembled that Huntly, Argyll, Maitland and Balfour had all subscribed the bond for Darnley's murder. This scarcely helped on the process of distraction. The hacked-off limbs of Hay, Powrie and Hepburn were in turn posted up on the gates of the leading Scottish towns, twenty-two shillings being paid to the boy who went on his way from Edinburgh to Leith, Haddington and Jedburgh bearing the grisly burden of a pair of legs.[35] But such public expenditure, such improving sights, still did not prevent Queen Mary's erstwhile subjects from clamouring against the lords in the government, that they too should 'suffer for their demerits'.

The marriageability of the queen became once more a matter of public comment and private speculation. Drury thought Mary asked her brother if she might marry George Douglas as early as December[36] – fresh evidence of the unenduring quality of her feelings for Bothwell; the regent was said to have refused on the grounds that his half-brother was an 'overmean' marriage for the queen. George Douglas had the advantage of being able to press his suit in person. Other names, some of them strange indeed in the context, were mentioned, including a Hamilton, son of the duke of Châtelherault, Argyll's brother, and a young Stewart (Lord Methven). The most optimistic rumour was that which advanced the name of Morton himself, although it was agreed that the queen might not take easily to the notion. The *junta* of nobles in power, in between scheming privately for their relations or themselves to marry the queen, jested publicly about what would befall them if the queen managed to escape.

As spring came to Lochleven, Mary was able to smuggle out a few letters to France describing her plight and appealing for aid. They have a determined and desperate tone. She begged Queen Catherine de Médicis, in a letter (written while her jailers were at dinner) which stressed her wretched condition, to send some French soldiers to deliver her – 'it is by force alone I can be delivered. If you send never so few troops to countenance the matter, I am certain great numbers of my subjects will rise to join them; but without that they are overawed by the power of the rebels and dare attempt nothing of themselves.'[37] She managed to write to Archbishop Beaton, her ambassador in Paris, describing her sufferings, but begged him to burn her letters, lest they be discovered and get some of her supporters, who had helped her smuggle them out, into trouble.[38] She also wrote to Queen Elizabeth, a letter dated 1st May, in a large sprawling handwriting, very unlike her usual even lines, showing the ravages of despair after ten months' captivity: she described movingly '*la langueur du temps de mon ennuieuse prison*' and the cruel slights of those to whom she had done nothing but good; how her brother Moray had taken all she has (this letter was written on the very day on which Queen Elizabeth was viewing those 'nonpareiled pearls', a fact of which Queen Mary was fortunately in ignorance). Mary also attached great importance to the ring which Elizabeth had once sent her, and considered it as a talisman which would bring good luck to their relations. To her great distress she had not managed to persuade Robert Melville to part with the jewel, for fear of Moray's vengeance, so that she could not dispatch it to England as she wished to move Elizabeth's heart with pity. The letter ended pathetically: '*Ayez pitié de votre bonne soeur et cousine.*'[39]

Yet within twenty-four hours of writing this anguished letter, the queen was able to escape from her prison largely by her own generalship, ably assisted by George Douglas and an orphan member of the Douglas household whom she had won over by her kindness and captivated with her charm. Her active temperament fortunately allowed her to cast about ceaselessly for some practical means of terminating her confinement, like the lioness pacing its cage to which Maitland had compared her, while at the same time pouring forth as many appeals for outside help as she could smuggle out of the island. In the end it was inside rather than outside assistance which proved effective. So long as George Douglas remained on the island itself, there was not a great deal he could do to help his heroine beyond organizing her correspondence by bribing the boatman. But in the spring George Douglas quarrelled with his brother the laird (they both seem to have had their share of the peppery Douglas temper) and was ordered out of the house and off the island.

This gave him the necessary opportunity to alert on the queen's behalf lords such as the faithful Lord Seton, on whose loyalty she knew she could rely. Not only did George Douglas incur his brother's wrath, but his rumoured plans to marry the queen seem to have also brought down the anger of Moray on his head, so that he was in a mood of fair rebellion towards his family, and the established government of Scotland, by the spring. Queen Mary was able to turn this to full advantage. The attitude of his mother Lady Margaret was more ambivalent; Melville hinted that she had been 'upon the counsel' of the plot, although if Nau's account is accepted, she was left in total ignorance of it all.[40] As a mother, she would be torn between ambition for one son, George Douglas, and fear for the fate of another son, Sir William Douglas, if Mary escaped from his custody – for this would surely bring down the wrath of a third son, Moray the regent.

Queen Mary's chief female companions during her incarceration were the laird's wife, young Lady Douglas, who often slept in her room, and generally accompanied her throughout the day, old Lady Margaret Douglas, and two young Douglas girls of fourteen and fifteen, daughter and niece of the laird. These girls conceived a hero-worship of their captive, and the younger one especially was so obsessed by her presence that thoughts of the queen filled her imagination, even when she was asleep. In the late spring, however, young Lady Douglas gave birth to a child. This gave Queen Mary a little more liberty during the period of the lying-in; she determined to avail herself of the opportunity to effect escape. One romantic attempt, variously placed at the end of March or the end of April, involved the queen disguising herself as a laundress and escaping by boat with a bundle of washing while Mary Seton took her place in the castle.[41] Unfortunately one of the boatmen, mortified at the way she refused to show her face, tried to take down the muffler with which she kept it covered. Instinctively the queen put up her hand to stay him. The whiteness of the hand – that hand with its long fingers like five unequal branches which Ronsard had once praised – betrayed her. She was returned to her quarters, although the boatman kept his silence and did not report the attempt to the laird.

The key element in any escape was obviously the crossing of the water itself. Having suborned the boatman, George Douglas's first idea was to carry off the queen in a box; but the boatman dissuaded him, and together they agreed that it would be far easier to abduct the queen in disguise. There was by now another spy within the castle dedicated to the queen's cause – young Willy Douglas, an orphaned cousin of the house called 'the little Douglas', who was also by now devoted to her interests, won over by the charm and kindness she had shown to him. Willy became involved in smuggling out the queen's correspondence, for which he received a number of gold pieces, and incurred suspicion as he flaunted them about. There were other similar minor hazards to overcome: the laird's daughter noticed Willy Douglas delivering some letters to the queen, one of which she dropped on the ground; as a result the girl had a nightmare in which she saw Willy Douglas bringing a black raven into the house which flew away with her precious queen from the edge of the loch. The girl was so distressed at this that Mary was frightened she might arouse suspicion, and had to make her promise not to mention either the letters or the dream, on condition that the queen would take her with her when she escaped. But, Mary quickly added, of this escape she had at present neither hopes nor means. The laird of Markyston, a notorious wizard, also predicted that the queen would have escaped by the beginning of May and made a bet on it – as a result of which unhelpful piece of prophecy or sportsmanship her guard was increased.

George Douglas now asked permission to revisit Lochleven in order to say farewell to his mother, using the pretext that he intended to leave Scotland altogether and go to France. Both his mother and brother were deeply upset at this decision, and tried to persuade him to live instead with his half-brother the regent; they even enlisted the queen to write to him to this effect, and it was in this letter, which the queen obligingly wrote at their request, that she was able to send George Douglas a secret message urging the need to act swiftly before young Lady Douglas recovered from her confinement. The day fixed for the attempt was 2nd May, but the fact that Mary took the trouble to write to both Queen Elizabeth, quoted earlier, and Catherine de Médicis, appealing once more for assistance by French troops, on 1st May, shows that there was a great deal of doubt in her mind at least as to whether the escape would be successful. As spring stole towards summer, life on Lochleven became somewhat less bleak, and there were even modest boating expeditions on the lake; in the course of one of these, in which the laird accompanied the queen, her servants played a joke pretending their mistress had escaped, and in the ensuing fracas, half-playful, half-serious, some of the crowd on the shore of the island were wounded, and had to be attended to by the queen's surgeons. This incident was later considered by the queen to have distracted attention from the plots of George Douglas in Lochleven village itself.[42]

As George Douglas remained on shore in this village, having alerted Lord Seton of what was on hand, Willy Douglas took charge of arrangements on the island. His first idea was that the queen should leap a seven-foot wall in the garden, but when a gallant lady-in-waiting attempted the drop as an experiment and severely injured her foot, the plan was abandoned. Willy Douglas decided that the only safe course was for the queen to march boldly out of the main gate of the castle. On 2nd May he therefore organized a May-Day pageant, with himself as Abbot of Unreason; in the manner of such celebrations, the queen was made to swear to follow the abbot about all day; whereupon Willy Douglas gave a splendid exhibition of drunken fooling, as a result of which by the afternoon the queen declared herself to be so exhausted that she must sleep; she then flung herself down on her bed, not exhausted but desperately excited. As she rested, she heard a woman in the next room chattering and saying that a great troupe of horsemen had passed through the village of Lochleven that day, including Lord Seton, saying that they were going to an assize, and also that George Douglas had been seen in the village that day.

There were still some dramatic dangers to be overcome: for example, Lady Margaret insisted on discussing the question of the queen's escape, saying how she would ruin the Douglases if she did so and, in the midst of the actual conversation, noticed some horsemen on the shore: she would have raised an immediate outcry if the queen had not distracted her by fulminating bitterly against Moray. The laird himself looked out of the window and noticed Willy putting pegs into the bottoms of all the boats on the shore except one (to hole them against pursuit); he began to exclaim against Willy's idiocy, without exactly understanding what he was up to, until the queen pretended to faint, and the laird was compelled to go and fetch her a glass of wine. He was still sufficiently suspicious to ask to be near the window at dinner so that he could keep an eye on the loch and the village. Finally George Douglas bade farewell to his mother before his theoretical journey to France. One of the queen's maids then brought her one of the pearl earrings which she habitually wore, saying that George Douglas had recovered it for her from the boatman who had found it and had wished to sell it to him; but George Douglas had recognized the earring as belonging to the queen. This little piece of by-play was the signal that everything was now ready for the escape.

The queen retired into her room an hour before supper and put on a red kirtle belonging to one of her women, and one of her own long mantles over it. Then she went into the garden to walk with Lady Margaret. The queen was served her own supper by the laird, according to custom; next the laird went across the courtyard into the main tower, to eat his own supper with his family. Drysdale, the chief soldier of the island's guard, who generally stayed in the queen's room, went too and played at handball (thus reinforcing contemporary suspicions that he was in the plot).* The queen now had to rid herself of her faithful escort of the admiring young girls. She went to the

---

* But these suspicions do not seem to have been justified. A later letter written by Mary from England shows that she continued to dislike and fear Drysdale.[43]

upper room of her own tower, announcing that she wanted to say her prayers; this was not solely an excuse to absent herself since she did indeed pray fervently for the success of her venture. Here she cast off her own mantle and put on a hood like those worn by the countrywomen; one of her *femmes-de-chambre* dressed herself similarly, the other stayed below and tried to allay the suspicions of the girls, who kept asking why the queen was so long upstairs.

In the meantime Willy Douglas dexterously removed the laird's keys as he was handing him his evening drink at supper.* He then gave a sign through the window to the queen's woman that all was ready. The queen, in her disguise, boldly crossed the courtyard, although it was full of servants passing to and fro, and went out of the main gate; having re-locked the gate, Willy Douglas threw the keys into a cannon near at hand. The queen and her attendant stood for a time in the shadow of the castle wall, fearing they might be seen from the windows of the house, before finally going to the boats. Here the queen laid herself down beneath the boatman's seat, partly to be hidden, partly to avoid cannon shot. Several washerwomen by the boats recognized her, and one of them made a sign to Willy that she had done so; but the boy called out to the woman to hold her tongue. Even now the last hazard was not at an end: as they neared the opposite shore, Willy thought he saw an enemy lurking. It turned out to be one of George Douglas's servants who was a stranger to him. Finally they landed.

Mary was welcomed by the faithful George Douglas and by John Beaton. By a piece of ironic justice, Beaton had with him the best horses belonging to the laird of Lochleven, stolen out of the laird's own stables, which lay on the mainland. The queen mounted, and taking only Willy Douglas with her – even her *femme-de-chambre* was left behind for the time being – she set off

* Some doubt has been cast on the possibility of this feat, which is related by Nau. But the story is confirmed by a report, received in Paris by the Venetian ambassador at the time of the escape, via John Beaton.[44]

to meet Lord Seton, the laird of Riccarton and their followers, about two miles away. They then crossed the sea at Queensferry, and were at the Seton palace of Niddry by about midnight. The country people, who recognized the queen, cheered as she passed, and even the laird's uncle, who saw her, did not try to stop her. The music of popular acclaim sounded sweetly in Mary's ears after her confinement: there is a tradition that when she greeted her people outside Niddry the next morning, her long auburn hair was still flowing about her shoulders, for in her eagerness to show herself she had not even paused to have it dressed.

Queen Mary was once more at liberty after ten and a half months of captivity on a tiny island. In the meantime a countryman of lesser loyalty had rowed back to Lochleven to report her escape. Her disappearance had already been made known by the eager young girls, who found the queen's mantle in the upper room and thought she was hiding. The laird of Lochleven fell into such a passion of distress that he tried to stab himself with his own dagger.* But it is pleasant to record that those two other Douglases, George and Willy, who had placed devotion to their queen above family interest, were duly rewarded by her continual gratitude in later life, for as Mary herself wrote later to Beaton, asking him to forward George Douglas's cause in France, *'tels services ne se font pas tous les jours'*[45] (such services are not performed every day). The dashing George continued in Mary's employ during her English captivity; although he did not succeed in winning the hand of the queen he loved, his romantic aspirations might not have been so quickly extinguished if she had remained longer at liberty in Scotland. As Moray's brother, a Protestant and a member of the powerful Douglas clan, he would have represented a good

---

* The laird later sent on the queen's belongings from Lochleven, and in a report on her character to Morton said that there was no vice in her. This still does not prove that he connived at the escape, as has been suggested. While Mary was on Lochleven, he had good reason to fear the wrath of his half-brother Moray if he failed in his trust; once she was at liberty, she was once more queen of Scotland in many people's eyes, and it would be worth trying to win her favour.

compromise candidate as a husband. Willy Douglas, the boy Mary plucked from Lochleven, whom she called 'her orphan', remained attached to her service until death, and was mentioned in her last will at Fotheringhay.

Reference Notes

The following abbreviations have been commonly used:

C.S.P. Foreign	Calendar of State Papers, Foreign Series, Elizabeth
C.S.P. Roman	Calender of State Papers relating to English affairs (Rome)
C.S.P. Scot.:	Calendar of State Papers relating to Scotland
C.S.P. Spanish	Calendar of State Papers relating to Spain, Elizabeth
C.S.P. Venetian	Calendar of State Papers, Venetian
D.N.B.	Dictionary of National Biography
Hamilton	Hamilton Papers
Hat. Cal.:	Calendar of manuscripts at Hatfield House
Keith:	R. Keith, *History of the Affairs of Church and State in Scotland*
Knox:	John Knox, *History of the Reformation*, translated and edited by W. C. Dickinson
Labanoff:	*Lettres de Marie Stuart*, edited by Prince Labanoff
R.P.C.:	Register of the Privy Council of Scotland

For further details of these and other books cited (which have been described below in the shortest convenient form) the reader is referred to the bibliography.

CHAPTER ONE: *All Men Lamented*

1 Leslie, *Historie*, II, p. 260
2 Knox, I, p. 28
3 *Letters of James V*, p. 172
4 See entry under *Lineage* for Moray in *Burke's Peerage*, etc., 1963
5 Michel, *Les Français en Ecosse*, p. 420
6 Pitscottie, *Chronicles*, I, p. 377 *et seq.*
7 Diurnal of Occurrents, p. 22
8 Hamilton, I, p. 329
9 *Balcarres Papers*, I, *passim*
10 *Ibid.*, I, p. 81 *et seq*
11 *Ibid.*, I, p. 83
12 *Ibid.*, I, p. 149
13 Pitscottie, *op. cit.*, I, p. 394
14 *Balcarres Papers*, I, p. 61
15 Knox, I, p. 29
16 Hamilton, I, p. 328
17 *Balcarres Papers*, I, p. 228
18 Knox, I, p. 37
19 Hamilton, I, p. 307
20 Knox, I, p. 38
21 Pitscottie, *op. cit.*, I, p. 406
22 *Letters of James V*, p. 417
23 Hamilton, I, p. 348
24 Knox, I, p. 39; Leslie, *op. cit.*, II, p. 259
25 Labanoff, VI, p. 68
26 Hamilton, I, p. 328; p. 340; p. 342; C.S.P. Spanish, VI (11), p. 189
27 Knox, I, p. 40
28 Leslie, *op. cit.*, I, p. 24; Hume Brown, *Early Travellers*, p. 236

29 Leslie, *ibid.*, II, p. 260; Hamilton, I, p. 342
30 Sadler State Papers, I, p. 115
31 Mathew, *Scotland under Charles I*, p. 152
32 Hay Fleming, *Mary Queen of Scots*, p. 180
33 Knox, I, p. 11–12; p. 40
34 Hamilton, I, p. 342
35 Sadler, State Papers, I, p. 88
36 Knox, I, p. 45
37 Pitscottie, *op. cit.*, II, p. 8
38 Hume Brown, *op. cit.*, p. 118
39 Hamilton, I, p. 633
40 Knox, I, p. 50
41 Hamilton, II, p. 33

CHAPTER TWO: *England's Rough Wooing*

1 Leslie, *History*, II, p. 310
2 Hamilton, II, p. 326
3 Dalyell, *Scottish Fragments: The Late Expedition in Scotland*, sent to Lord Russell, Lord Privy Seal, by a friend of his, 1544
4 Archivo di Stati di Napoli, Carte Famesiane, tascio 709
5 Pollen, *Papal Negotiations*, p. 528; Donaldson, *Accounts of the Collector of the Thirds of Benefices*, Introduction, p. xv
6 Knox, I, p. 19; Knox, II, Appendix V, p. 255; Donaldson, *Scottish Reformation*, p. 12; p. 33
7 Pitscottie, *Chronicles*, II, p. 84
8 *Ibid.*, II, p. 85; Knox, I, p. 95

9 R.P.C., I, pp. 77 *et seq.*

10 Fergusson, *The White Hind*, p. 19; Dalyell, *Scottish Fragments*; William Patten, *Diary of Somerset's Campaign*, 1547

11 R.P.C., I, p. 11

12 Leslie, *op. cit.*, p. 310; Fraser, *Red Book of Menteith*, I, p. 503; Hay Fleming, *Mary Queen of Scots*, p. 192

13 Brantôme, *Oeuvres Complètes*, II, p. 460

14 De Beaugué, *Histoir de la Guerre en Ecosse*, p. 12

15 Teulet, *Papiers d'Etat*, I, p. 662; C.S.P. Scot., I, p. 99

16 C.S.P. Scot, I, p. 157

17 Leslie, *op. cit.*, II, p. 311; Jamieson, *Etymological Dictionary of the Scottish Language*, Vol. 3

18 Hamilton, II, p. 618

19 Printed in full, Stoddart, *Girlhood of Mary Queen of Scots*, Appendix

20 W. M. Bryce, *Voyage of Mary Queen of Scots in 1548*

21 *Ibid.*

22 Knox, I, p. 103

CHAPTER THREE: *The Most Perfect Child*

1 De Ruble, *La première jeunesse de Marie Stuart*, p. 19

2 Albert le Grand, *Les Saints de la Bretagne Armorique*, Part II, p. 279

3 Stoddart, *Girlhood of Mary Queen of Scots*, Appendix, p. 416

4 Bouillé, *Ducs de Guise*, I, p. 225

5 *Balcarres Papers*, II, p. 6; p. 32

6 *Lettres de Catherine de Médicis*, I, p. 66

7 De Ruble, *op. cit.*, p. 17

8 *Lettres de Catherine de Médicis*, I, p. 6

9 Guiffrey, *Lettres inédites de Dianne de Poytiers*, Introduction, p. xxxiii

10 *Ibid.*, p. 35; p. 42

11 De Ruble, *op. cit.*, p. 30

12 Brantôme, *Oeuvres Complètes*, V, p. 85

13 De Ruble, *op. cit.*, p. 31; Labanoff, I, p. 10

14 *Balcarres Papers*, II, p. 135

15 De Ruble, *op. cit.*, p. 63

16 Guiffrey, *op. cit.*, p. 91

17 De Ruble, *op. cit.*, p. 69

18 *Shorter Oxford Dictionary*, Vol. I

19 *Tresorier des Enfants de France. Fonds français.* 11207f., pp. 128 *et seq.* Printed De Ruble, pp. 281 *et seq.*

20 De Ruble, *op. cit.*, p. 51

21 Brantôme, *op. cit.*, V, p. 83; Montaiglon, *Latin Themes of Mary Queen of Scots*

22 Brantôme, *op. cit.*, V, p. 86

23 Labanoff, I, p. 4

24 De Ruble, *op. cit.*, p. 300

25 Register House, Edinburgh: GD/97/3 no 7

26 Labanoff, VII, 2nd supplement, p. 277

27 *Balcarres Papers*, II, Introduction, p. xxvi

28 Cameron, *Scottish Correspondence of Mary of Lorraine*, p. 149

29 C.S.P. Foreign (Edward VI), p. 103

30 *Ibid.*, p. 97

31 *Ibid.*, p. 109

32 Pollen, *Papal Negotiations*, p. 414

33 Brantôme, *op. cit.*, IX, p. 490

34 Pimodan, *La Mère des Guises*, p. 380

CHAPTER FOUR: *Betrothal*

1 Labanoff, I, p. 10

2 Bouillé, *Ducs de Guise*, II, p. 27

3 *Balcarres Papers*, II, p. 110

4 Labanoff, I, p. 45

5 Claude de l'Aubespine, *Histoire Particulière de la Court de Henry II*

6 Labanoff, I, p. 14

7 Neale, *Catherine de Medici*, p. 12; C.S.P. Venetian, VII, p. 187

8 Bouillé, *op. cit.*, I, p. 229

9 Stoddart, *Girlhood of Mary Queen of Scots*, Appendix B, p. 450; Labanoff, I, p. 29

10 *Balcarres Papers*, II, p. 253; p. 271

11 *Ibid.*, II, p. 237; Introduction, p. li

12 Labanoff, I, p. 29

13 *Ibid.*, p. 41

14 *Ibid.*, p. 34

15 *Ibid.*, p. 21

16 Stoddart, *op. cit.*, Appendix B, p. 448

17 C.S.P. Venetian, VI, pt 3, p. 1365

18 *Ibid.*, pt 1, p. 532

19 Stoddart, *op. cit.*, p. 143

20 Regnier de la Planche, *Estat de France sous François*, II, p. 75

21 Baschet, *La Diplomatic Vénitienne*, p. 486

22 De Ruble, *La première jeunesse de Marie Stuart*, p. 35

23 Phillips, *Images of a Queen*, p. 14

24 Hume Brown, *Early Travellers*, p. 75

CHAPTER FIVE: *Queen-Dauphiness*

1 *Discours du Grand et Magnifique Triomphe Faict du Mariage de François et Marie Stuart*; Hamer, *Marriage of the Queen of Scots to the Dauphin*

2 De Ruble, *La première jeunesse de Marie Stuart*, p. 149

3 C.S.P. Venetian, VI, pt 3, p. 1486

4 Hay Fleming, *Mary Queen of*

Scots, Appendix, p. 491

5 Knox, II, p. 78; Ronsard, *Poésies choisie*, p. 353

6 Brantôme, *Oeuvres Complètes*, V, p. 83; Knox, II, p. 78; Hat. Cal., I, p. 400

7 Brantôme, *op. cit.*, V, p. 94

8 C.S.P. Venetian, VII, p. 383

9 Printed Maxwell-Scott, *Tragedy of Fotheringhay*, Appendix; Melville, *Memoirs*, p. 96

10 C.S.P. Foreign, III, p. 251; *Tudor and Jacobean Portraits* (N.P.G.), p. 219

11 C.S.P. Venetian, VI, pt 2, p. 1058

12 Brantôme, *op. cit.*, V, p. 86

13 See Arbuthnot, *Queen Mary's Book*

14 Blanchemain, *Ronsard*, VIII, p. 28

15 Hay Fleming, *op. cit.*, p. 29; p. 213 note

16 Arbuthnot, *op. cit.*, p. 131; Castelnau, *Memoirs*, I, p. 528

17 C.S.P. Foreign, II, p. 14

18 MacNalty, *Mary Queen of Scots*, Appendix 1, p. 214

19 Labanoff, I, p. 57

20 Leslie, *History*, II, p. 385

21 C.S.P. Venetian, VI, pt 3, p. 1571

22 Phillips, *Images of a Queen*, p. 12 *et seq.*; p. 237

23 C.S.P. Foreign, II, p. 145; C.S.P. Venetian, VII, p. 29

24 Melville, *op. cit.*, p. 49

25 C.S.P. Foreign, II, p. 382; p. 406; p. 434; p. 466

26 C.S.P. Venetian, VII, p. 167

27 *Ibid.*, p. 75

28 C.S.P. Foreign, I, p. 347

29 *Ibid.*, p. 256

30 Bouillé, *Duc de Guise*, I, p. 526

31 De Ruble, *op. cit.*, p. 173

32 Bouillé, *op. cit.*, I, p. 529

CHAPTER SIX: *The White Lily of France*

1 C.S.P. Foreign, I, p. 561

2 C.S.P. Venetian, VII, p. 113

3 De Ruble, *La première jeunesse de Marie Stuart*, p. 181

4 C.S.P. Venetian, VII, p. 138, 178

5 Baldwin Smith, *Elizabethan Epic*, p. 120; Belleval, *Les fils de Henri II*, p. 43

6 Bouillé, *Ducs de Guise*, II, p. 29

7 Stoddart, *Girlhood of Mary Queen of Scots*, p. 258

8 De Ruble, *op. cit.*, pp. 187–88; C.S.P. Foreign, II, p. 171

9 C.S.P. Venetian, VI, pt 3, p. 1486; De Ruble, *op. cit.*, p. 188

10 C.S.P. Foreign, II, p. 111

11 Hamer, *Marriage of Mary Queen of Scots*

12 Labanoff, I, p. 70

13 Knox, I, p. 319; p. 116

14 Teulet, *Papiers d'Etat*, I, p. 721; Regnier de la Planche, *Estat*

de France sous François, II, p. 279

15 Melville, *Memoirs*, p. 51; C.S.P. Foreign, II, p. 511; III, p. 73

16 C.S.P. Venetian, VII, p. 227; p. 234

17 C.S.P. Foreign, III, p. 394

18 *Ibid.*, p. 394; C.S.P. Foreign, II, p. 410

19 Forneron, *Ducs de Guise*, p. 290

20 C.S.P. Foreign, II, p. 186; Hay Fleming, *Mary Queen of Scots*, p. 220

21 Regnier de la Planche, *op. cit.*, p. 203

22 De Ruble, *op. cit.*, p. 202

23 See Dr Potiquet, *La Maladie et La Mort de François II*; Armstrong-Davison, *The Casket Letters*, Appendix A

24 C.S.P. Venetian, VII, p. 275

25 *Ibid.*; p. 269; Hardwicke State Papers, I, 156

26 *Ibid.*, p. 275

27 Foneron, *op. cit.*, p. 327

28 Stoddart, *op. cit.*, p. 316; C.S.P. Venetian, VII, p. 278

CHAPTER SEVEN: *Mary the Widow*

1 Froude, *History*, VI, p. 443

2 C.S.P. Foreign, III, p. 472

3 C.S.P. Foreign, IV, p. 201

4 C.S.P. Foreign, III, p. 472

5 Conyers Read, *Cecil*, p. 285

6 C.S.P. Foreign, III, p. 472;

Wright, *Queen Elizabeth*, I, p. 58

7 Labanoff, I, p. 80

8 C.S.P. Venetian, VII, p. 290

9 C.S.P. Foreign, III, p. 423

10 *Lettres de Catherine de Médicis*, I, p. 158; p. 576; Chéruel, *Marie Stuart et Catherine de Médicis*, pp. 17–28

11 Hat. Cal., I, p. 258

12 Strong, *Portraits of Queen Elizabeth*, I, p. 24

13 C.S.P. Foreign, III, p. 565

14 Melville, *Memoirs*, p. 62

15 Leslie, *History*, II, p. 453

16 Knox, I, p. 354

17 C.S.P. Foreign, IV, p. 84

18 Camden, *Annales*, p. 53

19 Melville, *op. cit.*, p. 62

20 C.S.P. Foreign, IV, p. 154

21 Keith, *History*, II, p. 268

22 Leslie, *op. cit.*, II, p. 256

23 C.S.P. Foreign, IV, p. 154

24 *Ibid.*, p. 200

25 Keith, *op. cit.*, III, p. 211; *Dispatches of Suriano and Barbaro*, p. 33

26 Hay Fleming, *Mary Queen of Scots*, p. 246

27 *Ibid.*, p. 246

28 Leslie, ed. Bannatyne Club, p. 297

29 C.S.P. Foreign, IV, p. 243

30 *Les Affaires du Conte de Boduel*, p. 7

31 C.S.P. Foreign, III, p. 409

32 Gore-Browne, *Lord Bothwell*, p. 128

33 Brantôme, *Oeuvres complètes*, V, p. 93

34 C.S.P. Foreign, IV, p. 263

CHAPTER EIGHT: *The State of the Realm*

1 *Lettres de Catherine de Médicis*, I, p. 605

2 Brantôme, *Oeuvres complètes*, V, p. 92

3 Hardwicke State Papers, I, p. 176

4 C.S.P. Foreign, IV, p. 260; p. 261

5 Knox, II, p. 7

6 Herries, *Memoirs*, p. 56; Knox, II, p. 8

7 Robertson, *Inventaires*, p. cxviii; Hume Brown, *Early Travellers*, p. 73; Cameron, *Scottish Correspondence of Mary of Lorraine*, p. xix

8 C.S.P. Foreign, III, p. 224; Pollen, *Papal Negotiations*, p. 132

9 Hume Brown, *op. cit.*, p. 83

10 *Painted Ceilings of Scotland*, p. 9

11 Hay Fleming, *Mary Queen of Scots*, p. 255

12 Knox, II, p. 8

13 Leslie, *History*, II, p. 281 footnote

14 MacQueen, *Alexander Scott and the Scottish Court Poetry*

15 Leslie, *op. cit.*, I, p. 116

16 C.S.P. Scot., I, p. 205

17 Michel, *Les Français en Ecosse*, pp. 9–10

18 Castelnau, *Memoirs*, I, p. 186

19 Hume Brown, *Scotland in the Time of Queen Mary*, pp. 7 et seq.

20 Leslie, *op. cit.*, I, p. 5

21 Hume Brown, *op. cit.*, p. 77

22 Hume Brown, *op. cit.*, p. 52; Levassieur, *La Population Française*

23 C.S.P. Scot., I, p. 649

24 Leslie, *op. cit.*, I, p. 95; Hume Brown, *Early Travellers*, p. 39

25 Pitscottie, *Chronicles*, p. 275

26 *Chronicles of the Families of Atholl and Tullibardine*, I, p. 32

27 Robertson, *Inventaires*, p. 49

28 G. Seton, *History of Seton Family*; Leslie, *op. cit.*, I, p. 93

29 Cameron, *Scottish Correspondence of Mary of Lorraine*, p. xx; Hume Brown, *Early Travellers*, p. 47

30 Hat. Cal., II, p. 285

31 Fergusson, *Lowland Lairds*, p. 14

32 C.S.P. Spanish, I, p. 381

33 Macqueen, *op. cit.*; C. S. Lewis, *English Literature in the 16th Century*, p. 94

34 Child, *Ballads*, VI, p. 411

35 Hat. Cal., III, p. 47

36 C.S.P. Scot., I, p. 206

CHAPTER NINE: *Conciliation and Reconciliation*

1 Knox, II, p. 8; C.S.P. Foreign, IV, p. 278
2 Laing, *Knox*, IV, p. 439
3 Eustace Percy, *Knox*, p. 59
4 Laing, *Knox*, IV, p. 373
5 Knox, II, p. 13 *et seq.*
6 C.S.P. Scot., I, p. 551; Knox, II, p. 20; Laing, *Knox*, VI, p. 132
7 Diurnal of Occurrents, p. 67; Knox, II, p. 21
8 C.S.P. Scot, I, p. 555
9 Diurnal of Occurrents, p. 69
10 Donaldson, *Scottish Reformation*, p. 45
11 Knox, II, p. 21
12 C.S.P. Scot, I, p. 566
13 R.P.C., I, Introduction, p. xl
14 Melville, *Memoirs*, p. 102; Castelnau, *Memoirs*, I, p. 179
15 Pollen, *Papal Negotiations*, p. 75
16 Skelton, *Maitland*, I, p. 305
17 *Ibid.*, II, p. 395
18 Levine, *Early Elizabethan Succession Questions*, p. 7
19 *Kervyn de Letterhoven*, II, pp. 24–5
20 Neale, *Queen Elizabeth*, p. 114
21 C.S.P. Foreign, III, p. 573
22 Labanoff, I, p. 110
23 *Ibid.*, p. 123
24 C.S.P. Foreign, IV, p. 523; Hay Fleming, *Mary Queen of Scots*, p. 295
25 Conyers Read, *Cecil*, p. 235

26 Wright, *Queen Elizabeth*, I, p. 84; p. 58
27 Philippson, *Marie Stuart*, III, p. 457
28 Robertson, *Inventaires*, p. lxxx
29 Conyers Read, *op. cit.*, p. 237

CHAPTER TEN: *Governor Good and Gracious*

1 C.S.P. Scot., I, p. 582
2 Knox, II, p. 33
3 C.S.P. Scot., I, p. 609
4 *Ibid.*, p. 613
5 *Ibid.*, p. 563; Mackinnon, *Constitutional History*, p. 276
6 Robertson, *Inventaires*, p. xii
7 Exchequer Rolls, Vol. 19, Introduction, p. lxxi
8 Donaldson, *Scotland: James v–James vi*, p. 133
9 Neale, *Queen Elizabeth*, p. 215
10 Donaldson, *op. cit.*, p. 169
11 C.S.P. Scot., I, p. 206; Hume Brown, *Early Travellers*, p. 43
12 Lythe, *Economy of Scotland*, p. 57
13 Hume Brown, *op. cit.*, p. 122
14 Chronicles of Atholl, p. 36
15 C.S.P. Scot., I, p. 621
16 Robertson, *op. cit., passim*
17 *Libraries of Mary Queen of Scots*; Robertson, *Inventaires*, p. cxliii
18 Melville, *Memoirs*, p. 96
19 *Ibid.*, p. 96
20 C.S.P. Scot., p. 675
21 C.S.P. Scot., II, p. 148
22 Knox, II, p. 43

23 Robertson, *op. cit.*, p. 125

24 *Ibid.*, p. 60

25 *Ibid.*, p. 75

26 Macgeorge, *Miscellaneous Papers*, p. 12; C.S.P. Scot., II, p. 448

27 Hume Brown, *op. cit.*, p. 121; Hesketh, *Tartan*

28 Brantôme, *Gallant Ladies*, II, p. 215

29 C.S.P. Scot., II, p. 148

30 C.S.P. Scot., I, p. 579

31 Robertson, *op. cit.*, *passim*

32 Knox, II, p. 32

33 C.S.P. Scot., II, p. 8

34 Knox, II, p. 102

35 Child, *Ballads*, VI, p. 379

36 Robertson, *op. cit.*, p. xlix, note 3

37 Hay Fleming, *Mary Queen of Scots*, Additional notes, p. 490

38 Neale, *op. cit.*, p. 65

39 Gatherer, *Buchanan*, p. 53

CHAPTER ELEVEN: *The Fall of Huntly*

1 Gatherer, *Buchanan*, p. 79

2 C.S.P. Scot., I, p. 513

3 Robertson, *Inventaires*, p. 49

4 Knox, II, p. 63; C.S.P. Scot., I, p. 665

5 R.P.C., I, p. 219

6 C.S.P. Scot., I, p. 651

7 *Accounts of the Lord High Treasurer*, II, p. 197; James Fraser, *True Geneologie of the Frasers*, 1666

8 C.S.P. Scot., I, p. 651

9 Batten, *Charters of the Priory of Beauly*

10 C.S.P. Scot., I, p. 665; Knox, II, p. 54

11 Knox, II, p. 59

12 Diurnal of Occurrents, p. 74

13 *Accounts of the Lord High Treasurer*, II, p. 205; p. 226

14 Dickinson, *Scottish Parliament*

15 Pollen, *Papal Negotiations*, p. 162; Labanoff, I, p. 175

16 Keith, II, p. 182

17 Labanoff, I, p. 112

18 C.S.P. Scot., I, p. 684

19 Knox, II, p. 69

20 Hay Fleming, *Mary Queen of Scots*, p. 315; Pollen, *op. cit.*, p. 251

21 C.S.P. Foreign, VI, p. 211

22 *Ibid.*, p. 260

CHAPTER TWELVE: *A Husband for a Girl*

1 Gatherer, *Buchanan*, p. 85

2 Hamilton, I, p. 358

3 C.S.P. Spanish, I, p. 312

4 C.S.P. Scot., II, p. 19

5 Keith, II, p. 213

6 Pollen, *Papal Negotiations*, p. 130

7 Knox, II, p. 73

8 *Ibid.*, pp. 82 *et seq.*

9 *Ibid.*, p. 85, note 6

10 C.S.P. Scot., II, p. 54

11 *Ibid.*, p. 28

12 Melville, *Memoirs*, p. 92

13 C.S.P. Foreign, VII, p. 264
14 *Ibid.*, p. 268
15 Strong, *Eworth*
16 Melville, *Memoirs*, p. 82
17 C.S.P. Foreign, VII, p. 299
18 Melville, *op. cit.*, p. 101; Read, *Cecil*, p. 315
19 Melville, *op. cit.*, p. 92
20 Hay Fleming, *Mary Queen of Scots*, p. 238; Knox, II, p. 203; Teulet, *Papiers d'Etat*, II, p. 112
21 Bannatyne M.S.S., II, p. 227
22 C.S.P. Scot., II, p. 126
23 Teulet, *op. cit.*, II, p. 42
24 Melville, *op. cit.*, p. 107
25 C.S.P. Scot., II, p. 126
26 *Ibid.*, p. 75
27 *Ibid.*, p. 129
28 Teulet, *op. cit.*, II, p. 32

CHAPTER THIRTEEN: *The Carnal Marriage*

1 Bannatyne M.S.S., *Oxford Book of Scottish Verse*, p. 176
2 C.S.P. Scot., II, p. 166
3 *Papiers de Granville*, XIV, p. 33
4 C.S.P. Scot., II, p. 168
5 *Ibid.*, p. 171
6 Bannatyne M.S.S., II, p. 227
7 Register House, Edinburgh, S.P., 70 A
8 Pollen, *Papal Negotiations*, p. lxxv; p. xcv
9 Hay Fleming, *Mary Queen of Scots*, p. 348

10 Wright, *Queen Elizabeth*, I, p. 202
11 Knox, II, p. 158
12 Robertson, *Inventaires*, p. lxxxiv
13 Hat. Cal., I, p. 33
14 Knox, II, p. 162
15 C.S.P. Scot., II, p. 201
16 *Ibid.*, p. 139
17 *Ibid.*, p. 213
18 Gatherer, *Buchanan*, p. 93
19 Melville, *Memoirs*, p. 102
20 C.S.P. Scot., II, p. 232
21 Melville, *op. cit.*, p. 104
22 Labanoff, I, p. 300
23 *Ibid.*, p. 296
24 C.S.P. Scot., II, p. 234; p. 236
25 Knox, II, p. 174
26 Gatherer, *op. cit.*, p. 92
27 Labanoff, I, p. 342
28 C.S.P. Scot., II, p. 213; p. 241; p. 243; p. 327
29 Leslie, *Defence*, printed Anderson, *Collections*, I, p. 11
30 C.S.P. Foreign, VII, pp. 539, 541; Stewart, *Scottish Coinage*, p. 89
31 Herries, *Memoirs*, p. 73

CHAPTER FOURTEEN: *Our Most Special Servant*

1 Pollen, *Papal Negotiations*, p. 232
2 C.S.P. Scot., II, p. 254
3 C.S.P. Foreign, VIII, p. 13
4 Knox, II, p. 178
5 Keith, II, p. 404

6 C.S.P. Scot., II, p. 255

7 Tytler, *History*, V, p. 334

8 Keith, III, p. 265

9 C.S.P. Scot., II, p. 258

10 Gordon, *Genealogical History of the Earldom of Sutherland*

11 Froude, *History*, VII, p. 44

12 Melville, *Memoirs*, p. 113

13 Wright, *Queen Elizabeth*, I, p. 234

14 Labanoff, I, p. 342; Keith, III, p. 260

15 Chambers, *Life of James I*, p. 21

16 Birrel, *Diary*, p. 5 footnote

17 Herries, *Memoirs*, p. 79

18 *Ibid.*, p. 77

19 Nau, *Memorials*, p. 4

20 *Ibid.*, p. 15

21 *Ibid.*, p. 16

22 Lennox Narrative: printed Mahon, *Mary Queen of Scots*, Appendix A, p. 129

23 Nau, *op. cit.*, p. 17

24 Labanoff, I, p. 351

CHAPTER FIFTEEN: *Breakdown*

1 Diurnal of Occurrents, p. 7; Hay Fleming, *Mary Queen of Scots*, p. 400

2 Nau, *Memorials*, p. 7; C.S.P. Scot., II, p. 282

3 Nau, *op. cit.*, p. 28

4 Labanoff, VII, p. 297

5 Donaldson, *Scotland: James v–James vi*, p. 130

6 C.S.P. Scot., II, p. 254

7 Gore-Browne, *Lord Bothwell*, p. 351; Herries, *Memoirs*, p. 80

8 Pitcairn, *Criminal Trials*, I, pt 1, p. 502

9 Nau, *op. cit.*, p. 41

10 Hat. Cal., XIII, p. 82

11 Robertson, *Inventaires*, p. xxvi

12 *Ibid.*, p. 93

13 Register House, Edinburgh: Clerk of Penicuik M.S.S. G.D. 18/1305

14 *Accounts of the Lord High Treasurer*, II, p. 512; p. 499; p. 501

15 R. Bannatyne's *Memorials*, p. 238; C.S.P. Scot., II, p. 289

16 Woodgate, *Reminiscences of an Old Sportsman*

17 Gent, 'The Edinburgh Castle Mystery', *Chambers Journal*, September and October 1944

18 Melville, *Memoirs*, p. 131

19 Hat. Cat., I, no 1116; Levine, *Early Elizabethan Succession Question*, p. 188

20 Herries, *Memoirs*, p. 79

21 C.S.P. Domestic (James i), I, no 102

22 Gatherer, *Buchanan*, p. 168

23 C.S.P. Foreign, VIII, p. 114; Keith, III, p. 349

24 C.S.P. Foreign, VIII, p. 118; Hay Fleming, *op. cit.*, p. 411

25 Nau, *op. cit.*, p. 30

26 Hay Fleming, *op. cit.*, Appendix, p. 500

27 Keith, II, p. 447; p. 450

28 Labanoff, I, p. 374

29 R.P.C., I, p. 494

30 Pollen, *Papal Negotiations*, pp. 282 *et seq.*

31 Tytler, *History*, new enlarged edition, II, p. 400

32 Nau, *op. cit.*, p. 31; Knox, II, p. 191

33 Nau, *op. cit.*, p. 32

34 Gatherer, *Buchanan*, p. 169

35 Stevenson's Introduction to Nau, *Memorials*, p. cxlii

36 Diurnal of Occurrents, p. 103

37 Keith, I, p. xcvi

38 Keith, III, p. 290

39 Hosack, *Mary Queen of Scots*, I, p. 532

40 Lee, *Moray*, p. 184; Donaldson, *op. cit.*, p. 124

41 Diurnal of Occurrents, p. 103

42 Robertson, *op. cit.*, p. 61; p. 63; p. 69

43 Melville, *op. cit.*, p. 143

44 Keith, I, p. xcvii

CHAPTER SIXTEEN: *The Murder of Darnley*

 1 *Les Affaires du Conte de Boduel*, p. 12; Diurnal of Occurrents, p. 105; Pitscottie, *Chronicles*, II, p. 91

 2 Pearson, 'Skull and Portraits of Lord Darnley'

 3 Armstrong-Davison, *Casket Letters*, p. 312

 4 Mahon, *Tragedy of Kirk o'Field*, p. 248

 5 Keith, II, p. 460

 6 C.S.P. Spanish, I, p. 597

 7 Labanoff, I, p. 395

 8 Keith, I, p. ciii

 9 Gore-Browne, *Lord Bothwell*, p. 293

10 *Les Affaires du Conte de Boduel*, p. 12

11 Nau, *Memorials*, p. 31

12 Henderson, *Mary Queen of Scots*, II, Appendix C, p. 664

13 Pitcairn, *Criminal Trials*, I, pt 1, p. 501

14 Nau, *op. cit.*, p. 33; Forbes-Leith, *Narratives*, p. 117

15 Gatherer, *Buchanan*, p. 111; Mahon, *Mary Queen of Scots*, Appendix A, p. 127

16 Robertson, *Inventaires*, p. ci

17 Gatherer, *op. cit.*, p. 115; Pitcairn, *op. cit.*, I, pt 1, p. 501; Robertson, *op. cit.*, p. 177

18 Hosack, *Mary Queen of Scots*, I, p. 535

19 Nau, *op. cit.*, p. 34; Mahon, *op. cit.*, p. 115

20 Pitcairn, *op. cit.*, I, pt 1, p. 496

21 *Ibid.*, pt 1, p. 498

22 *Ibid.*, pt 1, p. 502

23 Labanoff, II, p. 3

24 Mahon, *Mary Queen of Scots*, Appendix A, p. 127; C.S.P. Venetian, VII, p. 389

25 Nau, *op. cit.*, p. 34

26 Pitcairn, *op. cit.*, I, pt 1, p. 493

27 Mahon, *Tragedy of Kirk o'Field*, p. 57

28 Nau, *op. cit.*, p. 44

29 Knox, II, p. 201

30 C.S.P. Foreign, VIII, p. 182

31 Pitcairn, *op. cit.*, I, pt 1, p. 495

32 *Ibid.*, pt 2, p. 149

33 Mahon, *Mary Queen of Scots*, Appendix A, p. 128

34 Pitcairn, *op. cit.*, I, pt 1, p. 502; Herries, *Memoirs*, p. 84

35 Gatherer, *op. cit.*, p. 116

36 C.S.P. Roman, II, p. 223

37 Labanoff, VII, p. 108

CHAPTER SEVENTEEN: *The Mermaid and the Hare*

1 *Les Affaires du Conte de Boduel*, p. 13

2 C.S.P. Venetian, VII, p. 388

3 Labanoff, II, p. 3

4 *Les Affaires du Conte de Boduel*, p. 13

5 Knox, II, p. 202

6 Robertson, *Inventaires*, p. lviii

7 Keith, I, p. xcviii

8 Anderson, *Collections*, I, p. 24

9 C.S.P. Venetian, VII, p. 389

10 C.S.P. Foreign, VIII, p. 211

11 *Ibid.*, p. 182

12 C.S.P. Scot., II, p. 318

13 Tytler, *History*, VII, p. 372

14 C.S.P. Foreign, VIII, p. 185

15 R.P.C., I, p. 500

16 Robertson, *op. cit.*, p. 53; C.S.P. Foreign, VIII, p. 198; Gore-Browne, *Lord Bothwell*, p. 374

17 Keith, II, p. 532; C.S.P. Foreign, VIII, p. 198

18 Diurnal of Occurrents, p. 108

19 Keith, II, p. 562

20 Nau, *Memorials*, p. 37

21 Labanoff, II, p. 20

22 Pollen, *Papal Negotiations*, p. 386

23 C.S.P. Scot., II, p. 322

24 Pitcairn, *Criminal Trials*, I, pt 1, p. 502

25 Melville, *Memoirs*, p. 149

26 Labanoff, II, p. 31

27 C.S.P. Foreign, VIII, p. 217

28 Phillips, *Images of a Queen*, p. 44

29 Lang, *Mystery of Mary Stuart*, p. 210

30 *Les Affaires du Conte de Boduel*, Appendix XIV

31 Stuart, *A Lost Chapter in the History of Mary Queen of Scots*, *passim*

32 Hat. Cal., XIII, p. 82

33 Diurnal of Occurrents, p. 110

34 Hay Fleming, *Mary Queen of Scots*, p. 454

35 Mahon, *Tragedy of Kirk o'Field*, p. 182

36 Diurnal of Occurrents, p. 111

37 Robertson, *op. cit.*, p. 175

38 Anderson, *op. cit.*, I, p. 27; Keith, II, p. 588

39 Melville, *op. cit.*, p. 154

40 Teulet, *Papiers d'Etat*, II, p. 170

41 C.S.P. Foreign, VIII, p. 229;

Teulet, *op. cit.*, II, p. 170

42 Mahon, *op. cit.*, p. 184

43 Labanoff, II, p. 31

44 *Ibid.*, p. 55

45 Tytler, *History*, new edition, III, p. 3; Teulet, *op. cit.*, II, p. 156

46 Nau, *op. cit.*, p. 40

47 C.S.P. Scot., II, p. 336

48 Macgeorge, *Miscellaneous Papers*

49 C.S.P. Foreign, VIII, p. 246

50 Teulet, *op. cit.*, II, p. 711 *et seq.*; Keith, II, p. 628; Herries, *Memoirs*, p. 93

51 Labanoff, II, p. 23

52 Nau, *op. cit.*, p. 47

53 *Ibid.*, p. 48

54 *Ibid.*, p. 51

55 Melville, *op. cit.*, p. 156

CHAPTER EIGHTEEN: *Lochleven*

1 Melville, *Memoirs*, p. 156

2 Nau, *Memorials*, p. 52

3 Macgeorge, *Miscellaneous Papers*, pp. 12 *et seq.*

4 C.S.P. Scot., II, p. 730

5 Pitcairn, *Criminal Trials*, I, pt 1, p. 495

6 C.S.P. Foreign, VIII, p. 269; p. 287

7 Nau, *op. cit.*, p. 59

8 C.S.P. Scot., II, p. 356

9 *Ibid.*, p. 373

10 *Ibid.*, p. 372

11 *Ibid.*, p. 354

12 *Ibid.*, p. 355

13 Nau, *op. cit.*, p. 62

14 C.S.P. Foreign, VIII, p. 252; C.S.P. Spanish, I, p. 649

15 C.S.P. Scot., II, p. 231

16 Donaldson, *Scotland: James V–James VI*, p. 125, footnote

17 C.S.P. Scot., II, p. 376

18 Castelnau, *Memoirs*, I, p. 648; Labanoff, II, p. 63, footnote 2

19 Nau, *op. cit.*, p. 62

20 *Ibid.*, p. 64

21 Keith, II, p. 736

22 C.S.P. Scot., II, p. 390

23 Nau, *op. cit.*, p. 69

24 Keith, II, p. 738; Nau, *op. cit.*, p. 69; C.S.P. Scot., II, p. 845

25 Labanoff, II, p. 61

26 C.S.P. Foreign, VIII, p. 345

27 Macgeorge, *op. cit.*, pp. 12 *et seq.*

28 C.S.P. Foreign, VIII, p. 363

29 *Ibid.*, p. 333

30 *Ibid.*, p. 356

31 Henderson, *The Casket Letters*, Appendix D, p. 177

32 *Acts of Parliament of Scotland*, III, p. 27

33 Nau, *op. cit.*, p. 71

34 *Ibid.*, p. 59

35 Pitcairn, *op. cit.*, I, pt 1, p. 491; Diurnal of Occurrents, p. 128

36 Wright, *Queen Elizabeth*, I, p. 206

37 Labanoff, II, p. 69

38 *Ibid.*, p. 65

39 Hat. Cal., I, no 1172; Cecil Papers folio no 147/26; Labanoff, II, p. 67

40 Melville, *op. cit.*, p. 168
41 Keith, II, p. 790
42 Nau, *op. cit.*, pp. 84 *et seq.*
43 Labanoff, III, p. 15
44 C.S.P. Venetian, VII, p. 414 ,
45 Hay Fleming, *Mary Queen of Scots* (unpublished documents), p. 511

Index